Praise for *The League*

"Talk about a team of rivals ready to claw each other to death on Sundays and join forces to sell their game from Monday to Saturday, this is it! Halas, Mara, Marshall, Bell, and Rooney— this is their story. It is also the NFL's story. How the men and the league came though the ballyhoo of the 1920s, survived the Great Depression and World War II, and set the stage for football's ascendency as the national game is told by John Eisenberg with humor, heartbreak, and insight. Before the owners were billionaires, they were just a collection of scoundrels who believed in football and money."

—RANDY ROBERTS, coauthor of *A Season in the Sun*

THE
LEAGUE

THE LEAGUE

HOW FIVE RIVALS CREATED THE NFL AND LAUNCHED A SPORTS EMPIRE

JOHN EISENBERG

BASIC BOOKS
New York

Basic Books
Hachette Book Group
1290 Avenue of the Americas, New York, NY 10104
www.basicbooks.com

Printed in the United States of America
First Edition: October 2018
Published by Basic Books, an imprint of Perseus Books, LLC, a subsidiary of
Hachette Book Group, Inc. The Basic Books name and logo is a trademark of
the Hachette Book Group.

The Hachette Speakers Bureau provides a wide range of authors for speaking events.
To find out more, go to www.hachettespeakersbureau.com or call (866) 376-6591.
The publisher is not responsible for websites (or their content) that are not
owned by the publisher.

Print book interior design by Linda Mark.

The Library of Congress has cataloged the hardcover edition as follows:
Names: Eisenberg, John, 1956– author.
Title: The League : how five rivals created the NFL and launched a sports empire /
John Eisenberg.
Description: First Edition. | New York : Basic Books, an imprint of Perseus Books,
LLC, a subsidiary of Hachette Book Group, Inc., [2018] | Includes bibliographical
references and index.
Identifiers: LCCN 2018012386 (print) | LCCN 2018016380 (ebook) |
ISBN 9781541617377 (ebook) | ISBN 9780465048700 (hardcover)
Subjects: LCSH: National Football League—History. | Football—United States—
History.
Classification: LCC GV955.5.N35 (ebook) | LCC GV955.5.N35 E58 2018 (print) |
DDC 796.332/64—dc23
LC record available at https://lccn.loc.gov/2018012386
ISBNs: 978-0-465-04870-0 (hardcover), 978-1-541-61737-7 (ebook)

LSC-C

10 9 8 7 6 5 4 3 2 1

For my press box colleagues

Contents

PROLOGUE

WHEN THE NATIONAL FOOTBALL LEAGUE'S TEAM OWNERS met at the Victoria Hotel in midtown Manhattan on a cold Monday morning in December 1934, the media contingent covering the event consisted of a single photographer. Not one of New York's major newspapers bothered to send a reporter. And the one photographer did not stay long.

After fifteen years in business, the NFL was still languishing on the fringe of America's sports scene. Millions of sports fans around the country followed baseball, college football, horse racing, and boxing, but many did not even know a professional football league existed. A meeting of the men who ran the league could not possibly produce news that a majority of fans cared about.

A day earlier at the Polo Grounds in New York, the NFL had staged a championship game for just the second time. Before then, the league had simply recognized the team with the best win-loss record as that year's champion. But some teams played more games than others, and ties were commonplace, complicating the calculations. To end the confusion, the owners had decided to split their teams into two divisions and match up the division winners in a single game that

1

determined the league title. They hoped the championship contest might one day become a landmark event, like baseball's World Series.

The game at the Polo Grounds, a renowned baseball venue, had mixed results. A brutal ice storm hit New York, limiting the crowd to slightly more than half of the stadium's capacity. That was disappointing. But the game itself was memorable. The visiting Chicago Bears, undefeated and heavily favored, built a lead and seemed in control until the New York Giants switched from cleats to sneakers after halftime to improve their footing on the icy field. The Giants proceeded to score four straight touchdowns and win by a wide margin.

Some of the other team owners had attended the game as a show of support, and now they were meeting to review their season, consider rule changes, and present a championship trophy to Tim Mara, who owned the Giants. The second-floor conference room quickly filled. Mara, tall and grinning, was among the early arrivals. Known in New York sports circles more as a horseracing bookmaker and boxing promoter than as a football team owner, he was accompanied by his twenty-six-year-old son, Jack, who handled the Giants' business as the team's president.

George Halas, who owned and coached the Bears, also arrived early along with his older brother. A fiercely competitive midwesterner who had played for the Bears until he was thirty-four years old, Halas was in no mood to congratulate the Giants again after praising them in his postgame interviews with reporters the day before. But his scowl gave way to a sporting smile; Tim Mara was his rival on the field but a good partner in the football business, deserving of a handshake.

Wearing a high-collared suit and round glasses, Joe Carr, the league's president since 1921, sat at a head table, ready to run the meeting. Also present were Bert Bell and Lud Wray, former University of Pennsylvania football teammates who co-owned the Philadelphia Eagles, one of the league's newest teams; George Preston Marshall, an opinionated laundry magnate who owned the Boston Redskins; and Art Rooney, a diminutive, cigar-chomping sportsman

Joe Carr (with glasses) hands
the 1934 championship trophy
to Jack Mara, as Tim Mara
smiles. George Halas stands
by Carr's right shoulder.
(Associated Press)

and gambler who owned the Pittsburgh Pirates. The owners of the
Brooklyn Dodgers and Detroit Lions rounded out the group.

When the meeting began, the men gathered around Carr and the
Maras. Carr uttered "words of congratulation" to the elder Mara and
presented his son with the Ed Thorp Memorial Trophy, a silver-plated
cup named for a well-known referee, rules aficionado, and equipment
supplier who had died earlier that year. The lone photographer on
hand, representing a wire service, snapped a photo that would run in
the *New York Times* and other newspapers around the country the
next day, giving the NFL a rare moment of widespread publicity.

The photographer quickly departed after that, as the owners
returned to their seats. They had much to discuss. Although their
just-concluded season had produced several positives, it was not clear
the NFL was headed in the right direction. Its average per-game
crowd of 13,247 in 1934 set a record, but larger crowds in Chicago
and New York had pulled that figure up; other than the Bears and Giants, most teams drew poorly and lost money. The pitiful Cincinnati

Reds had suspended operations after scoring 10 points and allowing 243 in eight games, forcing Carr to take on a semipro squad, the St. Louis Gunners, as a late-season replacement. The Gunners then beat Rooney's Pirates in their first game, making quite a statement about the modest caliber of the league's lower echelon.

The NFL had formally organized in 1920 out of a loose coalition of semipro squads, mostly located in small and midsize towns in America's industrial belt. By 1926, twenty-two teams were competing for the league title. But most had since folded, unable to draw crowds or break even financially. Long gone were such squads as the Rock Island Independents, Pottsville Maroons, and Dayton Triangles. The Packers, in tiny Green Bay, Wisconsin, were the last surviving remnant of the NFL's industrial-town origins.

Carr had led a drive to make the league more of a big-city venture. The Frankford (Pennsylvania) Yellow Jackets had become the Philadelphia Eagles. The Portsmouth (Ohio) Spartans had become the Detroit Lions. The owners of those and the other surviving teams believed this was necessary; if pro football was ever going to compete with baseball, it needed to succeed in the nation's largest cities. But even after breaking into major markets, the NFL still had fundamental problems. With the country in an economic depression, Halas and several other owners continually borrowed money to keep their teams afloat. On the field, there was a dangerous competitive imbalance—the Bears and Giants dominated, along with the Packers, who had recently won three straight titles—and a general lack of action. In more than half of the games in 1934, the losing team had failed to score. No wonder attendance in most stadiums was so low.

As the owners began discussing possible rule changes at the Victoria Hotel, they understood they had to make their league more competitive and their sport more exciting. Marshall dominated the conversation, as he had since he joined the league in 1932. A former actor, he thought a game should be entertainment, like a Broadway production, and constantly suggested rules aimed at giving fans more to like. He had previously led the charge to make passing a much larger part of the game and had convinced his colleagues to give offenses more room to operate by moving the action away from the sidelines and into the middle of the field, with plays starting on a set of "hash marks." At this meeting, Marshall proposed eleven of the fourteen motions that were raised, many governing intricacies such as the marking-off of penalties and the placement of the ball after fumbles. In each case, the idea was to give offenses a boost.

Before Carr banged the gavel to close the meeting, the owners also voted to put Bell and Halas in charge of a finance committee and established a "waiver rule" preventing players from changing teams in the second half of the season. Historians would not recall it as a momentous session. The owners of the Packers, Gunners, and Chicago Cardinals were not even present. The new rules, although important, would not prove as transformative as Marshall's proposals in prior meetings.

But this meeting was historically noteworthy because it marked the first time Marshall, Halas, Bell, Rooney, and Tim Mara were together in the same room discussing league affairs. These five men would keep the league afloat during its difficult early decades through their innovations, resourcefulness, and resolve, laying the foundation for the NFL to emerge as a sports superpower in the 1960s.

Other important figures in the early decades of pro football included Curly Lambeau, who ran the Packers; Carr, who produced order out of disarray; and Dan Reeves, an owner who tore down racial barriers and brought the game to the West Coast when he moved the Rams to Los Angeles. But Mara, Halas, Bell, Rooney, and Marshall were the ones most responsible for keeping pro football alive. They spent years watching their teams play a brutal sport on Sundays, then argued with each other, at times bitterly, at league meetings over rules, referees, and the schedule. "They fought with each other more than today's NFL owners ever will," recalled Upton Bell, Bert's son. But they almost always put aside their hard feelings for the sake of the league, sometimes damaging their own team's prospects to achieve collective progress. "The credo of sharing became the foundation of our league," Halas said later. Indeed, it was the key to the league's survival and eventual success. Today, pro football is a multi-billion-dollar colossus, looming over all American sports, and is at times accused of prioritizing profits over all other goals. It is thus surprising, if not remarkable, that the men who made the league did not subscribe to an individualistic, capitalistic ethos.

Pro football's early history reveals another irony. Unlike today's NFL owners, these were not men of immense family wealth. Mara was an Irish cop's son who been schooled on the streets of Lower Manhattan. Rooney's dad owned a bar. Halas's parents lived modestly after emigrating from Bohemia, a territory in the Austrian Empire in what is now the Czech Republic. Marshall had to fend for himself as a young man after his father died. Bell was the only one born to the manor, but he wasted his fortune and disavowed his place in high society. "They were on their own. No one was going to save them," Upton Bell said.

Though the Victoria Hotel meeting was the first that found them all together, they were not strangers. Halas and Marshall had backed teams in a failed professional basketball league in the 1920s. Rooney, Bell, and Mara had spent many summer days and nights together in Saratoga, New York, the horseracing spa that attracted high-rolling gamblers. Rooney and Bell, in particular, were two-fisted bettors.

Halas was the only real founding father, having attended the meeting at a car dealership in Canton, Ohio, on September 17, 1920, where the American Professional Football Association—as it was originally known—was organized. Mara came along five years later, as the NFL staggered through its infancy. Marshall, Bell, and Rooney arrived in the early 1930s. They were unlikely devotees of "paid football," as it was known in its early years. Marshall's first love was the theater. Mara had never seen a football game when he started the Giants. Bell was a college football loyalist who had once sneered at the pros; his father helped found the National Collegiate Athletic Association. Rooney hesitated to disband his successful semipro team to join the NFL.

On this Monday in December 1934, no one could have envisioned the NFL's spectacular future. Sports fans across the country were not talking about the title game between the Giants and Bears the day before. They were still focused on the classic college game between Army and Navy, played a week earlier before 79,000 fans in Philadelphia—far more than Bell's Eagles had drawn *all season* in that city. Baseball fans were debating what might happen to Babe Ruth now that the New York Yankees had parted ways with their legendary slugger, who had grown too old and round to hit as many home runs as he once did.

As the football owners met at the Victoria Hotel, baseball's owners and executives were also meeting that morning, just blocks away in New York, at the Waldorf Hotel. Their "winter convention" received far more press coverage, befitting baseball's status as America's pre-eminent professional sport. Most of New York's major newspapers dispatched a reporter to cover the event and, in some cases, also sent a columnist on the expectation that important news would develop.

The NFL could not begin to match baseball or college football in generating headlines or interest—a persistent frustration for the men who ran the league. By 1934, their collaborative efforts did not seem to have much impact. Much of America continued to view pro football as little more than a lark, a cousin of professional wrestling. Halas, Mara, Marshall, Bell, and Rooney were about the only ones who believed the sport had any future. Many of their friends thought they were out of their minds to continue to support it, and they wondered, at times, whether those friends might be right.

PART ONE

1

HALAS: THE FOUNDER

IN 1920, GEORGE HALAS WAS A FORMER FOOTBALL MAN, seemingly done with the sport. He had played in college and in the military during the Great War, but there was no major professional league to advance to; once you graduated from college, your only option was semiprofessional ball, a sandlot game. Halas had tried it, suiting up on a half-dozen Sundays for a team near his Chicago home. After his experience with that ragtag group, he had decided to give up *all* sports, get a job, and get on with his life. He was twenty-five.

Putting to use the engineering degree he had earned from the University of Illinois, Halas now drew a salary of fifty-five dollars a week as a safety expert for the Chicago, Burlington and Quincy Railroad, testing bridges for "stresses and strains" to ensure they would not collapse. In his spare time, he courted his future wife, Wilhelmina "Min" Bushing, a pretty brunette from Pilsen, the Chicago neighborhood where he had grown up. Halas could see the outline of a contented, white-collar life coming into view. His mother was delighted that he had given up football, the roughest of the sports he enjoyed playing.

Then one morning in March 1920 he received a phone call in the bridge design department at the railroad office in downtown Chicago. A man named George Chamberlain was on the other end. The general manager of the A. E. Staley Manufacturing Company, a starchmaker in Decatur, Illinois, Chamberlain had a job in mind for Halas and was in Chicago hoping to discuss it with him in person. Could they meet that evening at the Sherman Hotel?

Hours later, Halas entered the hotel lobby and strode across the carpet with a natural athlete's loose-limbed, rolling gait. Broad through the chest and just under six feet tall, he sported tousled, dark bangs that fell at an angle across his pale forehead. He shook hands with Chamberlain, who was bald and had a Teddy Roosevelt moustache and round, steel-rimmed spectacles. "I found Mr. Chamberlain to be a very determined man, about fifty, well-muscled; he had played football and baseball in his younger days," Halas wrote. Both men were engineers. They hit it off.

Chamberlain got down to business. His boss, Eugene Staley, believed sports could boost employee morale and help sell Staley products. Three years earlier, Staley had started a company baseball team coached by a former major league pitcher, Joe "Ironman" McGinnity. It competed in an industrial league against other major company teams through the Midwest, including the Samson Tractors of Janesville, Wisconsin; the Indian Refining Company Havolines of Lawrenceville, Illinois; and the Republic Trucks of Alma, Michigan. The Staley team drew crowds and newspaper coverage, and now Staley wanted to start a football team.

Chamberlain asked whether Halas was interested in coaching the football team, as well as playing for it. Halas quickly said yes. Although he was challenged by his railroad job, he remained an athlete at heart. He had played football, baseball, and basketball in both high school and college, showing enough potential on the diamond to briefly make the majors as an outfielder for the Yankees. For as long as he could recall, he had always had a new season to prepare for, more games to anticipate. But the Yankees had found a better right fielder, someone named Babe Ruth, and Halas had reached a dead end in football. He missed having games to look forward to. Staley's offer could provide a new outlet for his competitive energies.

There was no doubt Halas was qualified to coach a team. He had been mentored by two of the greats during his career. At Illinois, he played football for one of the sport's shrewdest coaches, Robert Zuppke. While with the Yankees, he played for thoughtful, pipe-smoking Miller Huggins, destined to manage the team to three World Series wins. Halas already had begun transitioning into coaching, having helped run a team of former college stars at the Great Lakes Naval Training Base, near Chicago, during the Great War.

Halas asked Chamberlain several questions. Could he recruit players? Yes, Chamberlain said, he could offer prospects full-time work at Staley as well as the chance to play football. The response excited Halas. Several of his Great Lakes teammates had been All-Americans; he could field a powerful team. His next question: Could the team practice two hours a day? It sounded like more than any team needed, but Chamberlain assented, telling Halas, "You're the expert." Finally, Halas asked whether those long practices could occur on company time. Sure, Chamberlain said.

The salary offer was modest, around what the railroad paid him, but it was not about money for Halas. He would get to coach and play for the company football team, play on the baseball team, and maybe start a basketball team. His calendar would positively overflow with sports and games. Meanwhile, he would learn to make starch, continuing to put his engineering and chemical training to use. Within a week, he quit the railroad, took the job with Staley, and moved 170 miles to Decatur, no longer a former football man. His mother was disappointed. Halas was thrilled.

BARBARA HALAS WAS JUST SHY OF THIRTY-ONE YEARS OLD WHEN she gave birth for the eighth time on February 2, 1895, in Chicago, delivering a boy given the name George Stanley Halas. Barbara had been a child herself, no more than five, when she arrived in the United States from Bohemia, a territory in the Austrian empire, later to become part of the Czech Republic. Little is known about her journey or early life in Chicago, but we do know she married a man named Frank Halas and soon started a family.

Frank had also come from Bohemia as a youth. Weary of the domineering rule of the Hapsburgs and frustrated after a failed revolt, Bohemians immigrated to America in waves in the 1860s. They "were tired of constant wars that were sapping the best blood of their nation, wasting their fields, and fastening still more grievous tax burdens upon shoulders that were already crushed," journalist Josefa Humpal Zeman wrote. Lured by stories of religious freedom and available land and jobs, so many Bohemians settled just south of downtown Chicago that they called their neighborhood Pilsen, after the city many had inhabited in the old country. Chicago's Pilsen had Czech newspapers, Czech churches, and Czech businesses. You could walk its streets without hearing a word of English.

Like the Germans, English, and Irish immigrants arriving in America around the same time, the Bohemians fled difficult circumstances at home only to encounter more hardship in America. Their Chicago neighborhood was crowded and chaotic, rampant with disease. But there was hope, as among the immigrants were some of Bohemia's most talented, literate, and ambitious citizens. "One would find men of education and high social standing engaged in street-sweeping, cigar-making, and other humble occupations," Zeman wrote. Frank Halas, intelligent and resourceful, started out as a reporter at a Czech newspaper, but he had an eye for fashion and soon found more profitable work as a tailor. Working with Barbara, who cut the buttonholes, he built a successful business preparing men's suits for large clothiers.

The couple built a three-story house, lived on the first floor, and rented the other two, thankful to be raising their family in America. Of the eight children they produced, only four, including George, survived childhood. But, despite their loss, Frank and Barbara retained a positive outlook, demanding that George and his siblings speak English rather than the Czech they heard on the street. It was necessary, the parents said, if they wanted to make something of themselves in America.

Frank's business grew so large that he built a workshop behind the house. But then he suffered a stroke, forcing drastic changes. He sold the business, leased the workshop and apartment building, and built another structure nearby—a three-story brick residence with apartments above a ground-level grocery, which Barbara ran. The Halas family lived on the second floor. They were far from wealthy, but between what the grocery and apartment rentals brought in, there was enough. Years later, one of Halas's players, Mike Ditka, would scoff that he "threw nickels around like manhole covers." But, rather than take offense, Halas agreed, saying he was proud that he had learned a dollar's worth as a boy.

Halas's two brothers and sister called him "Kid." In a household that was loving but strict, they were all expected to dress neatly, excel in school, and worship at St. Vitus, a Roman Catholic church. Frank and Barbara emphasized education as the path to success, and George took note, building a strong academic record. But sports were his passion. As a youngster, he played street softball and cheered for the Chicago Cubs. At Crane Tech High School, he played baseball and lightweight football and ran track.

As was true for millions of other young Americans raised by immigrant parents in these years, sports were an integral part of Halas's assimilation into the country's cultural mainstream. At the ballpark, he was not viewed by others as a young man of Czech parentage, from a neighborhood where little English was spoken; he was just a Cubs fan, his passion shared with people of a variety of ethnicities and religions, who spoke many languages. Alike in their support of the home team, they became friends, or at least compatriots, rather than strangers.

Frank Halas died "quite suddenly," as Halas would later write, on Christmas Eve in 1910. Halas was fifteen. His mother, determined to see her children go to college, sold the building where they lived,

closed the grocery, and opened a tavern. After his high school graduation, George worked for Western Electric for a year, mostly because
he needed to add weight to play college sports. Once he was at the
University of Illinois, he tried out for the football team but absorbed
fearsome hits in scrimmages, suffering a broken jaw and a broken leg.
He fared better in baseball, cracking the varsity lineup as a sophomore
outfielder hitting .300 and making plays behind his brother Walter, a
star pitcher.

But Zuppke, the Illini football coach, admired Halas. The young
man played such combative defense for Illinois's basketball team
that the coach had to pull him off the floor at times to keep fights
from breaking out. Believing that intensity could help the football
team, Zuppke kept giving Halas chances. Finally healthy as a junior
in 1917, Halas returned kickoffs and punts. At the team banquet after that season, Zuppke gave a speech that resonated with him. "Just
when I teach you fellows how to play football, you graduate and I lose
you," Zuppke said. Those words, Halas later recalled, "would govern
the rest of my life."

But he did not know that yet. It was the winter of 1917–1918,
and, with the country at war in Europe, Halas volunteered for the
navy and asked to be sent to sea on a submarine chaser—a small vessel
designed to destroy German subs. Instead, the navy put him in the
sports program at Great Lakes. Though disappointed, Halas threw
himself into his duties, playing on the base's basketball and baseball
teams, which took on college teams and squads from other military
institutions to boost morale.

In the fall of 1918, Great Lakes fielded a magnificent football
team. The quarterback, Paddy Driscoll, had been an All-American
at Northwestern. The center, Charlie Bachman, had been an All-
American at Notre Dame. The coach oversaw the base's officer training school, leaving him little time for football, so Halas, Driscoll, and
Bachman ran practices.

Great Lakes went unbeaten and received a bid to play in the Tournament of Roses football game, soon to become known as the Rose

Bowl, in Pasadena, California, on January 1, 1919. They faced another military team, the Mare Island Marines, before a packed house of 27,000 fans. On his finest day as an athlete, Halas scored a touchdown on a pass from Driscoll and returned an interception 77 yards, setting up another touchdown. Great Lakes won, and Halas earned the game's Most Valuable Player award.

After that game, Halas told his mother he was through with football and would stick to the relative safety of baseball. His military service ended, and the Yankees, who had seen him play in college, invited him to their spring training camp in Florida in 1919. Miller Huggins liked that he was a switch hitter who could cover ground in the outfield. Halas made the club, but once the season began, he managed just two hits in twenty-two at bats, his inexperience plainly evident as he flailed at major league curveballs. A hip injury set him back, and the Yankees finally dispatched him to a minor league team in St. Paul, Minnesota, for seasoning. When the season ended, he went home to Chicago and took the railroad job.

But he could not stay away from sports, especially football, which resonated with him on a fundamental level. Having been denied the chance to fight in a real war, he relished football's militaristic nature. What was the sport, with its scripted "plays," if not an approximation of two military units clashing on a battlefield? The rugged altercations between linemen certainly resembled hand-to-hand combat.

Although he had told his mother he was through with the sport, he longed to continue playing. "I ached for the excitement of a good game, for the competition, for the challenges to the muscles, for the thrill of victory," he later wrote. When he heard from a doctor who ran a semipro team in nearby Hammond, Indiana, he jumped at the chance to join. The pay was one hundred dollars a game. The team played other semipro squads such as the Canton (Ohio) Bulldogs, led by Jim Thorpe, the nation's most famous athlete, a broad-shouldered Native American who had won the decathlon at the Olympics in 1912. Playing for the Hammond team meant fitting weeknight practices and weekend games into his busy schedule, but it was worth the trouble. Halas was back alongside Paddy Driscoll. The pay was good. The team won all six games it played in 1919, including two against Canton.

"The season deepened my love for football," Halas wrote, "but I assumed my future rested with the railroad. Now and then, I would look at some of the other engineers doing the same thing day after day for thirty years. The prospect did not excite me as on cold winter days I rode the streetcar to and from the CB&Q offices. My real love was football." It was near the end of that cold winter that his office phone rang and Staley's offer beckoned.

In his first months at Staley's sprawling plant in Decatur, Halas played shortstop for the company baseball team and worked as a scale-house clerk. As summer waned, he began building his football team with a recruiting trip through the Midwest, finding plenty of takers for his unusual offer of a full-time job and the chance to play football. "I assured the men they would get paid at the end of the season for their football, depending on the size of the gate, and also told them they'd get paid weekly wages for the various duties at the plant. They all seemed to like the prospect of stability in a corporate setup," Halas would recall.

His talent haul included former All-Americans from Wisconsin, Nebraska, Illinois, and Notre Dame. Unfortunately, Paddy Driscoll had already signed with the Racine Cardinals, a Chicago semipro team that played near the city's Racine Street (some historians would later erroneously assume it played in Racine, Wisconsin). Staley had actually fielded a football team the year before, but it was a modest squad quarterbacked by Charlie Dressen, who would later play major league baseball and manage the Washington Senators. With Halas in charge, the team was far more organized, skilled, and purposeful. He handed out cloth-bound playbooks, tested players on their assignments, and schooled them in dark football arts such as how to get away with kicking and gouging opponents at the bottom of a pile.

Most American sports fans considered football a spirited amateur endeavor, a character-building exercise for high school and college boys. Played with few rules, and with some participants bare headed, it had been popular since the 1870s. "I believe in rough games and in rough, manly sports," President Theodore Roosevelt exclaimed around the turn of the century. After a spate of on-field deaths from violent collisions in the early 1900s, Roosevelt threatened to abolish the sport with an executive order unless college administrators instituted rules that made it safer. He wanted football to continue to be played, viewing it as an ideal training ground for soldiers.

Once players stopped dying on the field, college football developed a fanatical following almost rivaling that of professional baseball, a sport so preeminent that fans and sportswriters had called it the "national pastime" since the 1850s. By 1920, many college teams were playing in new, football-specific stadiums, before screeching crowds, on Saturday afternoons.

A postcollege version of the sport sprouted in the 1890s but was never nearly as popular. The first prominent teams represented athletic clubs such as the Chicago Athletic Association, Pittsburgh Athletic Club, and Latrobe (Pennsylvania) YMCA, amateur organizations that fielded teams in multiple sports. They sought to lure former college stars with under-the-table payments until they grew tired of the contrivance and simply began paying players, horrifying purists who believed that violated football's amateur essence. That version of the game, thus, did not develop a following.

Companies and independent sports entrepreneurs in the East and Midwest also began fielding football teams in the early 1900s. But unlike college football, which organized into conferences operating under a governing umbrella, the "paid" sport was a free-for-all. Players jumped from team to team during seasons in search of better pay. Active college players suited up under assumed names to make extra money, not that much was available. Teams passed a hat through the stands at games to bring in funds, hoping for a few coins and bills the players could divide up. Most games drew few fans.

Halas believed his Staley team deserved better. But when he wrote to other teams about scheduling games in the fall of 1920, he received "indifferent and vague" replies. He decided on another course. A league of semipro teams in Western Pennsylvania had become fairly popular, and several other circuits also had gained traction. Halas sent a letter to Ralph Hay, manager of the Canton Bulldogs, suggesting they start a league.

It turned out Hay, owner of an automobile dealership, had already broached the idea at a meeting with the owners of the Massilon (Ohio) Tigers and teams in Akron, Cleveland, and Dayton. They had another meeting scheduled at Hay's dealership on September 17. That day, Halas took a train to Canton with Morgan O'Brien, another Staley engineer who was helping him run the team. En route, Halas and O'Brien talked about the advantages of belonging to a league—principally, that it would give shape to their season and offer them a title to play for, meaning each game was important.

That evening, Halas and representatives from eleven other teams met in Hay's showroom, located on the first floor of the three-story Odd Fellows Building on Cleveland Avenue. "Chairs were few," Halas recalled, so the men stood around gleaming Hupmobile and Jordan cars while they drank beer, which Hay provided, and discussed football. "I sat on a runningboard," Halas recalled. The local paper covered the meeting and listed Halas as representing the Staley Athletic Club. He had many ideas and spoke frequently. The league needed rules, referees, a scheduling protocol, and a president, he told the others. Chris O'Brien, a painting contractor from Chicago, also was present; he operated the Racine Cardinals. Andrew "Doc" Young, a physician and athletic trainer, ran the team Halas had played for, the Hammond (Indiana) Pros. During the two-hour meeting, the men formed what they called the American Professional Football Association, agreeing to put up one hundred dollars each to solidify their commitment. They elected Thorpe as their commissioner even though he had no background in management, on the assumption that his selection would bring attention to their new endeavor.

The Staleys played their first game in Decatur on October 3, 1920, a sunny Sunday afternoon. Nearly two thousand fans sat in wooden bleachers and cheered as they trounced the Moline Tractors, 20–0, with Edward "Dutch" Sternaman, Halas's former teammate at Illinois, scoring three touchdowns. A week later, they routed the Kewanee Walworths, 25–7, as Halas, an end, and ten of his teammates played every snap, never leaving the field. The Staleys soon played six straight road games, mostly against outmatched squads such as the Rockford Athletic Club and Champaign Legion. Twice, they traveled to Rock Island, Illinois, to play the Independents, coming away with a victory and a tie.

The typical game was little more than a brawl loosely governed by rules poached directly from college football. Passing was legal, but the ball was fat, almost round, making it difficult to throw. That discouraged offenses and limited scoring, as did the rules. A clipping penalty set a team back 25 yards. When a pass fell incomplete in the end zone, the team lost possession. Moving the ball downfield was such a challenge that teams routinely punted on second or third down, hoping the round ball would roll farther if the opponent did not have a deep back waiting to field it. Playing for field position was a popular strategy as teams simply sat back and waited for their opponent to make a mistake. Though safer now, the sport was still rugged and bloody. Halas suffered a sprained ankle and a fractured cheekbone during the 1920 season. The Staleys' center, George Trafton, was a square-jawed roughneck described by a teammate as "the meanest, toughest player alive." Trafton injured so many opponents during one game at Rock Island that vengeful fans chased him to the team bus after the final whistle.

In late November and early December, the Staleys played three games in a row in Chicago. They defeated the Tigers, 6–0, on Thanksgiving, then lost three days later to the Racine Cardinals. It was the Staleys' only defeat in 1920. A week later, they won a rematch with the Cardinals, 10–0. As winter enveloped the Midwest, the Staleys and Akron Pros had the league's best records. The Pros had eight wins, two ties, and no defeats, and had allowed only one touchdown all season. The Staleys had ten wins, one defeat, and a tie. It was common for teams to arrange to play with little advance notice, as the league had no scheduling protocols, and Halas arranged for the Staleys to play Akron at Cubs Park in Chicago, later known as Wrigley Field, on December 12.

Halas wanted to win so badly that he signed Paddy Driscoll, his friend, to a one-game contract, even though Driscoll had played and coached all season for the Cardinals. Halas had helped write the league rule that forbade players from jumping from team to team during the season, but he reasoned this was a fair move because the Cardinals' season was over. There was no attempt to hide Driscoll's presence. He was listed with the Staleys on the lineups printed in the *Chicago Tribune* and other papers on the morning of the game.

Twelve thousand fans paid fifty cents apiece for tickets and shivered through the contest as a cold rain fell. The Pros' best player, Fritz Pollard, a speedy halfback, was one of two African American players in the league, along with Robert "Rube" Marshall, an end for Rock Island. A Chicago native, Pollard had studied chemistry at Brown University, where, as the school's first black football player, he helped his team earn an invitation to the Rose Bowl. Opposing defenses had struggled to contain him all season, but the Staleys kept Pollard bottled up on the muddy field. The game devolved into little more than a scrum of colliding bodies, with most plays consisting of runners simply plunging into the line. Nineteen of the twenty-two starters contested every snap; Halas's squad, like most, consisted of only a few players more than the eleven-man minimum. Neither team had scored when the referee blew his whistle to end the game.

Newspaper coverage of the contest, what little there was, did not note the presence of a black player. It was potentially significant; major league baseball maintained a strict color line, permitting no blacks on its teams. But pro football was so obscure that its racial practices went unnoted. A trickle of black players would continue to suit up in the 1920s and early 1930s, until the owners abruptly adopted baseball's restrictive, racist approach. An end from Rutgers, Paul Robeson, played for Akron in 1921, switched to another team in 1922, then quit pro football, destined to become famous as an actor and activist. Most of his admirers had no idea he had ever played football.

Before the 1920 season, the APFA's owners had agreed that they would vote to select a champion rather than have the title decided on the field or by record. After the scoreless tie between the Staleys and Pros in Decatur, Akron, and Buffalo's team, the All-Americans, all claimed they deserved the title. The vote to determine a champion was scheduled for the next league meeting at the Portage Hotel in Akron on April 30, 1921.

Halas would later write that the 1920 season "confirmed my belief that professional football had a great future." But he was disappointed by the quality of many teams and the league's general mismanagement. Pro football was a pale imitation of college football's sold-out stadiums, traditional rivalries, and energetic newspaper coverage. Halas skipped the Akron meeting in April 1921, sending O'Brien in his stead. In Akron, some teams dropped out of the league, others applied to join, and most owners claimed they were losing money. They agreed they needed to organize more effectively and establish a realistic business model. Thorpe obviously had to go. He was a terrific player but had no idea how to run a league. Joe Carr, manager of the Columbus (Ohio) Panhandlers, was elected president to replace Thorpe. The Panhandlers had struggled in 1920, but they had been around for more than a decade, almost entirely because of Carr's deft management. Carr had also run a baseball minor league and now wrote a sports column for the *Ohio State Journal,* a newspaper in Columbus. He had covered the World Series and championship boxing matches. The other owners believed he could bring order, and true know-how, to their nascent enterprise.

It was an astute decision: Carr would serve as the league's president and de facto commissioner for almost two decades. Few men would do more to ensure its eventual success. "There were a lot of pioneers, but Joe Carr was the one who kept it going," said Dan Rooney, owner of the Pittsburgh Steelers, years later. "He had a passion for it and did the right things. He knew you had to have uniforms, a rulebook, a head of officials. He worked to get the right people and the right places in the league. He doesn't get the credit but I see him as similar to Pete Rozelle and other commissioners who came later. Carr really knew what he was doing."

Minutes after Carr was elected president, Halas's surrogate, O'Brien, was elected vice president. It was a testament to the respect the other owners had for Halas and the Decatur squad. But the vote to determine the 1920 league champion went against Decatur. It was an Ohio-based league. The owners were meeting in Akron. They voted for the Pros over the Staleys because Akron had finished the season with no losses and three ties, while Decatur had one loss and two ties. According to a biographer, Halas "seethed about that 'lost title' for the rest of his life."

JOE CARR BEGAN TO RUN THE LEAGUE FROM HIS DESK AT THE *Ohio State Journal.* Within months, he had drafted a constitution and set up bylaws, which the other owners approved before the 1921 season. Carr wanted to stop teams from using disguised college players, a piece of chicanery in which many indulged. Carr also wanted to take a harder position against players jumping from team to team during the season, which caused a great deal of confusion and undermined the notion that each city, in fact, fielded its own team.

When the APFA kicked off its second season that fall, it had seventeen teams, including a new one in Green Bay, Wisconsin, a tiny shipping and meatpacking outpost on the Fox River. Halas anticipated another winning season for the Staleys. He had taken another recruiting trip and signed a fresh haul of talent that included Chic Harley, an All-American back from Ohio State. Harley's brother, Bill, had stepped in as a negotiator and asked for a cut of the Staleys' profits in exchange for the opportunity to sign Chic and two other players. Halas had agreed to the arrangement.

Shortly before the season began, Eugene Staley called Halas in and delivered a shock: he could not afford to keep funding the football team. It had cost him $16,000 in salaries and expenses in 1920—more than $200,000 in twenty-first-century dollars—and, in a town as small as Decatur, he could not possibly sell enough tickets to offset those expenditures. The team needed to play in a larger city where it could lure more fans, Staley explained.

Feeling remorseful about having convinced Halas to switch careers and move to Decatur only to cancel the enterprise after one year, Staley offered a deal. He would pay Halas $5,000 to establish the team in Chicago as an independent, for-profit concern. All Staley asked in return was that Halas continue to use the Staley name for the upcoming season, thus advertising his starch in the big city. After the season, Staley would no longer back the team, and Halas could become the owner.

Halas accepted Staley's offer. He was excited by the prospect of running a team in his hometown. Although Chicago already had the Racine Cardinals, Halas was confident he could win enough games and draw enough fans to get by. He quickly struck another deal, this one with Bill Veeck, the president of baseball's Cubs, to play his home games at Cubs Park. Veeck only asked for 15 percent of the gate and concession sales, terms Halas found eminently fair.

Halas chose orange and blue for the team's uniform colors, copying those of his alma mater, the University of Illinois. To house his players, he rented rooms at the Blackwood Apartment Hotel, near the ballpark. He also decided to take on a partner, expecting that he would need financial help once Staley's payments ceased after the season. Paddy Driscoll was his first choice, but Driscoll was under contract to the Cardinals. Dutch Sternaman, Halas's former college teammate, became his partner in the pro football business.

The Chicago Staleys played their first game at Cubs Park on October 16, 1921. They rallied to beat the Jeffersons of Rochester, New York, 16–13, which delighted Halas, who played the entire game on the edges of the offensive and defensive lines, giving and taking

George Halas, the player.
(Associated Press)

shoves and punches. He loved to play, but he was more excited that the game had attracted almost 8,000 fans, more than quadrupling the attendance for the team's opener in Decatur the year before.

The Staleys registered six wins and a tie before losing to the Buffalo All-Americans on Thanksgiving. Halas arranged a rematch for early December, billing the game as a "championship" that would determine the league's top team. The All-Americans were without several key players, who had been suspended by the league when Carr discovered they were also playing for a nonleague team in Philadelphia, another practice he was determined to stop. The All-Americans also stopped off in Akron and played the *day before* they took on the Staleys, leaving them worn out for the game in Chicago.

Not surprisingly, the Staleys defeated Buffalo. It appeared they had earned the title. Halas, though, scheduled another home game, against the Canton Bulldogs, hoping to draw a crowd and generate more revenue. The extra game stirred confusion among the league's owners. What if Canton won, dealing the Staleys their second defeat of the season? Would Buffalo then deserve the title because it only had one defeat? Carr issued a ruling, declaring the league season over, the window for scheduling games closed. The outcome of this extra game between the Staleys and Bulldogs would have no bearing on the championship. In fact, Carr said, he believed it was already decided that the Staleys would be awarded the title at an upcoming league meeting, which surprised and delighted Halas.

The Staleys defeated Canton, encouraging Halas to schedule yet *another* game, against the Racine Cardinals, shortly before Christmas. In frigid conditions, fewer than 3,000 fans watched Chicago's teams slip around on a frozen field in a scoreless tie. But the Staleys had already concluded their league season with nine wins, one defeat, and one tie, which, for the first time, and not the last, made Halas a pro football champion.

Now that he was home, Halas bought an engagement ring and proposed to Min. They were married on February 18, 1922. Within three years, they had a son, George Jr., and a daughter, Virginia. There was no doubt the growing family's future would have been more secure if Halas had kept his railroad job. The success of the APFA was hardly ensured. It was under constant attack from some of college football's most prominent and respected advocates.

In a widely lauded speech in New York in January 1922, Fielding Yost, head coach at the University of Michigan, said that paying men to play football "robs the great American game of many of its greatest character-building qualities. The ideals of generous service, loyalty, sacrifice, and whole-hearted devotion to a cause are all taken away. The game is robbed of the exhilarating inspiration of achievement merely for achievement's sake." Most fans agreed, it seemed, taking a dim view of the pro game mostly because money was involved. In a *Chicago Tribune* "man on the street" question-and-answer column printed in the fall of 1922, five fans were asked whether they preferred college or pro football. None liked the pro game. "College athletes have something to fight for, but in the pro game they're just fighting for money," one fan told the paper.

In truth, college football was not so clean; the desire to win had so overtaken some chancellors and deans around the country that recruiting scandals and academic improprieties had become commonplace. Nonetheless, the college game remained a hallowed, puritanical endeavor in the public's eyes. By comparison, pro football seemed a tawdry imitation. Late in the 1921 season, the Green Bay Packers, coached by Curly Lambeau, a former Notre Dame player, were caught using three current Notre Dame stars in a game against the Staleys. Halas turned them in, and, though the APFA responded by kicking Lambeau and his squad out of the league after the season, the incident made the league look second rate.

Amos Alonzo Stagg, the University of Chicago's head coach, was so disturbed by the professional game that he advocated taking away the varsity letters of college players who eventually turned pro, an idea the Big Ten briefly adopted. On November 1, 1923, Stagg pleaded with "all friends of the game" to help eliminate the scourge of paid football, which, he said, was ruining the high school and college games by tempting athletes with money. "Under the guise of fair play but countenancing rank dishonesty in playing men under assumed names, scores of professional teams have sprung up within the last two or three years, most of them on a salary basis of some kind," Stagg said. "Football, when played with the amateur spirit, possesses more elements for the development of character and manhood than any sport I know. To patronize Sunday football games is to cooperate with forces which are destructive of the finest elements of interscholastic and intercollegiate football."

With the sport's powers and many fans lined up against him, Halas was cautious in his public comments. "Professional football will never replace college football and we won't want it to," he said. But he pressed ahead with his notion that pro football could survive and eventually succeed. Although he would always claim he had merely broken even in his first season in Chicago, court records would soon indicate he sold enough tickets to turn a $21,600 profit. That alone offered him sufficient encouragement to keep going.

At his suggestion, the APFA changed its name at an owners' meeting in Cleveland on June 24, 1922. "I lacked enthusiasm for our name," Halas wrote, because the word "association" connoted minor-league status in baseball. He suggested the National Football League, explaining that baseball's National League was that sport's most established, respected circuit. The other owners approved unanimously.

He also changed his team's name to the Bears. He was a Cubs fan, and his team played in the Cubs' ballpark. "Football players are bigger than baseball players, so if baseball players are cubs, then certainly football players must be bears!" he would write. Before he could proceed, however, Halas first had to gain official possession of his franchise. Staley had registered the rights with the league, so Halas applied for a transfer, seemingly a simple transaction. But Bill Harley, who had negotiated a minor ownership stake in exchange for his brother's services, also applied for the franchise. The other owners deliberated for hours before voting on who owned the Bears. Halas won, 8–2. (Harley took the league to court over the matter, and, though he lost, the case forced Halas to open his books.)

In the fall of 1922, Halas introduced his Bears to a big city rollicking through the early years of America's Roaring Twenties. With a population of 3 million, Chicago was filled with speakeasies and jazz clubs, big dreams and new ideas. Its newspapers fought to print the most outlandish tales about mobsters and murder. Its skyscrapers rose so high you had to squint to see the top floors. That summer, two women sauntered onto a beach wearing one-piece bathing suits that bared their legs, a shocking impropriety that led to their arrests.

College football riveted the city's sports fans in the fall. On October 28, 1921, a packed house of 31,000 fans watched the University of Chicago host Princeton in a matchup of top-ranked teams, as millions listened to a nationwide radio broadcast of the game, college football's first. While the University of Illinois varsity trudged through a losing season in 1922, the team's fans exchanged exciting accounts of a dashing back running wild on the school's freshman team. His name was Harold "Red" Grange.

Amid the energy and spirit of innovation prevailing in Chicago, Halas was optimistic about his team's prospects. Sports fans around the country were agape at the exploits of baseball's Babe Ruth, boxers Jack Dempsey and Gene Tunney, and tennis star Bill Tilden. Soon, Grange would join their ranks as a headline-making sensation. Was there any reason pro football and the Chicago Bears could not attain a similar level of renown?

But Halas's optimism was sorely tested. Aside from coaching his team and playing for it, he wrote press releases, courted sports editors, and traveled around the city selling pro football, but the Bears received little coverage and cultivated few fans. If 8,000 attended a game, that was a good day. Many games drew far fewer. Although Halas had turned a profit in 1921, his expenses mounted, and he continually borrowed money from a football-loving bank officer to keep the Bears afloat over the next few years. In the summer and early fall months, before his ticket revenue started rolling in, he needed help paying his bills. "In truth," Halas would write, "the Bears lived hand-to-mouth."

2

MARA: THE PROMOTER

I N 1900, IN THE THICKLY POPULATED LOWER EAST SIDE OF
Manhattan, a young man named Timothy James Mara began to
carve out a life. He was thirteen years old, tall and pale and husky, a
cop's son living with his parents and an older brother in a neighborhood dominated by Irish expatriates. Mara attended public schools
and worked a newspaper route that took him straight up Broadway
from Wanamaker's to Union Square, through crowds of newly arrived
Chinese, European, and Jewish immigrants.

Although the city was full of young men with similar backstories,
Mara would never be lost in a crowd. Outgoing and irrepressible, he
had a glib tongue, quick mind, and wry smile that seldom faded as
he worked the city's nooks and crannies. Decades later, his grandson,
John Mara, said, "He was one of those people who filled up a room."
That was true even as he delivered papers as a youth. His route took
him into bookmaking parlors and Tammany Hall political meetings,
where he met the wealthy, famous, and connected. He did not cower
from them, awestruck. He thrust out his hand and introduced himself.

As with young George Halas in Chicago, sports helped Tim
shed stereotypes as a son of immigrants; he became part of America's

cultural mainstream through horse racing, one of the country's popular diversions at the time. While on his newspaper route, he met and befriended legal bookmakers who operated out of hotel rooms and storefronts, taking bets on races. Mara noticed they seemed to "live best and work the least," he later said. The bookies liked him, and several hired him to "run" bets. While delivering papers in the morning, he took his customers' wagers and passed the money on to the bookies. That evening, he distributed any winnings. The job required him to be organized, sharp, and, above all, honest. Some customers tipped him when they won or gave him a nickel for every bet he toted.

When Mara was fifteen, in 1902, his father died suddenly, and he quit school, which seldom interested him, anyway. He ushered at the Ziegfeld Theater, sold peanuts and programs at Madison Square Garden, and worked at a lawbook bindery. But he craved action and soon was booking bets himself. He already knew the fundamentals of the trade. He studied the horses, set odds, paid off the winners, and pocketed the rest. His clientele swelled. "He didn't have a lot of education but he had street smarts," his grandson said. "His father dying young impacted him greatly. He was forced to grow up, and he met a lot of Damon Runyon-like characters and developed certain instincts that served him well for his whole life."

In 1910, when anti-gambling legislation shut down New York horse racing for four years, Mara, operating out of a hotel suite, took bets on races in other states. In 1921, he set up a stand in the betting enclosure at Belmont Park—a hall where bettors shopped among a row of bookies for favorable odds in the frantic minutes before a race, then bet directly with the bookie they selected. Mara sat on a high stool with a fistful of bills in one hand, an odds board in the other, and a noisy jumble of bettors around him, winking at customers, making jokes and change as he constantly recalculated odds. The work introduced him to the glittering world of wealthy racing families such as the Vanderbilts, Astors, and Whitneys. They befriended Mara and invited him to their parties, quite a leap for an Irish kid from Lower

Manhattan. In the summers, he followed them upstate to the races at Saratoga, where he opened another betting stand.

If horse racing was his favorite sport, boxing was his second favorite. He rooted for Gene Tunney, the champion heavyweight and light heavyweight who, like Mara, had Irish roots and had made a name in New York. Mara longed to get into the fight game. One of his best customers at the racetrack was a wealthy building contractor who had been a childhood friend of Al Smith, the governor of New York. That connection Mara helped obtain licenses to stage Tunney's fights and several others at Madison Square Garden and the Polo Grounds. While promoting fights, Mara became friendly with Tunney's manager, Billy Gibson, a prominent figure in New York boxing. Gibson had previously managed a lightweight champion and other successful fighters, and had provided some of the financial backing for a pro football franchise that flopped in New York in the early 1920s.

The football team was known as Brickley's Giants. Charlie Brickley, a former Harvard star, now in his early thirties, was the head coach, co-owner, and only well-known player on the roster. College fans recalled him as a drop-kick specialist who had once booted five field goals through the uprights as Harvard defeated Yale, 15–5. After graduating, Brickley coached at Johns Hopkins, Boston College, and Fordham while occasionally playing semipro ball. Optimistic about the future of "paid" football, he organized the Giants and joined the APFA in 1921. Unfortunately, New York's first pro football team was badly outmanned. Brickley's Giants played only two official league games, losing both by a combined score of 72–0. "Little can be said for the brand of football displayed," the *New York Times* reported. The only interesting moment was a drop-kicking contest between Brickley and Jim Thorpe, now with the Cleveland Indians, at halftime of one of the games. The Giants dropped out of the APFA and played a few exhibitions before folding in 1923.

In the summer of 1925, Joe Carr, president of the enterprise now known as the National Football League, came to New York to convince Gibson to invest in pro football again. The NFL was flailing.

The league's roster of teams, located mostly in midwestern and eastern factory towns, changed significantly every year. After watching so many clubs struggle and fail in his three years as the league's president, Carr believed the whole enterprise would collapse if it could do no better than the Duluth Kelleys and Kenosha Maroons and failed to develop fans in metropolitan areas.

When Carr traveled to New York, the start of the 1925 season was two months away. On a summer afternoon hot enough to make the men grateful for ceiling fans, Carr sat down in Gibson's office, having brought along Dr. Harry A. "Doc" March to help twist Gibson's arm. A pipe-smoking, white-haired physician, originally from Canton, Ohio, March was a man of many interests. He ran a musical troupe, March's Musical Merry Makers, which toured the East and Midwest. He had been the team physician for the Canton Bulldogs in Jim Thorpe's day. Football was his true passion—not playing it but running a team. He now lived in New York and wanted a role if the NFL put another team there. But he did not have money to buy the franchise. "Doc March was looking for an angel," Mara said later, "and I was it."

When the meeting began, only Gibson, Carr, and March were in the room. It is not known whether Mara showed up coincidentally or had been invited by Gibson; he may have come to ask for a piece of Tunney, his favorite fighter. Regardless, he knocked on the door and joined the meeting, unaware of how much the next hour would shape the rest of his life.

Despite the heat, Mara was formally dressed down to his derby hat, and he was more wealthy and prominent than he ever could have imagined when he was delivering newspapers on Broadway at the turn of the century. He was thirty-eight years old and devoutly Catholic, with a wife, Lizette, and two sons, Jack and Wellington, ages sixteen and nine. His bookmaking business was booming. He also owned a coal company, Mara Fuel, and a lawbook bindery, the latter serving primarily to facilitate racing bets from lawyers and judges. He promoted boxing matches and would soon also try his hand at stock trading and selling scotch. "I never passed up the chance to promote anything. Not just for the profit, but for the challenge," he would say later. Decades later, Mara's grandson shook his head and smiled at the thought of his grandfather's multifaceted business world. "I'm not sure you can still live the kind of life he did, get involved in so many things, take so many chances. I'm not sure that works today," John Mara said.

In a bookie's vernacular, Tim Mara was the longest of shots to join a pro football league. He did not follow college football and barely knew the sport was played professionally. "He knew about boxing and horse racing, but nothing about football, that's for sure," John Mara said. When he sat down with Carr, Gibson, and March, Gibson had just rejected the idea of funding a new NFL team in New York. Gibson had lost money on Brickley's Giants and was not about to place another bet on such a risky proposition.

"Say, maybe you'd be interested in this, Tim. These men here have something you may want to buy," Gibson said.

"What is it?" Mara asked.

"A professional football franchise in New York," Gibson said.

"How much does it cost?" Mara asked.

No one knows who replied, though it was probably Carr, and the answer was either $500 or $2,500, depending on which version of the story one believes. "I was told it was $500, but it doesn't matter," John Mara said.

Mara initially balked. What did he know about football? The other men tried to persuade him, with Gibson offering to become a minority investor. Carr admitted Mara "might lose money at first" but eventually would turn a significant profit because "the future of pro football is tremendous." Carr's honesty and optimism were persuasive. Mara soon came around.

"I'll take it," he said, reportedly adding, "Any franchise in New York ought to be worth $500." Then he paused and said, "Now what do I do?"

Doc March jumped in. "Just leave that to me," he said.

Thus were born the New York Giants, owned by a man who barely knew football's basic rules. "He just thought, 'I'm a promoter . . . in New York . . . this is sports . . . it can work,'" Mara's grandson explained later. Mara himself would eventually laugh about the team's unusual origins. "The Giants were born out of a combination of brute strength and ignorance," he said. "The players supplied the brute strength and I supplied the ignorance."

But though he knew nothing about football, he did know how to run a business. Before leaving Gibson's office, he made Gibson the team president and March the secretary, responsible for building the squad. Mara was responsible for writing checks, and he wrote many in the coming weeks, quickly discovering this was not a small investment. The team needed uniforms and equipment, not to mention players and coaches. Seeing that he was spending more than he wanted, Mara asked friends to join him in the venture. Most turned him down and suggested he had lost his mind. A few said yes. Even with help, though, most of the cost still fell to Mara.

Meanwhile, March began to construct the team. He started by hiring a coach, Bob Folwell, a former wrestler whose penchant for foul language had cost him several college coaching jobs. March then signed "name" players such as Century Milstead, a tackle from Yale, and Henry "Hinky" Haines, a Penn State running back.

Mara, the innate promoter, believed the roster needed more exciting players for the Giants to compete, both on the field and for the attention of fans. It was a thrilling time for sports in New York City. Babe Ruth was bashing home runs. Tunney fought regularly at Madison Square Garden, Yankee Stadium, and the Polo Grounds, and Jack Dempsey, the world heavyweight champion, also fought in the city. The Army-Navy college football rivalry drew sellout crowds, as did games featuring Notre Dame. Fordham and New York University fielded popular football squads. Desperate to get the Giants noticed, Mara struck a deal with Jim Thorpe, hoping his presence on the team would generate newspaper coverage. But March doubted that Thorpe, now thirty-eight, could still play, given his sore knees and fondness for alcohol, so while his teammates would be paid either by the game or for the season, Thorpe would earn $250 per half, in case he tired and had to sit on the bench after halftime.

The Giants debuted on Sunday, October 11, 1925, taking on the Providence Steam Roller in Rhode Island. The setting underscored pro football's hardscrabble status. The Steam Roller's home field was the Cycledrome, a 10,000-seat oval stadium built for bicycle racing. The field was surrounded by a banked track that cut 5 yards off the corners of one end zone. There was only one cramped locker room and no public-address system. An announcer walked the sideline shouting the score, substitutions, and down-and-distance details through a megaphone. Some 8,000 fans attended the game and sat in temporary bleachers on the banked track, close to the action. Players frequently tumbled into the crowd, eliciting cheers. The Steam Roller, another new team, whipped the Giants, 14–0, eliciting more cheers. Thorpe had a few decent runs, but the Giants never came close to scoring. Mara, traveling with the team, was disappointed.

The next day, the *New York Times* published a five-page sports section dominated by extensive coverage of the fourth game of the World Series between the Washington Senators and Pittsburgh Pirates. There was also a lengthy roundup of the college football weekend and articles about horse racing and soccer. The Giants' game received no coverage.

To drum up interest for the team's first home game on October 18 against the Frankford Yellow Jackets at the Polo Grounds, Mara hired a publicist, bought newspaper ads, courted sportswriters, and paid for sound trucks to drive around the city blaring details about the game. He walked around with packs of tickets in his pockets but gave most away, unable to sell them. It was a humbling experience. He was accustomed to his ventures enjoying immediate success.

A day before the game, the Giants and Yellow Jackets played at Frankford's tiny home field near Philadelphia. The Giants lost, 5–3, with the decisive points coming on a safety when the Yellow Jackets blocked a New York punt through the back of the end zone in the second quarter. Yet again, the game received no coverage in the *New York Times,* which devoted its eight-page sports section the next day almost entirely to college football results. Army had defeated Notre Dame, 27–0, before 80,000 fans at Yankee Stadium.

The Giants took a Saturday evening train back to New York after their game. The next day, Mara and his wife and sons attended morning mass at Our Lady of Esperanza Church on 156th Street, then stood outside the church for a few minutes before heading to the game. "Well, I'm going to see if I can put pro football over in New York," Mara told a friend before leaving. The game attracted 27,000 fans. Although less than half had paid for their tickets and the crowd was meager compared to the big college game the day before, Mara was encouraged. This was more interest than he had expected. He hoped the Giants would put on a show. Early in the first quarter, Thorpe took a handoff and stumbled a few yards downfield. Mara, sitting on the bench, turned to his publicist and exclaimed, "Isn't that the greatest run you've ever seen?" A football expert he was not.

Mara's teenage son, Jack, was on the field with him, working a sideline yard marker. Mara's wife and younger son, nine-year-old Wellington, were seated in the stands behind New York's bench. Their side was in the shade, and Wellington came home with a cold, prompting Lizette to suggest moving the Giants' bench to the other side of the field, where the sun shone. "He made that switch and we've been on that side ever since," John Mara said.

In the end, the game was a disappointment. The Giants lost, 14–0, and the Thorpe experiment came to an inglorious conclusion. After losing a fumble in the second quarter, the once-great star limped to the sidelines and pitched forward onto a tarpaulin, either exhausted or drunk, possibly both. He would not earn $250 for playing in the second half. Mara and March had seen enough; the Giants were through with Thorpe.

The good news for Mara was the *New York Times* finally paid attention to his team, sending a sportswriter, Alison Danzig, to cover

Tim Mara had never seen a pro
football game when he started
the Giants. (Associated Press)

the game. "Pro Elevens Clash Before 27,000 Here," read the headline
in the next day's paper. Danzig was reasonably impressed, it seemed,
writing that the game was "a far cry" from the lamentable pro contests
staged by Brickley's Giants a few years earlier. Given the size of the
crowd, Danzig wrote, "New York evidently is ready to support a professional league team."

The game was the first of nine in a row at home for the Giants;
they would spend all fall at the Polo Grounds, trying to develop a
following. They delivered a victory in their next game, surprisingly
routing the Cleveland Bulldogs, the defending league champions,
19–0. But without Thorpe, the game drew fewer than 10,000 paying
customers. However, the victory marked the start of an encouraging
turnaround on the field. The Giants' defense stiffened, and Folwell's
single-wing offense flourished, with Hinky Haines breaking so many
runs from his halfback slot that Mara built an advertising campaign
around him: "Come See Hinky Haines and His New York Giants!"
The Giants proceeded to win seven games in a row.

Their prospects were less bright off the field. Their uniforms were stolen out of their locker room before one game (seized and returned an hour before kickoff), and March and the quarterback were arrested after another game when a minister convinced a policeman that it was illegal to play football on the Sabbath. (It was indeed illegal in Pennsylvania, but not in New York, and a judge quickly dismissed the charges.) Most discouragingly, New Yorkers showed little interest even though the team continued to win. One game drew just 1,200 paying customers. Mara's financial losses piled up. He was paying $4,000 a week in expenses and at least $2,500 a week in gate guarantees to his opponents. By late in the season, he had lost $40,000, a large sum for anyone, including him.

He lamented the situation one day to Governor Smith. "Pro football will never amount to anything; why don't you give it up?" Smith responded. Mara replied that his sons enjoyed the Giants and would "run me right out of the house" if he folded the team. But Mara's patience had a limit and he was nearing it. If he could not figure out how to stop hemorrhaging money, he would have to shut the team down.

THOUGH STILL NO FOOTBALL EXPERT, MARA FOLLOWED THE college game now, recognizing that any responsible pro owner should be able to identify the sport's best young players. In the fall of 1925, Red Grange, the halfback who had exhibited such promise on Illinois's freshman team in 1922, was easily the sport's most dazzling player. Now a senior, Grange delivered so many electrifying performances for the Illini that he made the cover of *Time* magazine, an honor usually reserved for world newsmakers. Fans across America were desperate to see Grange. Wherever he played, the stadium was full, and the crowd stood and shrieked when he took a handoff, shed tacklers, and broke into the clear, heading for the end zone. That sounded good to Mara. Why not try to lure him to New York? With Grange on the team, the Giants probably would sell enough tickets to wipe out the debt they had rolled up.

To that point, college players never contemplated turning pro until they graduated. But Grange, in a shocking development, had signed a personal management contract with an ambitious theater owner, C. C. Pyle. Informally known as "Cash and Carry," Pyle had convinced Grange to quit school and turn pro as soon as he played his last college game. College coaches such as Stagg and Yost were horrified, as were fans loyal to the college game.

Undaunted, Mara booked a stateroom on a train to Chicago and told March he planned to return with Grange. But he was too late. Pyle had already struck a deal with George Halas: Grange would play for the Chicago Bears for the rest of the 1925 season. Like Mara, Halas was in debt and had been struggling to attract fans to his games. He envisioned Grange as a savior, recognizing that signing him would come at a personal cost. Sure enough, his college coach, Robert Zuppke, a close friend, was furious with him for tempting Grange. Halas hated that, but he was desperate to survive, so desperate he agreed to give Grange almost half of the Bears' gate proceeds—an arrangement so lucrative for the player it would have wiped out most NFL teams.

But there also was good news for Mara. Halas and Pyle were planning a cross-country tour for the Bears, expecting to sell tens of thousands of tickets and rake in a fortune. More than anything, they wanted to play in New York. Mara left Chicago with a date for a game at the Polo Grounds. The Bears and Giants would play on Sunday, December 6. Mara sent a telegram to March:

> Partially successful STOP
> Returning on train tomorrow STOP
> Will explain STOP
> Tim Mara

March had no idea what that meant. Mara elaborated when he arrived. "Grange will play in the Giants-Bears game," he said, "but he will play for the Bears." It was shame Grange had signed elsewhere, Mara said, but hopefully New York fans would still pay to see him.

After the game was publicly announced, "there was almost a riot" among fans clamoring for tickets at Mara's office at the Knickerbocker Building, where the Giants were headquartered. They sold 15,000 tickets on the first day and another 25,000 in the next two days. Mara bought newspaper ads, rented sound trucks, and kept the story in the papers, building momentum in the days before the game. Babe Ruth had bought tickets, Mara announced. Gene Tunney would speak to the Giants in the locker room before the game, he said. Soon, all the Polo Grounds' 3,482 box seats were gone, and one hundred sportswriters had wired for credentials.

Meanwhile, Grange and the Bears were playing their way toward New York. Their barnstorming tour began with a pair of games at Cubs Park in Chicago. The Bears and Cardinals played a scoreless tie before a capacity crowd of 36,000 on Thanksgiving. Three days later, Grange threw a touchdown pass in a win over the Columbus Tigers that drew 28,000. The Bears then went on the road. An exhibition in St. Louis drew 8,000 fans in a blizzard. A league game against the Yellow Jackets at Shibe Park in Philadelphia drew 36,000, a capacity crowd, and Grange scored two touchdowns in Chicago's 14–7 win. For the first time, pro football was making front-page news. New York was the next stop.

After a week of rain, the skies cleared on game day. Hours before kickoff, fans began to gather on the streets around the Polo Grounds. Scalpers sold tickets for three and four times face value. Squadrons of extra police assigned to the event were overwhelmed. The crowd swelled close to 70,000, well over the stadium's capacity. Fans stood in stairwells and on landings, straining to see the field. As the teams warmed up, a marching band played, and several thousand fans wandered the field, having been assigned temporary end-zone seats. Shortly before the opening kickoff, Mara had to clear the field so the game could begin.

The fans roared as Grange led the Bears onto the field, his red hair glinting in the sun. The Giants had not lost in several months, but the

Bears brought them back to reality, taking a 12–0 lead. Grange gave a solid all-around performance; by the end of the day, he would rush for 53 yards on eleven carries, catch one pass for 23 yards, and complete two of three pass attempts. The crowd went wild when he touched the ball, but quieted after he was kicked in the arm late in the first half, resulting in an injury that would linger for weeks. Grange spent the third quarter on the bench with a jacket over his shoulders, his day seemingly over.

When the Giants scored a touchdown to make the score 12–7, Grange threw off his jacket, returned to the field, and provided the magical moment the fans had come to see. When a pass by the Giants' quarterback sailed over a receiver's head, Grange grabbed the ball out of the air and raced to the end zone for a touchdown that clinched a victory for Chicago. The final score was 19–7.

Counting the gate receipts after the game, Mara was stunned when they added up to $143,000. Even after Grange, Halas, and Pyle received their sizable cuts, Mara had made enough to erase his debt and even put the Giants in the black for the season. "I was about ready to toss in my hand until Grange turned pro," Mara said later. "He proved that pro football didn't have to be a losing proposition. That more than anything else kept me in pro football."

HALAS AND PYLE HAD ARRANGED A BRUTAL SCHEDULE FOR Grange and the Bears. Two days after playing in New York, they took on a sandlot all-star team at Griffith Stadium in Washington, DC. Only 5,000 fans attended. Grange was limited by his arm injury. The promoter lost money. The very next day, the Bears were in Boston, playing the Providence Steam Roller before 18,000 fans. Grange left the game in the third quarter because his arm was sore. The day after that, the Bears lost badly in Pittsburgh to a local all-star team, with Grange unable to perform after the first quarter. He was booed as he walked to the locker room, where it was determined his injury was a broken wrist. Two days later, he did not suit up in Detroit, the Bears absorbed a 21–0 defeat, and the promoter refunded the proceeds from 9,000 of the 15,000 tickets he had sold.

But after taking a break, Halas and Pyle resumed the barnstorming tour in late December with three games in Florida, one in New Orleans, and five on the West Coast. Grange's injury had healed. He raced 70 yards for a touchdown in Tampa, tossed a scoring pass in Jacksonville. A crowd of 75,000 watched the Bears defeat a club team in Los Angeles. By the time the tour concluded in late January with a victory over an outmatched local all-star team in Seattle, the Bears had played seventeen games before slightly fewer than 300,000 spectators since leaving Chicago in early December. Although the show flopped at some stops, it had attracted the interest of famous syndicated sportswriters such as Grantland Rice, Damon Runyon, Westbrook Pegler, and Ford Frick, whose columns on Grange, although not always positive, introduced the idea of "paid football" to millions of readers. For the first time, pro football was treated as more than just a sandlot game.

The publicity came at a good time for the NFL. While the press followed Grange, several embarrassing incidents revealed the league's status as a precarious, small-time endeavor. The Milwaukee Badgers were caught using high school players in a game. The Pottsville (Pennsylvania) Maroons were suspended and stripped of the league title for defying a rule against playing an exhibition game in another team's home territory. (The game was in Philadelphia, home of the Frankford Yellow Jackets, against a team that included the members of the famed "Four Horsemen" backfield, who had led Notre Dame to a national championship.) But these incidents received little newspaper coverage because of Grange's dominance.

While partnering with Halas on the tour, C. C. Pyle had recognized that the NFL was not a sturdy institution; many of its franchises were barely surviving. But Pyle had just become the first person to make real money on pro football. He and Grange netted some $250,000 apiece on the Bears' tour, while Halas made $100,000. Now

Pyle wanted to make more. At an NFL owners' meeting on February 6, 1926, shortly after the end of the tour, he announced that he and Grange had secured a five-year lease on Yankee Stadium covering every Sunday and holiday date from October 15 to December 31. He was starting his own team in New York with Grange as the star.

"I have the biggest star in football and I have the lease on the biggest stadium in the country and I am coming into your league whether you like it or not," Pyle declared. Several owners practically shouted with joy. They envisioned Grange coming to their cities, selling tickets, and stirring excitement. A sense of euphoria spread through the room. But Tim Mara sat silent, stewing. He had started the Giants with the understanding that New York was his territory. Living in Grange's shadow was not his plan. And although his own interests dominated his thoughts, he also had the league's interests in mind. Should a player and his "representative" be able tell the owners how to run their business? Would the owners also allow the next great player to just invade another team's turf?

Mara stood and stated his case. Joe Carr, who was running the meeting, recognized Mara was correct and professed his support. But the president also arranged for Pyle and Mara to meet, hoping they could agree on a deal that satisfied both. Could the new team play in Brooklyn, perhaps? Carr hoped so; he naturally saw the benefit of having Grange in the NFL.

The meeting was bound to fail. Mara had found Pyle obnoxious from the day they met. When Carr brought them together in Detroit, Mara made it clear he loathed the idea of Pyle operating a team anywhere in New York. Pyle had a shrewd, innovative cast of mind, but he had met his match. Mara reportedly almost took a swing at Pyle, who stalked out of the meeting even more determined to proceed. "No blasted Irishman is going to keep me out of New York!" Pyle supposedly told Grange.

At Carr's urging, the other owners supported Mara, leaving Pyle outside of the NFL. Pyle quickly pivoted, devising a plan to start a new league with a Grange-led New York franchise as its flagship. The team would be called the Yankees, Pyle said, and New York's fans surely would flock to see Grange. He suggested the new team would run Mara and the Giants out of town.

In the coming years, several upstart pro football leagues would form and challenge the NFL, seeking to take over, or at least share, the nascent sport. Each time, as with this first challenge from Pyle, the NFL's defense of its turf began with Mara and the Giants. The upstart leagues all put teams in New York, recognizing the necessity of success in America's largest market. The new teams challenged Mara at times when the Giants were not consistently profitable, testing Mara's patience, fortitude, business agility, and, very likely, his cash reserves. If Mara had ever tired of it all and ceded New York to a newcomer, the NFL might have been eclipsed.

But he did not. When he heard about Pyle's new league, Mara dug in for a fight, fearing that the likeliest outcome was both teams would struggle. There just was not enough interest in pro football to support two New York teams, Mara believed. "I didn't make enough money last year to stuff a hat brim," he told a reporter. "If Grange carries out his threat to put a team in New York and conflicts with our Sunday dates, neither one of us will make a nickel."

By the fall, Pyle had organized a ten-team venture known formally as the American Football League and informally as the "Grange League." It featured one former NFL squad, the Rock Island Independents, and new teams such as the Boston Bulldogs and Los Angeles Wildcats. It kicked off with high hopes and an optimistic motto: "Football for all and all for football." Carr, in an interview with Don Maxwell, sports editor of the *Chicago Tribune,* said he welcomed the challenge of a rival league and warned Pyle about thinking it was a get-rich venture. "Oh, it's a great game, this pro football. But it's never been a great money-making game," Carr said. "Take that old team we called the Columbus Panhandles. I organized that bunch 20 years and more ago. We made some money, but I didn't get rich. No one has in this pro grid game, and a lot of us have gone broke thinking we would."

The AFL's season began encouragingly, with the Yankees drawing 22,000 fans to games in Cleveland and Philadelphia, the latter
more than double what an NFL game at the same stadium drew
a week later. But fans quickly lost interest. Grange, playing on an
injured knee, could not replicate the dazzling runs that had made
him famous. Crowds for most games shrank to a few thousand fans.
Several AFL franchises folded in October, more in November. Only
four were operating by the end of the season.

The NFL was also struggling badly. Its product simply was not
exciting. Of 116 official league contests in 1926, almost three-fourths
ended with one team having failed to score. Almost 10 percent of the
games ended scoreless. There were twenty-one teams vying for the
league title, but many drew meager crowds. Mara was among those
experiencing problems. His usual arsenal of marketing tricks failed to
lure fans to the Polo Grounds. A succession of rainy Sundays did not
help. Just 5,000 fans attended one game. The return of Jim Thorpe,
back with the Canton Bulldogs, drew 35,000, but most of the crowd
came for a high school game that preceded the pro game, and Thorpe
never left the bench.

Trying to attract attention before a mid-November game against
a team from Los Angeles, Mara and the Giants resorted to a stunt.
One of their players carried a football to the top of the twenty-three-
story American Radiator Building on West Fortieth Street. Hinky
Haines was stationed on the sidewalk below, by the building's entrance. The idea was to complete "the longest forward pass on record,"
according to the *New York Times*. On the first attempt, the ball hurtled
downward, hit the sidewalk, and exploded. A third attempt knocked
Haines over. He finally made the catch on the fifth try, and onlookers
applauded, but that Sunday's game drew another small crowd.

Obsessed with the Yankees, Mara ascended to the top of the Polo
Grounds one Sunday when both teams had games and trained binoculars on nearby Yankee Stadium. "There's no one over there, either!"
he exclaimed. His fears had been realized. Pyle and the Yankees lost
$100,000 during the season, after which the AFL folded. Mara lost

$40,000 and was also tempted to give up. He again had doubts about pro football's future. How could he not? But he still believed it was possible the sport could become a winner, and, more importantly, his sons, Jack and Wellington, loved that he owned the Giants. "It was a challenge just to stay afloat. I think he was tempted many times to get out. He had a hand in many businesses, and this one was not profitable," his grandson, John Mara, said. "He enjoyed going to the games and being a part of it, but his sons were the ones who developed a passion for it. He would have sold the team and gotten out if they hadn't been so excited. I'm sure of it."

WHEN PYLE APOLOGIZED TO MARA AFTER THE DISASTROUS 1926 season, the NFL's owners relented and permitted him to bring his Yankees, with Grange, into their league. But, at Mara's insistence, the deal with Pyle put severe limits on the Yankees, who were permitted to play just a few games per season at Yankee Stadium, never conflicting with a Giants game at the Polo Grounds. In essence, Mara controlled when Pyle's team played. It was a terrible deal for Pyle, whose fate was further sealed when Grange suffered a serious knee injury early in the 1927 season and was unable to play. The football Yankees would fold before the decade ended. The Giants, meanwhile, won the NFL championship in 1927, as if to reward Mara for having triumphed in pro football's first war. It would not be the last.

3

MARSHALL: THE SHOWMAN

EVEN AFTER GRANGE'S TOUR IN 1925 AND EARLY 1926, most American sports fans viewed pro football as a dubious enterprise, believing it lacked tradition, class, and consistent quality—the elements that had helped make college football so popular. But pro football had company at the bottom of the nation's sports ladder. Pro basketball, also in its infancy, was even more obscure.

Unlike football, basketball still was not popular on college campuses. The pro game consisted of a scattershot collection of club teams located in the East and Midwest. Some had formed leagues such as the Central Basketball League, Eastern League, and Interstate Basket Ball League, but these tenuous coalitions never lasted long. Players jumped from team to team, sometimes from one night to the next, in search of better pay. Owners ran up debts. Meager crowds were the norm.

As with pro football, though, the sport featured zealous team owners who believed it would eventually attract a larger following. Max Rosenblum, a department store magnate in Cleveland, owned a team, as did George Preston Marshall, the operator of a chain of laundries in Washington, DC. In 1925, they and several other owners convinced Joe Carr to help them put together a "major" league. The American Basketball League tipped off in the fall.

Carr talked Halas into starting a team in Chicago. Halas had played basketball at Illinois, so he understood the game. He hoped the team would provide revenue in the winter and early spring, when the Bears were not playing. Carr, becoming a close friend, was optimistic about basketball's future. Halas called his team the Bruins, continuing with his Cubs/Bears theme.

Of the basketball league's other owners, Marshall most impressed Halas. Tall and ruddy faced, with slick-backed hair and blazing blue eyes, Marshall had taken a small laundry business and built a chain with several dozen locations. Palace Laundry and Dry Cleaning was ubiquitous in the nation's capital and had made Marshall a wealthy man. He ate at expensive restaurants, drank at stylish clubs, and lived out of hotel suites. A driver chauffeured him around Washington in a limousine. He had just turned thirty. Halas had never met anyone like him.

A former actor, Marshall promoted his laundries with a theatrical flair. The presentation was just as important as the product, he believed. His stores were always freshly painted blue and gold, with bright flower arrangements in the front windows. His employees wore crisp linen uniforms, also blue and gold. His delivery trucks—painted blue and gold—were everywhere. And Marshall had a knack for devising effective sales campaigns. Once, he took out a full-page newspaper ad that was entirely blank except for a disclaimer at the bottom: "This page cleaned by Palace Laundry and Dry Cleaning Company." Thinking a basketball team could help promote his business, Marshall bought a Washington-area semipro team known as the Yankees in 1923. Marshall renamed them the Palace Five. Some fans called them the Laundrymen. Their best player, George "Horse" Haggerty, was a hulking interior player best known as the first man able to palm a basketball.

When the Palace Five joined the ABL in 1925, Marshall moved their home games to the Arcade, a 4,000-seat arena in the city's northwest quadrant. Game nights became spectacles. There was a preliminary competition, usually a matchup of local high school basketball squads, followed by a game between the Palace Five and a league rival. The evening culminated with a dance on the court, with the Meyer Davis Palace Five Orchestra providing music.

Like Tim Mara, Marshall knew how to draw a crowd. The Palace Five developed a following. After several winning seasons, though, the team lost eight straight games at the start of the 1927 campaign. With his crowds dwindling, Marshall gave up, selling the franchise to a Brooklyn club in another league. Pro basketball had become "a big business requiring more of my personal attention than I can give it without neglecting my laundry interests," he told the *Washington Post*. In truth, it remained a failing sport.

Halas was disappointed about Marshall's departure from the league. Halas had brought his Bruins to Washington and thoroughly enjoyed Marshall's lively game-night show. Games in other cities seemed drab by comparison. Halas's own home games at the Illinois National Guard Armory, on Chicago's North Side, were hardly spectacles. Instead of following Marshall's lead and giving up, though, Halas doubled down on his investment, moving the Bruins' home games to the larger Chicago Stadium. "I went to a few games. I remember the coach's wife became good friends with my mother. But there was never much attendance," Halas's daughter, Virginia McCaskey, recalled.

When the ABL suspended operations in 1931, Halas finally disbanded the team. Pro basketball would not gain traction with the public until the late 1940s. But the ABL, nevertheless, had quite an impact on American sports. It was where Carr, Halas, and Marshall first worked together, a partnership that eventually produced a sporting success story unimaginable at the time.

IF THE STORIES MARSHALL LIKED TO TELL ABOUT HIMSELF can be believed, he began honing his flair for showmanship as an eleven-year-old in Grafton, West Virginia, a railroad and coal mining town where he was born in 1896. He had a business selling rabbits, using the proceeds to buy marbles and minor league baseball tickets. Unable to sell a common momma rabbit, he took out a newspaper ad offering a "fine Jacksonville hare" for sale. That was inaccurate, but the ad attracted customers, and Marshall sold the rabbit for three times the normal price. "I've been guilty of promotional ideas and being a showman ever since I can remember," he later wrote.

Grafton, a town of 5,200, was almost entirely white and had a distinctly southern sensibility. Marshall, the only child of the local newspaper publisher, was descended from Confederate officers. His segregated upbringing nurtured views on race that he would carry into adulthood.

Though not an outstanding athlete, Marshall enjoyed sports. In the summer, he was the batboy for the local minor league team. In the fall, he organized his friends into a sandlot football squad that competed against boys from other towns. Marshall did not play, but he sold tickets to the games, making as much as twenty-five dollars per contest. Already, he was interested in the business of sports.

When he was a teenager, his father took possession of a laundry store in Washington, DC, as payment on a debt. The family moved from Grafton to the nation's capital. Marshall attended Central High, a segregated public school, and the private Friends Select School. He also attended Randolph-Macon Academy in Front Royal, Virginia. But schoolwork bored him. Tall, slender, and darkly handsome, he dreamed of becoming an actor and joined a troupe at Poli's Theater in Washington. Falling in love with the lights, music, and applause, he quit school to pursue an acting career. He liked to call himself the Magnificent Marshall; he would never be known for modesty. Initially, he enjoyed relative success, cast in roles both in New York and with a touring company. "I persisted in the conviction that I was a budding Barrymore," he would write, but, in the end, "a number of producers differed" with his assessment, and he had to admit he "was not much of an actor."

From early 1917 until late in 1918, he served in the army during the Great War, mostly in a machine-gun company at Camp Meade in

Maryland. He never left the United States and returned to a changed family dynamic. His father had died during the war, and now Marshall had a $5,000 life insurance payout, a mother to support, and a laundry business to run. "My playing days were over," he explained. It was time to make money, ideally lots of it. The Magnificent Marshall did not intend to live quietly.

He dabbled in the theater business, investing in Broadway shows and producing performances at segregated venues in Washington and Baltimore. One of his favorite plays was *Getting Gertie's Garter,* a bawdy sexual farce set in a hayloft. But he soon gave up the theater business, finding his father's modest laundry operation more profitable. In Washington, a growing city with a transient population of federal government employees, there was a need for laundry services. Marshall beat out his competitors with catchy slogans and relentless promotion, which included the blue and gold uniforms of his basketball team, with "Palace Laundry" emblazoned across the chest. His laundry chain expanded from two stores to two dozen and kept growing. "Showmanship provided the answer," he wrote.

Besides promoting his business, Marshall shamelessly promoted himself, making himself the center of attention on Washington's social circuit with his good looks, loud voice, and opinions on all subjects, many reflecting his conservative politics. Every night became a performance. Marshall could be found at Duke Zeibert's, the popular bar and eatery, or the Shoreham Hotel, where beautiful people gathered on the terrace to talk politics. Even in a city of large egos, Marshall stood out. Whatever situation he was in, he "considered it a lost opportunity were he not the center of attention," a *Washington Post* sportswriter would write. Another journalist would say that Marshall "is not always offensive but he is never merely inoffensive. He dominates any group of people he finds himself in. He does not hold conferences, he holds court."

Marshall married a Ziegfeld Follies showgirl, but his incessant carousing doomed their union. He made no secret of his true goal. Raised in Appalachia, he sent out Christmas cards featuring himself

George Preston Marshall. (Associated Press)

with a laundry sack over his shoulder as he climbed a ladder marked "society." He realized his grandiose ambitions, becoming a staple of newspaper society columns in both Washington and New York, where he kept a suite at the St. Regis Hotel and was often seen attending Broadway openings and staying out late at fashionable nightspots such as the Stork Club.

Nothing derailed him. When his nocturnal lifestyle ended his first marriage, he began dating starlets and actresses, including Louise Brooks, the former silent-movie star who glamorized the bobbed haircut. She playfully called Marshall "the West Wash King." When the stock market crashed in 1929, plunging millions into economic hardship, Marshall again stood out, this time by surviving in style.

His continued business success afforded him "more time for baseball, football, and basketball games," as he later put it, and he still corresponded with Joe Carr, his friend from the basketball league. Now Carr wanted him to buy into the NFL; running the football league was still Carr's primary job. Marshall was skeptical. Even by

1929, almost a decade after George Halas had founded the Chicago Bears and helped bring pro football into existence, the NFL was not an impressive venture. Twelve franchises had disbanded in the past four years. Four new ones had joined the league, all destined to fail. Carr wanted Marshall to back a team in Boston, where a previous franchise had lasted just one season. Putting another team in Boston did not sound like a good idea, Marshall thought.

But Carr was persistent, and Halas, another friend from the basketball league, also kept prodding Marshall to try the NFL. Finally, Marshall agreed to take the prospect seriously. On November 15, 1931, he and several friends were among a crowd of 20,000 at a game between the New York Giants and Halas's Chicago Bears at the Polo Grounds. The Bears won, 12–6. After what he called the "thrilling" contest, Marshall and company gathered for drinks. The others were Jay O'Brien, a New York investment banker; Vincent Bendix, a midwesterner who had made a fortune manufacturing starters and brakes for automobiles; Larry Doyle, a New York stockbroker; and John "Jack" Hearst, the son of newspaper publisher William Randolph Hearst. They met at Hearst's apartment in Manhattan.

According to Marshall's version of the evening's events, O'Brien asked, "Why can't we have a football team, the best in the country?" Marshall explained that it cost at least $25,000 to get a team going and operate it for a season, and "we probably don't want to shoot that sum on an enthusiasm." But the others, except for Hearst, were interested. Even when Marshall said the league wanted them to run a team in Boston, they wanted to invest. In fact, one said he knew the owner of baseball's Boston Braves and could arrange a cheap lease deal for the team at Braves Field. By the end of the night, everyone had agreed to invest $7,500 to get the project started. "My worst nature got the best of me," Marshall would later say. He called Carr with the news. The NFL president was delighted. Marshall's Boston team would kick off in 1932.

4

BELL: THE PROFLIGATE SON

As the twentieth century began in the United States, the richest 10 percent of the population amounted to a royal class. They owned 75 percent of the country's assets. They paid no income tax. They lived in ornate mansions on Fifth Avenue in New York; along the seaside boulevards of Newport, Rhode Island; and in other bastions of power and prestige such as Philadelphia's Rittenhouse Square, "home to more millionaires per square foot than any other American neighborhood except New York's Fifth Avenue," according to one account. This was Bert Bell's world as a boy.

Rittenhouse Square itself was a public park designed by William Penn, the English entrepreneur who founded Pennsylvania in 1681. Beginning in the 1850s, wealthy families seeking refuge from immigrants and increasing commercial development had surrounded the park with brownstone and marble mansions designed by leading architects. By 1900, the area's residents included John Wanamaker, founder of the famous department store; Alexander Cassatt, president of the Pennsylvania Railroad; and William Weightman, a chemical manufacturer who became Philadelphia's leading real estate owner.

John Cromwell Bell and his wife, the former Fleurette de Benneville Myers, fit right in. Bell was a well-known corporate attorney with a future in politics. Fleurette's relatives had wielded influence in Philadelphia since the colonial era. They were the quintessential young power couple. Indeed, we know far more about Bert Bell's family history than we do about Halas's, Mara's, or Marshall's because his family had been prominent for centuries before his birth.

Born in 1862 in central Pennsylvania, John Bell had moved to Philadelphia when he was fourteen. A strong student, he ended up at the University of Pennsylvania, where he studied law and earned a prize for his thesis. He also played varsity football at a time when many of the sport's fundamental rules, such as the scoring worth of a touchdown, were still being debated and frequently revised.

In 1884, Bell's final season, Penn defeated Harvard for the first time. Though he put away his uniform sweater after that, he would continue in the sport for years as a chairman of Penn's football committee and one of the sport's foremost rules experts. In the 1890s, he was second in command to Yale's Walter Camp on the rules committee of the Intercollegiate Athletic Association, the forerunner of the National Collegiate Athletic Association. When the NCAA was formed in the early 1900s out of Theodore Roosevelt's determination to make football safer, Bell was among the organizers.

After college, he rose quickly through Philadelphia's lawyerly ranks and attained prominence. The city's Republican elite eyed him as a potential district attorney candidate, but he turned them down; between his football obligations and his corporate clients, his days were full.

In 1890, at age twenty-eight, he married Fleurette at her family's mansion in northwest Philadelphia. Fleurette's father, Leonard Myers, was a lawyer and Civil War veteran who had been a Republican congressman and close confidant of two presidents, Abraham Lincoln and James Garfield. But it was Fleurette's maternal ancestry that provided her social bona fides; her great-great-grandfather, George de Benneville, was born in London in 1703 to aristocratic French Huguenot parents and raised in the royal court of Queen Anne.

De Benneville eventually renounced the privileged life of an aristocrat after a spiritual awakening and came to America in 1741. Settling in Pennsylvania's Oley Valley, north of Philadelphia, he married Esther Bertolet, the daughter of another influential settler. They had seven children and built a homestead that included a school, church, and medical practice. Trained as a doctor, de Benneville treated and tutored Native Americans as well as local citizens while becoming the first person in the colonies to preach a Universalist faith of salvation for all souls. After his wealthy father-in-law died in 1758, de Benneville moved to Bristol Township, near Philadelphia, where he built an estate and continued to treat patients and preach. Siding firmly with the rebels in the Revolutionary War, he ministered to soldiers but also offered his family's burial yard as a final resting place for a British general who died in combat. Two of his sons became doctors, and a daughter married into the wealthy Keim family of Reading, Pennsylvania. A bountiful family tree sprouted. By the time John Bell and Fleurette de Benneville Myers married in 1890, some 150 descendants of George de Benneville were buried in the family cemetery adjacent to the mansion where the ceremony took place.

The Bell nuptials were labeled "one of the interesting weddings of the week" by the *Times of Philadelphia*, though it was "a quiet affair, owing to a recent death in the bride's family." (Fleurette's mother had died the year before.) Bell was described as "the well-known lawyer and member of the university football team." Fleurette wore a "gray traveling suit," and "immediately after the brief reception, the newly-wedded couple left on a wedding tour." They settled into a "handsome" three-story home at 334 South Twenty-Fourth Street, a half mile from Rittenhouse Square and across the street from another park, Fitler Square. The Bells employed servants to keep house and a cook to prepare their meals. Their first child, John Cromwell Bell Jr., was born on October 24, 1892, and another son, De Benneville Bell, was born on February 25, 1895.

Philadelphia's Republican leaders continually sought to lure Bell into politics, but he turned down a judgeship and a job in the district attorney's office. Finally, when the district attorney job itself opened up in 1902, Bell "yielded to the persistent demand of the people" and accepted the position "after receiving a petition signed by fifteen hundred members of the bar and many leading citizens of Philadelphia." As district attorney, Bell secured the second-ever first-degree murder conviction of a woman in Philadelphia, and, in a "brilliant" performance, won a verdict in a complex case in which "the leading chemists of the world were pitted against the district attorney's contention that the use of sodium sulfide as a food preservative was deleterious." Upon completing his term, he ran for reelection and won "by a very nattering majority, receiving the support of many opposed to him politically."

In 1907, Bell declined to run for another term and returned to private practice. At a testimonial dinner, the chief justice of Pennsylvania's supreme court said Bell had "followed faithfully the traditions of the office and has given them additional luster." But Bell was enticed back into politics when Pennsylvania's governor appointed him the state's attorney general in 1911. In a history of Philadelphia published the next year, it was written that Bell's "position is evident to all who know aught of the history of the Philadelphia bar and the work of the courts during the last quarter of a century. Throughout his entire professional career he has united the intensely practical with high ideality. Words, looks and actions are the alphabet by which we spell character, and in the life of John Cromwell Bell these have had no uncertain sound."

BELL AND HIS WIFE LIVED "AMID SUCH TURN OF THE CENTURY wealth and prominence that it took John O'Hara more than a dozen books to describe it," the sports journalist Phil Musick once wrote, referencing the Pennsylvania-born novelist who depicted those times. Although 1900 signaled the end of America's Gilded Age in some ways, the Bells enjoyed the trappings of their great fortune well into the twentieth century.

In the early 1900s they hired architect Horace Trumbauer to design a home for them. Trumbauer did not work on a small scale; his previous work included a 110-room mansion for industrialist Peter Widener. Trumbauer would later design the main library at Harvard. For the Bells, he created a commanding three-story brick residence at 229 South Twenty-Second Street, just west of Rittenhouse Square. With a marble staircase and marble archway framing its front door, the home featured three floors of high-ceilinged rooms that looked onto Twenty-Second Street. The staff lived on the fourth floor. It was a home befitting American royalty, destined for the National Register of Historic Places. In 1906 the Bells moved in, when their sons were fourteen and eleven. Like many in their circle, they continued to split time between their city residence and a summer estate, in their case an eleven-acre retreat in Radnor, on the Main Line. According to the Social Register of 1900, the home was known as Blithewold.

The Bells indulged their two sons. De Benneville "had a nanny when he was 2, a pony when he was 6, a tux when he was 12 and a Marmon roadster when he was 17." One of his friends, Lou Little, destined to become a college football coach, later told sportswriter W. C. Heinz, "For a fellow like me, that beautiful city home with the servants and everything was like walking into a hotel. And that summer home was like walking into a country club."

John Bell's sons grew up hearing about the law, politics, and football, their father's passions, and it was assumed they would take a similar path, utilizing the advantages their parents' success and lineage afforded them. John Jr., the dutiful and obliging eldest son, known as Jack, "wanted to follow in his father's footsteps," according to the Pennsylvania Historical and Museum Commission, and he mimicked those steps almost exactly. After his graduation from Philadelphia's Episcopal Academy in 1910, Jack attended his father's alma mater, the University of Pennsylvania. Although he did not play football, he excelled at soccer and tennis while earning a liberal arts degree. Then it was on to Penn's law school, a lucrative private practice, and political appointments that included stints as Philadelphia's assistant city solicitor and assistant district attorney—all before he turned thirty-three. A conservative Republican, Jack Bell was destined for the highest levels of state government.

Though raised in the same circumstances, young de Benneville was different from his older brother. Whenever his nannies lost track of him, they knew they could find him playing football in the park across the street. As a youth, he rejected his fanciful first name, considering it snobbish. He wanted to be called Bert. When friends teased him for it, he slugged them. "If you don't think I had to fight many times to get people to call me Bert, then I must have dreamed of all those schoolyard battles," he said later. At the Haverford School, a prestigious private academy, he was an indifferent student but was described in his senior yearbook as a "hero of countless football, basketball, and baseball battles," and "one of the best athletes in the history of the school." Though he would make his name in football, he also batted .510 as a senior baseball captain. He was a jock and something of a class clown. His classmates voted him "most sarcastic" and "best kidder."

Decades later, Bert's son, Upton, said of him, "Although he came from a proper conservative Republican family, Bert walked with a swagger as a kid and found a way to talk out of the side of his mouth. He didn't want to talk like all of those proper, jut-jawed society people. He decided that everything he was going to do was going to do was in some ways different from the way they acted."

His determination to be different did not include his college choice. That was not negotiable. "He'll go to Penn or he'll go to hell!" his father roared near the end of his high school years. But, unlike his father and brother, Bert meandered through his classes at Penn, uninterested in academic excellence or becoming a lawyer. He "never came to class if the weather was bad outside," according to some football teammates. He would eventually leave Penn without earning a degree.

But, as in high school, he attained prominence in college as an athlete, now as a quarterback for his father's beloved Quakers. Though just five feet eight and 155 pounds, Bell was a "peppery little guy," according to one sportswriter, and "a great field general who is never bluffed and never at a loss for what to do," according to another. His coach praised him as "brainy" after he started in his first varsity game in 1915. He would start at quarterback for the Quakers for most of his time on campus.

While at a preseason training camp outside Philadelphia in 1916, he received word that his mother was gravely ill. Fleurette had suffered a stroke and undergone surgery. Bell set out for home, but his mother died before he reached her bedside. Six days later, he started at quarterback for the Quakers in their season opener and tossed a long pass that set up the only points in a win over West Virginia.

The 1916 season would be the high point of his college career. Bell was briefly benched after an early-season loss to Swarthmore in which he completed just two of twenty passes, but he quickly regained his starting job and "piloted the team in masterful fashion" during an upset win at Michigan. Five thousand fans greeted the team upon its return to Philadelphia. Bell then gave a "faultless" performance in a rout of archrival Cornell. With a record of seven wins, two losses, and a tie, the Quakers were invited to take on Oregon in the Tournament of Roses football game in Pasadena, California.

Played on January 1, 1917, before 27,000 fans, the game was easily the most significant in Penn football history to that point. Outweighed by fifteen pounds per man on average, the Quakers competed well as decided underdogs, generating thirteen first downs to Oregon's eight. But Oregon's Webfoots prevailed, 14–0, scoring both of their touchdowns in the second half. Bell endured such a beating from his rugged opponents that a substitute took his place in the fourth quarter.

Like many teams across the country, Penn's 1917 varsity was impacted by America's expanding involvement in the Great War. Most upperclassmen went into the armed forces, leaving freshmen to man key positions. The Quakers still won nine of eleven games with Bell

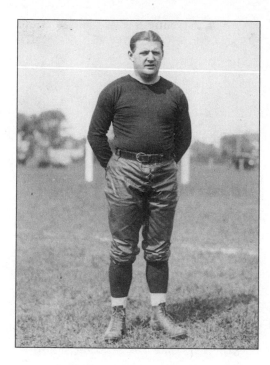

Bert Bell, quarterback of the Penn Quakers. (Penn Athletics Archives)

leading the way. In a decisive victory over a Michigan squad thought to be stronger, he "used such a varied selection of plays that at times he had the Michigan defense bewildered," according to the *Philadelphia Bulletin*.

At the team's end-of-season banquet, Bell was selected as a captain for the 1918 season. But, in another act that belied his rarified social background, he volunteered for military duty with an army mobile hospital unit based out of Philadelphia. Several teammates also volunteered, as did Jack Kelly, a noted oarsman who would later win three Olympic gold medals and gain renown as a developer and the father of actress Grace Kelly. Deployed to France in the spring of 1918, Bell and his friends served at Châtel-Guyon, a health resort that had been converted into a hospital for wounded American and French soldiers as well as German prisoners. It was not a cushy assignment. Germans shelled the hospital, killing several of Bell's comrades. The unit received commendations for helping move patients to safety during the shelling.

Bell "almost never talked about his war experience," his son, Upton, would recall. But he did share lighthearted stories about cavorting through the French countryside in his off-duty hours with Jack Kelly, who became a lifelong friend. They dreamed up a bait-and-switch that worked to good effect. Bell, the big talker, would pick a fight with a tough guy in a bar, but, rather than throw a punch, he offered to bet that his friend, Jack, could whip the tough guy. Frenchmen invariably accepted the challenge, and Kelly, a muscular former bricklayer, invariably won the fight. Many nights ended with Bell and Kelly hurriedly skipping town with their pockets full and grins on their faces.

The armistice brought Bell home, and, in the autumn of 1919, he resumed his life as a big man on Penn's West Philadelphia campus, serving as the football captain and starting quarterback. His return sent expectations for the Quakers' season soaring. Bell is a "brilliant player" and "Penn seems destined to take the leading position in the intercollegiate football world in the East this fall," one columnist wrote. The Quakers overwhelmed their first five opponents by a 237–7 margin, delighting local fans. Penn added 5,000 seats at Franklin Field to meet an increased demand for tickets. But the team's initial success did not last. Bell shanked three punts, missed a field goal, and tossed a crucial interception in a stunning home loss to underdog Penn State. The Quakers then suffered a disappointing loss to Dartmouth at the Polo Grounds in New York when Bell missed a key field goal and failed to bring down two runners on their way to the end zone—a performance lambasted by the *New York Times*, which pinned the blame for the 20–19 defeat "squarely" on Bell.

He realized he no longer needed football. He was twenty-four, a man among boys in the huddle. He had been to war and back, and now he wanted to enjoy the peace that followed. Although he still enjoyed playing football, he was ready to don a raccoon coat and take part in the Philadelphia high life, with his father paying the bills. "My father and mother gave me everything I ever asked for, and I was a pretty good asker," Bell told W. C. Heinz later.

Three days after the loss to Dartmouth, the *Philadelphia Inquirer* reported that Bell had lost more than just the game. It turned out he had wagered his Marmon roadster. Bell confirmed the story years later, explaining that his father had just given him the thousand-dollar car, which he added to his stake after he had bet "all the money I had and could borrow" that the Quakers would defeat Dartmouth. Bell's father was surely not pleased to learn the car now belonged to a Dartmouth football fan. John C. Bell Sr., by this point one of Philadelphia's wealthiest citizens, knew his older son, Jack, would never embarrass the family in such a way. Jack was out of law school, married, and working as an assistant city solicitor. But the elder Bell continued to tolerate his rakish younger son's shenanigans. Bert was the one who had played college football, his father's favorite sport, and the one who had volunteered for frontline military service. "Despite their philosophical differences, Bert was my grandfather's favorite child," Upton Bell said. "Jack was the prized one, but my grandfather absolutely loved Bert because Bert was all the things he wasn't. Bert was a gambler, a chance-taker."

Months after playing in his final college game (the Quakers tied Pitt, 3–3, to end their ballyhooed 1919 season with a 6-2-1 record), Bell withdrew from Penn without a degree despite having been on campus since 1914. There was no chance that he would follow his father and brother into the law. Football was what he knew best. He took a job as an assistant coach at—where else?—Penn, which in 1920 hired a new head coach, John Heisman, a Penn grad and former Quaker player who had become a renowned coach at Auburn, Clemson, and Georgia Tech. New York's Downtown Athletic Club would later put Heisman's name on its prestigious award honoring the nation's top college football player.

In 1920, Heisman put Bell in charge of the backfield. Bell's close friend and former Penn teammate, Lud Wray, coached the line. They would hold those jobs for almost a decade as Penn fielded winning teams and drew big crowds. Heisman left after three seasons, but his replacement, Lou Young, kept Bell and Wray and led the Quakers to a 9-1-1 season in 1924. That success prompted speculation that Bell and Wray might soon become head coaches elsewhere, but they stayed at Penn.

When not coaching, Bell was one of Philadelphia's most prominent playboys. A staple of the high-society party scene, he stayed out late, chased girls, drank, and gambled on everything from cards to horse racing to boxing matches and football games. He spent several weeks of every summer with other scions of wealthy families at the horse races in Saratoga, New York. While betting on races during the day and staying out at supper clubs until dawn, Bell met Tim Mara, then known primarily as a bookie from New York, and became friendly with Mara's son, Jack. He also spent time with George Preston Marshall, still a laundry chain owner from Washington, and Art Rooney, a shrewd sportsman from Pittsburgh.

Bell's meager salary as an assistant football coach did not begin to fund his escapades, which included sizable gambling losses, but Bell's father always provided whatever was needed to settle his scores. The elder Bell made only one request of his younger son: that the two eat breakfast together every morning, with Bert wearing a coat and tie, regardless of how much money Bert had lost the previous day or how late he stayed out.

The family never revealed an official tally of Bert's losses, but he squandered so much money that his father eventually demanded that he work off some of the debt. The elder Bell had ventured into real estate and now owned two of Philadelphia's landmark Center City hotels. By 1928 Bert was managing the Ritz-Carlton while continuing to coach at Penn, and he later managed the St. James. But he continued to lose money. Picking the wrong time to try the stock market, he suffered losses at a brokerage house located in the Ritz-Carlton, then reportedly dropped $50,000 in the 1929 crash. His father finally ran out of patience and lashed out angrily at his son during breakfast one day. "Dammit, you're thirty-something and still drinking and gambling and running around. I'm tired of bailing you out! It's time you settled down," he exclaimed. John Bell suggested his son marry the debutante daughter of a friend. When Bert resisted, his father offered to pay him $100,000. Bert "reluctantly" agreed and the engagement was set. But, when he received a chunk of the money, Bert drove straight to Saratoga and lost it at the betting window. He returned to Philadelphia and confessed to his father that he had blown the wedding gift.

"And I ain't marrying that broad!" he exclaimed.

His father responded, "Well, Bert. If that's the way you want it, no more money. You can go run my hotels and do your coaching, or do whatever you want, but that's the last penny you're ever going to get from me. You're not going to see another red cent." Bert Bell had always relied on the safety net his family's wealth provided, but, after testing its limits for years, he could count on it no longer.

PHILADELPHIA WAS A COLLEGE FOOTBALL HOTBED IN THE 1920S and early 1930s, when Penn was a national power. Temple and Villanova opened new stadiums, aspiring to greater prominence. By 1932 the city had hosted more than a dozen Army-Navy games.

There also was pro football in Philadelphia. The Frankford Yellow Jackets, named for the small northeast Philadelphia neighborhood where they played, joined the NFL in 1924 and became consistent winners. C. C. Pyle's infamous American Football League, built around Red Grange, included a Philadelphia team called the Quakers. As elsewhere, the pros lived in the shadows of the college teams. The Quakers won the AFL title in 1926 but folded with the rest of the league. The Yellow Jackets fashioned a 55-22-8 record in their first five NFL seasons and won the league title in 1926, but many of their home games at tiny Frankford Stadium drew no more than 5,000 fans. Pro football was an afterthought in the city.

Though steeped in the college game from a young age—his father had literally helped write the rulebook—Bert Bell did not entirely ignore the pros. In 1926 he served as an informal coaching advisor for the Quakers, whose roster featured several of his former

Penn teammates, including Lud Wray. Bell even suited up for one AFL game, against Jim Thorpe and the Canton Bulldogs. But he remained a loyal college football man and continued to coach Penn's backfield through the 1928 season, when he resigned over a difference of opinion with Wray and the head coach about the need for practice scrimmages. (They wanted more; Bell feared they wore the players out.) Without a coaching job in 1929, he still spent his Saturdays at college games, studying tactics. Then, in 1930, he became the backfield coach at Temple, a job he would keep for three years.

Throughout these years, Bell paid little attention to the Frankford Yellow Jackets, who began to struggle after the stock market crash. Unable to sign quality players, they lost eight straight games at one point and finished the 1930 season with a 4-13-1 record. Their attendance plummeted, and not only because the team was bad; many fans simply could no longer afford tickets. When a fire destroyed their stadium before the 1931 season, the Yellow Jackets began splitting their home games between the Baker Bowl, home of baseball's Phillies, and Municipal Stadium, the giant facility that was packed for Army-Navy games. But few of their supporters came to watch them. The press began calling them the Philadelphia Yellow Jackets in hopes of improving attendance, but they were shut out in seven of eight games, further quelling interest. Finally, the owners suspended operations in early November, leaving Philadelphia without a pro team.

As much as we know about Bert Bell's lineage, we know curiously little about how he eventually got involved with the NFL. He had met Tim Mara and Jack Mara at Saratoga. He also knew George Preston Marshall and Art Rooney, who were not in the league yet but, like Bell, would soon gain admittance. The league began looking for new ownership in Philadelphia after the Yellow Jackets collapsed, not wanting to abandon the market. Bell probably seemed like an ideal candidate with his football background and enough family wealth to withstand a downturn in interest, attendance, and revenue. Few people knew his father had cut him off. One way or another, Bell became interested in owning a pro team. It would not cost a lot—the fee for a franchise was $2,500, less than he blew at the horse races on some days—and it surely sounded more interesting to him than running a hotel.

In 1932, when Marshall joined the NFL with a franchise in Boston, he wanted to hire Lou Little as his coach. Little and Bell had been childhood friends and teammates at Penn, and Little was now a winning head coach at Columbia. He turned Marshall down after consulting with Bell but recommended Wray, who took the job.

That fall, Bell patched up his differences with Wray that had led to his departure from Penn's staff several years earlier. While following his friend's team in Boston, he and Wray discussed the fact that their hometown was without a team. They could easily step in, they agreed. For someone in Bell's position, there was little downside. One can imagine John C. Bell Sr.'s reaction to the news that his son was considering buying into pro football. Now seventy and near the end of his life, he had always looked down his nose at the pro game, practically sneered at it. He could not imagine anyone wanting to watch football played by adults. The college game was popular, he believed, because it helped shaped the character of young men.

Bert Bell was undeterred. In one of his final rebellious acts, he disavowed his father's opinion, rounded up several minority investors, and bought the dormant Frankford franchise. The group paid a $2,500 guarantee to the NFL and assumed $11,000 in debts the Yellow Jackets owed the Bears, Giants, and Packers. On the day the purchase was finalized in 1933, Bell was walking in Center City Philadelphia. At the corner of Broad and Chestnut, two major streets, he glanced up and saw a billboard promoting President Franklin Roosevelt's National Recovery Act, emblazoned with its symbol, a bald eagle. Bell had an idea. He would call his new team the Philadelphia Eagles. When John C. Bell died two years later, he went to his grave believing Bert had once again done something foolish.

5

ROONEY: THE GAMBLER

H E IS RECALLED IN THE FAMILY AS THE "FIRST ART Rooney," distinguishing him from his grandson with the same name who became famous as the Pittsburgh Steelers' cigar-loving owner. The first Art was a red-bearded ironworker who wandered the globe in search of steady work in the 1800s. His Irish parents fled the potato famine for Montreal, where Art was born and lived until he was twenty-one. When Canada's economy collapsed, he relocated to Wales, married an Irish girl, and started a family, then moved back to Canada. Eventually, he crossed the border into the United States—on foot and without a passport, according to family legend—and found work in Youngstown, Ohio, before continuing east. By 1890, he was nearly forty and living with his wife and six children in Pittsburgh, at the time a "clanging, smoke-belching metropolis" in the heart of America's industrial belt.

In a city full of immigrant laborers, the Rooneys were better off than most. Art's father had taught him how to "puddle" molten iron, that is, to stir it to maintain a certain temperature and consistency. The skill allowed him to ascend the ranks from laborer to crew chief, tripling his paycheck. Art owned a home near the giant American

Iron Works mill, across the Monongahela River from downtown, and he also owned another property where he took in boarders. But in the early 1890s steel plants began taking over, and Art's union went on strike. Briefly reduced to working menial jobs, he eventually bought a boarding house with a ground-floor saloon that catered to the mill population—a wise investment, Art thought, because men drank even in tough times, when they could not afford it. Saloons became the family business. Art's oldest son, Daniel, opened one in Coulterville, a small coal town northeast of Pittsburgh, where he fell in love with Margaret Murray, a petite Irish redhead. They married and soon had a son, Arthur Joseph Rooney, born on January 27, 1901, in a room over the Coulterville saloon.

The first Art Rooney died in his early fifties in 1903, before his grandson of the same name knew him. But the first Art greatly influenced the life of the second. The first Art brought the Rooneys to Pittsburgh after years of wandering; the second Art would call Pittsburgh home for his entire life. The first Art took up the saloon business; the second Art grew up on top of one.

Daniel and Margaret Rooney moved back to Pittsburgh and bought a building in the Ward, a neighborhood on the city's north side. Located at the corner of Robinson and Corry Streets, adjacent to Exposition Park, home of the Pirates, Pittsburgh's National League baseball club, the building housed Dan Rooney's Café and Bar on the ground floor. Daniel and his family lived upstairs, while below them ballplayers, bookies, union leaders, gamblers, and ironworkers congregated, with no women allowed.

Broad shouldered and muscular, Daniel was deemed one of the toughest guys in the Ward. On Saturday nights, he broke up fights in his saloon, trudged upstairs to his wife and children, wiped off the blood, put on a clean shirt, and went back downstairs to tend bar until it was time to break up another fight. His oldest sons, Art and Dan, shared a tiny room. On some winter mornings, they awoke to find snow on their blankets that had blown through cracks in the walls. But they did not complain. They thought they lived at the center of the universe. In their father's saloon they met ballplayers and ward bosses, giving them an early introduction to their city's social and political life. By age thirteen, Art was paid to "run errands," which meant participating in political shenanigans. Years later, he told an interviewer he had no idea he was breaking the law by voting more than once in an election.

His mother attended mass every day and raised him and his siblings in the Roman Catholic faith. Once, when Art was fifteen and she was ill, he spent an entire day at church praying for her. He would become a daily communicant himself as an adult. His mother also made sure he tended to his schoolwork, but Art was more interested in sports than anything else. Unlike his grandfather or father, who worked from a young age to help support their families, Art had the freedom of leisure time, a relatively new concept among working-class families in America. Art and Dan, eventually the eldest of nine children, spent their days at the neighborhood park, dreaming of becoming baseball players like the ones they watched at Exposition Park and met in their father's saloon. They also played football, boxed, and brawled. Their father bought them boxing gloves and a punching bag for Christmas one year. "Boy, could they punch, and boy, could they fight," a family friend recalled.

Dan topped out at nearly six feet tall and inherited his father's broad shoulders; tangling with him was usually a mistake. Art would later joke that his menacing younger brother amassed more knockouts than Jack Dempsey. Art stopped growing at five feet eight but was naturally athletic and just as tough minded as Dan, especially in a boxing ring. A successful amateur fighter, he was runner-up twice in the American Athletic Union's national tournament and won an international competition in Canada. Although he never boxed in the Olympics, he defeated a lightweight who later won the gold medal at the 1920 games.

He was also a standout on the gridiron. At the University School, a prep academy, he played halfback and led the team with what the school newspaper described as "wiggling, squirming, and serpentine runs," standing "head and shoulders above his companions." Though small, he was talented enough to attract the attention of college coaches. Notre Dame's then-unknown coach, Knute Rockne, sent him a recruiting letter. Penn State offered him a cut of the proceeds from game-day program sales; the NCAA, barely a decade old, was not yet a strict, rules-obsessed overseer. Art turned down Rockne and Penn State. In an arrangement unimaginable today, he played simultaneously for Indiana Normal (now Indiana University of Pennsylvania) and Duquesne. It was an era when many schools played fast and loose with rosters and eligibility rules, and "tramp" players abounded. Art actually did not try hard to fool anyone. He played under his real name for both teams, whose games were covered by the same newspapers in Western Pennsylvania. If anyone noticed that he was playing for two schools, no one said anything.

In 1921 he left Pennsylvania to play baseball, his true love among sports, at Georgetown University in Washington, DC. He had played for semipro teams since he was fifteen and still hoped to reach the major leagues. A speedy outfielder, he hit for a high average with a left-handed swing and stole a lot of bases. To his great disappointment, though, Georgetown's coach barely allowed him on the field. A scout for the Boston Red Sox still saw enough potential to offer him a contract, but Art turned it down, reasoning that he could earn more money playing for semipro teams around Pittsburgh. That fall, he was back on the football field, playing for just one school now, Duquesne.

When his college football days ended in the early 1920s, he faced a common predicament. He wanted to keep playing, but how and where? The NFL was not an attractive option; it was lurching forward, with franchises coming and going. Pro football's potential in Pittsburgh was limited by state ordinances, known as blue laws, prohibiting commercial activity on Sundays to avoid conflicting with church services. Sundays were when NFL teams played, so as not to compete with college games on Saturdays. Instead of supporting an NFL team, Pittsburgh boasted a league of semipro squads. Art started his own team, calling it the Hope-Harveys. Hope was the name of the Ward firehouse where the players changed and showered after games. Harvey was the name of the team doctor who never charged Art for his services. The team played at Exposition Park, which the Pirates had abandoned for the newly built Forbes Field.

The Hope-Harveys were a Rooney family affair. Art was the owner, coach, and halfback. Dan was the quarterback. Two of their younger brothers, Jim and John, also played on the team. The *Pittsburgh Press* called Art "the Red Grange of the independents," and Dan was also a formidable player, with his notable size and speed. Their games were deemed important enough to merit newspaper coverage. On November 28, 1924, the *Pittsburgh Daily Post* reported that Art returned an interception 60 yards for a touchdown in a victory over the Boston Bulldogs. On December 13, 1925, the same paper commented that "Art Rooney, little Northside lad, had a great campaign." The Hope-Harveys were among Western Pennsylvania's best sandlot teams.

Art and Dan continued to play semipro baseball for a succession of teams, including the Pittsburgh Collegians, and in 1925, they suited up for the Wheeling (West Virginia) Stingers of the Mid-Atlantic League, a fully professional circuit. Art led the league in runs, hits, and steals, and almost won the batting title. Dan, for his part, batted an impressive .369. They loved the minor-league life, the bus rides, late nights, and camaraderie with teammates. One night in Frostburg, Maryland, anti-Catholic taunts from the opposing dugout resulted in a brawl that halted the game and then eventually resumed later, at a restaurant. Frostburg's city council sent a letter to the Wheeling team's owners, informing them that Art and Dan were banned from the city.

The Rooney boys were sportsmen for all seasons, and, eventually, they wore down. Dan entered the priesthood and went to China as a missionary. Art continued to run the Hope-Harveys, who became known as the Majestic Radios after an electronics store became a sponsor, and then Art changed the name again, to the J. P. Rooneys, to promote his brother Jim's successful run for a seat in the Pennsylvania

General Assembly. By this point, Art was thirty and had given up his uniforms for a coat and tie.

For as long as he lived, Art relished telling the story of the one day he actually worked for a living. It came in the summer of 1918, after his senior year in high school. His mother had ideas about what he should do next. Rather than attend college, she thought he should get started in the iron mills, where so many men she knew worked, including Art's uncle, Mike Concannon, who was a foreman at a blast furnace. The family pulled a few strings, and Art reported for duty at the mill. The job was tough, sweaty, and dull. Art quickly realized he did not like it. After working all morning, he sat with Uncle Mike at lunch. "How much money do you make?" Art asked.

Mike told him and explained that Art, too, could make that much as a foreman after fifteen years. Art was not impressed. He packed up his lunch and went home without even bothering to collect his wages for a half-day's work. He had bigger ideas about how to provide for himself. He had a quick mind, a facility with numbers, and a knack for spotting opportunities—qualities that helped him make money at, of all places, the racetrack.

When Art was a boy, his father had introduced him to horse racing and gambling on an outing to a track in Cleveland. His father liked to bet, and Art loved everything about the scene: the roar of the crowd, the speed of the horses, the money on the line. Racing was illegal in Pennsylvania, but bookmakers could always be found at Dan Rooney's Bar and Café. Soon enough, Art was carrying wagers to horse parlors for some of his father's saloon customers. When he started making his own bets, he shocked his elders with his instincts and aptitude. He was "born to play the horses," his son would write, and "quickly surpassed in expertise his teachers, the touts and bookies and racing-form readers who recognized his precociousness and took him under their wings." Long before he stopped playing sports in the 1920s, Art came home from racetracks with more than enough

Art Rooney. (Pittsburgh Steelers)

money to live on. When a baseball team in the Southern League, a reputable minor-league circuit, offered him a contract, he turned it down and told the manager, "I can make more money at the racetrack."

He had grown up around hustlers, quick-witted men who always seemed to have an idea and an angle, and he became one himself. Instead of getting in the boxing ring, he promoted fight cards. Instead of playing football, he ran a team. In the late 1920s he became co-owner of the Showboat, a floating casino-nightclub on the Allegheny River. Drinking and gambling were illegal, but Art knew the right cops. His co-owner was a notorious card shark, and, according to his biographers, his acquaintances also included bootleggers and ward heelers. Art "was no angel," those biographers concluded, but other than "uncorroborated hearsay," there is "scant evidence indicating that he was more than peripherally engaged" in any illicit schemes.

Whenever he really needed money, he just went to the track. Art's winnings funded a unique honeymoon with his bride, the former Kathleen McNulty, in 1931. Kathleen, known to all as Kass, was six years younger and also from the Ward, where her father made pickle barrels. Art had paid her little attention until adulthood, when he saw her for what she was: a willowy, witty brunette. Her father was lukewarm about her taking up with a gambler and sportsman with dubious friends, but she defied him, and they eloped in a civil ceremony in New York, where they had traveled to watch the Belmont Stakes.

Art made $10,000 on the race, and, flush with cash, the couple headed across the country, traveling on trains, at times with a small entourage, visiting "every racetrack from here to Tijuana," Kass recalled. They stopped in San Diego, holed up in an elegant hotel, and crossed the border for the races at Tijuana's historic Agua Caliente racetrack. America was in the throes of the Great Depression, but life was grand and exciting for Art and Kass. They eventually came home, and, when they did, it was to families still upset they had eloped, so they were married again, this time at St. Peter's Church.

The couple settled into a Northside apartment. Every morning Art rose, kissed Kass goodbye, and commuted to his office at the Fort Pitt Hotel, a downtown landmark, where the phone rang constantly as he oversaw his interests and holdings, including the Showboat, the football team, local politics, and his racetrack wagers. He knew everyone and everything, it seemed. Years later, when one of his grandchildren visited and was asked to describe what granddad did for a living, the grandchild replied, "He answers the phone."

AT FIRST, ART WAS LUKEWARM ON THE IDEA OF BUYING INTO the National Football League. His sandlot team played in a creditable league—no less creditable than the NFL, as he saw it. But after the birth of his first child, a son, in 1932, he thought he needed a more dependable way to support his family besides playing the horses. His sandlot football league was never going to bring in a great deal of revenue. The NFL was hardly prospering, but its teams played in major cities, offering more potential for growth. He knew Tim Mara, Jack

Mara, and George Preston Marshall from the racing world. They told him Joe Carr wanted a team in football-mad Western Pennsylvania, and Art's political friends pointed out that there was growing support for an easing of the blue laws, a fundamental obstacle to an NFL franchise in the state.

With Carr's encouragement, Art put together a group of minority investors and presented himself to the NFL owners when they came to Pittsburgh for a meeting in late February 1933—a clear signal Pittsburgh was on their radar. The meeting was held at the Fort Pitt Hotel, where Art kept his office. At another league meeting five months later in Chicago, his franchise application was accepted along with bids from Bert Bell in Philadelphia and a Cincinnati group fronted by a local coroner.

Art was taking a gamble. A referendum on the repeal of blue laws would not take place until November, and if the vote went the wrong way, his team could not play on Sundays and would have trouble remaining in the league. But he never minded a bet, and certainly was an expert on reading odds. He liked his chances.

PART TWO

6

ALMOST BROKE

G EORGE HALAS DID NOT JUST POCKET THE WINDFALL HE received from the Bears' barnstorming tour with Red Grange in 1925 and early 1926. He was thirty, with a wife and two children to support—three children, really, the third being the Bears. Unlike many later NFL owners, as well as most of the founding fathers, Halas neither came from money nor earned a lot, forcing him to continually scrounge for cash to keep his team afloat. The Grange money enabled him to start business ventures that, he hoped, would make things easier. He opened a real estate company, invested in the stock market, and put more into his pro basketball franchise. The 1929 stock market crash curtailed his plans. Halas, along with millions of other Americans, was almost ruined by the subsequent economic depression. His broker sold his stocks for relative pennies. His real estate company folded, as did his basketball team. His Grange money was gone.

The Bears were already struggling. They slipped from nine wins in 1927 to seven in 1928 to just four in 1929. In the latter season, they lost to the Packers and Giants by a combined 67–0 score, and the crosstown Cardinals obliterated them, 40–6. Their attendance slipped with their performance. Their final home game in 1929 drew just 2,123 fans. "We couldn't pay our guarantee to the visitors from Frankford," Halas wrote.

In addition to coaching the team, Halas still suited up and played. Dutch Sternaman, his ownership partner, helped him coach, an arrangement that had become problematic. Halas favored a more wide-open offensive style, while Sternaman wanted to keep things simple. "The split hurt the team," according to Halas. "I would tell the team to do this and Sternaman would tell them to do that."

On many Sunday evenings, Halas brought Joe Carr back to his apartment for a postgame dinner with his family. Halas's daughter would recall that it was typical for the men to remain at the table long after the plates had been cleared. They had much to discuss—league affairs, refereeing controversies, team issues. Everyone in the league understood that Halas could influence Carr. "I think Pete Rozelle was the first commissioner he didn't control," Halas's grandson, George McCaskey, said decades later, referencing the NFL commissioner hired in 1960. But, in 1929, their Sunday night conversations almost surely centered on Halas's efforts to keep the Bears from folding. When the season ended, Halas studied his financial ledgers and was stunned to see that his modest proceeds from program sales were all that had kept the team in the black. Carr, too, was alarmed. The NFL could live without the Duluth Eskimos, Dayton Triangles, and most of the other teams that had already failed, but if the Bears went under, they might take the whole league down with them.

Halas continued to look for ways to generate money to pay his bills and keep the Bears in business. "He would try anything, whatever came along, just to keep things going," his daughter, Virginia McCaskey, said. "His timing on going into real estate was very bad. He tried being a car salesman, but the only car he sold was to himself. The basketball team was another one of those things."

In the end, he had no choice but to ask for help. His mother loaned him money, as did his mother-in-law, another widow, "who never let him forget it," his daughter said. He received help from one of his best friends, Charles Bidwill, a corporate attorney and sportsman who avidly supported the Bears. A brother-in-law provided a loan, too, and finally, in what surely was a low point for him, Halas asked his children for permission to "borrow" from their college savings accounts. "I was probably ten or eleven," Virginia McCaskey recalled. "All the birthday and Christmas checks my grandmother had sent me were in an account. He sat Mugs and me down in our living room and explained that he needed the money but was just borrowing it. He kept saying, 'I'll pay you back, I'll pay you back.' I didn't mind. He could have had anything I had. I was just happy he could use it."

It was clear after the 1929 season that Halas needed to stop putting on a uniform on Sundays. It was also clear the Bears needed new leadership. "The time had come for Dutch and me to stop coaching, or more accurately, mis-coaching," Halas wrote. His choice for a new coach was a surprise: Ralph Jones, the athletic director at the Lake Forest Academy, a private high school north of Chicago. The public was "astonished" by the hire, Halas wrote, but he had played for Jones on the freshman football team and varsity basketball at Illinois and liked his cerebral approach. Jones promised Halas that the Bears would win a championship in three years "and I believed him," as Halas later put it.

An original thinker, Jones was not a devotee of the run-oriented "single wing," the most popular offensive alignment at the time. It called for the center to snap the ball to a tailback lined up 5 yards deep, with a wingback and quarterback positioned nearby, on the same side. Halas employed the single wing at times with the Bears, but he preferred the T formation, in which the quarterback lined up directly behind the center, with two backs behind him. Upon taking over the Bears, Jones, with permission from Halas, tweaked the T. He had the blockers line up farther apart to create more room for ball carriers. He moved a split end wide of the blockers as a designated pass receiver. He put a halfback in motion, running parallel to the line of scrimmage, before the ball was snapped. These new ideas were intended to confuse defenders and bolster the Bears' passing game.

Jones and Halas also overhauled the team's roster. Halas had already brought back Grange; though no longer a dazzling, game-changing player after a serious knee injury, he still had a knack for finding running room while toting the ball and was a savvy defender. He was, Jones thought, perfect for the split end role in the modified T. And to keep defenses from focusing on Grange, Halas signed Bronko Nagurski, a 240-pound fullback from the University of Minnesota who often flattened defenders when he plowed into them.

After failing to score in three of their first four games in 1930 as they adjusted to Jones's new T, the Bears jelled on an October afternoon; with Grange running outside and catching passes, and Nagurski running inside, they ran over the Cardinals, 32–6. They ended the season with five straight wins and an overall record of nine wins and four losses.

But although the news on the field was better, the Bears' financial situation remained discouraging. As the Depression wore on, fans could not afford tickets and banks could not offer loans. "We had a drawer full of bills and we were overdrawn at the bank, and no change was in sight," Halas recalled. For the second straight year, he was unable to pay the Frankford Yellow Jackets their guaranteed percentage of the gate when they played in Chicago. By the end of the 1930 season, Halas owed more than $10,000.

No one at the time would have suggested pro football was a thriving concern. Twenty-two teams had competed for the NFL title in 1926, but by 1931 only ten were still in business. When the Providence Steam Roller, Cleveland Indians, and Frankford Yellow Jackets folded after that season, the number of franchises that had failed since the league's inception in 1920 rose to thirty-five. With the addition of George Preston Marshall's Boston franchise in 1932, the league consisted of just eight teams, most of them concentrated in the country's two largest cities. The Giants, Brooklyn Dodgers, and

Staten Island Stapletons played in and around New York City, while the Bears and Cardinals played in Chicago. Beyond the nation's first and second cities, pro football barely existed. There was a team in Portsmouth, Ohio, one in Green Bay, Wisconsin, and another in Boston. That was it.

The NFL's fortunes did not resemble an arc pointed ever higher on a graph, continuously climbing; rather, its fortunes rose and dipped unpredictably, often changing from year to year, producing a permanent state of unease among those in charge. Halas and Tim Mara had seen enough go right to continue believing in the sport's potential, and though Marshall, Bert Bell, and Art Rooney were newcomers, they also saw the possibilities. But there was inherent risk in being a pro football man, especially during the Great Depression.

Interest in *other* sports remained high across America, despite the economic collapse. Fans could escape their troubles for a few hours at an event or over the radio. When a horse named Twenty Grand won the Kentucky Derby on May 16, 1931, "a colorful crowd of nearly 60,000 spectators offered roaring acclaim," the Associated Press reported, while millions listened to a national radio broadcast. Later that year, baseball's St. Louis Cardinals and Philadelphia Athletics so mesmerized the country with a seven-game World Series that thousands of fans gathered in the streets just to listen to the broadcasts together. College football still generated crowds and headlines. Traditional powers such as Michigan, Pitt, Notre Dame, and Southern Cal played in packed stadiums. On November 26, 1932, Notre Dame trounced Army before 78,000 fans at Yankee Stadium. Two weeks later, Notre Dame lost to Southern Cal, with a crowd of 93,000 watching at the Los Angeles Coliseum, a magnificent edifice that had just hosted the Olympics.

Pro football did not compete for the attention of America's sports public. Even more than a decade in, the NFL was widely dismissed as something of a carnival act, played largely by men who took part only because they had nothing better to do. The league's best team, the Green Bay Packers, played in a tiny, horseshoe-shaped wooden structure located behind a high school. That encapsulated pro football in its early years.

Granted, their stadium situation notwithstanding, the Packers were a success story. A decade earlier, the NFL had kicked them out of the league after Halas caught them using college players in a game against the Bears. They were allowed to return but were on the verge of collapse a year later. Local leaders devised a unique plan to sell stock in the team to the public for five dollars per share. Hundreds of fans invested, turning the team into a community-owned, nonprofit enterprise. That put the Packers on relatively sound footing, and they started to win. The team's coach, Curly Lambeau, was a handsome and intensely competitive tailback who had briefly played at Notre Dame. He energetically recruited new talent and put his squads through long practices. The Packers went 43-20-8 between 1923 and 1928 and leapt to the top of the league after Lambeau signed Clarke Hinkle, a powerful fullback and linebacker; Mike Michalske, a rugged guard; and Johnny "Blood" McNally, an elusive back. All three would become Pro Football Hall of Fame inductees along with Lambeau.

The team prospered partly because it was community owned, which helped attendance, and partly because the publisher of the local newspaper, the *Green Bay Press-Gazette*, was a major supporter, guaranteeing consistent coverage. Mostly, though, the Packers prospered because they won. Early in the 1931 season, which would end with them securing their third straight NFL title, they defeated the Bears, Giants, and Cardinals on successive Sundays in Green Bay. Sportswriters delighted in recounting little Green Bay's victories, casting the Wisconsin team as David and the big-city clubs as Goliaths.

Notre Dame's Knute Rockne had died in a plane crash earlier that year, prompting some columnists to suggest Lambeau was America's next great football coach. The men of the NFL were pleased to see one of their own recognized—it seldom happened—although Halas grumbled about it. The relationship between Halas and Lambeau was distantly civil at best, Halas having been the one to turn Lambeau in for using college players. Their teams and fans had since forged an intense rivalry. Whenever the Packers played in Chicago, 2,000 Green Bay fans traveled with the team to Cubs Park. But, despite the Packers' success, their home stadium held just 10,000 fans. (Fire marshals reluctantly let in another 3,000 when the Bears came to town.) There was no visiting locker room, so the Packers' opponents dressed for the game in their hotel rooms in downtown Green Bay, gathered in the hotel lobby, and shared a bus to the stadium. There also were no rest rooms, so when nature called, fans simply relieved themselves under the stands.

IN THE SUMMER OF 1931, DUTCH STERNAMAN APPROACHED Halas with a proposition. He had invested in an apartment building and a gas station rather than the stock market, so he was doing better than most. But, facing steep mortgage payments, he wanted to unload his 50 percent share of the Bears and offered it to Halas for $38,000. Halas accepted without hesitating even though he did not have the money; he wanted control of the team. He arranged to pay Sternaman in three installments over three years, then set out to find $25,000 for an initial payment. Miraculously, Charles Bidwill "raised $5,000 from a bank that was already closed," Halas wrote. The mother of George Trafton, who had played for the Bears for more than a decade, loaned Halas the bulk of the initial payment.

After making a second payment following the 1931 season, in which the Bears won eight of thirteen games, Halas needed to make a final payment of $7,000 on August 1, 1932, to gain sole control of the Bears. But he only had $2,000 as the date approached, and no bank would loan him the rest. A clause in the deal stipulated that all stock in the team, including Halas's, would revert to Sternaman if Halas missed a payment. The deadline passed. On August 3, Halas received a letter from Sternaman's lawyer stating that the Bears would be put up for sale on August 9. Halas was desperate. "I called everyone I knew. No one would help me," he later wrote. Finally, on the morning

of the scheduled sale, he received a call from a banker willing to loan
him the balance of the payment. Halas raced to the bank, got a check,
raced to Sternaman's lawyer's office, and handed it over. Somehow, at
the nadir of the Great Depression, he finally had sole ownership of
the Bears.

EVEN THOUGH HE HAD BEEN REDUCED TO BORROWING FROM HIS
children to pay his debts, Halas continued to look for new business
opportunities. One presented itself in 1932 when William Hauk, a
laundry owner who advertised in the Bears' game program, told Halas
of a competing laundry service that was on the verge of going out of
business and could be bought cheaply. Halas did not have the money
and knew he could not keep asking friends and family members for
loans. He turned to Jim McMillen, a former offensive lineman for
the Bears. Like Halas, McMillen had played at Illinois and earned
an engineering degree. As a senior in 1923, he helped open holes
for Grange, then a sophomore sensation. After graduating, McMillen
played for the Bears through 1929, but his small football salary paled
next to what he earned during the offseason as a professional wrestler.

A careful investor, McMillen had plenty of money, enough to sail
through the depression. He also had great respect for Halas, and he
helped his former coach buy the failing laundry. Halas renamed it
White Bear Laundry and hired William Hauk to run it. McMillen
provided the necessary operating capital with a loan, which Halas
repaid over the next decade. White Bear was a commercial laundry,
serving restaurants and hotels, and Hauk was a savvy partner. Unlike
his forays into real estate and basketball, Halas's laundry investment
survived the Depression and became solidly profitable.

"He had a good partner. They had big White Bear Laundry trucks
roaring all around Chicago," Virginia McCaskey said. "I remember
going to see the business. It was fascinating to me. There was the
machinery with large mangles for sheets and tablecloths. You would
feed a sheet into one end and it would go through the rollers. There

were women on one end to feed the material properly. The women on the other end were the folders. . . . It was understood that my father was all football during the season, but in the offseason, he went to the laundry offices in the morning before he went to the Bears offices, and then he stopped at the laundry on the way home."

By 1932, Charles Bidwill was more than just a loyal fan of the Bears. He helped Halas run the team in the role of vice president. They were good friends with similar biographies. Both were Chicago natives, born in 1895. Bidwill was never the athlete Halas was, but he shared Halas's zeal for sports. A natty dresser with a chatty personality, Bidwill had served in the Great War, earned a law degree from Loyola University, and worked as a corporate counsel in the 1920s, making good money in the process. That enabled him to buy a printing company, develop a winning thoroughbred racing stable, and manage Hawthorne Race Course. He also ran the Chicago Stadium Operating Company, which promoted events at the vast indoor venue. Inevitably for someone so well connected in Chicago, his associates included questionable characters, including a lawyer with ties to Al Capone. But that did not tarnish the respect Bidwill earned as an energetic, self-made success.

One evening in the summer of 1932, Bidwill hosted Halas and Min on an evening dinner cruise aboard his yacht. The other guests included Arch Ward, sports editor of the *Chicago Tribune,* and David Jones, the physician who owned Chicago's other pro football team, the Cardinals. Although their teams competed during the season, Halas and Jones were friendly. Four years earlier, Halas had arranged for Jones to buy the Cardinals for $25,000 from Chris O'Brien, the painting contractor who had started the Cardinals as a sandlot organization in the late 1800s. But Jones was already weary of competing with Halas for the favor of Chicago's sports fans. As Bidwill's elegant yacht cruised around Lake Michigan that evening, Jones expressed a willingness to sell the Cardinals.

"If I get my price," Jones said.

"What is that price?" Bidwill asked.

"Fifty thousand dollars," Jones said.

Several nights later, Bidwill called Jones and said he would buy the Cardinals. Halas was excited to bring Bidwill into the NFL's inner ranks. With his wealth and social network, he was just the kind of owner the NFL needed. Bidwill was so fond of Halas that he kept his Bears season tickets and even remained the team's vice president for a year after he bought the Cardinals. In fact, at Halas's request, Bidwill also bought a minority stake in another franchise, the Portsmouth Spartans, who would soon move to Detroit and start anew as the Lions. After that transaction, Bidwill owned one team and a piece of two others. It was a blatant conflict of interest—one the NFL never would allow decades later—but in the 1930s, the owners of the league's other teams had no problem with it.

WHEN THE 1932 SEASON BEGAN, THERE WAS MOUNTING PRESsure on Ralph Jones. The Bears' coach had promised Halas a championship within three years. This was his third year. The Bears started slowly; their first three games were scoreless ties. Then they lost to Green Bay by the pitiful score of 2–0, with the only points coming on a blocked punt that produced a safety when the ball rolled out of the back of the end zone. The *Chicago Tribune*'s Wilfrid Smith described the game, played before 17,500 fans, as "one of the old-fashioned brawls for which the Bears and Packers are famous." Smith certainly had an up-close view: he worked the game as a member of the officiating crew, the head linesman, before writing his game story in the press box. It was another blatant conflict unimaginable today, but sportswriters in the 1930s routinely doubled as NFL officials—in hindsight, one of the most obvious signs that the league lacked professionalism.

The conflict seemingly impacted Smith, who kindly did not point out in his game story that the Bears had now played 240 minutes of football that season without scoring a point. Halas surely approved of the omission. But the Bears' fans had not lost faith. More than 27,000 attended a home game against Staten Island on October 23 and watched Grange and Nagurski run wild in a 27–7 victory. Two weeks later, the Bears easily defeated the Giants, 28–8, inaugurating a winning streak. By the end of the season, the Bears had a 6-1-6 record, while Green Bay was 10-3-1 and Portsmouth was 6-1-4. The owners had decreed that the league title would go to the team with the best winning percentage, with ties excluded from the calculation. The NFL would not begin to include ties in the math, counted as "half victories," until 1972. As a result, Chicago and Portsmouth had higher winning percentages than Green Bay, even though the Packers boasted quite a few more wins. It was not the fairest approach.

Halas and Portsmouth's owner arranged for their teams to play at Wrigley Field, formerly known as Cubs Park, on December 18. The winner would lay claim to the title, and, oddly, the loser would finish third, behind Green Bay. When heavy snow and bitter cold battered Chicago in the days before the game, Joe Carr decided to move it to the Chicago Stadium, an indoor venue. What is surely the most unusual game in NFL history ensued. A circus had just left town, leaving a six-inch bed of tanbark on the floor. Though an advantageous cushion for the players, "the elephants had been there, and most of all, what I remember about the game is the odor," said Virginia Mc-Caskey, who attended the game with her mother. A capacity crowd of 11,198 filled the arena as snow continued to fall outside, but the fans struggled to follow the action because of a unique set of ground rules. The field was 80 yards long, including the end zones, and 8.5 yards narrower than usual. When a team crossed midfield, it was immediately moved back 20 yards. There was a goal post at one end only. Field goals were prohibited. "It was all a bit puzzling at times," Virginia McCaskey said. "Whenever I had a question, I would ask my mother and she would know the answer."

The Spartans were playing without their biggest star, Dutch Clark, a halfback destined for the Hall of Fame. Although he enjoyed being

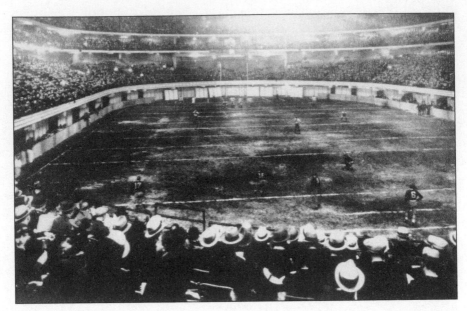

The indoor championship game at the Chicago Stadium, December 18, 1932. (Pro Football Hall of Fame via AP)

on the team and wanted to see the Spartans win, he had more important matters to consider, namely, making enough money to live on. He had taken a job as the head basketball coach at Colorado College, and when his team's season opener conflicted with the hastily arranged extra game, Clark elected to coach basketball rather than play football. The NFL's championship was still not a prized commodity.

Neither the Bears nor the Clark-less Spartans had scored when the fourth quarter began. But a Bears halfback intercepted a pass and returned it to the Portsmouth 7 yard line. After three runs up the middle, the Bears were at the one. On fourth down, Nagurski faked a plunge into the middle of the line, stepped back, and lobbed a pass to Grange, who was open in the end zone. When Grange made the catch, an official raised his arms, signaling a touchdown. The Spartans erupted. According to NFL rules, which the league simply copied from the college game, a forward pass had to originate from at least five yards behind the line of scrimmage. Nagurski had been within five yards of the line when he threw the ball, the Spartans argued. The officials did not change the call. The touchdown stood. The Bears wound up winning, 9–0, earning their first NFL title since 1921.

But Halas did not have time to revel in the victory, as he lacked the funds to pay the salaries he had promised his players and coach for the season. Instead of asking the banks and his friends and relatives for more loans, he tried another strategy, offering IOUs. According to Halas, Jones took one IOU for $1,000 and another for $500. Grange took one for $1,000. Nagurski took one for $500. "Some of the greatest players in history, and he's giving them promissory notes? They could have told him to take a flying leap, but they stayed with him," said Halas's grandson, George McCaskey. "I can only speculate, but at some level, it had to be the result of relationships that were more than typical coach-player or typical employee-employer. They had to have some measure of faith in his vision for the sport's future. They also had to respect his sheer doggedness, the fact that he simply would not give up."

7

NEW IDEAS

WHEN THE NFL EXPANDED TO BOSTON AT AN OWNERS' meeting in Atlantic City, New Jersey, on July 9, 1932, the national sports media could not be bothered to notice. The next day's *New York Times* included an eight-page sports section with articles about major league baseball, horse racing, polo, tennis, sailing, minor league baseball, and the Olympics. There was no mention at all of the NFL. A day later, *Times* sportswriters covered golf, rowing, shooting, more baseball, more horse racing, but still no pro football.

The Associated Press eventually reported the news, as did Boston's newspapers. But Boston's sportswriters were indifferent. The NFL had already tried their city once, with a team called the Bulldogs, formerly the Pottsville Maroons, in 1929. The Bulldogs folded after one miserable season, and there was no reason to believe another pro football venture would end differently. Boston was a busy sports town, with fans supporting two major league baseball clubs, the Red Sox and Braves, as well as teams from Harvard and Boston College in various sports. Local sportswriters believed there was no future for pro football, which had flopped not only in Boston but almost everywhere else, too.

Yet the city's general enthusiasm for sports was the reason Joe Carr wanted a team there. George Preston Marshall, leader of the group that owned the new team, had preferred to put his team in Washington, where he lived. But the nation's capital was not yet the sprawling metropolis it would become within several decades. Buffalo, Milwaukee, Pittsburgh, St. Louis, San Francisco, and Baltimore all were larger, as was Boston.

Washington's cause also was not helped by the fact that it was south of the Mason-Dixon Line. A southern mentality prevailed in the city, as did Jim Crow laws, with many restaurants, theaters, and public venues strictly segregated. That was potentially a problem for the NFL. Many Washington fans did not want to cheer for black athletes, or so it was believed, but unlike baseball, which maintained a strict, if unofficial, "color line," NFL teams occasionally used black players. The owners feared that might cause problems in Washington. Still, Marshall tried to talk Carr into Washington, but the league president was adamant, mainly because of Boston's potential. Marshall finally gave in. At the Atlantic City meeting, which he attended with two members of his ownership group, the first order of business was admitting their team to the league. Tim Mara presented a motion. Halas seconded it. The vote was unanimous: Marshall was bringing a team to Boston.

He quickly struck a deal with Emil Fuchs, an attorney who owned the Boston Braves, the baseball team. The new football team would play at Braves Field, a roomier stadium than cramped Fenway Park, home of the Red Sox. With that deal done, Marshall decided to call his team the Braves, too. He figured he could use the Indian theme as a marketing ploy, but mostly he was just following the lead of other NFL teams: the Brooklyn Dodgers, Cleveland Indians, and New York Giants had all taken the names of the major league baseball clubs that played at their stadiums, hoping the association with the more popular sport would make them appear more legitimate and worthy of attention.

In their first season, the Braves fielded a young squad, with rookies making up more than half of the roster. The backfield included the incomparably named Honolulu Hughes, pro football's first Hawaiian-born player, and Cliff Battles, also no slouch in the name department. Battles was a promising rookie back from West Virginia Wesleyan, and Marshall, the West Virginia native, wanted players from the state on his team. He outbid several other clubs for Battles by offering him $175 per game, $25 more than any other team offered. The Braves' head coach was Lud Wray, Bert Bell's former Penn teammate and fellow assistant coach. The Braves played their first game on October 2, 1932, losing at home to Brooklyn, 14–0, before 6,000 fans. The outcome hinted at what lay ahead. After surprisingly defeating the Giants, 14–6, the Braves were shut out by the Cardinals on October 16 and played a scoreless rematch with the Giants at the Polo Grounds on October 23. The following week, the largest crowd of the year at Braves Field came to a game against the Bears, and after each team scored a touchdown in the first quarter, the fans witnessed a scoreless scrum over the final forty-five minutes, producing a 7–7 final score.

Marshall was increasingly frustrated. He believed in putting on a show for his customers, but the Braves were not exciting. They had scored three touchdowns in five games and played two ties. How could you expect fans to keep buying tickets to such dull shows? Marshall would soon become infamous for interfering in his coach's business, sometimes even demanding to call the plays, and Wray was the first to experience his meddling. Marshall wanted the Braves to pass more, but Wray stuck to the ground game. Cliff Battles would rush for more yards than any other NFL back in 1932, while Honolulu Hughes would toss just one touchdown pass and nine interceptions in his only NFL season. Marshall stewed.

Tensions briefly eased when the Braves engineered their version of an offensive explosion on November 6, defeating Staten Island, 19–6. But then the Green Bay Packers drummed them, 21–0, and the Portsmouth Spartans shut them out, 10–0. The Braves ended their season on the road, defeating the Cardinals and Dodgers by a combined score of 15–6. Their final record was respectable, four wins, four defeats, and two ties, but in those six hundred minutes of football, their offense had crossed the goal line just five times.

The lack of scoring was not limited to Boston. The Bears, who won the league title, played six ties out of fourteen games in 1932 while scoring just twenty-three touchdowns. On average across the NFL, teams scored just 8.2 points per game, a 23 percent drop from two years earlier. Marshall had recognized before the season that there was a problem. At the July 1932 owners' meeting where his franchise was formally approved, he had seconded a motion, introduced by the Giants' Dr. Harry March, to move the goal posts from the back of the end zone to the goal line. Intended to cut down on ties by making field goals easier to convert, the proposal "lost by a roll call vote after considerable discussion," according to the official minutes from the meeting. That "discussion" included the first on-the-record exhibit of Marshall's show-business sensibility, which would eventually produce profound changes in pro football. "I realize you men know your football inside and out," he told the other owners, "but the way I look at it, we're in show business. And when the show becomes boring, you throw it away and put a more interesting one its place. That's why I want to change the rules. I want to give the public the kind of show they want."

Months later, after his team's drab inaugural season, Marshall led a charge to enliven the game. From the outset, the NFL had simply followed college football's rules, which, among other things, required that forward passes originate from at least five yards behind the line of scrimmage. When the NFL owners met at the Fort Pitt Hotel in Pittsburgh in February 1933, Marshall gave another impassioned speech about the league needing to set its own rules rather than just follow the college game.

"Gentleman, it's about time we realized that we're not only in the football business; we're also in the entertainment business," Marshall declared. "If the colleges wants to louse up their game with bad rules, let them. We don't have to follow suit. The hell with the colleges! We should do what's best for us. I say we should adopt rules that will give the pros a spectacular individuality and national significance. Face it, we're in show business. If people don't buy tickets, we'll have no business at all."

When Carr opened the floor, Marshall was ready. Before the meeting he had talked with Halas, who loved football's brutal nature but was encouraged by Marshall's bold temperament to consider fundamental changes to the status quo. They had put together a list of amendments to the rules, and one by one, Marshall introduced them as motions. The first, and most important, was to allow forward passes from anywhere behind the line. Halas seconded the motion, and, in a fateful moment, it passed. College football still placed limits on the passing game, but now it was unrestricted in the pros. "Nagurski will pass from anywhere so why not make it legal?" muttered Potsy Clark, Portsmouth's coach, still bitter about the "indoor" title game in Chicago several months earlier. Marshall also introduced a motion to spot the ball ten yards in from the sideline after plays that ended with the ball either out of bounds or within five yards of the sideline. The idea was to bring more action into the middle of the field and give offenses more operating room. The motion passed, introducing hash marks on the field, an idea the colleges had long debated but declined to use.

The push for change became infectious. Tim Mara advocated doing away with the extra point and instituting a ten-minute overtime period to break ties. "In every sport but football, the authorities have sought to avoid a tie score," Mara said. Neither proposal passed, but Marshall reintroduced the idea of positioning the goal posts on the goal line rather than at the back of the end zone. Halas seconded the motion. It had failed a year earlier mostly because Nagurski was a strong kicker and the other owners believed Halas wanted primarily to help the Bears. This time, the rule change passed.

After the meeting, Carr told the press the owners hoped the new rules would make their game significantly more exciting. "We think we have overcome the balance previously held by the defense. In fact, if we can give the offense a slight edge, it doubtless would improve the game for both the players and the spectators," Carr said. "We are primarily interested in developing a spectacular scoring game. We haven't the pageantry associated with college games, hence as a substitute we must offer wide-open play with frequent scoring."

Five months later, at another owners' meeting at the Blackstone Hotel in Chicago in July, Marshall continued his assault on the status quo. It had been determined that the league would have ten teams in 1933. Marshall proposed that they be split into East and West divisions, and that the division winners play for the league title after the regular season. For years, the owners had discussed the idea of a postseason championship game patterned after the World Series, the biggest event on America's sports calendar. Determining the league title on the field was obviously preferable to using regular-season records, a method that often produced controversy. Hopefully, a single, decisive game would draw the attention of the national media and most of the sport's fans, whatever team they rooted for. The interest generated by the "indoor game" in Chicago convinced Marshall the time had come. His motion passed unanimously. The NFL would stage its first championship game at the end of the 1933 season.

Marshall had only been in the league for a year, and, already, he had turned it upside down. Many years later, Wellington Mara, Tim's son, would say, "Marshall was way ahead of everybody. He saw that pro football should be a family game. Anything to make it a show."

Start-up expenses and in-season costs had mounted during the Braves' first season in Boston, and, by the end of the year, the operation was $46,000 in the red. Marshall's partners, concerned that the losses would not stop, expressed a desire to sell their interests. Marshall bought them out and became the team's sole owner. Although he lamented pro football's shortcomings in league meetings, he was still optimistic about its potential, both in Boston and elsewhere.

It was clear he needed to try a different approach in his second season, though, and, always unafraid of making big changes, he moved his home field to Fenway Park. That ended his association with the Braves, so he also needed to change the team's name. Keeping with the Native American theme, he selected Redskins. It appeared he wanted to continue using Native American imagery to help market the team. In 1932, his players had taken publicity photos in feathered headdresses. Marshall would later allude to several players having Indian blood, which was probably not true. In a broader way, he thought the theme gave his team an identity distinct from that of other teams in the league. The name also allowed him to keep the franchise's Indian-head logo.

When Lud Wray left after one season to coach his friend Bert Bell's new NFL team in Philadelphia, Marshall went as far as to hire a coach with a Native American connection. William "Lone Star" Dietz had played college football in the early 1900s with Jim Thorpe at the Carlisle Indian Industrial School in Carlisle, Pennsylvania. He had gone on to coach at Washington State, Purdue, and several other colleges, always selling himself as a Native American, born on a South Dakota reservation to a Sioux mother and German father. Although there remained a great deal of prejudice against Indians in America in the 1920s, Dietz embraced the identity, believing it set him apart in the coaching fraternity. Decades later, journalists would discover Dietz had, in fact, been born in Wisconsin to white parents.

From the start, Marshall denied hiring him because of his ethnicity. In an Associated Press article about the name change from July 6, 1933, Marshall said, "The fact that we have in our head coach, Lone Star Dietz, an Indian, together with several Indian players, has not, as may be suspected, inspired me to select the name Redskins." He just wanted to avoid any confusion with baseball's Braves, he said. He may also have selected Redskins to achieve a connection with the Red Sox, who also played in Fenway Park. Whatever his rationale, the new name and the switch to Fenway Park in 1933 did not bring much change in the team's fortunes. The Braves had drawn an average crowd of 15,500 per game in 1932. The Redskins averaged 15,619 in

1933. And with Dietz in charge, the team went 5-5-2, giving it a .500 record for the second straight season.

THE OPENING GAME OF THE 1933 NFL SEASON WAS A WEDNES-day night affair between the Pittsburgh Pirates and Chicago Cardinals at Pittsburgh's Forbes Field. The midweek date was necessary because a referendum to ease Pennsylvania's blue laws was still a month away. Art Rooney's Pirates drew a small crowd of 5,000 fans to their franchise debut, and they won, 14–13, in a game that was forgettable except for one feature: it pitted the NFL's only African American players against each other. The Pirates had Ray Kemp, a tackle who had grown up in Pittsburgh, worked in the coal mines, and played for Duquesne and Rooney's semipro team. Joe Lillard, a speedy back, played for the Cardinals.

Their presence on the field was not deemed newsworthy. Black players suited up fairly regularly for NFL teams in the 1920s and early 1930s. Before he was the league's president, Joe Carr had covered black athletes as a sportswriter and welcomed them as competitors against his sandlot football team. Fritz Pollard, a black halfback, was one of the league's first stars, and nine black players had competed in the NFL in 1926. Although the number dropped after that, the league never went all white, like major league baseball. Duke Slater, a black offensive lineman, played for the Cardinals in 1927. Harold Bradley, another black lineman, played for the same team in 1928. Dave Myers, a black quarterback from New York University, played for Staten Island and Brooklyn in 1930 and 1931.

Lillard joined the Cardinals in 1932. Nicknamed "the Midnight Express," the six-foot-two, 195-pound back had starred at the University of Oregon until he was suspended for having played semipro baseball, a violation of his amateur status. Lillard said he had been paid only to drive the team bus, but, regardless, he was through with college football. In his third game with the Cardinals in 1932, he ran for gains, completed passes, returned kicks, and tallied an extra point on a drop kick against the Braves in Boston. The *Boston Globe*'s headline read, "Negro Star of the Chicago Eleven Thrills 18,000 by Dazzling Runs as Cardinals Down Boston."

One can imagine George Preston Marshall stewing as he watched Lillard run circles around his Redskins. Marshall's racism, which he had first learned in segregated Grafton, West Virginia, was further hardened in segregated Washington. The otherwise shrewd businessman did not think blacks were good for business, on the football field or anywhere else. The official minutes from NFL meetings in the early 1930s do not reference discussions about forbidding teams from using African American players. But the owners' meetings often consisted of several hours of official business followed by long, boozy evenings at restaurants and hotel bars, where off-the-record business was conducted, and it seems clear in hindsight that race was a consistent topic on those evenings after Marshall became an owner in 1932. His quest to make pro football more pleasing to the public, in his view, included more than just rule changes aimed at increasing passing and scoring. Within two years of his arrival, the league no longer fielded African American players. In this respect, as with financial matters, the league's history is not one of continuing upward progress. It went backward before it went forward.

During the first half of the season-opening game between the Pirates and Cardinals at Forbes Field in 1933, Lillard was the best player on the field. "Great player, elusive as all outdoors. In the first half, he ran us crazy," according to Kemp. In the locker room at halftime, Kemp later recalled, the Pirates' player coach, Forrest "Jap" Douds, told his team, "We've got to get that damn nigger the hell out of there." Kemp said later, "I was mad, naturally. And as we were going back out, Jap pulls me aside and says, 'Ray, you know I didn't mean *you* when I said that.'" Marshall was clearly not the only intolerant person in the NFL. It was no surprise, then, that the Pirates cut Kemp three games into the 1933 season. When Kemp complained to Rooney, the Pirates' owner refused to overrule Douds, who also played tackle, Kemp's position.

Kemp went back to a job at a steel mill until the Pirates asked him back late in the season. When he accompanied the team to New York for a game, he could not stay at the team hotel, which did not serve blacks. According to Kemp, Walter White, head of the National Association for the Advancement of Colored People, wanted to sue the hotel and the Pirates for discrimination. "He said, 'There's no reason this should be happening, you being a college graduate an all,'" Kemp recalled. "But I told him I'd prefer not to go to court. I said, 'I know Art Rooney. He invited me to play for his team. He just has a couple of guys running it, no doubt, who are racist. But give him a little time and he'll straighten all this out. He probably doesn't even know this is going on,' which he didn't." The New York trip culminated with Kemp starting against the Giants at the Polo Grounds. It was his final game as an NFL player. "It was my understanding that there was a gentleman's agreement in the league that there would be no more blacks," Kemp said later.

Lillard's career also ended unceremoniously. The Cardinals had suspended him in 1932, supposedly for clashing with the head coach and some teammates over missing practices and breaking team rules. He continued to be seen as a disruptive force in 1933, even though the real problem may have been that some white players resented that a black man was the team's best player. In any case, he did not start the Cardinals' season finale and was soon dumped from the roster, never to return.

Carr and the owners would always vehemently deny that they agreed to ban black players beginning in 1934. "For myself and most of the owners, I can say there never was any racial bias," Rooney said years later. In a 1970 interview, Halas said, "in no way, shape, or form" had the owners formally agreed to follow baseball's lead and exclude blacks. The record suggests otherwise. From 1934 to 1945, the NFL was completely white, a development many historians trace to the influence of Marshall, whose Redskins, infamously, would not integrate until 1961.

8

BENNY AND THE GIANTS

A FTER THE NEW YORK GIANTS STAGGERED THROUGH THE 1928 season, winning just four of thirteen games, Tim Mara had no trouble paying off the $40,000 debt the team accrued. Horse racing in New York was prospering, with crowds filling track grandstands and bettors wagering record amounts. Mara, one of the sport's most popular bookies, had become a wealthy man and used his profits to fund a stock portfolio and his lawbook bindery and coal company. He was not pleased to see the Giants losing money, but he could afford it.

That changed in 1929. The stock market crash liquidated his portfolio. Several of his businesses closed. He was still better off than many New Yorkers, who lost everything, but if his football team could not pay for itself, he would have to fold it. Mara knew that would devastate his sons, who loved that their father owned a team, but he felt as if he had no choice. Fortunately, the Giants engineered a dramatic reversal in 1929. Mara had taken charge of personnel matters during the offseason, reconfiguring the roster himself rather than letting his partner, Dr. Harry March, make decisions—as March, the more knowledgeable football man, had always done. Mara had joked about his lack of football knowledge, but it turned out he knew more than he thought.

His key move was acquiring Benny Friedman, a former University of Michigan backfield star who had played in the NFL for the Cleveland Bulldogs in 1927 and Detroit Wolverines in 1928. The five-foot-ten, 185-pound Friedman was a daring downfield passer who could also run for large gains and kick field goals. He had led the Wolverines to a 28–0 victory over the Giants early in the 1928 season, greatly impressing Mara. After the season, Mara told March, "We need Friedman. Spend what you have to spend, but get him."

March began negotiating with the Wolverines' coach, Leroy Andrews, who did not want to part with his talented young player. Detroit had finished third in the league in 1928, winning eight of ten games. But March kept haggling until Andrews agreed to one of the more unusual deals in NFL history, one that is unimaginable today. Mara would acquire every Detroit player, not just Friedman. The Detroit franchise would fold. Andrews would take over as the Giants' coach, replacing Potty Potteiger, a former baseball minor leaguer who had led New York to an NFL title in 1927. The scale of the deal indicated how badly Mara wanted Friedman, as did the $10,000 salary Friedman negotiated for the 1929 season. It was an unheard-of amount in an era when most players earned $125 a game. The other NFL owners were aghast. George Halas grumbled that Mara had lost his mind.

But Friedman was worth the money, Mara thought. The year before, as the Giants' debts mounted, Mara had asked his players to travel to road games on an old bus rather than in the private Pullman rail car they were used to. On one trip, they stayed at a YMCA rather than a hotel. If they wanted to become a first-class outfit, the Giants needed to sell more tickets. Mara, believing Friedman could make a difference, built a marketing campaign around him. Handsome and glib, the quarterback spoke to school and business groups all over New York before the 1929 season, extolling the virtues of pro football. Mara had bet on the right horse, it turned out. Red Grange was a bigger name, but Friedman was an exciting, unique offensive force, as well as a forward-thinking strategist. The idea of passing the ball in any situation other than third and long was deemed foolish by many coaches, but Friedman believed "the time to pass is on first or second down. Why wait until third down, when the defense is looking for it?" Fans flocked to see him and the Giants' new aerial attack.

Mara and March had surrounded him with former teammates from Detroit, a group of returning Giants, and several newcomers, including Ray Flaherty, a receiver from the New York Yankees, C. C. Pyle's franchise, which had folded. The Giants opened the 1929 season with a scoreless tie against a new team based in East Orange, New Jersey, that would collapse after one year. But, after the disappointing start, the Giants went on a long winning streak. They traveled to Rhode Island and defeated the Providence Steam Roller at the Cycledrome, then opened their home schedule a week later with a 19–6 win over Staten Island before 20,000 fans. The next week, 30,000 came to the Polo Grounds for a game against the Frankford Yellow Jackets. Friedman raced around the backfield, sidestepping defenders and hitting open receivers for touchdowns in a 32–0 rout. "Polo Grounds Crowd Watches Brilliant Aerial Display," read a headline in the *New York Times*.

The sport's rules conspired against Friedman. In 1929, passes still had to originate from at least five yards behind the line, and, on top of that, two straight incompletions resulted in a 5-yard penalty. The league's official ball was so fat it was difficult to grab and toss. Undeterred, Friedman hurled passes all over the field. Fans stood in anticipation when he took the snap, and they were riveted when he threw the ball downfield. It was far more exciting than the usual war of attrition, mostly composed of short runs and punts, that constituted a football game, college or pro.

Three days after the win over Frankford, on October 23, a panic that had infiltrated the country's financial markets triggered a massive selloff that continued for almost a week. The country was plunged into an economic nightmare. It was the beginning of what would soon be called the Great Depression. But enthusiastic crowds continued to come to the Polo Grounds to cheer on Friedman. On November 24, the Giants hosted the Green Bay Packers in the most important game of the NFL season. Curly Lambeau's Packers were 9-0 and had given up only two touchdowns in total to that point. More than 25,000 fans arrived at the Polo Grounds. Although that was paltry compared to the nearly 80,000 that Army and Notre Dame would draw at Yankee Stadium a week later, it indicated a markedly higher level of interest in the sport in New York than just the year before.

The imposing Packers featured a pair of dominating interior players, Cal Hubbard and Mike Michalske. They also had a pair of nimble backs, Verne Lewellen and Johnny Blood, who helped Green Bay's offense bound down the field. They were too much for the Giants. Hubbard and Michalske harassed Friedman on pass attempts, while Lewellen boomed punts of more than 60 yards to keep the Giants stuck in their own territory. Somehow, the Giants kept the game close and pulled within a point on a Friedman touchdown pass in the third quarter. But the Packers' physical superiority prevailed, and they won, 20–6, before what the *New York Times* called "the most enthusiastic professional crowd of the year."

The Giants played five more games in 1929 and won them all, mostly by wide margins, to finish the season with a superb record of thirteen wins, one loss, and one tie. Friedman finished with twenty touchdown passes, easily setting the league's single-season record. But the Packers finished with a 12-0-1 record, and there was no question the owners would vote them the championship. The Giants had to settle for second place. Mara lamented the lone defeat that had cost his team the title, but he was thrilled with the season. Owing to Friedman, the Giants had sold enough tickets to turn an $8,500 profit for the season. Mara could no longer count on his other business to keep the Giants afloat, but he hoped the team would no longer need help.

By the summer of 1930, Mara was caught in a tangle of legal cases. A bank was suing him to collect on a $50,000 note he had signed for his friend Al Smith's 1928 presidential campaign. He was suing Gene Tunney and Billy Gibson, his friends and former business partners, for money he believed he was owed for promoting a championship fight. Fearing he could lose control of the Giants if the cases went against him, Mara transferred ownership of the franchise to his sons. Although he still ran the team, his sons would eventually take command. Jack, who was twenty-two, had just graduated from Fordham and was headed to law school. He went on the team's road trips and enjoyed spending time with the players. But Wellington, who was fourteen, was the family's true football devotee. In 1930 he wrote a detailed scouting report on the Staten Island Stapletons before the Giants played them, his precociousness and knowledge leaving his father dumbfounded.

The move led to a major change in how the team operated. Within two years, Harry March sold his minority share to Mara and departed. March had worked alongside Mara since the Giants' inception, and though neither publicly commented on what caused their split, the timing suggests March realized, at this point, that he would never own the team. March took a job with the league office but soon lost that, too, after butting heads with George Preston Marshall.

The Giants, meanwhile, began the 1930 season with great optimism. Freidman was back, and Mara was trying to sign Chris "Red" Cagle, a former Army halfback whose slashing run so electrified fans that he had made the cover of *Time* magazine. Rather than turn pro, Cagle had become a coach at Mississippi State. In the Giants' opener, Friedman ran for one touchdown, threw for another, and kicked two extra points in a 32–0 win over the Newark Tornadoes. One week later, the Giants lost at Green Bay, 14–7, before an overflow crowd of 13,000. Regrouping, they won their next eight games before losing to the Bears, giving them an 11-2 record heading into a home game against the Packers on November 23. More than 37,000 fans—the Giants' biggest crowd since the "Grange game" in 1925—trekked to the Polo Grounds, mostly to see Cagle, who had finally signed and was making his debut. Unlike in their home game against the Packers the previous year, the Giants built an early lead and held on to win, 13–7. The victory elevated the Giants to first place, but they lost their next two games, and, when the season ended, they had a 13-4 record and the Packers were 10-3-1. With ties excluded, the Packers had a miniscule advantage in winning percentage, .769 to .764. For the second straight year, Green Bay won the title with the Giants right behind them.

Despite that disappointment, the Giants were more profitable than the previous year, coming out more than $20,000 ahead. And, by December, the championship race seemed unimportant in comparison to a new event on the Giants' calendar—a charity exhibition game at the Polo Grounds against a squad of past and present Notre Dame stars, coached by the legendary Knute Rockne.

In the early 1930s, college football remained significantly more popular than the pro game. And no team embodied college football's preeminence more than Notre Dame, which had emerged as a powerhouse in the 1920s thanks to Rockne and his glamorous Four Horsemen backfield. National radio broadcasts and fawning newspaper coverage had turned the Irish into their era's "America's team," and, even though their campus was in South Bend, Indiana, their second home was New York, with its large Irish American population. After a roaring sellout crowd watched them upset Army at the Polo Grounds in 1924, the Fighting Irish played at least one game in the city every year.

Mara, with his Irish roots, supported Rockne's team. Seeking to raise money to help New Yorkers who had been ruined by the market crash, Mara proposed a game between the Giants and the 1930 Notre Dame varsity. Not only would it draw a crowd, but it also would give the Giants a chance to demonstrate that pro football was no longer a second-rate sport. Rockne liked the idea, but his team, on its way to another national title, had no room on its schedule. He proposed that a blend of former and current Irish players travel to New York for a game against the Giants. Mara readily agreed, and a date for the game was set: December 14, 1930.

Mara had no difficulty mounting a successful promotional campaign for the game. He took out newspaper ads that read, "See the Four Horseman Ride Together Again." Many football fans, especially those who rooted for Notre Dame, were not going to pass up such an opportunity. More than 50,000 tickets were sold.

Rockne's squad gathered in Indiana and practiced for four days before taking a train to New York. Mara was confident; his players were in better condition and physically larger, especially along the offensive and defensive lines. By the day of the game, Rockne had made the same realization. "Take it easy on us," he told Friedman when they met before kickoff to discuss the rules. Friedman was now the Giants' head coach as well as the quarterback, Andrews having been fired late in the season.

Sure enough, the Giants dominated. The Four Horsemen had nowhere to run. Friedman passed and ran for big gains. By halftime, the Giants led, 15–0, and Rockne was angry. When Harry March visited the Irish locker room, Rockne complained that he had scheduled the game for charitable reasons and was being embarrassed. The Giants played backups in the second half. The final score was 22–0.

The game raised more than $100,000. Mara and Friedman traveled to City Hall and presented a check to Jimmy Walker, the mayor of New York. Mara had never felt better about his team. The Giants had turned a profit during the season, won a slew of games, and contributed to the city. Their pummeling of Notre Dame sent a message to the country's sports public. Baseball and college football fans could no longer dismiss the NFL with a scornful laugh.

Best of all, the Giants were becoming a fixture in New York. The city's crowded sports landscape included baseball's Yankees and Giants, championship boxing matches, big college football games, and America's best horse racing. The Giants had sought a place among that company, and, after two seasons with Friedman, they were close to that goal. When the NFL's owners met after the 1930 season, they had plenty to fret about. Teams were losing money. Franchises were folding. The league's future had never seemed shakier as the effect of the Great Depression set in. But all the owners, not just Mara, found hope in the Giants' success in America's first city and largest media market. And as at other points in the NFL's early history, hope was about all they had.

LIKE MILLIONS OF AMERICANS, FRIEDMAN FOUND HIMSELF dealing with grave financial issues. Although he earned more than any other player in the league, he had invested in the stock market before the crash and suffered heavy losses. To make up for them, he took a part-time coaching job at Yale in 1930. Yale's head coach wanted him to show the team's backs how to mount a passing attack. During the 1930 season, Friedman left his apartment in Brooklyn early in the morning, took a train to New Haven, Connecticut, to coach at Yale, then took a train back to New York for the Giants' practice in the afternoon. It was an exhausting regimen. That Friedman played as well as he did for the Giants was somewhat miraculous.

Shortly after the season, in February 1931, Friedman was married at a Long Island country club, with Guy Lombardo and his orchestra providing the music. The guest list, composed of many of the most famous people in New York, was a testament to his celebrity, but marriage changed Friedman's view of his future. Even after the Giants' successful 1930 season, pro football was hardly a reliable way to make a living. Now that he had a wife to support, with kids surely on the way, he needed more stable and lucrative employment. He retired from the Giants, telling the *Brooklyn Daily Eagle*, "I've got to build for the future. Professional football doesn't hold for me all the promise it might from a business angle. If I have a future in football, it's not as a player."

Yale offered him a full-time job as an assistant coach, and several of the school's alumni said they could try to find him a position on Wall Street, too. It was a major disappointment for Mara. Now he needed not only a new star player but also a new head coach. He hired Steve Owen, one of the team's linemen, as an interim head coach in 1931. A gravelly voiced, tobacco-chewing midwesterner, Owen played with uncommon intensity and worked as a foreman at Mara's coal yard during the offseason. The other players on the team respected him.

After opening the 1931 season with a win, the Giants lost three straight games, mostly due to a lack of offense. Mara had remained in contact with Friedman and tried to convince him to come back, especially after the promises of a Wall Street job came to nothing. Mara even offered to move the Giants' practices to the mornings so Friedman could continue to coach at Yale in the afternoons. Halfway through the season, Friedman agreed to return. The Giants won their first two games with him as attendance picked up, but then they lost three in a row. When the season ended, they had seven wins, six losses, and a tie—their worst record with Friedman—but had cleared a $35,000 profit.

Soon after the season ended, Friedman stopped by Mara's office. The two men were close, and their conversation that day was friendly until Friedman explained the reason for his visit. He wanted to invest in the Giants, to become a minority owner. He thought he deserved the opportunity after helping turn the team around. Mara delivered a sobering reply. "I'm sorry, Benny, but this is a family business," he said. "We've been friends and I like you a lot, but the Giants are for my sons. I'd like you back next year as a player-coach, but that's up to you to decide."

Friedman did not take the news lightly. He severed ties with Mara. "My timing was off," he said later. "If I had asked him in the years when the team was like a plaything to him, I probably would have gotten what I wanted. But at the time I asked him, it was his sole asset. He said, 'No, I'm keeping it for my sons.' That was that. I thought I deserved a piece of the club because I had played a big part of moving it from the red ink to black ink. And when Tim turned me down, I felt I should move along, that I couldn't stay with him."

George Halas wanted to sign Friedman and put him in the backfield with Grange and Nagurski, but Friedman's wife did not want to leave New York, so he signed with Brooklyn's struggling football Dodgers. They hoped he could help them gain on the Giants in the New York market, but it quickly became clear that Friedman could not be a one-man team; he needed talent around him, too, and the Dodgers did not have much. They ended the season with three wins and nine defeats, losing twice to the Giants.

The Giants, for their part, also endured a losing season in 1932, but Mara stuck with Owen, who would go on to coach the team for more than two decades. A year later, in 1933—the first year the NFL went with two divisions and a championship game—Owen had a lot to work with, including star players such as Mel Hein, a powerful center and linebacker who would play for the team for fifteen years without missing a game; Harry Newman, a young tailback from Michigan who could run and pass; and Ken Strong, an aptly named all-league fullback who had previously rejected the Giants to play for Staten Island. The Giants won the East division with an 11-3 record and played the Bears in the NFL's inaugural title game at Wrigley Field on December 17, 1933.

The game served as evidence that Marshall's new rules had enlivened pro football. As 25,000 fans watched, the Giants and Bears both moved the ball easily, utilizing deep passes and trick plays. The Associated Press described it as "probably the most spectacular game of the year" and "a brilliant display of offensive power." It was anything but a scoreless, muddy scrum. The Giants led by one point at halftime and by five early in the fourth quarter, but with less than two minutes to play, the Bears' Bronko Nagurski tossed a "jump pass" to a receiver who then lateraled the ball to a teammate. The resulting touchdown gave Chicago a 23–21 lead, and the Giants ran out of time on a final drive. They had fallen just short of the title for the third time in five years.

The next year, with many of the same players back, the Giants brought a 5-2 record into a regular-season rematch with the Bears

It became clear in the 1933 championship game that rules changes made pro football more exciting. (Pro Football Hall of Fame)

in Chicago on November 4. The undefeated Bears humbled them, 27–7. When the teams met in New York two weeks later, a crowd of 55,000 packed into the Polo Grounds, offering the best proof yet that the Giants were no longer an afterthought, or an unsteady enterprise. The Bears outweighed the Giants by an average of fifteen pounds per man, but Owen had the Giants ready. With Hein dominating the interior, they took the lead with a second-quarter touchdown as their defense blunted Chicago's relentless attack. The immense crowd loosed a roar every time a swarm of red-clad Giants buried Nagurski or Grange.

Holding a 9–0 lead early in the fourth quarter, the Giants appeared on their way to an important win. But Chicago's physical superiority had worn them down. The Bears drove to a touchdown, got the ball back, and drove into field goal range. Their kicker booted a game-winner with less than a minute to play. "It was a game worthy of its surroundings, a game of savage tackling, of irresistible power and of spectacular ball-carrying. It was football at its best in a display that had the huge gathering limp with excitement," the *New York Times'* Arthur Daley wrote.

The Giants quickly recovered, winning two of their remaining three games to capture the East division again. For the second straight year, they would face the Bears for the league title, this time at the Polo Grounds. Though the teams had played a close game on the same field a month earlier, the matchup had all the makings of a rout. The Bears had finished the regular season with a perfect record, winning thirteen straight games, as Beattie Feathers, a rookie from Tennessee, became the first NFL back to rush for more than a thousand yards in a season. Halas's squad figured to dominate the Giants, who had finished the regular season with an 8-5 record after losing their finale to the weak Philadelphia Eagles. "I know it doesn't look good," Owen told reporters, "but we'll give them a battle."

Mara still anticipated another sellout, but, when a storm coated New York with ice several hours before kickoff, thousands of fans stayed home, preferring to listen to a live radio broadcast of the game. The Bears led, 10–3, after a first half in which players slipped around the field. At some point in the second half, though, the Giants changed their footwear. Ray Flaherty, a veteran end for the Giants, had told Owen before the opening kickoff that rubber-soled sneakers probably would provide better footing on the ice than metal cleats, prompting Owen to send a friend, Abe Cohen, on a search for enough sneakers for the entire team. Cohen, a diminutive tailor who helped on the sideline during games, tried several sporting goods stores, which were closed, before ending up at Manhattan College, where the athletic director gave him the basketball team's sneakers. The second half of the game was underway by the time he hurried back to the Polo Grounds. He handed out the shoes to the Giants' players on their sideline.

The Giants still trailed early in the fourth quarter, 13–3, but, after their footwear change, they were able to race around the field while the Bears still struggled for decent footing. In a stunning reversal, the Giants scored four touchdowns in the final ten minutes and won, 30–13. Halas was furious, almost inconsolable; the Bears' loss in what would become known as "The Sneaker Game" would forever rank among his bitterest memories. "It was a freakish way to lose, but it was legal and it cost us the championship!" he would write. Mara, though, would forever recall the surprising victory as one of his happiest moments as a team owner. After enduring several seasons ending in frustration, New York fans responded to the Giants' fourth-quarter rally with a show of support so wild it turned chaotic.

"Enthusiasm turned to delirium," the *Chicago Tribune* wrote. "Hats spun down from the heights of the stands. Hundreds poured over the retaining walls and banked solidly around the gridiron. Only when a cordon of police, with the Giants' substitutes assisting, had lined up, could the crowd be controlled. After each touchdown, hundreds ran onto the field to slap the backs of their heroes." Mara could scarcely believe the scene. It was what he had always hoped for but feared might never happen. His city had lost its mind for his football team. There was, in his estimation, no sweeter sight.

9

INSTITUTING A DRAFT

Bert Bell could not have grown up more differently from Tim Mara, who quit school as a teenager, or Halas, a son of immigrant parents who worked hard just to get by. Bell attended elite schools and spent his summers at his family's country estate. "They had maids and butlers. He even had his own horse!" his son, Upton, would recall. But Halas, Mara, and the other NFL owners took to Bell from the day he joined the league in 1933. As they quickly discovered, he was a bon vivant who walked into rooms with a smile and a wink. "In those days, he was a man about town," Upton said. "He didn't have any money in his pocket, except his father's, but he knew how to live as if he did. In other words, he liked to party and he liked to gamble and he liked to have a drink."

His powers of persuasion would eventually help him attain the NFL's highest office; more than a decade later, his colleagues would elect him commissioner. But in 1933, he was failing in his efforts to convince one person in particular to see things his way. He had been courting Frances Upton, a willowy, dark-haired comic actress who had starred on Broadway. More than once, Bell had asked her to marry him. She always declined. "She was the only person who could ever

say no to Bert Bell," Upton Bell would write. The daughter of a deco-
rated New York police sergeant, Frances demanded that Bell give up
drinking before she would consider marrying him. After Bell finally
agreed to do it, they were married in early 1934. Bell was almost forty.
The pieces of his life were coming together. He had married a woman
he truly loved, not one his father had suggested was appropriate. Yes,
he had wasted a small fortune and no longer had his family's financial
backing—a fact of which the other owners were unaware—but he
had a knack for getting by. When he decided to start a pro football
team, his future wife loaned him the necessary money.

Surveying his circumstances after the 1934 season, he saw only
one real regret. As much as he enjoyed being in the NFL, it had a fundamental problem. The league's franchises were split into two groups,
those that consistently won and those that consistently lost. Bell's
Philadelphia Eagles were just two years old but already entrenched
as a "have not." It was going to be nearly impossible for them to join
the Chicago Bears and New York Giants in the top tier, Bell believed.
In the two years since they joined the league, the Eagles had won just
seven games. They had experienced a few highs, including a 3–3 tie
with the Bears in 1933 and a 6–0 win over the Giants in 1934. Bell
found the tie especially satisfying because it was played on a Sunday in
Philadelphia just days after the blue law referendum passed; Bell had
campaigned hard for that outcome. But the Eagles' victories, whether
moral or real, were few compared to the many defeats they had suffered.

Their first league game was a disaster, a 56–0 loss to the Giants at
the Polo Grounds on October 15, 1933—a staggering blowout in a
year when NFL teams averaged 9.7 points per game. Three days later,
only 1,750 fans attended the franchise's first home game, a 25–0 loss
to the Portsmouth Spartans. Late in the 1933 season, so few fans
were coming to the Eagles' home games that Bell offered a free car
wash to anyone who bought a ticket. In 1934, the Eagles lost five of
their first six games before defeating the miserable Cincinnati Reds,
soon to fold, before a crowd so sparse that no official attendance figure was announced.

Pro football was going nowhere in Philadelphia. The 80,000 fans Army and Navy drew to their game in the city on December 10, 1934, was more than the Eagles had drawn all season. The man once known as De Benneville Bell was unaccustomed to being second-class in any endeavor, but the Eagles were second-class NFL citizens along with other losing teams such as the Brooklyn Dodgers, Chicago Cardinals, and Art Rooney's Pittsburgh Pirates. It was hard to envision any of them competing with the Giants and Bears, whose larger crowds generated more revenue, providing an edge in the competition to pay for top college players turning pro.

All the owners were affected by their team's losses, but Bell, like Halas, was a former player and felt them almost viscerally. He had played in the Rose Bowl and later coached winning college teams. He simply hated losing, and not just because it meant he might sell fewer tickets to the next game. Determined to improve the Eagles' prospects after the 1934 season, he began recruiting a player he thought could help turn the team around: Stan Kostka, a burly fullback and line-backer from the University of Minnesota. The Golden Gophers had won college football's national championship that fall, earning accolades as one of the greatest teams of all time by going 8-0 and out-scoring their opponents, 270–38. Kostka, a square-bodied, 210-pound bruiser, led the offense in touchdowns and leveled opposing runners as a defender. Bell envisioned him battling the formidable linemen who made the Bears and Giants so daunting.

Bell placed a call to Kostka. The young man told him the Dodgers, Giants, Bears, Packers, and Pirates also had contacted him. "I asked him point blank if he would sign with the Eagles if I came out there to Minnesota and offered him a contract for more money than any other team in the league would give him," Bell told the Associated Press. "He said yes so . . . I went to Minneapolis."

As Bell told the story, he and Kostka met at a hotel. Bell pledged to top the highest offer Kostka received, which, according to Kostka, was $3,500 in salary for the 1935 season. Bell offered $4,000. When Kostka asked for time to think about it, Bell gave him an hour. "I knew what was in his mind. He wanted to get to a telephone and call the club that had offered him $3,500 and see if they'd top my offer," Bell said. "Apparently, he couldn't make the connection, because when he came back he still hadn't made up his mind. I told him, 'Look, I'll give you $6,000 if you sign now and let me go home.' He hedged. So I left."

Kostka eventually signed with the Dodgers for $5,000. Bell was furious. That was more than Bronko Nagurski made, and Bell thought a rookie should not earn more than the league's best player. And even more ominous, in Bell's view, was that Kostka had all the leverage. When teams bid against each other, the player prospered, but the teams suffered. How was that good for the league?

Bell was not the only frustrated owner. The recruitment of another college star, Alabama's Don Hutson, created more bad feelings and underscored the need for change. Hutson, a speedy receiver, had put on a show in the Rose Bowl on January 1, 1935, catching seven passes, two for touchdowns, against Stanford. The Packers' Curly Lambeau attended the game in Pasadena, California, and contacted Hutson several days later, suggesting he come play in Green Bay. Other teams also reached out to him, and like Kostka, Hutson played them off one another, driving up his price. Eventually, only Lambeau and John "Shipwreck" Kelly, the Dodgers' twenty-five-year-old player-coach, pursued him.

"Finally, Curly sent me a contract and I just went ahead and signed it," Hutson would recall years later. The contract called for him to earn $300 a game. But, according to Hutson, on the day he put the contract in the mail, Kelly showed up at his home in Tuscaloosa and offered to match Green Bay's offer. "I told Kelly I couldn't do that because I had already signed with Curly and put the contract in the mail that morning because I hadn't heard from him," Hutson remembered. "Kelly said, 'Don't worry. Sign a contract with me, too, and let me worry about it.'" Hutson signed another contract, which Kelly immediately mailed.

Both contracts reached Joe Carr's desk at the league office on the same day. Carr could not believe Hutson had signed with two teams and tried to figure out how to resolve the situation. Glancing at the postmarks on both envelopes, he saw that Lambeau's had been posted seventeen minutes earlier. That informed Carr's ruling. Hutson belonged to the Packers.

Kelly and the Dodgers were frustrated, as was Art Rooney, who had lost out in the bidding to sign several other players. "Something has to be done," Rooney told a Pittsburgh sportswriter. "Our club lost a bit less than $10,000 last year, yet when we try to sign a new man from the college ranks, we find other clubs immediately jack up the price. It becomes a wild scramble with the players in the end getting ridiculous first-year salaries from the richer teams while the tail-enders, who need new talent most, get slim pickings."

After losing Kostka, Bell proposed the idea that would forever change pro football. Why not institute a draft? Pool the top college players and let teams select them one at a time, starting with the team with the worst record—which therefore needed the most help—and proceeding through the standings in inverse order, with the best teams picking last. That would be fairer and more orderly than the mad scramble each year for the top college players. The talent entering the league would now be spread around more equitably, leading to more competitive games, and, ideally, eliminating the class line between the Giants and Bears on one hand and teams like Bell's Eagles on the other. Just as important, in Bell's view, was that only one team would then own a player's rights, eliminating the battles driving salaries so high.

In the first months of 1935, Bell quietly sold his idea to the other owners. Some did not need convincing; Rooney and others in the lower echelon immediately saw it could help them. But what about Halas and Mara? As owners of the most dominant, profitable teams, they would be relinquishing one of their primary advantages over the other teams. It was a pivotal moment. Halas and Mara saw they would suffer if a draft was instituted, but they also understood the league would benefit. "I thought the proposal sound. It made sense," Halas said. "Tim Mara also approved. He and I had more to lose than any other team. With our support, the proposal was adopted."

Mara said the possibility of the Giants being less dominant "was a hazard we had to accept for the benefit of the league, of professional football, and of everyone in it." He grasped that the NFL, still in its relative infancy, needed to change. "People come to see competition," Mara said. "We could give them competition only if the teams had some sort of equality, if the teams went up and down with the fortunes of life."

On May 18, 1935, Carr and eight owners met at the Fort Pitt Hotel in Pittsburgh. Bell stood and addressed the group. "Gentlemen, I've always had the theory that pro football is like a chain," he said. "The league is no stronger than its weakest link, and I've been a weak link for so long that I should know. Every year, the rich get richer and the poor get poorer. Four teams control the championships, the Giants and Redskins in the East, and the Bears and Packers in the West. Because they are successful, they keep attracting the best college players in the open market, which makes them successful." He made his pitch for an annual draft. The other owners liked it, and, after Bell sat down, they hammered out details. A motion was proposed, seconded, and passed unanimously. The inaugural NFL draft was scheduled for the following winter, shortly after the 1935 season.

"Bert was a very persuasive man. You have to remember that he was a politician at heart," Art Rooney said later. "He had come from a political family. His father and brother were active in politics. That must have been where he acquired the finesse to work with strong men like George Halas and Tim Mara and George Preston Marshall and persuade them to work together for the common good."

IF ANYTHING, THE 1935 EAGLES ILLUSTRATED THE NEED FOR the draft that would follow that season. They played eleven games, lost nine, scored just 59 points, and didn't win a single home game. Bell tried various tricks to boost attendance. He announced that clergymen of varying faiths would sit on the Eagles' bench every Sunday. He signed a halfback who had been in prison, thinking the curiosity factor might sell a few tickets. His desperation was evident.

The prison halfback, Edwin "Alabama" Pitts, was a navy veteran who had been convicted with three accomplices of robbing a grocery store in New York. Though he had never played organized sports, he starred on the football and baseball teams at Sing Sing Prison in upstate New York, becoming a media sensation. Upon his release, he signed with a minor-league baseball team in Albany, New York, but lasted fewer than fifty games before being released. Turning to football, he signed a four-game, $1,500 contract with the Eagles.

As Bell hoped, the press jumped all over the story, which helped lure 20,000 fans, the Eagles' largest crowd ever, to their 1935 season opener. But Pitts never played in a 17–7 loss to Pittsburgh, not even when the fans chanted, "We want Pitts!" Lud Wray, the head coach, gave Pitts some snaps in the next few games, and he caught a few passes. But the team kept losing, and fans lost interest. When Pitts's contract expired after four games, he was gone. "Bert, the only thing you haven't done is hire a good football team. Have you thought about trying that?" Halas told Bell after the Bears routed the Eagles, 39–0, on October 13, 1935.

The Eagles' dismal season ended with a 13–6 home loss to the Packers before 4,000 fans. A week later, the Lions defeated the Giants in the league championship game in Detroit. Bell attended the game, returned to Philadelphia, and began to organize the draft. Because it was his idea, the other owners had put him in charge. He reserved a suite at the Ritz-Carlton, a hotel that Bell's father owned and Bell had once managed.

On February 8, 1936, the owners gathered at the hotel for a meeting set to start at 1:30 p.m. Bell directed them to his suite, which featured a conference table, piano, and chalkboard resting on an easel, which Bell had brought in for the occasion. Tim Mara was joined by his sons, twenty-seven-year-old Jack, by now the Giants' president, and twenty-year-old Wellington, more knowledgeable than ever about the talent in the college game. George Halas and Charles Bidwill, the owners of the Chicago teams, arrived together. Curly Lambeau represented the Packers by himself, as did Pittsburgh's Art Rooney and Boston's George Preston Marshall. Lud Wray, the Eagles' coach, was on hand to help Bell.

The men took off their jackets and went to work. Their first job was determining the group of college players they could select from. The owners and coaches volunteered the names of players who had exhausted their college eligibility. Someone—likely Bell or Joe Carr, who ran the meeting—wrote the names on the chalkboard. When the list swelled to nearly one hundred, the men agreed they should draft more than five each, the number they had agreed to initially. Bell offered a motion to raise the number of rounds to nine. Halas seconded the motion and it passed unanimously.

In the coming years, as the owners came to see the draft as one of the most crucial events on their calendar, teams would employ scouts and turn the study of college talent into a richly funded science. But the first draft involved little sophistication. To gauge the skill and talent of outgoing college players, the owners and coaches had done little more than read newspapers and magazines, check college media guides and All-American lists, and attend a few games. Their idea of advanced scouting was soliciting opinions from their friends in the college ranks. Their budgets included no funds for scouting.

When the nine teams were ready to start the 1936 draft, the Eagles went first, as they had the worst record. Bell picked Jay Berwanger, a darting halfback from the University of Chicago, who had won the Downtown Athletic Club Trophy, a new award given by one of New York's foremost sports organizations to the nation's top college player. It would become the Heisman Trophy a year later, in honor of John Heisman, the club's athletic director, after he died. Picking second, Marshall's Redskins selected Riley Smith, an Alabama quarterback who had thrown passes to Don Hutson. Art Rooney took

Bill Shakespeare, a Notre Dame halfback nicknamed "the Merchant of Menace." The other six teams quickly made their first selections, with the champion Lions going *before* the runner-up Giants because the Giants had a higher regular-season winning percentage.

The Eagles began the second round by taking John McCauley, a halfback from Rice Institute in Texas. After the other eight teams made their second selections, Bell started the third round by drafting Wes Muller, a center from Stanford. The meeting, which had started shortly after lunch, continued into the early evening and evolved into a football stag party. "There were plenty of cigars, and the liquor flowed," according to a Philadelphia sportswriter. The event featured none of the fanfare the draft would eventually attract. Without offering details, the Associated Press simply reported that the league had adopted a "new ruling" about how college talent would be dispersed. The *New York Times* did not immediately report that a draft had occurred.

By the end, after teams had selected eighty-one players in total, the owners took the next step, negotiating with their picks to see whether they could agree on a price. The players had not agreed to this method of distributing talent, and it did not benefit them; now that one team "owned" their rights, they could not solicit multiple offers and pit bids against each other. It was the first example of the kind of broad differences between owners and players that would ultimately produce labor strife. The players selected in the inaugural draft had only one bargaining tactic: they could threaten not to play, and many did just that. The NFL was, after all, hardly a path to riches. Most players earned around $250 per game. Many prospects, even the best ones, went into business instead. Only twenty-four of the eighty-one players selected in 1936 suited up for a game that season.

Long before the Eagles made Berwanger the first overall pick, he publicly suggested he might not play. He wanted to finish his studies and graduate, he said, and wanted to maintain his amateur status so he could try out for the 1936 US Olympic team as a decathlete. "I haven't decided what I will do. I may play professional football next fall because of its practical advantages. I might take a coaching job, although it is my ultimate intention to enter business in preference to making a career in professional athletics," he told the Associated Press in the fall of 1935.

When he failed to make the Olympic team, he began considering the NFL more seriously. Bell contacted him and asked what he had in mind as a salary. Berwanger reportedly asked for $1,000 a game. Bell countered with $150. Seeing that a deal was unlikely, Bell traded Berwanger's rights to the Bears, receiving in return a tackle, Art Buss. Halas coveted Berwanger, a front-page sensation in Chicago. But Berwanger only raised his price after the trade, and, when Halas refused to meet it, he decided not to sign. He never played in the NFL.

"He asked me what I wanted," Berwanger said of Halas years later. "I said $25,000 for two years and a no-cut contract. We shook hands, said goodbye, and he and I have been good friends ever since. They just couldn't afford to pay that kind of money." Instead of playing in the NFL, Berwanger coached at his alma mater until it dropped its football program in 1939. After serving as a navy flight instructor during World War II, he founded a company that made plastic and sponge-rubber strips for car doors, car trunks, and farm machinery. It was grossing $30 million annually when he sold it in 1992.

Bell's frustrations with the Eagles' inaugural draft class went beyond his failed negotiations with Berwanger. None of the nine players he selected ended up signing with the team. John McCauley, the second pick, took a job with a tool company in Midland, Texas. Another back from Rice, Bill Wallace, also went into business. Harry Shuford, a back from Southern Methodist University, went to law school. Al Barabas, a Columbia running back, chose minor league baseball. John "Jac" Weller, an All-American guard from Princeton, opened a real estate and insurance business. Pepper Constable, a Princeton back, went to Harvard Medical School.

Other teams faced similar problems. Shakespeare, the third overall pick, opted to work for the Thor Power Tool Company in Aurora, Illinois, rather than play for Rooney in Pittsburgh. The Giants' first pick, tackle Art "Pappy" Lewis, played just one season with the team. The most enduringly famous name among the eighty-one draftees never played in the NFL. Paul Bryant, an Alabama end taken in the fourth round by the Brooklyn Dodgers, decided to go into coaching. Nearly a half century later, "Bear" Bryant retired as the most successful coach in college football history.

The point of the draft was to give lesser teams a better chance to compete, and that eventually happened, but the 1936 draft did not immediately produce parity. Mostly, the rich got richer. Of the four future Hall of Fame inductees selected, tackle Joe Stydahar and guard Dan Fortmann went to the Bears, and running back Tuffy Leemans went to the Giants. The fourth, Wayne Millner, an end from Notre Dame, went to Marshall's Boston club.

Sixty-four players were drafted before Millner, offering the owners an early example of what would become one of the great truths about the draft: outcomes for individual players are hard to predict. A player everyone regards as a future star can quickly become a bust, while a player taken in a later round, almost as an afterthought, can turn out to be one of the greatest of all time. It was true in the first draft and remains true today, even with teams now relying on detailed, time-intensive scouting practices.

When the draft was instituted, the owners saw it as a means of solving their own problems, and, while Halas and Mara graciously agreed to a plan that ended up undermining their own teams' dominance, what was absent from the owners' discussions was any sense of the players' interests. At the time, the owners cared little about what players might think. Indeed, one of the selling points of the draft was that it would keep player wages in check. That many would-be NFL players decided not to sign up under the new terms should not have shocked the owners, many of whom were savvy businessmen, but it did. The owners did not count on pushback from the players. But more of that, much more, was coming.

10

BETTING BONANZA

O N THE FIRST SUNDAY OF THE 1936 SEASON, THE PITTS-burgh Pirates hosted the Boston Redskins at Forbes Field in Pittsburgh. Almost 16,000 fans came to the stadium, mostly to see whether Art Rooney's team demonstrated any signs of improvement. The Pirates had won just nine of thirty-five games in their first three NFL seasons.

Following his usual game-day routine, Rooney attended a morning mass before making his way to the game. He was optimistic, believing his team was in capable hands. Joe Bach, the Pirates' head coach, was a flinty midwesterner who had suited up for Notre Dame in the 1920s as one of the "Seven Mules," the blockers who opened holes for the Four Horsemen. Now thirty-five, he had worked as a college assistant after his playing days and then produced a winning team as a head coach at Duquesne. He was in his second year with the Pirates.

George Preston Marshall was also optimistic about what the Redskins might achieve in 1936, although when he spoke with Rooney before the game, he offered his customary lament about Boston's lack of interest in his team. It might force him to do something drastic one day, he warned.

When the game began, the defenses dominated. In the second quarter, a Boston halfback fumbled, and the Pirates' George Kakasic scooped up the ball and raced 26 yards for a touchdown. That remained the game's only score until Kakasic booted a field goal in the fourth quarter to finish off a 10–0 victory for the Pirates. Ten days later, they traveled to Brooklyn for a weeknight game at Ebbets Field and won again, 10–6, to give them a 2-0 record for the first time. That was all it took for the Pirates to pique the interest of fans in football-mad Western Pennsylvania. A crowd of 25,800 attended their next game at Forbes Field, against the New York Giants, on September 27. The Pirates had never beaten the Giants. The year before, the Giants had annihilated them in Pittsburgh, 42–7.

Rooney hoped his friend from the horse racing scene, Tim Mara, would accompany the Giants on their trip. Next to Bert Bell, Mara was his closest ally among the league's owners. Rooney remained cautious around Marshall and George Halas, large personalities who dominated league meetings. But he had known Mara for years and trusted him. Mara, though, did not travel to Pittsburgh. He had steadily ceded more and more authority over the Giants' affairs to his sons. Jack, the team president, was on the trip. When the game began, Jack was on the press box roof, running a film camera. The Giants had started filming their games, hoping to learn more about their players by studying the film afterwards.

New York had lost its season opener to the weak Philadelphia Eagles, a disappointing result, and now the Pirates struck first with a touchdown in the second quarter. The Giants answered with a touchdown in the third quarter, and the game was tied when the Pirates drove to the New York 4 yard line in the final minutes. Three plunges into the line went nowhere, so Bach called on his kicker, who booted an 11-yard attempt through the uprights for the decisive points that gave Pittsburgh the victory. After the game, Rooney bid farewell to Jack Mara with a handshake, asking the young man to convey greetings to his father. Then he retired to his office to count his gate, his biggest ever.

ROONEY'S FIRST YEARS IN THE NFL HAD BEEN ONE LONG LESSON in humility. His semipro teams had ruled Western Pennsylvania for many years, but he quickly found that NFL squads were bigger, faster, better coached, and considerably more skilled. Nonetheless, Rooney continued to field teams comprised of working-class Pittsburghers, the same kind of players who had filled his semipro rosters. Harp Vaughan and Warren Heller were two of Rooney's old friends from the Northside. Cap Oehler had worked in the coal mines. Dave Ribble carried a Teamsters card. Winning was important, but, with jobs scarce in a depressed economy, Rooney thought it was more important to help out the men he had played cards and sports with since his youth.

The quintessential early Pirate was Mose Kelsch, a running back who played without a helmet. He had grown up an orphan in Troy Hill, a Northside neighborhood, and received little formal education. But Rooney met him on the city's sandlots, and he became a fan favorite on the semipro circuit, directly challenging defenders in his path with a straight-ahead running style. When Rooney joined the NFL in 1933 and formed the Pirates, Kelsch, thirty-six, became the league's oldest player. Still playing without a helmet, as NFL players could do until 1943, he no longer ran over defenders, but he could kick field goals and extra points. In one of the Pirates' first games, he waddled onto the field in the waning minutes, bald head glistening in the sun, and booted a game-winning kick.

With Jap Douds as the head coach, the Pirates had gone 3-6-2 in their first season. The local talent on their roster helped sell tickets, but the Pirates were no match for the NFL's established teams. Their first-ever road trip produced a 47–0 loss to the Packers. The Giants defeated them twice by a combined 50–5 score.

Rooney tried a different coach, Luby DiMeolo, in 1934, and traded for Johnny "Blood" McNally, a hell-raising halfback who had been kicked out of Notre Dame. He had caused so much trouble while playing in Green Bay that the Packers finally traded him, even though he was one of their star players. Neither move worked. McNally barely played because of injuries, and DiMeolo's primary qualification was being a friend of one of Rooney's brothers. The Pirates lost ten of twelve games, and the fans even turned on Kelsch when he missed several key extra points.

Near the end of the season, Rooney and DiMeolo were having a conversation in Rooney's office when DiMeolo mused that football players were tougher than boxers. Rooney, a former ring champion, took offense. The argument escalated until Rooney suggested they settle it with their fists. Someone brought in gloves and Rooney proceeded to batter his coach. When the season ended, DiMeolo was out of a job and Rooney hired Bach. (Kelsch never had a chance to play his way back into the fans' favor. He died in an automobile accident in July 1935. Rooney served as a pallbearer at the funeral.)

Bach put a greater emphasis on conditioning, blocking, and tackling, and in 1935, his first season with the Pirates, they opened with a victory over the Eagles and won back-to-back games against the Cardinals and Redskins in late October. With a 3-4 record, they were just a game out of first place in the East division. But, when they suffered key injuries, Rooney lacked the funds to pay for capable replacements. They won just one of their last five games.

That season, the Pirates drew an average of 12,489 fans per game, slightly above the league average but not enough for Rooney to turn a profit. His tickets were among the league's cheapest. He received no money for radio broadcasts of his games; in fact, he paid a station to air them. He had to schedule a slate of exhibition games against semipro teams to stay in business, and the extra contests exhausted the players, as evidenced by their late-season swoon. "In those days, nobody got wealthy in sports," Rooney said later. "You got two thrills.

One came Sunday, trying to win the game. The next came Monday, trying to make the payroll."

Always looking for different ways to bring in money, Rooney had accepted an unusual offer from Tim Mara before the 1936 season. Seeking to bring a semblance of order to the league schedule—there had been little before—the owners had instituted a set of protocols after they split the teams into two divisions in 1933. But the rules were flexible. If both owners wanted to change the date and location of a game, they could. They could even swap one opponent for another. Mara wanted to avoid playing the Bears twice in 1936, thinking the Giants' win-loss record would benefit. He offered to pay Rooney to take the Giants' place on the Bears' schedule. Rooney agreed to the deal, which meant the Pirates had to play the fearsome Bears twice in a three-week span, first in Pittsburgh on October 4, then in Chicago on October 18. With a 3-0 record going into their home game against the undefeated Bears, the Pirates sold out Forbes Field for the first time. The Bears toyed with them, building a 27–0 lead before the Pirates made the final result more respectable with a couple of scores in the fourth quarter. Two weeks later, before 20,000 fans at Wrigley Field, the Bears defeated the Pirates again, 26–7. Bach bristled about Rooney's deal with Mara slowing his team's momentum.

The Pirates righted themselves, though, and, after they defeated the Eagles, 6–0, in a Thursday night game in Philadelphia in early November, they had a 6-3 record and a grip on first place in the East. The Giants were having a down year. The Redskins were the only other winning team in the division. With three games to go, bookies listed the Pirates as 7–5 favorites to win the East and host the league championship game at Forbes Field. But their final three games were on the road, and they lost the first two, to the Lions and Cardinals. Their season came down to their final game against the Redskins on November 29 in Boston. The winner would take the East and play for the NFL title.

Rooney was optimistic because the Pirates had beaten the Redskins earlier in the season and had two weeks to prepare for the rematch. But he also had promised a friend in Los Angeles that the Pirates would come to the West Coast for an exhibition game in the interim. The players dutifully boarded a train for the cross-country journey, played the game, and returned, but the trip wore them down, and Bach was so incensed that he and Rooney came to blows during the ride home. The team's mood was grim heading into the big game in Boston, and the Redskins won easily, 30–0. The players each received a $65 bonus from the league for finishing second, but Rooney was disappointed, and Bach simply fled the scene, taking the head coach position at Niagara University. Rooney would say later that one of his worst mistakes was letting Bach go. His team would not win more than four games in a season again until the early 1940s.

In his first years in the NFL, Rooney was careful in his dealings with the other owners. He was quite a bit younger than most of them and neither as accomplished in business as Marshall or Bidwill nor as savvy about football as Halas or Lambeau. But that did not stop him from courting them, a natural inclination for someone so innately sociable. He took them to his favorite restaurants, in Pittsburgh and elsewhere. He attended mass with the Catholic owners. The others found him funny, kind, and likeable. It helped that Mara vouched for him.

But he could see he was different. The others, especially Halas and Marshall, were deeply competitive by nature, willing to do almost anything to beat you or somehow take advantage of you. When Halas and Rooney were dividing up the gate after the Pirates played at Wrigley Field in 1936, Halas shortchanged Rooney by several thousand dollars. "Halas, mistrustful by nature, may have been testing this younger man," Rooney's biographers wrote. Rooney pointed out the error. Halas denied it. Rooney insisted he was owed more. Halas held his ground. Eventually, they stood within inches of one another, and a fistfight seemed inevitable. Then Halas backed down, smiled, and said he was glad they had not fought. "George, you were no sure thing to win that fight," Rooney declared.

Football and the affairs of their teams consumed the other men, or so it seemed to Rooney. He cared about the Pirates, but they were not his top priority, and that showed in their performance. "Aside from Halas, Marshall, Curly Lambeau and Mara, I guess I, like most of the other owners, didn't pay enough attention to football," Rooney said later. He was busy in local politics, even serving as Pittsburgh's Republican Party chairman in 1936. He had obtained a license to promote boxing matches. He still played some semipro baseball in the summers. And, of course, there was his primary source of income— gambling on horse racing.

In the midst of tending to his various affairs, playing baseball, and preparing for the Pirates' season (he had named Johnny Blood the team's player-coach) in the summer of 1937, he drove to Empire City, a racetrack in Yonkers, New York, to bet on the races one weekend. It was a social occasion; he was accompanied by Buck Crouse, a retired middleweight boxer. Once he was at the track, Rooney made his way to the betting enclosure, where a stable of bookmakers, including Tim Mara, held court. In the days before tracks managed gambling with pari-mutuel machines, legal bookies ran what amounted to small businesses; they set odds on the horses and agreed to wagers in individual transactions with their customers. Mara hailed the short, cigar-chomping Rooney, assuring the other bookies his credit was good.

Mara always had the scoop on which horses were running well; several months earlier, Rooney had turned a tip from Mara into a $7,000 score at Belmont Park. Now, after a conversation with Mara, Rooney went to another bookie and placed a $200 bet on the first race at Empire City. (He never bet with Mara, not wanting to compete with his friend.) His horse came in, earning $800. Feeling bad

Art Rooney (left) and Tim Mara study the horse racing odds. (New York *Daily News* Archive via Getty Images)

about taking so much from the bookie, he went back with more bets, giving the man a chance to even the score. But Rooney won "three or four" races to raise his winnings to $5,000, which he then bet on a 5-1 shot. When that horse came in, Rooney was up somewhere between $19,000 and $25,000.

He was not betting strictly on Mara's advice. Rooney was a keen student of horses' performance records, which were published in the *Daily Racing Form.* He also was unafraid to play a long shot on a hunch or back a favorite when he thought it was warranted. In the feature race that day at Empire City, he bet $10,000 on heavily favored Seabiscuit to win the Jerome Handicap, and Seabiscuit won, earning Rooney almost twice his original wager. He lost several late-day bets but still ended up well ahead. Seldom, if ever, had Rooney experienced such a profitable day at the races. Mara advised him to take his winnings and go home. "Stick that dough in your kick and forget about the horses. I should know. I'm a bookmaker. It's my business to take money from guys like you," Mara said.

Rooney planned to take Mara's advice. While eating a celebratory streak dinner at a Broadway saloon that night, his dinner companion, the saloon's owner, asked, "What's your next move, Artie?" Rooney replied, "Back to Pittsburgh." But the owner, a classic New York hustler, talked Rooney into heading north to Saratoga, where the summer racing meeting was set to open. Rooney arrived at the famous track early on Monday, July 20, 1936, and began to gather information before making his wagers. The weather was foul— lightning struck a barn, killing a horse and knocking eight others unconscious—but expected to improve later. Rooney found Mara in the betting enclosure and asked which horses were running well. He ate breakfast at the track kitchen with the backside clockers, who timed morning workouts.

Mara had advised him to wait several days before starting to bet because the track was sloppy and a batch of unfamiliar horses had arrived from California. Rooney paid no heed. He approached another bookie in the enclosure and bet on Taken, a 5–1 shot, in the first race. Taken, ridden by famed jockey Eddie Arcaro, won the race. Rooney then won the second race with a colt named Little Marty, and, after losing the third, won two straight with bets on "mudders," horses that enjoyed running on a sloppy track. Rooney did not stop there, but rather began to bet even larger sums. When his horse came in at 7–1 in the sixth race, he had brought a track cliché to life: he needed a wheelbarrow for his winnings. By the end of the day, Bill Corum, a sports columnist for the *New York Journal-American*, estimated that Rooney hade made close to $100,000—nearly $2 million in today's dollars.

Corum, on hand to cover the races, had heard about Rooney's streak as word spread through the grandstand that a "plunger," racing's description for a high-risk gambler, was making a killing. He found Rooney and accompanied him as he bet. Corum wrote a column published the next day headlined, "It's Art but They Don't Like It," depicting Rooney as a heroic underdog, a canny native of hardworking Pittsburgh who had outmaneuvered the big-city bookies. Other New York columnists at the track picked up on the story and wrote about Rooney as his streak continued the next day with winning bets in the first three races. By now, crowds were following him around the grandstand and cheering him as he approached the betting window with fistfuls of cash. The publicity had turned him into a sensation. Rooney was suddenly the most famous horse player in America. He ended up far ahead for a second straight day.

When his hot hand finally began to cool, he took Mara's advice and headed back to Pittsburgh. His wife, Kass, had been holed up in their apartment with their two young boys and was pregnant with their third child. He told her their lives were about to change because they would never have to worry about money again. After a few days at home, he headed back to Saratoga and added to his winnings. An urgent phone call from home interrupted his run. Kass was going into labor. Rooney promised Mara that he would name the newborn for him, in honor of the touts Mara had supplied. Timothy James Rooney was born on August 8, 1937. Rooney returned to Saratoga later that month and kept winning. It was hard to know exactly how much he had won when the meeting ended, but Mara estimated it was between $250,000 and $380,000—a life's fortune in Depression-era America, between $4.3 million and $6.5 million in today's dollars.

As summer waned and football season approached, Rooney began to focus on the Pirates. The other NFL owners had read about his run in the newspapers. Several sent congratulatory telegrams. Never again would Halas test the younger man. Apparently, Rooney was not to be trifled with. Back in Pittsburgh, Rooney continued to field interview requests from journalists. One day, a New York columnist called and explained that Marshall had expressed concern about Rooney being both a gambler and an NFL owner. Rooney replied, "When George gives up the broads, I'll give up gambling."

Rooney would eventually become one of Pittsburgh's most beloved citizens, but he was not yet a legendary figure in the 1930s.

Around his city, he was mostly recognized as a down-to-earth local entrepreneur who promoted boxing matches and owned a losing
football team. Sports fans did not begrudge him his success. In fact,
they were pleased to see one of their city's own receive national attention. They hoped his run at the betting window would translate into
better days for the football Pirates. But they would soon discover that
it made no difference at all.

11

MOVE TO DC

Like Bert Bell, George Preston Marshall was court-ing an actress, Corinne Griffith, a lithe, dark-haired beauty who had been known as "the Orchid Lady of the Screen" during her hey-day in Hollywood's silent-movie era. Marshall wanted to marry her and went all out to convince her to say yes. When he proposed early in 1936, he arranged a theatrical-style backdrop that included Afri-can American performers singing about slaves in the Old South and serving mint juleps in *Gone with the Wind* costumes. When Griffith agreed to marry him, Marshall's engagement gift to her was a Con-federate flag that had been in his family since the Civil War.

After marrying, the couple spent most of the fall of 1936 in Bos-ton, where Marshall ran the Redskins from a hotel suite. Many of their conversations followed a similar course. Griffith told her his team's games were boring. Marshall admitted she was right. Though new to football, she knew the entertainment game. She certainly knew a spectacle from a flop, and, by any measure, the Redskins were the latter. They had fewer than five hundred season ticket holders after five years in business. They often drew just a few thousand fans to their games, which were quiet affairs, only slightly louder than Griffith's silent films.

Marshall had gone into pro football believing he could rule it. None of the other team owners could match his business acumen. Though they were good men and he got along well with them, they were bookies and gamblers for the most part, sports guys, while Marshall had built a lucrative laundry empire. The others knew football, but Marshall was sure he was the one who could make the NFL into a big enterprise, with his team on top.

From the outset, convinced he knew best, he had meddled with his team on such matters as which players made the roster, what plays to call, even whether the captain should call heads or tails at the coin flip before kickoff. Other owners watched games from the stands and press box, but Marshall stalked the sidelines, cursing officials and shouting plays and substitutions to his coach. To his surprise, the Redskins did not win in the manner that he had won in the laundry business—that is, efficiently and completely. They won some games but lost more. In 1935, they went 2-8-1. Marshall cursed his players, his coaches, the referees. He churned through three head coaches in the Redskins' first four years. In 1936, he made an effort to improve the team, spending more on player salaries and hiring Ray Flaherty, a respected former Giants player, as the team's latest head coach. But he also nearly doubled his ticket prices, giving Boston's sports fans another reason to ignore a team and sport they had never been excited about, anyway. The Redskins performed better on the field, building a winning record, but continued to draw puny crowds. Boston's sportswriters criticized Marshall, suggesting in print that his prices were too high, his meddling hurt the team, and his sport was dull. The football teams at Harvard and Boston College garnered more headlines, as did baseball's Red Sox and Braves. "There were times on game day when the papers played the Radcliffe girls' field hockey team above our game," Marshall groused later.

With his movie-star wife, stretch limousine, and full-length raccoon coat, Marshall believed he was much too big and important to be ignored. He began to consider moving his team to another city. In November he invited Joe Carr to a home game against the Packers, an attractive opponent, primarily to demonstrate why he was so upset. Seeing a crowd of just 11,220 fans, Carr understood Marshall's concerns. The owner snapped after the game, telling reporters, "The nice thing about owning a pro football team is that all you have to do to move is pack your trunks."

Quietly, he scheduled a scouting mission in Washington, his hometown. He had concocted a plan. If he moved the Redskins to the nation's capital, he could market them not only to sports fans there but also to fans in Virginia, his native West Virginia, and the entire Deep South, where the football-mad public only had college football and, thus, lacked a rooting interest on Sundays. It was a grand idea, Marshall thought. Washington was ready for pro football, he believed. He could build the team with players from popular southern college teams such as Florida, Georgia, Tennessee, and Texas. The Redskins could become the pro team for the entire Deep South. It meant he could not use African American players from schools with integrated teams such as Michigan State or UCLA, but Marshall wanted an all-white team, anyway.

Marshall's wife thought it was a great idea. Boston had all but given up on the Redskins, it seemed, especially after Marshall publicly threatened to move. On November 29, 1936, they pounded the Pirates at Fenway Park, 30–0. Suddenly, all they had to do was beat the Giants at the Polo Grounds on December 6 and they would win the East division and play in the league championship game. But only 4,283 fans attended the home game against Pittsburgh. That was truly pathetic. The low turnout convinced Marshall it was time for bold action. If the Redskins did win the division, he decided he would yank the championship game out of Boston. He had not run the idea past Rooney, Mara, or any of his friends, but because he would be hosting the game, he could do what he wanted. He decided the Redskins would play the Packers, who had won the West, in New York.

Griffith nodded when he suggested the idea. On autumn evenings in their hotel suite in Boston, the two began to plot the rollout of the team once it was in Washington. Marshall would court the city's sportswriters and win them firmly to his side, preventing a reprise of what had happened to him in Boston. The *Washington Times* was looking for a publisher; if he took that job, he could control the paper's coverage and feature the Redskins at the top of the sports page. The longer Marshall discussed the idea with his wife, the better it sounded. They could start a team band and stage elaborate halftime pageants featuring music, jugglers, maybe even live animals. They would give the fans in Washington something besides football, perhaps even a Christmas extravaganza with a plane flying over the stadium and dropping a parachuting Santa Claus onto the field. One way or another, Marshall would make sure "the Orchid Lady of the Screen" never again complained that the Redskins' games were dull.

RAY FLAHERTY HAD BEEN WARNED ABOUT MARSHALL. Confident and purposeful, he demanded that his contract with the Redskins include a clause forbidding the owner from stalking the sidelines during games. Marshall reluctantly agreed to watch from a field box behind the bench, but he soon devised another way to continue to interfere. He had a pair of telephones installed, one by his seat and one on the bench. Whenever he had an idea, he called Flaherty . . . during the game.

Although Marshall's team may not have been able to win over many fans, his officiousness entertained the rest of the league. Before the Redskins played the Giants on December 6, 1936, with the East division title on the line, a reporter asked Giants coach Steve Owen whether Marshall's "coaching" bothered him. "Bothered? I hope George Preston Marshall is in good voice. It ought to be worth at least a couple of touchdowns to us," Owen replied.

Marshall got the last laugh. Playing in a driving rain, the visiting Redskins took the lead with an early touchdown while their mud-splattered defenders handily controlled New York's offense. In the fourth quarter, Boston's Cliff Battles splashed 80 yards for a touchdown. The Redskins earned their first division title and a place in the league championship game with a 14–0 victory. Unable to hide his delight, Marshall sent a telegram to the Bears' George Halas, his friend and nemesis, whose team had finished behind the Packers in the Western division:

> george, stop
>
> guess what, stop
>
> you get to watch us in the big game, gpm, stop

After the game, when Marshall told Carr about wanting to move the championship game to New York, Carr did not attempt to dissuade him. The league announced that Boston and Green Bay would play at the Polo Grounds that Sunday. Marshall was done with Boston and its disinterested press and fans. "We'll get a much bigger gate in New York," Marshall told reporters. "We certainly don't owe Boston after the shabby treatment we've received. Imagine losing $20,000 with a championship club." Though the teams and the league had less than a week to drum up interest, the game drew 29,545 fans—unquestionably more than it would have attracted in Boston. New Yorkers rooted for the Redskins, their fellow East division team, but were disappointed as the Packers scored early on a 48-yard touchdown pass from Arnie Herber to Don Hutson and went on to win easily, 21–6.

After the game, Marshall told reporters he was uncertain where he would move his team, suggesting Newark as a possibility. But he was being coy. He had hosted a contingent from Washington at the title game, including Clark Griffith (no relation to Corinne), who owned baseball's Senators and the city's largest sports venue, Griffith Stadium. The two men discussed a lease arrangement after the game, and four days later, on December 16, 1936, Marshall announced he was moving the Redskins to Washington. The *Boston Globe* buried the story. The *New York Times* barely paid attention, printing a short blurb at the bottom of a sports page. But it was big news in Washington. "Marshall Moves Boston Redskins to District," blared a *Washington Post* headline. It was understood that the other team owners and Joe Carr would officially approve the move at a later date; they were not going to interfere with Marshall's plans.

Even before that approval came several months later, Marshall began to sell his team and his sport to a new city. The Redskins' success was hardly guaranteed. Washington was not known as a sports town. Attendance for the Senators had plunged when they no longer challenged for the pennant every year, unlike in their heyday in the 1920s. The best local college football teams, Georgetown and George Washington, elicited modest support. Marshall certainly recalled the failure of his own Palace Five basketball team in the 1920s. But against the evidence, Marshall believed the Redskins could thrive. He had been an outsider in Boston, a stranger to the city's leaders, but in Washington he knew just about everyone there was to know. He was already a success in the city, owing to his laundry dynasty, and he was sure he could succeed again.

His timing was fortuitous. Washington would grow from 486,000 residents in 1930 to 663,000 by the end of the decade. Thousands of newcomers arrived every year, lured by federal government jobs generated by President Roosevelt's New Deal programs. That Marshall opposed the New Deal on principle did not stop him from benefitting from it indirectly. Long a relatively sleepy, southern-style outpost, Washington was evolving into a sophisticated metropolis.

In another stroke of good fortune, Marshall drafted Sammy Baugh, a star quarterback from Texas Christian University, days before the move to Washington was announced. Marshall hoped Baugh would energize the Redskins' offense. He would do that and much more, it turned out.

Marshall and Baugh did not get off to an auspicious start. Baugh held out, turning down the owner's initial offer of a $5,000 contract for the 1937 season. Utilizing his only leverage now that one team owned his rights, he threated to play baseball for the St. Louis Cardinals, with whom he had also signed, explaining to Marshall that he had dreamed of playing in the major leagues since he was a youngster in Sweetwater, Texas.

For his part, Marshall was too busy to focus strictly on Baugh. Aside from the Redskins, he still ran his laundries and had signed a $100,000 deal to produce the Greater Texas and Pan-American Exposition, a World's Fair–like event that took place in Dallas from June through October in 1937. Assisted by his wife, a native Texan, he staged a months-long variety spectacular that included an auto race, historical reenactments, nightly activities, and sports contests featuring athletes from twenty-one nations.

As Marshall's negotiations with his top draft pick dragged on, he brought Baugh to Dallas and squired him around the exposition. Baugh was impressed with Marshall's showmanship and bombast, but the stalemate continued. Finally, just before the Redskins opened their inaugural Washington training camp in September, Baugh signed for $8,000, becoming the NFL's highest-paid player. After they agreed to terms over the phone, Marshall asked Baugh to bring a Stetson hat and some cowboy duds to Washington when he arrived to sign his contract.

"What size do you wear?" Baugh asked, thinking Marshall wanted the clothes and hat for himself.

"They're not for me, son, they're for you!" Marshall exclaimed.

He planned to market Baugh as a gun-slinging Texas cowboy coming to the big city to play football. Never mind that Baugh had grown up in a town, not on a farm, and was too busy playing sports to ride horses or lasso livestock. Marshall wanted him in cowboy garb when he came to the nation's capital. Reporters gathered at the airport for his arrival, and Baugh stepped off the plane wearing a Stetson, checkered shirt, whip-cord pants, and a pair of high-heeled cowboy boots. "My feet hurt," he whispered to Marshall, who met him on the tarmac. Baugh limped to his welcome-to-Washington luncheon at the Occidental Hotel, the *Washington Post*'s Shirley Povich wrote later. But the ploy worked. It would not take long for Baugh to become known as "Slingin' Sammy."

When he reported to training camp, Ray Flaherty put him in a passing drill and encouraged him to hit a receiver "in the eye." "Which eye?" Baugh drawled. He might not have been an authentic cowboy, but he possessed a quality every successful quarterback must have: supreme self-confidence. A new era for Marshall's franchise was underway.

SHORTLY BEFORE THE REDSKINS BEGAN TRAINING CAMP THAT summer, the telephone rang one evening in the suite at Washington's Shoreham Hotel, where Marshall and Corinne Griffith lived. She picked up. Barnee Breeskin, leader of the hotel's orchestra, was on the line. Washington's new team should have a fight song, he said, just like college teams do. In fact, Breeskin said, he had already written one, titled "Hail to the Redskins." When Breeskin played the tune over the phone, Marshall was initially unenthusiastic. But Griffith had the opposite reaction and quickly penned lyrics to go with the music. "Braves on the warpath," she wrote, would "fight for old D.C." Some of the lines required a clichéd Native American dialect: "Scalp 'um, swamp 'um, we will / Take 'um big score. / Read 'um, Weep 'um, touchdown, / We want heap more."

The Redskins had their fight song. Now they needed a band to play it. Marshall heard about a brass ensemble composed of milk deliverymen from the Chestnut Farms Dairy, located just over the Maryland line from the District, and he soon hired them. The band debuted at the team's first home game in Washington, a Thursday night contest against the Giants on September 16. Marshall was excited to see the matchup draw 24,000 fans to Griffith Stadium, and he put on a show. In a pregame ceremony, the players were introduced, and the band played "Hail to the Redskins." Jesse Jones, chairman of a powerful Depression-era government agency, the Reconstruction Finance Corporation, tossed a ceremonial first pass.

A defensive game unfolded. Although Baugh had set passing records at TCU, Riley Smith lined up under center with Baugh and Battles behind him in a double wing formation. The Giants' defense kept them in check. (The Redskins' top pick in the inaugural NFL draft, Smith had actually signed and proved useful on the field.) The score was 3–3 early in the fourth quarter, with a field goal by Smith providing Washington's only points. As the Giants tried to move into scoring range, Smith intercepted a pass and ran 58 yards for a touchdown. A few minutes later, he kicked another field goal. The Redskins won, 13–3, with Smith having scored every Washington point.

The Redskins followed their promising start with a home loss to the Chicago Cardinals, and their attendance soon fell off. Only 7,320 fans witnessed a 14–0 loss to the Philadelphia Eagles at Griffith Stadium on October 10. Marshall fretted. The meager crowd was reminiscent of what he had endured in Boston. So far, he had sold fewer than a thousand season tickets in Washington.

In the latter half of the 1937 season, though, the Redskins surged. Flaherty handed more of the offensive responsibilities to Baugh, who mostly lined up at halfback, alongside Cliff Battles and behind Smith, the quarterback. All three attempted passes in Flaherty's progressive scheme, but Baugh threw the most, befuddling defenses with sharp tosses that sliced through the autumn air to open receivers. The Redskins won three straight games, lost one, and won two more as the fans returned. Leading up to a home game against the Packers, the reigning NFL champions, on November 28, tickets sold so briskly that Marshall anticipated a capacity crowd. "Mark me, there will be a new record for football crowds in Washington," he told the *Post*'s Povich, who wrote that Marshall "envisions the Green Bay crowd as the last convincing argument to fling into the teeth of the doubters who said pro football would not take root here. He would like to send a set of record figures back to Boston where fans avoided his ball team as if the Redskins were lepers with the black plague running interference."

When the gates to Griffith Stadium opened on the morning of the Green Bay game, hundreds of fans rushed inside and quickly filled the general admissions sections. The streets around the stadium were clotted with traffic, keeping thousands from their seats when John Garner, Roosevelt's vice president, tossed a ceremonial first pass just before kickoff. But soon enough, as Marshall had promised, a record crowd of 30,000 filled the stadium.

The game was a low-scoring affair. The Packers led at halftime, 6–0, but the Redskins took the lead on a run by Battles in the third quarter and sealed the victory when Baugh threw a touchdown pass. With the win, the Redskins improved their record to seven wins and three defeats. If they won their regular-season finale the following Sunday, they would capture the East division and play in the league championship game for the second straight year.

But their final regular-season game was a tough assignment: a re-match with the Giants at the Polo Grounds. With a 6-2-2 record, the Giants also would capture the East if they won the game. The contest was effectively a championship semifinal. Bookmakers favored the home team; a mixture of rain and snow was predicted, and the Giants' powerful squad was better suited to playing on a bad field. Ignoring the prognosticators, Marshall told reporters his team would "sweep the Giants aside like rubbish." Washington fans fed off his enthu-siasm, immediately snapping up 350 tickets at the Redskins' offices. Another thousand tickets were ordered and quickly sold. The Penn-sylvania Railroad scheduled special trains to run between Washing-ton and New York on the Sunday of the game, arriving before kickoff and returning that evening. In the end, 8,000 Redskins fans traveled to New York by car, bus, plane, and train.

"The invading Washington rooters were much in evidence on the Eighth Avenue subway from Penn Station to the Polo Grounds. It wasn't difficult to distinguish them," *New York Times* columnist John Kieran wrote. "They wore feathers in their caps and whooped. One hung up a big pasteboard sign in a subway car. It read: 'Redskins Special.'"

In a surprise that delighted the fans, the members of Marshall's band mustered on Seventh Avenue outside Penn Station. Marshall not only had brought them to New York, but he had outfitted them in "new costumes of burgundy and gold, with white feather head-dresses, imported straight from Hollywood. The leader and two drum majors wore chief's war bonnets with streamers of white feathers that fell all the way to the ground." As the band marched up Seventh Avenue toward Columbus Circle playing "Hail to the Redskins," hundreds of fans fell in behind it, roaring the lyrics. "They were simply full of loyalty and red feathers and other things," Corinne Griffith would write later, recalling the scene. Marshall, sporting a new raccoon coat, strode confidently in front of the band. "George Preston Marshall slipped unobtrusively into town today at the head of a 150-piece band and 10,000 fans," *New York Journal-American* columnist Bill Corum wrote.

The traveling Washington supporters filled several sections of the Polo Grounds' seating bowl, but New York fans still dominated the crowd of 58,285, the second largest ever to watch a pro football game, behind only the massive gathering of curiosity seekers who had turned out to watch Red Grange in New York in 1925.

Once the game began, it became apparent that the Giants' defense was not prepared to check the Redskins' attack. With Battles rushing for large gains and Baugh hitting open receivers, the Redskins mounted a drive that produced a touchdown. Then Battles broke free for a 75-yard run down the sideline, setting up another score. In the second quarter, Baugh completed four passes on yet another scoring drive. With their team holding a 21–0 lead at halftime, the visiting Washington fans were almost delirious. Hundred stormed onto the field and "paraded in a wild demonstration," marching behind Marshall's band as it gave a halftime concert on the field.

But the Giants returned to the field with renewed purpose. They scored a touchdown on a 62-yard interception return, and, a few minutes later, their offense drove steadily until quarterback Ed Danowski hit Tuffy Leemans on a short pass for a touchdown. Washington's lead was reduced to seven, and the stadium "was in a frenzy," the *New York Times* reported. "Complete strangers slapped one another on the back. The Giant benchwarmers came perilously close to rushing on the field and parading their mates around the gridiron on their shoulders. Pandemonium hit the Polo Grounds with a lusty hand." But the Redskins "hauled out their tomahawks and went to work again," according to the *Times*. Baugh completed four straight passes, the last to a wide-open Ed Justice for a touchdown. The rally had been blunted, and the Redskins overwhelmed the Giants in the fourth quarter. Danowski dropped back to punt near his goal line, but "the gargantuan form" of the Redskins' 258-pound Turk Edwards was "on him in a flash." Edwards blocked the punt, and a teammate fell on the loose ball in the end zone.

New York fans remained in their seats, mesmerized by the Redskins' performance. "There is not a superlative in the English language that can quite describe the magnificence of the Washingtonians," Arthur Daley would gush in the *New York Times*. "There was no Cliff Battles or Slingin' Sammy Baugh in the New York lineup. The way Battles carried the ball had to be seen to be believed." Shortly after the blocked punt and resulting touchdown, Battles intercepted Danowski at the Redskins' 24 yard line and headed in the other direction, weaving between lunging Giants trying to bring him down. Exhausted after 75 yards, he was tackled one yard short of the goal line. Riley Smith bulled into the end zone on the next play, and the Redskins later added yet another touchdown. The final score was stunning: 49–14. The Giants had only allowed 60 points all season before this game.

When the last whistle blew, the 8,000 Washington fans "joyously stampeded onto the field," the *Washington Post* reported. "Then, fighting off police who attempted to defend the goal posts, the wildly cheering contingent seized the uprights, rent them in splinters and bore the remains on the field in a triumphant procession. Long into the darkness the wild celebration continued until the Capital fans were forced to scurry downtown to board special trains back to Washington."

Marshall was euphoric. Not only had his players backed up his pledge to "sweep the Giants aside like rubbish," they had scored more points in a game against the Giants than any opponent in New York's franchise history. When the Redskins returned to Washington, 5,000 fans greeted their train at Union Station. The city had fallen in love. The Redskins' season ticket total would soar from 958 in 1937 to 10,951 in 1940 and 31,444 by 1947. To this day, the team's fan base remains one of football's largest and most loyal.

In the 1930s, the league championship-game site alternated every year between the homes of the East and West division winners. Having "hosted" the game in New York the year before, the Redskins now traveled to Chicago to face the Bears for the 1937 title at Wrigley Field. Unable to stop himself, Marshall again pledged a victory, and, again, his players backed him up. The Redskins won, 28–21, with Baugh tossing touchdown passes of 55, 78, and 35 yards.

The bizarre "indoor" title game between the Bears and Portsmouth Spartans had been played in the same city just five years earlier, but already it seemed like an event out of football's distant past. There had been just one touchdown in that game, which was dominated by the defenses. But the league had instituted important rule changes since then, hoping to open up the pro game, and the changes had worked. In 1937, the Redskins and Bears combined for seven touchdowns and more than 800 yards of offense in the championship game. Football's future had arrived, ushering Marshall to the pinnacle of the pro game—right where he had always thought he belonged.

PART THREE

12

BROTHERHOOD OF RIVALS

IN THE SECOND QUARTER OF THE 1937 CHAMPIONSHIP GAME
between the Bears and Redskins at Wrigley Field, Sammy Baugh
absorbed a brutal hit and limped to the sideline with a hip injury. He
missed more than a quarter but returned in the second half. In the
final minutes, Baugh, playing defense, tackled a Chicago halfback,
Dick Plasman, near midfield. Plasman, one of the last NFL players
still performing without a helmet, believed Baugh was playing too
rough and punched him as they tumbled out of bounds. A fight between the teams broke out, and George Preston Marshall leapt from
his field box to join it, eventually finding himself jaw-to-jaw with
George Halas. They exchanged obscenities and insults and nearly
came to blows.

When tempers finally cooled, Marshall returned to his box. His
wife was livid. "That man Halas is positively revolting!" Corinne Griffith sputtered.

Marshall roared back at her, actually shaking a finger under her
nose. "Don't you dare say anything against Halas! He's my best friend!"

For Griffith, who was still relatively new to football, it was a star-
tling introduction to the curious brotherhood of men who governed

the NFL. Even though they fought at league meetings, and even occasionally on the field, all was quickly forgotten amid their efforts to see their sport survive and prosper. "They were the most unique set of men in American sports history. They argued and fought like crazy, but the air was always cleared the next day," Bert Bell's son, Upton, said. "Through it all, they developed respect for each other and became the closest of friends."

Halas and Marshall had known each other since the 1920s, when they owned teams in the same pro basketball league. Each was headstrong, intensely competitive, and wanted desperately to beat the other. At league meetings, neither took a bathroom break out of fear that the other might take advantage of his absence and pass a rule favoring his own team. But they also were "drawn together" in what amounted to "love at first sight," Corinne Griffith later wrote. Within days of their near-fight at the 1937 championship game, Halas and Marshall were on the phone, exchanging jokes while they arranged postseason exhibition games between their teams in Dallas and Miami.

Texas and Florida were populated by zealous college football fans who had never seen a pro game. Marshall wanted to convince them not only that pro football was a quality product but also that they should support the Washington Redskins. Halas had a more immediate reason for wanting to schedule extra games. He needed the money. Just a few years removed from giving his players IOUs instead of their salaries, Halas, unlike Marshall, was not a wealthy man. The Bears always walked a thin financial tightrope. The proceeds from exhibition games might keep Halas from having to take out a loan.

The Redskins and Bears split the two reenactments of the championship game, with the game in Miami disintegrating into a brawl that led to eight player ejections. When the other NFL owners read about the games in the newspapers, they were dismayed. The Redskins and Bears were making money. It could create a competitive advantage for what were already two of the league's best teams. When the owners convened at the Ritz-Carlton Hotel in Philadelphia for a league meeting in late February, they quickly passed a resolution banning offseason games for every team except the champion, which could only play one—a late-summer contest against a team of college all-stars, which had already become a popular annual event.

As always, much of the meeting was given over to finalizing the schedule for the upcoming season—an exhausting debate. Every owner had issues, either stadium conflicts or the desire to play certain opponents on certain dates. Satisfying everyone's agenda was impossible. The owners had put a scheduling protocol in place after they split the league into two divisions in 1933. Every season, a team played two games against each of its four in-division opponents (one in each city) and faced two opponents from the opposite division on a rotating basis. Another opponent from the opposite division was selected out of a hat, completing an eleven-game schedule for each team. Scheduling had been haphazard since the league's earliest years, but, finally, it made a modicum of sense. Still, even in 1938, the situation was flexible. If both owners wanted to change the date and location of a game, they could, with permission from the league office. They could still even swap one opponent for another if all three teams agreed.

Year after year, the schedule generated more ill feelings among the owners than all other matters combined, with the debates inevitably becoming heated and personal. Halas, Marshall, Rooney, Bell, and Mara had different goals. As the owners of losing teams, Bell and Rooney cared more about their bottom lines than their win-loss records and did not mind giving up home dates; they needed to play before larger crowds on the road just to stay afloat. Halas and Marshall, as the owners of winning teams, were always looking to add home games they could win, even if it meant playing a lesser team and selling fewer tickets.

Year after year, no one made out better than Mara. Every other team was always happy to come to New York because the visitors' take of the Giants' gate was the largest in the league. The Giants wound up playing more home games, which helped them continue to dominate on the field. Between 1936 and 1941, they faced the Bears and Packers eight times during the regular season, and all eight games were at the Polo Grounds; a game in Green Bay, especially, would not produce nearly as much revenue for the teams to split.

No matter where they were situated in the league hierarchy, though, the influential owners knew it was important to attend meetings and fight doggedly for their teams' best interests. "The owners with the staying power were the ones who came away with the decent schedules," Rooney said. "The guys who snuck out to get some sleep or go night-clubbing wound up getting murdered the next season because when they weren't there to defend themselves, we'd give them all the dates we didn't want."

On the first day of the Philadelphia meeting in February 1938, a tentative schedule for the upcoming season was put on a chalkboard. So many issues ensued that the session did not adjourn until two in the morning. As usual, Marshall's voice was the loudest in the room. He was not pleased that the Redskins were scheduled to return to Chicago to play the Bears. Washington had just played the championship game in Chicago, and, though Marshall had won, he did not want to go back that fall. He was still trying to sell pro football to a new city, and he believed a home game against the Bears, a championship rematch, would help immensely. Marshall and Halas had argued about it during their teams' postseason exhibition tour, and Marshall brought up the issue at the league meeting. "It is absolutely vital to us, as far as the press and public are concerned, that the Chicago Bears play a game in Washington this year," Marshall thundered. "We have played the Bears in the (title) game in Chicago. We have played them in several exhibition games. We have been, naturally, as we should be, as good members of the league, very reasonable with Mr. Halas, and we expect him to be so with us."

The other owners suggested Marshall was putting his own interests first and did not deserve an extra home game. He explained that this was not about him getting an extra home game; he believed a rematch of championship-game opponents from the prior season should always take place in the city that did not host the title game. The fans in that city deserved to see the top teams play.

One of Halas's favorite tactics was to say little at certain times, and he did that now, believing the other owners would not side with Marshall, who continued to speak. "I don't think there is a member here who would think it unreasonable if I offered that idea as a resolution," Marshall said. "I don't think my request is unreasonable. But I am perfectly willing to abide by the judgment of the league and put it to a vote."

Tim Mara could stay silent no longer. "I don't think that is a legal form of procedure," the Giants' owner said. He had never cared for Marshall, even before their teams became rivals for East division supremacy. Marshall's loud officiousness set off Mara's temper. Art Rooney would later recall watching the two "get redder and redder as they yelled each other at league meetings. Maybe it was the schedule, or a change in the rules. It didn't make any difference. They just liked to fight." Now, after listening to Marshall propose a vote on switching the site of his game with Halas, Mara snapped. "There is no use putting to a vote something that is not right," he said, staring at Marshall. Taken aback, Marshall appeared to relent. "I didn't say I think there should be a vote on it. I did not mean to put it in that form, Mr. Mara," he said. "But I think it ought to be a question of whether it is acceptable to Mr. Halas."

After being prodded by Carl Storck, the league secretary, who was running the meeting, Halas finally spoke: "I don't see any reason why he should have six games at home and the Chicago Bears only have four. I think the public of Chicago is entitled to an even split. Why should he not have five home games in Washington and we have five home games in Chicago? The fact that he won the pennant does not mean a thing. The pennant has been won before by the Bears, and it was won by New York, and by the Packers and Lions, and they never asked for the best of it."

Storck finally asked for a vote on Marshall's resolution that would make it compulsory to reverse the site of any championship-game

rematch played the next season. Mara, Bell, and three other owners supported Halas, giving him a majority. Rooney and three others
sided with Marshall. "The motion is lost," Storck said.

Hearing that, Bell asked to change his vote. He felt the issue
should be decided in private, between the two owners, not by a vote.
Now the tally was five against and five for. Storck declared a recess so
that Halas and Marshall could settle the dispute, which was holding
up the scheduling process for the whole league. But Halas and Marshall had been arguing over the matter for several months, and there
was no hope of either changing his mind. Halas had the NFL law on
his side, but he liked Marshall and wanted his rival to feel any decision was fair. He offered to flip coin, a magnanimous gesture from a
fierce competitor with the upper hand. Marshall agreed, and a coin
was produced.

Halas won. That fall, the Redskins traveled to Chicago and played
the Bears on November 13 at Wrigley Field. The Bears, in the midst
of a down season, came into the game with a .500 record, while the
Redskins held first place in the East—but the Bears won the game
easily, 31–7.

AFTER THE DECISIVE COIN FLIP AT THE PHILADELPHIA MEET-
ing in February 1938, the owners spent an entire afternoon trying
to finalize a schedule tolerable to each of them. But they failed and
finally just tabled the matter so they could turn to others before the
meeting adjourned.

Their first piece of other business was addressing a letter from
Damon Runyon, the famous writer, who was presenting an offer to
the league from a business group in Miami. The group wanted to
move the NFL championship game to their South Florida city for
the next five years, and it was offering attractive financial terms—a
guaranteed $40,000 payout every year, with a percentage of gate re-
ceipts beyond that also going to the teams. The owners were tempted.
The championship game had never generated that much money, and

it was seldom played in good weather because most of the teams in the league were in the Northeast or Midwest. Wintry conditions had hurt the gate for several of the championship games, including the most recent one in Chicago. Only 15,878 fans had braved frigid temperatures to watch the Redskins and Bears.

Nearly three decades later, pro football's owners would approve the idea of playing their championship game at a warm-weather neutral site. The game would quickly become known as the Super Bowl. But in 1938, the owners still believed the drawbacks outweighed the upside, primarily because each of them could not imagine abandoning his fans for such an important game. "I move that the president be directed to thank Mr. Runyon for his kind offer," Mara said, "and advise him that it would be impossible for the teams in this league to play the championship game in Miami for the reason that it would be unfair to the fans who support our games during the season."

Rooney second the motion, and it passed unanimously. The meeting soon turned to weightier matters. Halas stood, and the room fell silent. He said Runyon's offer indicated that their championship game was growing in stature. Obviously, the league had taken a step in the right direction when it established the two-division setup and post-season title game. Those changes had instilled order where chaos once ruled. But although its seasons were better organized now, the NFL still had problems, Halas said. One of the biggest, in his opinion, was the continuing disparity between the "have" and "have not" franchises. Bert Bell's draft should eventually level the playing field, he said, but at this point, the predraft status quo endured. The same teams won year after year—Packers and Bears in the West, Giants and Redskins in the East. With their superiority assured, it was no surprise, Halas claimed, that some teams had strong attendance while others could not get anyone to come to their games.

The Giants were in a class by themselves, having drawn an average of 35,717 fans to their home games over the course of the 1937 season. Their total season attendance of 250,025 represented more than a quarter of the entire league's attendance for the season, more than double any other team's total. Halas did not need to point out how auspicious these facts were. If the Giants did not yet match the stature of baseball's Yankees and Giants in New York, they were gaining ground.

After the Giants, there was a tier of teams that were at least not failing at the gate. The Bears had averaged 22,752 fans per game in 1937, while the Redskins averaged 18,837 and the Lions averaged 18,830. Those were decent if unspectacular figures. Aside from those teams, though, the news was depressing. None of the other six teams was faring well. After eight years in Brooklyn, the Dodgers still played in the Giants' shadows, drawing less than half as many fans. Pittsburgh's Pirates had averaged 13,089 fans per game in 1937, not enough to make a profit. The Packers, though winners on the field, averaged just 12,888 fans per game, almost solely because of their stadium's limited capacity. The league's newest team, the Cleveland Rams, had flopped in 1937, averaging just 11,160 fans per game, but they still outdrew the Chicago Cardinals and Philadelphia Eagles. One of the league's oldest teams, the Cardinals had drawn just 25,812 fans all season. Bert Bell's Eagles had attracted just 23,698.

The absence of parity was a problem, Halas said, but an even more pressing one, he believed, was the way the game itself was played. Although loosening the rules to promote more passing and scoring had made pro football more entertaining, NFL games were still dogged by issues that could serve only to repel fans. Many games seemed to drag, lasting more than two and a half hours, with long lags between snaps. The pace was too slow. The officiating also needed to be addressed, Halas said. The owners strived to pick competent officials and educate them about the rules, but almost every game was marked by disputes and controversies. That was bad for the league. Fans needed to have faith that the officiating was unbiased and competent.

Several other owners surely smirked at his last suggestion. Throughout the league, it was widely believed that the Bears received favorable treatment because of Halas's relationship with Joe Carr. Officials who either lived in Chicago or were intimidated by the famously imperious Halas always seemed to work the Bears' games. Exhibit A was the jump-pass touchdown that decided the indoor championship game in 1932. It almost surely was illegal, but the officials had let it stand. The next year, Carr even allowed Halas's own brother, Walter, to officiate a Bears game.

More evidence of Halas's sway had come at a 1934 league meeting. Some owners had proposed making a dropped lateral a live ball, a change Halas feared would inhibit his T-formation offense, which relied on laterals. "You gentlemen will destroy me and the modern T-formation," he cried. Wellington Mara would recall that Halas "was bitterly opposed" and "gave one of his most passionate speeches. He really cried. Real tears." The owners voted in Halas's favor. They could not bear to cross him.

Wellington Mara also remembered a minor incident at Wrigley Field that, he believed, spoke volumes: "An official went to retrieve a punt that had gone out of bounds. He dropped his cap to mark the spot. George took his foot and moved it a foot or so in favor of the Bears. The distance meant nothing, but the action was typical. Halas just couldn't resist getting every possible advantage for the Bears."

As he spoke at the 1938 league meeting in Philadelphia, though, Halas seemed to truly have in mind the league's best interests, not those of the Bears. The men in the room were his partners in the pro football business. Their game, their product, needed help. And Halas believed he knew who could provide that help: Hugh "Shorty" Ray, an official and rules aficionado from Chicago.

Halas and Ray had both attended Chicago's Crane Tech High School and the University of Illinois. Like Halas, Ray had played football for the Illini, even though he stood just five feet six. After studying mechanical engineering in college, Ray took a job as a mechanical drawing instructor at a Chicago high school. He also became a high school football official and found his calling. In 1917, he started an association that oversaw the training and licensing of high school officials throughout Illinois. When college football became popular in the 1920s, he officiated Big Ten games.

Halas respected Ray. He was aware that Illinois *high school* football possibly had better officiating than the NFL. At the 1938 league meeting in Philadelphia, Halas suggested to the owners that they bring in Ray as a consultant. The officiating was bound to improve, Halas said. The other owners agreed to the proposal. Although Halas exasperated them at times, they bowed to his knowledge and ideas about football; aside from Bell, he had the most storied career as a player and coach.

Ray did not seem like a man who would significantly change pro football. He was fifty-four years old, short, and nebbish, wore horn-rimmed glasses, and spoke in a high-pitched monotone. But he would leave a lasting mark on the NFL. Within two years, he had organized four-man teams of "followers," as he called them, who traveled to every game with stopwatches in hand, studying penalties, timeouts, and other fine-point mechanics of the game. After reviewing the data his teams produced, Ray proposed changes both big and small. He noticed that seconds were wasted almost every time the ball went out of bounds and prompted the owners to add sideline crews tasked with retrieving the ball quickly and getting it to the officials. Ray also discovered that many controversies resulted from the officials not clearly signaling their rulings. A set of hand gestures was already in place, but Ray encouraged the officials to gesture with greater clarity and enthusiasm.

In the coming years, Ray would become a fixture around the league and a major influence. He changed the shape of the pro ball, streamlining the more rugby-ball-like original. He helped make the officiating more professional. Every summer, Ray would give his officials a written test, demanding that they correctly answer 95 percent of his rules questions. "He pounded the rules into his officials," said Mark Duncan, the NFL's supervisor of officials, in a 1966 interview. Ray also transformed the game itself. With less time wasted, a given game had more plays, more action. The pace improved, and scoring rose, in part because of new strategies implemented by forward-thinking coaches, but also because teams simply had more time with the ball.

Every year, Ray traveled to training camps and presented the latest rule changes to the players and coaches. Some snickered while he spoke; he had none of the bravado of most men in football. Some coaches believed he had made the game too complicated. But, as Halas would later put it, hiring Ray was "my great contribution to the National Football League. Every team in the league has benefitted from his efforts." Indeed, although Halas, Marshall, and the other large personalities deserve the most credit for putting the league on firm footing, unsung figures such as Ray and Joe Carr also helped make the game what it is today.

13

A STEP FORWARD

A FTER THE GIANTS' LOPSIDED LOSS TO THE REDSKINS ON
the last Sunday of the 1937 season, Tim Mara did not want to
attend the league meeting in Chicago a few days later, knowing he
would encounter George Preston Marshall. But he knew he needed
to be present at the Sherman Hotel for the gathering, scheduled for a
day before the championship game between the Bears and Redskins.
The league's annual college draft was on the docket.

Mara traveled to Chicago with his sons, Jack and Wellington.
Now a twenty-one-year-old Fordham University graduate, Wellington Mara had talked his father into allowing him to skip law school
to work for the Giants. Given the title of secretary, he was in charge
of everything from arranging travel to purchasing equipment to negotiating player contracts. He also handled the team's scouting efforts,
and it was in this role, as a talent evaluator, that he truly distinguished
himself. The league's other football men relied mostly on newspaper
articles to learn more about notable college talent, but Wellington
spent his fall Saturdays in the stands at college games. Then he contacted administrators, coaches, and even professors to get the inside

scoop on his favorite prospects. He had maintained files on players since his middle school days.

In 1935, while at Fordham, Wellington took a train to Washington one Saturday to watch George Washington play Alabama. He was there to see Tuffy Leemans, a fullback for George Washington. They arranged to meet in front of the school's gym after the game, with Wellington having signed his father's name to the telegram to increase the chances that Leemans would show up.

"When I got there, he thought I was a kid who wanted his autograph. He looked at me strangely suspicious," Wellington recalled later. Leemans protested that he was supposed to meet with Tim Mara, "but I was able to convince him that I was in fact a legitimate emissary, and he did listen to me," Wellington remembered. The Giants eventually selected Leemans as a second-round pick in the 1936 draft, and he became an immediate contributor, leading the league in rushing as a rookie before settling in as a vital offensive "triple threat" who piled up yards rushing, passing, and receiving.

Two years after Wellington's first meeting with Leemans, when he was on his way to Chicago for the draft in December 1937, Wellington shared with his father the extensive files he had amassed on that year's prospects. None of the other teams had nearly as much information. In the parlance of the racetrack, which the elder Mara understood, the Giants were lengths ahead of their rivals coming down the stretch. Nonetheless, Mara insisted that his son share his research with the others. When the owners and coaches met to select players at the Sherman Hotel, Wellington unveiled his list of the top 166 prospects on a chalkboard. To his father, Wellington protested that teams that failed to pay attention to the college game did not deserve the help, but Tim Mara was adamant, heeding an ethos that Joe Carr had preached and that Halas also subscribed to and embodied: They might be enemies on the field, but the owners were partners in a business. They needed to strive for the betterment of the group, even if those on top suffered in the process. As they had understood during the debates over scheduling, a few successful teams would not make for a successful league. They all needed to do well. "The thinking was, 'If you don't all stand together, you're going to die,'" said Upton Bell, Bert's son.

"It was a pretty remarkable thing, when you think about it," said Virginia McCaskey, Halas's daughter. "They were all very strong-minded, strong-willed individuals, but they understood they had to give up personal considerations if they were going to make it. The draft, no league had ever done that. I remember hearing my mother questioning my father on some things, 'Why are you doing that when it might hurt the Bears?' His response was what happens on the field was different from the business of the league."

The draft began at the Sherman Hotel shortly after noon when Carl Storck, the league's secretary-treasurer, called the meeting to order. Originally instituted to promote competitive balance, the draft had been only marginally effective so far. The additions of Baugh and Riley Smith had helped turn the once-lowly Redskins into winners, but the perennially strong teams still dominated, and neither the Eagles nor the Pirates, losing teams both, had signed any of their top picks. Frustrated, Rooney opened the Chicago meeting by proposing that losing teams receive twice as many picks as winning teams, but the motion failed. The powerful owners were not willing to go that far.

With the fourth pick in the first round, the Pirates selected Byron "Whizzer" White, a speedy halfback from Colorado regarded as the most naturally gifted player in the draft. But he also was a top student and was competing for a Rhodes Scholarship, which would take him to Oxford University in England. The teams drafting ahead of the Pirates had avoided White for that reason, but Rooney, always a gambler, picked him anyway. His bet paid off when Oxford allowed White to postpone his studies for a semester, enabling him to play for the Pirates in 1938. White's $15,000 contract immediately made him the league's highest-paid player, and, when he signed it, the ceremony was covered in a live national radio broadcast, a rarity for the Pirates.

White proved he was worth the investment in the short term, leading the NFL in rushing as a rookie. But the Pirates still finished last in the East, winning just two games. Shortly after the season, White left for England to begin his studies at Oxford and never again played for Pittsburgh. When he changed his academic track a year later and returned to the United States to attend Yale Law School, he played for the Detroit Lions for two seasons, leading the league in rushing once more, before joining the navy in 1942.

The Chicago draft did help several teams in more substantial ways. The Lions selected Alex Wojciechowicz, a sturdy two-way lineman who would become an All-Pro and later gain induction to the Hall of Fame. The Packers found a new tailback, Purdue's Cecil Isbell, who would become a league-leading passer and part of a championship squad. The Dodgers added Frank "Bruiser" Kinard, a tackle from Ole Miss who would earn all-league honors in six of his nine pro seasons.

In all, the teams combined to pick 110 players, and when the process ended late that afternoon, the owners joined in applause in the room for Wellington Mara, who had helped guide their selections. But, ironically enough, the Giants did not fare well in the draft. Their high picks, Gonzaga back George Karamatic and Northwestern back Fred Vanzo, failed to contribute to the team. Quietly stewing over those failures, the young Mara continued to amass information on college players during the 1938 season and again filled a chalkboard with prospects' names at the next draft meeting, held in New York on December 9, 1938. But when it was the Giants' turn to pick in the first round, they drafted a player who was not listed on the board. Asked about the omission, Wellington shrugged. "I didn't think I had to put every name on that list," he said. The all-for-one philosophy had its limits.

NO ONE WAS GETTING RICH OFF PRO FOOTBALL IN THE LATE 1930s. Many owners continued to rely on other businesses to offset the losses from their teams. "They would gather for league meetings, get their business done, and get back home to their other work," Virginia McCaskey said. Marshall still ran a laundry chain. Rooney still promoted boxing matches and gambled. Halas was still a partner in a commercial laundry. Tim Mara was invested in coal and liquor, but his bookmaking operation required more of his time than anything else. He had been a fixture at New York's racetracks for nearly two decades, fearful of delegating his business to underlings even for a day. With horse racing making front-page news almost year-round, the public still knew him as a bookie more than as the Giants' owner.

By the late 1930s, Mara believed the Giants' present and future were stable enough for him to step back from their daily operations. Jack and Wellington Mara ran the team adeptly, in his view. The Giants were championship contenders, and their attendance was the envy of the rest of the NFL. When the 1938 season began, Mara was especially optimistic. The Giants appeared to have another winning team—and they had vanquished a New York team from a rival league.

The American Football League had kicked off in 1936, in the hope and belief that the public's appetite for pro football could support two leagues at once. It amounted to a personal attack on Mara. Doc March, his cofounder and longtime assistant with the Giants, had dreamed up the idea of the AFL and brought it to life. March had soured on the NFL after Mara turned the Giants' future over to Jack and Wellington, and then, after he joined the league office, he clashed with Marshall, leading to his ouster. Seeking revenge, he gained the backing of Wall Street investors, solicited franchise bids from fifteen cities, and announced a new league with eight teams would kick off in 1936.

The AFL's New York franchise, the Yankees, immediately declared war on the Giants. They hired a former Giant player as their head coach and signed three players from the existing roster, including Ken Strong, a back who had been the team's leading scorer. The Yankees were offering more money. Harry Newman, the Giants' quarterback, also departed for the AFL, signing with a Brooklyn franchise.

But the challenges that starting a new league entailed were more daunting than March and his backers imagined. It turned out American sports fans did not want more pro football. Franchises in the AFL began folding before the season began. In the end, six took the field in 1936. Two moved to different cities within weeks. Playing at Yankee Stadium, the Yankees averaged around 14,000 fans per game, easily the best in the league. With a 5-3-2 record, they finished third in the standings behind the Boston Shamrocks and Cleveland Rams. March left the league after the season in the wake of contentious arguments with several owners. The NFL quickly annexed the Rams, choosing Cleveland as its tenth franchise, over Buffalo and Los Angeles. The AFL picked up the Los Angeles team and hung on for another season, but key players defected from the Yankees, whose attendance dropped precipitously, and the league itself folded after the 1937 season.

The threat gone, Mara was pleased that the Giants had Manhattan to themselves again. After losing two of their first three games in 1938, they faced the Redskins for the first time since Washington's epic rout the previous December. The matchup drew a sellout crowd of 37,500 to Griffith Stadium in Washington, and the Giants won, 10–7, on a late touchdown pass. Both teams continued to dominate the East division through the fall, and, for the second year in a row, they concluded the regular season by playing at the Polo Grounds in early December, with the division title at stake.

For the practices leading up to the game, the Giants' coach, Steve Owen, wrote a simple message on the locker room chalkboard: "49–14." Owen wanted the players to remember how badly the Redskins had beaten them in New York the year before. He did not have to worry.

On Sunday morning, eleven special trains from Washington arrived at Penn Station bearing Redskins fans and the hundred-piece Redskins Band. Marshall had given the band an official title. The league's other owners were incredulous that he had spent thousands of dollars on uniforms for a *band*. But it was Marshall's favorite toy.

Repeating the scene from the year before, the owner and his band mustered outside Penn Station and marched through the streets of Manhattan toward the Polo Grounds, with hundreds of fans trailing them and shouting the words to "Hail to the Redskins." Marshall's intent, clear enough, was to show himself and his team to be conquerors.

From the outset, though, it was clear this game would be markedly different. The Redskins' first possession was halted when the Giants' Ward Cuff intercepted Baugh and returned the ball 32 yards to the Washington 42. On the next play, Giants fullback Hank Soar dashed through a gaping hole and sprinted to the end zone for a touchdown. A few minutes later, the Giants recovered a Redskins fumble and drove to another touchdown.

The Redskins were not the same team as the year before. Cliff Battles, their magnificent back, had retired before the season and taken a job as a college coach when Marshall refused to give him a raise. (He had made half as much as Baugh in 1937.) They also were without Riley Smith, their quarterback, who had suffered a major knee injury halfway through the season. Focusing on Baugh, Giant defenders intercepted an incredible six passes, denying the Redskins any chance to build momentum. The Giants increased the lead to 17–0 in the second quarter and did not hold back in the second half. With the score 36–0 in the waning minutes, Marshall's bandsmen marched out of the Polo Grounds. "The band had seen enough," the *New York Times'* John Kieran reported.

Eddie Reeves, a vice president in the Redskins' front office, congratulated Wellington Mara after the game. "A great game," Reeves said, "but what you need is a band like we have." The young Mara smiled and said, "Eddie, we don't need a band. We have a football team."

THE NFL HAD INSTITUTED A POSTSEASON CHAMPIONSHIP GAME aiming to establish a major event on the American sports calendar, on par with the World Series. After five years, though, the comparison was still impossible to justify. The first five title games had drawn a

The Giants stop the Packers' Clarke Hinkle just short of the goal line in the 1938 championship game. (Associated Press)

disappointing average crowd of just 24,295. Moreover, the failure of the AFL in 1937 served as a reminder to the NFL owners that the continued existence of a pro football league was not assured.

But the championship game between the Giants and Green Bay Packers at the Polo Grounds on December 11, 1938, indicated that the faith the owners had placed in the sport and clung to for years was not misguided. The game drew 48,320, easily the largest crowd in the event's brief history. The fans witnessed a mesmerizing exhibition of the drama, skill, and violence that pro football alone could offer. The college game had remained more popular until now largely because it was viewed as an endeavor that helped turn boys into men—a process that transcended sports. But pro football's fan base would increase exponentially over the next quarter century, and it would eventually become the more popular version of the sport, in part because of its sheer brutality. Pro players were older, more physically developed, and thus their collisions were more breathtaking than those in college football. Long fascinated with violence in all forms, Americans lusted to see bodies crunching, and as pro football developed, they found it hard to turn their heads away.

The 1938 championship game between the Giants and Packers hinted at what lay ahead. It was an "absolutely ferocious" event, according to the *New York Times'* Arthur Daley. Early on, the Giants blocked two punts and took a 9–0 lead. But Green Bay's Arnie Herber tossed a long touchdown pass to start a rally that culminated with the Packers going ahead, 17–16, in the third quarter. "No such blocking and tackling by two football teams had ever been seen at the Polo Grounds," Daley wrote. "Tempers were so frayed and tattered that stray punches were tossed all afternoon."

The Giants took an uncommonly brutal beating. One player went to the hospital with a spinal contusion. Another suffered a fractured sternum. Mel Hein, New York's All-Pro lineman, suffered "a contusion of the brain that left him temporarily bereft of his memory," but Hein returned to the field after the Giants regained the advantage and led a defensive stand that denied Green Bay on several late drives. There was no thought given to the possible detrimental effect of his playing with what obviously was a concussion; a connection between football and serious brain trauma would not be made for decades. After the final gun sounded with the Giants ahead, 23–17, Daley intimated in the nation's foremost newspaper that the game had been compelling not in spite of its violence but because of it. "This was the gridiron sport at its primitive best," he wrote, adding that the display had gone so far as to legitimize the NFL: "Professional football, once a shabby outcast among sports, has become a dignified and honored member of the American athletic family."

On the field, the Giants' players lifted their coach, the 265-pound Owen, onto their shoulders in celebration. In the stands, Tim Mara shook hands with Joe Carr and reflected on how far the Giants had come. They had endured difficult times in the late 1920s and early

1930s, losing so much money at times that Mara could imagine the team failing. More recently, he had weathered the challenge posed by a rival league. There was always something. But while some of the NFL's other teams still struggled financially, the Giants would turn a $200,000 profit in 1938—an inconceivable sum. Mara would have to spend many days in the betting enclosures to make that much. For the first time in the NFL's history, someone was making real money in pro football. That it had happened in New York was perhaps little surprise to the other owners, and Mara deserved the credit, even if his main skill as an owner was knowing precisely when to let the true football minds, including his sons, take over.

14

THE GREATEST ROUT

VIRGINIA McCASKEY WAS AROUND TWELVE YEARS OLD ON the day in the mid-1930s when George Halas took her, her brother, and her mother to Riverview, a sprawling amusement park on Chicago's North Side. They were out with Arch Ward, sports editor of the *Chicago Tribune,* and his family. "I was about the same age as their daughter, Ruth, and [my older brother] Mugs was about the same age as their son, Tom," Virginia recalled. "Our parents were friends and we lived in the same parish, a few blocks from each other. We did a lot of things together."

Spread over acres and acres of land and featuring massive wooden roller coasters as well as other rides that whirled and dropped, Riverview drew large crowds. But no one bothered the Chicago Bears' owner and coach as he walked the grounds with his family while talking with Ward and munching on one of the park's signature foot-long hot dogs. "No one asked for his autograph or bothered him. No one knew who he was," Virginia recalled. "It would have been a nice problem, having people recognize him and interrupt our day, but the Bears were not a big deal. We were just another family at the park."

Today, pro football's prominent figures are celebrities, as familiar to the public as entertainers and politicians. The head coach of a successful team would need a security detail to enjoy a day at an amusement park. In the 1930s, though, pro football's coaches and players did not enjoy any measure of renown. Boxers, college football stars, and major league baseball figures could cause a commotion when out in public, but not a pro football coach—not even a good one.

In Chicago, baseball's Cubs riveted sports fans. They had led the National League in attendance for six straight years beginning in 1927, selling more than a million tickets in each of the first five seasons. Babe Ruth's Yankees were the only other major league club that drew comparable crowds, and the Cubs even outdrew them in 1928, 1929, and 1930. The Cubs' popularity was partly attributable to the tradition of excellence they established while winning five National League pennants and one World Series between 1906 and 1918. But their crowds had remained relatively modest until their forward-thinking owner, William Wrigley, began broadcasting the team's home games on the radio beginning in 1923.

Radio's popularity soared in the 1920s. The number of radios in use in America rose from 60,000 in 1922 to 3 million in 1924 to 16.6 million by 1932. The number of radio stations also rapidly grew, from 382 in 1922 to 681 in 1927. Those stations needed programming, and Wrigley had what they wanted—hours of baseball, day after day.

The other major league owners were terrified of live game broadcasts, fearing the practice would destroy attendance, their primary source of revenue. Why would fans buy a ticket when they could stay home and follow a game for free? Eleven of the sixteen major league owners were skeptical enough to consider banning all radio game broadcasts in 1931. That never happened, but in 1934 the Yankees, Giants, and Dodgers did agree on a five-year radio ban in the New York market.

William Wrigley saw the new medium differently, as a promotional opportunity, not a threat. In 1925, he allowed WMAQ, a major Chicago station, to broadcast the Cubs' home games, hoping that fans who listened to games might be encouraged to come to the ballpark and buy tickets. Stations and networks eventually would pay for broadcast rights, but in 1925, before radio's power became evident, Wrigley gave his games to WMAQ for free. It was not an exclusive deal, either; by the end of the decade, most major Chicago stations would also broadcast the Cubs' home games, creating an overwhelming presence on the AM dial.

Just as Wrigley predicted, the broadcasts prompted his team's attendance to soar, not sink. The Cubs' gate rose 140 percent between 1925 and 1929. In 1927, they became the first major league club other than the Yankees to draw more than 1 million fans in a season. In 1929, they drew almost 1.5 million, more than any club would draw in a season until after World War II. Radio created loyal fans in Chicago and throughout the Midwest, and many wrote letters to the club thanking it for the broadcasts. One farmer rapturously wrote, "Don't stop it. I have a radio in the field with me. I plow one turn, sit down for a cool drink out of the jug and listen to the game. It's grand."

Halas was still a baseball fan. He had played the game adeptly enough to receive at-bats with the Yankees in 1919 and had followed the Cubs since he was a boy. "He loved them," Virginia said. So did the boys at her coed middle school. "It wasn't a big deal to them that my father was with the Bears. They were all Cubs fans," she said.

Halas did not seriously believe the Bears could become as popular as the Cubs. He believed in pro football's future, but he was a realist. The Bears were among the NFL's best franchises, and they struggled for attention. He did what he could to change that. After witnessing Wrigley's brilliant use of radio, he found a station that would broadcast the Bears' games in the 1920s. But the arrangement did not last, and the Bears were absent from Chicago radio in the years when the Cubs dominated it.

Finally, in 1933, Halas found a radio partner when WGN agreed to broadcast the home games of the Bears and Cardinals, the city's other NFL team. Using his newspaper connections, Halas made sure the broadcasts were promoted. He still believed print was the best way to win new fans to his team. He did not have time to run a newspaper and thereby guarantee the Bears better coverage—a stunt George Preston Marshall had pulled in Washington—but he did become friendly with sports editors, above all the *Chicago Tribune*'s Don Maxwell. "I remember him having dinners with us," Virginia McCaskey said of Maxwell. "Don realized he needed something for his Monday morning sections and that helped the Bears." When Maxwell was elevated to the paper's city editor in 1930, he turned the sports section over to Arch Ward, an Iowa native who had served as Knute Rockne's first publicist at Notre Dame before joining the *Tribune* sports staff in 1925. Having risen through the ranks, he now authored the iconic In the Wake of the News column, a daily compendium of notes and opinions covering sports across the country, with a focus on Chicago and its teams.

But Ward was an impresario more than a journalist, more interested in staging events than writing about them. In 1933 Chicago put on a world's fair celebrating its centennial, and the mayor asked Ward to find a sports event that could be included. Ward convinced major league baseball to hold an exhibition contest between the best players from the American and National leagues. Dubbed "the Game of the Century" by the *Tribune,* it was held on July 6, 1933, at Comiskey Park, home of the White Sox, and drew almost 50,000 fans. Babe Ruth hit a home run, the American League won, and baseball's All-Star Game was born.

The next year, Ward conceived the idea of a late-summer football exhibition pitting the NFL champions from the previous year against a team of college stars who had graduated. Halas and the other NFL owners eagerly went along. Many fans still believed college football was superior to the pros—it certainly remained more popular—and the pros jumped at the chance to dispel what they saw as a myth. The first game drew 79,432 fans to Chicago's Soldier Field on August 31, 1934. The college team had been selected by a fan vote, orchestrated by the *Tribune,* and featured well-known players. They faced off against the Bears, who had won the NFL title the previous December. The game ended in a disappointing scoreless tie.

Like baseball's All-Star Game, football's College All-Star Game quickly became a staple on the national sports calendar. It was much more popular than the NFL's championship game, another relatively new event. In 1935, the Bears, subbing for the NFL champion Giants, defeated the college stars, 5–0, before a crowd of 77,450. In 1936, the Detroit Lions and All-Stars tied, 7–7, before 76,000 fans. The results helped the pros' campaign for respectability. Many fans remained dubious, but more and more top college players were continuing their careers in the NFL, raising the league's caliber of play.

Ward named his event the College All-Star Game, with no reference to the pros, for a simple reason: he wanted to sell tickets. Pro teams still were not especially attractive commodities in the wider sports marketplace. The Bears enjoyed playing before giant crowds in the exhibition game, but they did not draw nearly as well on their own, without being associated with an opponent from the college ranks. Averaging 22,752 fans per game during the 1937 regular season, they were championship contenders, but still afterthoughts in Chicago, at least when compared to the Cubs.

AT A BANQUET IN 1935, CLARK SHAUGHNESSY, THE HEAD coach at the University of Chicago, approached Halas and introduced himself. Halas knew who he was. Shaughnessy, a cerebral Minnesota native, had replaced Amos Alonzo Stagg, the legendary coach who built the University of Chicago into a national power during a forty-year tenure that ended when the school administration believed he had grown too old for the job.

Shaughnessy wanted to talk to Halas about the Bears' T formation. With its pre-snap man in motion, end split wide, and quarterback lined up directly under center, it had helped the Bears win NFL titles in 1932 and 1933 and complete an undefeated regular season in 1934. When Shaughnessy began asking questions, Halas could see he possessed a keen strategic mind. Within two years, Halas was paying Shaughnessy a consultant's fee even though Shaughnessy still coached at the University of Chicago.

Over the years, as the two men discussed how to make the T more effective, the need for Halas and the Bears to do *something* became evident. The balance of power in the NFL's West division shifted after the Packers signed Don Hutson, the speedy receiver who "roamed the ball field, pulling down impossible passes," according to Halas. The Packers won three division titles and two league titles in a four-year span beginning in 1936. The last NFL game of the 1930s was Green Bay's 27–0 victory over the Giants in the 1939 championship game.

The Bears still fielded winning teams in these years. In 1939, they went 8-3 and their offense was one of three in the league that produced an average of more than 300 yards per game. It was clear the pro game was becoming more offensive-minded—before 1939, only one offense in league history had averaged as much as 300 yards per game during a season—and the Bears were at the forefront of the evolution. Still, Halas was tired of losing enough games to finish behind the Packers. The league's better defenses had adjusted to his T, he believed, by widening their alignments, which prevented the Bears' halfbacks from getting around the edges of the line. He decided it was time to introduce a new T, one that he and Shaughnessy had designed over the course of several years of conversations. In the new version, the quarterback assumed a larger role. Before, he was mostly a traffic cop whose job it was to take snaps and pitch to tailbacks, who in turn threw the passes. Now, he would become more of a centerpiece, throwing passes himself while making sure the offense ran smoothly.

Halas scouted the college ranks for a quarterback who could handle the job. He found Sid Luckman, a Columbia University star with a strong passing arm and the intelligence to run an intricate offense. Luckman was expected to be taken by the time the Bears picked in the first round of the 1939 draft, but, in a trade with Rooney's Pirates, Halas obtained the second overall pick and took Luckman. A year later, Halas again moved up in the first round, this time in a trade with

Bell's Eagles, and used the second overall pick to draft George Mc-Afee, a Duke halfback whose 165-pound frame belied his uncanny knack for breaking big gains. Some other owners rolled their eyes at how Halas manipulated the draft process, obtaining the best players even as the Bears continued to win. That went against the spirit of the draft, which had been designed to level the playing field. But Halas did not care. He wanted to win, and he was sure he had put together a powerful team. "When the 1940 season began, I felt we were fit for anything or anybody," he would write.

In their season opener, the Bears routed the Packers, 41–10, in Green Bay—a promising start. The Cardinals upset them the next week, but they rebounded with five straight wins, the last another victory over the Packers. Believing they were nearing a division title, the Bears carried a 6-2 record into a game against the Redskins at Griffith Stadium in Washington on November 17.

The Redskins, who led the East division, were ready with a 5-3-3 defensive alignment that stunted Luckman and the Bears' attack. The Redskins led at halftime, 7–3, and that was still the score when Luckman drove his offense deep into Washington territory in the final minute. After McAfee ran the ball to the 1 yard line, he faked an injury to stop the clock and give the Bears time for one more play. Luckman tossed a pass toward Bill Osmanski, his fullback, who had circled the defense and was open in the back of the end zone. But the Redskins' Frank Filchock wrapped his arms around Osmanski, denying the receiver a chance to make a catch. The ball hit Osmanski in the chest and fell to the ground for an incompletion.

Halas screamed about what he thought was an obvious pass interference penalty, but no flags fell, and the Redskins celebrated a victory. "I was ready to tear the referee limb from limb. I knew his ruling of no interference must stand, but I wanted to make my feelings known," Halas later wrote. "He popped into a dugout. All I could do was shout abuse after him. I probably used all of the words I had learned in the Chicago streets and in ball parks and training camps and maybe even made up a few new ones."

Hearing of Halas's complaints, George Preston Marshall responded with his own loud criticism. "The Bears are a bunch of crybabies. They can't take defeat," Marshall told reporters. "They are a first-half club. They are quitters. They are the world's greatest crybabies." Marshall never minded needling Halas. The two spoke regularly on the telephone during the season, mostly about league affairs, but the intense competition between their teams brought out the nastiness in both.

The Bears finished the regular season with two lopsided wins to earn the West division title and set up a rematch with the Redskins in the 1940 championship game at Griffith Stadium. "I did not let the players forget" what Marshall said, Halas later wrote. "You can understand why the game for the championship took on special importance."

Marshall did not back down, telling reporters the Redskins had beaten the Bears before and would do so again. He also sent a bombastic telegram to Halas after the Bears secured the division title: "Congratulations. I hope I will have the pleasure of beating your ears off next Sunday and every year to come. Justice is triumphant. We should play for the championship every year. Game will be sold out by Tuesday night." Seldom had an NFL championship game generated more anticipation, in part because of the public exchanges between Marshall and Halas. Although the league owners, as a group, believed in harmony, this was one instance where animus paid off. More than 36,000 tickets were sold, more than 150 press credentials issued. The Mutual Broadcasting System paid $2,500 for the right to broadcast the game nationally on the radio.

The game was set for December 8, 1940. Shaughnessy, now coaching at Stanford, traveled from California to Chicago to help Halas prepare. Shaughnessy's Stanford team, also wielding the updated T, had gone undefeated and would play in the Rose Bowl on New Year's Day. In Chicago, Halas and Shaughnessy devised a plan for challenging the Redskins' defense. Halas's preparations also included motivational tactics. In the locker room before the game, Halas hung newspaper clippings of Marshall's negative comments about the Bears. "When we were ready to go out, he pointed to the clippings and said, 'That's what the people in Washington are saying about you gentlemen. I know you are the greatest football team ever. Now go out and show the world.' We almost broke down the door," Osmanski recalled.

Before the kickoff, Halas huddled with Luckman and gave the quarterback three plays to run to begin the game. "They will show you whether the Redskins are staying with the defense they used in the last game against us. If they are, you will attack it as we have worked out," Halas told him.

The Bears won the toss and began the game with the ball. Luckman called a fake reverse with a man in motion. The Redskins reacted as they had three weeks earlier and held McAfee to a 7-yard gain. Yet Halas was thrilled, now certain his reconfigured offense would work. On second down, after McAfee went in motion to the right, Osmanski headed in the opposite direction, and Luckman pitched him the ball. The Redskins were fooled, and a hole opened. Osmanski straight-armed a linebacker and broke into the clear down the sideline. With help from a final clearing block, he ran 68 yards for a touchdown without being touched. "I could see this was going to be a great day for the Bears," Halas wrote.

After a long kickoff return put the Redskins in scoring range on their first possession, Sammy Baugh dropped back to pass and spotted a receiver open at the 4 yard line. But the receiver, Charley Malone, dropped the perfect pass, possibly because the sun got in his eyes. The Redskins settled for a field goal attempt and the kick flew wide. With the ball again, the Bears moved steadily downfield, entirely on the ground. A 27-yard run by Osmanski put them near the end zone, and Luckman plunged over the goal line for the score. "Our adjusted plays had them confused. They didn't know where the runner was going," according to Halas.

Minutes later, a partially blocked punt put the Bears in position for another score. Halas sent in a play that befuddled the Redskins more than any other to that point. The right halfback went left. The left halfback went right. Luckman lateraled to the fullback, Joe Maniaci,

The Bears' Bill Osmanski races 68 yards for a touchdown on the second play of the 1940 championship game. (Associated Press)

who ran to the left with the right halfback blocking for him. Without being touched by a defender, Maniaci ran 42 yards for a touchdown. The Bears had a 21–0 lead, and the first quarter was not over. The score was 28–0 at halftime, and somehow the second half was worse for Marshall and his team. The Bears' Hamp Pool intercepted a Baugh pass and ran it back 15 yards for a touchdown. Minutes later, McAfee also ran an interception back for a score. Before the end of the third quarter, yet another Washington pass was intercepted and returned for a touchdown.

The score was 54–0 by then, and, though Halas and Washington coach Ray Flaherty used backups in the fourth quarter, the rout continued with the Bears scoring one more touchdown, another, a third. The supply of new balls for the game ran out because the Bears had kicked them all into the stands on extra points. (Teams had not yet thought of putting up nets.) In the final minutes, the teams played with old practice balls, and, to avoid running out of those, the Redskins asked Halas to attempt the Bears' final two extra points on plays from scrimmage rather than on kicks. Halas complied.

When the final gun sounded, the Griffith Stadium scoreboard reflected a score that astonished sports fans across America: 73–0. "We wanted revenge and we got it," Bears tackle George Musso said. Actually, Halas and the Bears had done more than just exact revenge. With the most lopsided victory in league history, they had humiliated Marshall beyond measure—on his home turf, no less.

The Redskins' fans, furious with Marshall for having riled up the Bears, heckled him in his box seat throughout the second half. When Marshall ordered the stadium announcer to promote 1941 season ticket sales with the Redskins trailing by 60 points, the crowd booed. After the game, Washington's players were crestfallen, some near tears and barely able to respond to reporters' questions. When it was suggested to Baugh that the outcome might have been different if Malone had not dropped that sure touchdown early in the first quarter, Baugh shook his head. "If Charley had caught it, the score would have turned out 73–7," he said.

The Redskins admitted they had played poorly, but the Bears deserved credit, as they saw it, for a brilliant performance bordering on perfection. Some newsmen picked up on the theme. Arthur Daley began his *New York Times* story with a simple declaration: "The weather was perfect. So were the Bears."

The winning locker room, meanwhile, was crammed with reporters seeking an explanation. One reporter wore an official's uniform. The head linesman that day had been Irv Kupcinet, a Chicago sportswriter who was a friend of Luckman's and covered the Bears for the *Chicago Daily Times*. Destined to become a popular Chicago media personality, Kupcinet moonlighted as a football official. Although it was not unusual for sportswriters to officiate NFL games in the 1930s, the fact that it happened in a championship game, with a writer who covered the Bears, was precisely the kind of sly maneuver that Halas often employed, pushing ethical boundaries and infuriating the other

owners. But Kupcinet's judgment was not a factor in the result. The
Bears' lopsided victory was honest and deserved. The *Chicago Tribune*'s
Wilfrid Smith wrote that the rout was attributable to the Bears being
"the greatest team professional football has ever produced." The *Washington Post*'s Shirley Povich wrote, "The Bears were wonderful, weren't
they? The T formation is really dread stuff and Coach George Halas
comes pretty close to being the No. 1 offensive genius in the land."

For two decades, Halas had struggled to colonize the minds of
Chicago's sports fans. The 73–0 game ushered the Bears into the
limelight, almost by itself. Their attendance spiked the next season,
with crowds at Wrigley Field routinely surpassing 40,000 for mean-
ingful games against other strong teams. Chicago's sports tastes were
changing. The University of Chicago had dropped football. The Cubs
had fallen on hard times, their attendance dropping by more than 50
percent as years of losing mounted. Two radio stations now broadcast
the Bears' home games. Never again would Halas stroll anonymously
through a Chicago amusement park.

15

SAME OLD PIRATES

A FTER ART ROONEY MADE HIS FORTUNE AT THE BETTING window, he let his wife pick out any house she wanted as long as it was in the Ward, the Pittsburgh neighborhood they had grown up in. In 1939, they moved into a rambling three-story home with a center entry hall and enough space for the Rooneys' growing brood of young boys. It was not on a fashionable street and cost just $5,000. Though pleased about the purchase, Rooney quietly fretted about paying for its upkeep. His luck had turned. No longer did he return from the races with cash bulging his pockets. The ponies were beating him. Meanwhile, his football team continued to lose games and money. In 1938, the Pirates finished $35,000 in the red, pushing Rooney's deficit since he joined the NFL to more than $100,000.

His losing streak extended to politics. In 1938, a friend talked him into running for the registrar of wills in Allegheny County. He did not truly want the job but campaigned as only he could, donning suits, smoking cigars, and speaking honestly. He told one crowd he did not even know what the registrar of wills did. A victory in a crowded primary led him to believe he might win, but he lost in the general election. His ballot-box defeat was actually a relief. He had enough other responsibilities and needed to focus on his finances. Never lacking for ideas, he noticed boxing had reached a new peak of popularity in Pittsburgh, where the stable of local fighters included Billy Conn, a light heavyweight world champion. Rooney began promoting fight cards at Forbes Field, running the business out of his office at the Fort Pitt Hotel. The new business helped his overall bottom line.

He held out hope that his football team would also eventually become successful. Few in the city shared his optimism. The University of Pittsburgh's Panthers, a national power coached by Jock Sutherland, completely dominated the local football scene. The Pirates were rightfully seen as pitiful in comparison. Even with Whizzer White as the NFL's leading rusher, they won just two games in 1938. That fall, the United Press International polled the nation's newspaper sports editors on whether they thought Pitt could beat an NFL team. Forty-six percent of the editors responded yes, and, no doubt, many envisioned the Pirates as that NFL team losing to Pitt.

Part of the Pirates' problem was that their player-coach, Johnny Blood, was not only a mediocre coach but completely unreliable. He forgot to show up one Sunday to his team's game. Instead, he went to the Bears' game in Chicago and was sitting in the press box when a reporter asked why he was not with his own team. "We're not playing this week," Blood replied just as the stadium announcer gave the Pirates' score. In Blood's defense, sometimes it was difficult to know where the Pirates were playing. In 1938, they took on the Philadelphia Eagles in Buffalo, New York, and Charleston, West Virginia, because of lagging tickets sales. Rooney then moved the final game of the season, against Cleveland, from Forbes Field to New Orleans in hopes of luring a bigger gate; again, he had sold few tickets to the game, which he had postponed earlier in the season because the Pirates had so many injured players. (The Rams were furious, but Joe Carr allowed it.) When Rooney asked the mayor of New Orleans for promotional help upon arriving in the Big Easy, the mayor admitted he had thought the Pirates were a college team in town to play Tulane.

Every year, Rooney began the season with a full roster, but, as the losses mounted, he shed players to save expenses and the outmanned Pirates absorbed savage beatings, both figuratively and literally: there was often not a quality substitute on the bench, so the injured player had to stay in the game. Sportswriters lambasted him for failing to field competitive teams. He was too kind, they suggested, and it was true: he was loyal to the local players who needed the work, even if they were not helping the Pirates win. The gregarious Blood was good company at the racetrack, which kept him employed even though he set a terrible example. "On most teams, the coach worries about where the players are on the night before a game; on our team, the players worry about the coach," Rooney said.

After the 1938 season, Rooney seized on an opportunity to turn the Pirates around. Suddenly, Pitt's Sutherland was available. The tall, commanding coach had won 111 games while losing only 20 during a fifteen-year run at the school. His tenure had been marked by sold-out home games, undefeated seasons, and trips to the Rose Bowl; he was seen as sporting royalty in Pittsburgh. But Pitt's administration, increasingly uncomfortable with football's growing importance to the school, had instituted a series of changes that reemphasized academics, prompting Sutherland to resign after the 1938 college season.

Rooney praised Sutherland publicly, telling reporters he had "felt for a long time that Sutherland was the best coach in the profession." The two men knew each other, and Rooney wooed Sutherland, but Sutherland elected not to coach at all in 1939. Instead, Rooney brought Blood back. Fortunately for all concerned, Blood quit early in the 1939 season, after a 32–0 loss to the Bears that dropped the Pirates' record to 0-3. Walt Kiesling, a former player also frequently found alongside Rooney at the racetrack, took over, and he fared no better. By late in the season, the Pirates were 0-8-1 and on a fifteen-game winless streak. Only two games remained in their season, both against the Philadelphia Eagles, owned and coached by Bert Bell, Rooney's closest friend in the league and partner in football misery. The Eagles were 0-7-1.

PEOPLE WHO HAD KNOWN THEM BOTH FOR A LONG TIME laughed at the idea: Bert and Art, the best of friends? It could not have happened when they were younger. Bell was raised in opulence as a scion of America's ruling class. Rooney grew up over a bar, among gamblers and steel workers. "In that sense, they were opposites," Bell's son, Upton, said. But, by the 1930s, they were more alike. Bell had rebelled against his sniffy upbringing, even rejecting the name his parents gave him. And Rooney retained a certain personal modesty even after his famous run at Saratoga in 1937. That day, after he finished placing his bets, he walked the halls of the fabled track selling dollar raffle tickets to benefit his brother's church.

Both had been successful athletes as young men. Both worked their political connections to overturn Pennsylvania's blue laws and clear the way for games on Sunday and for Pennsylvania teams in the NFL. Their differences receded, and a role reversal of sorts occurred. As Rooney's gambling winnings soared, Bell, having wasted his fortune, needed his wife's money to start the Eagles. But nothing brought them together more than their shared misfortune in the NFL. By the end of the 1930s, even after the institution of a draft, it seemed as though the Pirates and Eagles would never compete with the Bears, Giants, Redskins, and Packers.

Like Rooney's Pirates, Bell's Eagles had never produced a winning season. After absorbing $90,000 in losses in their first three seasons, they went bankrupt, and Bell had no choice but to offer them for sale at a public auction house in downtown Philadelphia in 1936. Bell himself made the only, and thus winning, bid—$4,500. No one else wanted the team. That year, Bell added the title of head coach to his duties as general manager, ticket manager, trainer, scout, and publicist. His debut season on the sidelines did not go well. The Eagles threw a total of thirty-six interceptions while winning just one of a dozen games. Bell would coach the team for five years and register just ten victories against forty-four defeats. At one point, he lost fourteen straight games. Convincing his city's fans to buy tickets became all but impossible. On September 21, 1937, a meager crowd of 3,107 attended the Eagles' game against Cleveland at Philadelphia's Municipal Stadium, a massive edifice that could seat 100,000, as it did when Army played Navy.

In 1939, Bell tried to postpone a game against the Brooklyn Dodgers because of slow ticket sales and a forecast of driving rain. But Dan Topping, who owned the Dodgers, was already in town with his girlfriend and future wife, the Olympic figure skater Sonja Henie. Topping demanded that the game go forward as planned. Bell brought the fifty or so diehards who attended the game into the press box and served them free coffee and hot dogs while the teams splashed to a sodden, scoreless tie on the field. "It's days like that when it takes a very good sense of humor and an utter lack of regard for your bank balance to stay in professional football. I'm glad I had both," Bell said later. If the Eagles led the league in any category, it was financial struggles. The other owners were well aware of Bell's plight. Despite facing his own issues, George Halas offered to loan Bell $2,500 to help him get through the 1938 season. Bell accepted the loan, which he repaid the following year. Rooney likewise offered to loan Bell money.

The Eagles managed their best-ever season on the field in 1938, winning five games. Then, for the first time, they signed their first-round draft pick, Davey O'Brien, a star quarterback from Texas Christian University. Bell gave him a $12,000 bonus and a two-year contract, and O'Brien immediately showed that he was worth it, leading the league in passing as a rookie in 1939. But the Eagles fell apart around him and sank back to the bottom of the standings, forcing Bell to resort to extreme measures to keep from having to disband the team. Instead of taking trains to away games, the Eagles traveled on an old bus and spent nights at rooming houses rather than hotels. Bell told the players to pack lunches for their trips. As the bus motored down the road, Bell would spot flat farmland from his front seat and bellow at the driver to stop. "Everyone out, time for practice!" he shouted. Though the NFL had been in business for nearly two decades, it still retained much of the haphazardness of its early decades.

LED BY O'BRIEN, BELL'S EAGLES WON THE FIRST OF THEIR TWO meetings with Rooney's Pirates near the end of the 1939 season. When the teams met again three days later at Forbes Field, Rooney partnered with the Polish Refugee Relief Fund to make the game a fundraiser benefitting Poles fleeing the Nazis, who had invaded Poland that fall. That resulted in a much larger crowd than originally expected, and this time the Pirates prevailed. They and the Eagles both finished the season with one victory.

The Pirates had lost $8,000 during the season, but that was good news, relatively speaking; they had lost more during other seasons. Nonetheless, sportswriters speculated that Rooney could not afford to back his dismal franchise much longer. Fans filled high school stadiums across Western Pennsylvania on Friday nights and avidly supported Pitt, Duquesne, and Carnegie Tech on Saturdays, but little of that enthusiasm carried over to Pirates games on Sundays.

Offering his friend a way out after the 1939 season, George Preston Marshall found a wealthy Washingtonian willing to buy 50 percent of the Pittsburgh franchise. The offer was fair, but the man wanted to move the team to Boston, and Rooney, against the evidence, still believed he could succeed in Pittsburgh. "They tell me around here that I'm fighting a losing battle, that I'll never be able to make a go of it against the three college teams we have in Pittsburgh, and all of those fine high school teams. But I know different," Rooney said. But he did admit he was near his breaking point. "I'm definitely going to keep the team in Pittsburgh for another season," he told the press. "I hope I can always keep it here. But I can't go on losing money with the team here. I'll try it once more in Pittsburgh. But if I lose for the seventh time in eight seasons, I guess I'll have to take one of those offers."

Seeking a fresh start in 1940, he held a contest to change the team's nickname. Three thousand entries were submitted, and Rooney announced the winner in March. From now on, in a nod to the city's primary export, his team was the Pittsburgh Steelers. But sportswriters doubted the change would make a difference. "No matter what you call a grapefruit, it still squirts in your eye," Chet Smith wrote in the *Pittsburgh Press*. Rooney also took another stab at hiring Jock Sutherland, who was ready to return to coaching. Rooney had no doubt the move would boost attendance and change the team's fortunes. But he offered Sutherland only a $7,500 annual salary, which Dan Topping easily doubled. "I wish Art Rooney all the luck in the world," Sutherland said as he became the coach of the Brooklyn Dodgers.

Rooney still hoped his team could begin to establish itself in 1940. The schedule provided an opportunity, with four of the first five games at home. Rooney spent a little more money than usual acquiring talent, and when Halas brought the powerful Bears to Erie, Pennsylvania, for a preseason game, planning to easily dispatch Rooney's squad as they usually did, the Steelers did not quickly fold.

Shortly before the kickoff in Erie, as Halas exhorted his players in the visiting locker room, the door creaked open, and in walked Rooney with his eight-year-old son, Danny. Halas was stunned to see his rival in his team's locker room just before a game. It was a breach of basic football protocol. "Say, George, I hope you're giving them that keep-the-score-down talk," Rooney said. A few players chuckled. Then Halas smiled. Eventually, the entire locker room dissolved in laughter. The practical joke "broke the Halas spell," the *New York Times*' Art Daley wrote later, and the Steelers surprised the Bears that night, 10–9, further bolstering Rooney's hopes for the 1940 season.

They opened with a 7–7 tie against the Cardinals before 22,000 fans at Forbes Field, then also tied the Giants, 10–10, before 18,000. After winning in Detroit, they hosted the Dodgers and Sutherland. Rooney believed Pittsburgh fans would fill his stadium to get a look at the revered coach, but there were empty seats, and Sutherland's team won. The next week, the undefeated Redskins visited, bringing their band and a thousand fans along with Sammy Baugh, and they routed the Steelers, 40–10.

By early November, it was clear to all that it had been a fantasy to think a new name would make any difference. Rooney's team carried a 1-6-2 record into a rematch with the Redskins in Washington. Rooney indulged his habit of saving payroll expenses now that his team was out of the division title race. The Steelers dressed only twenty-five players, eight below the maximum limit, while Washington dressed the full thirty-three. After watching the Redskins win by four touchdowns, the *Washington Post*'s Shirley Povich criticized the shorthanded Steelers as a "woeful gang" that "made a mockery of themselves and the league." Povich estimated that Rooney had saved $2,000 but damaged the NFL's credibility.

For the second straight year, the season concluded with the Steelers and Eagles playing a pair of games. Bell's team was in even worse condition than Rooney's, winless in 1940 and playing to sparse home crowds. The Eagles' few remaining fans had given up on them, it seemed, after they suffered the worst possible indignity in late October, losing an exhibition game to a minor-league team, the Wilmington (Delaware) Clippers. Bell had scheduled the game to make extra money, but the result embarrassed the entire NFL.

Every Sunday night, Bell and Rooney commiserated on the phone, comparing their latest league defeats and lamenting their prospects. But although Rooney was struggling, he knew his friend was losing more money and asked whether Bell needed help. "After I turned him down three times in a row, I got a special delivery letter the next Monday. There was nothing in the envelope except a check for $5,000," Bell told the *New York Times* later.

Both men enjoyed being in the NFL and had earned the respect of the other owners. After proposing the draft, Bell had gained a seat on the league's executive committee, which handled major decisions. Rooney, a calm voice in a group dominated by headstrong competitors such as Marshall, Halas, and Mara, was "more effective resolving NFL matters than he was in addressing the Steelers' woes," Rooney's biographers would write. By 1940, both Rooney and Bell understood that it was time to act. No longer could they tolerate the losing on the field, or the expenses they incurred.

In late November of that year, Bell heard from the East-West Sporting Club, an organization formed by Alexis Thompson, the grandson of the founder of Republic Iron and Steel. A twenty-six-year-old sports-loving Yale graduate, Thompson had inherited millions as a teenager and bolstered his fortune selling eye-care products in New York. He wanted to buy the Eagles and move them to Boston, where his family was from. Bell did not want to sell but told Rooney about the offer. Rooney authorized Bell to serve as his agent in a potential sale of the Steelers to Thompson. If Bell could negotiate a sale within thirty days, he would receive a 25 percent commission. On December 9, 1940, Rooney and Thompson agreed to a complex deal. Thompson would pay Rooney $160,000 for the Pittsburgh franchise and the contracts of twenty-four players—seventeen Steelers and seven Eagles. The Steelers would send eleven players to the Eagles. Bell would receive a $32,000 commission.

The news broke at a league meeting in Washington the day after the Bears' 73–0 rout of the Redskins in the 1940 championship game. Most Pittsburgh sportswriters did not criticize Rooney for selling after so many years of losses. "You can't blame the guy," the *Pittsburgh Sun-Telegraph*'s Harry Keck wrote. But Pittsburgh fans feared the sale meant they would lose the Steelers. Loyal as ever to his hometown, Rooney quickly set out to fix the problem. Aided by the proceeds from his sale of the Steelers, he bought a 50 percent stake in the Eagles; he and Bell were going into business together. While fans in Philadelphia cheered the move, hoping Bell could straighten out the Eagles with the large sale commission and Rooney's infusion of cash, Rooney quietly rooted for Thompson to move the Steelers to Boston. He and Bell could then realize their ultimate goal: to own a franchise together that played home games in *both* Philadelphia and Pittsburgh.

The other owners quickly scuttled the plan, telling Thompson they did not want a team in Boston so soon after Marshall's disastrous experience there. They also told Rooney and Bell that they could not abide two cities sharing a team. After several weeks of uncertainty, Thompson announced in February 1941 that his team would stay in Pittsburgh with a new name—the Iron Men.

Rooney plotted another move. When Thompson missed a March deadline to open team offices, Rooney took him out for an evening at a popular Pittsburgh saloon, plied him with drinks, and suggested they exchange franchises. Thompson could have Philadelphia and the Eagles. Rooney and Bell would take Pittsburgh and the Steelers. Though shocked at first, Thompson listened intently as Rooney explained that Philadelphia was more Thompson's kind of town with its arts scene and the high society of the Main Line. By the end of the night, Thompson agreed to swap teams. The three men presented their unusual idea to the other owners. To their surprise, it was approved. Thompson's East-West Sporting Club now owned the Eagles. The Bell-Rooney partnership, which was now officially called the Philadelphia Eagles Football Club, Inc., owned the Steelers. That was awkward, but Bell and Rooney would not change their partnership's name for another three years.

For a head coach, Thompson hired Greasy Neale, who had played with Jim Thorpe years earlier and coached at Virginia and West Virginia. Neale would bring championships to Philadelphia by the end of the decade. Bell and Rooney contacted several notable names about coaching the Steelers, but none wanted the job. In the end, Bell became the head coach. He did not fare as well as Neale.

Between the exchange of Philadelphia and Pittsburgh players in Thompson's original purchase and the subsequent franchise swap, it was almost impossible to know which players belonged where. In the spring of 1941, Neale, Thompson, Bell, and Rooney met at the Racquet Club in Philadelphia to divide up the players on the two teams. After that meeting, Bell thought he and Rooney had ended up with better players. As he prepared the Steelers for the 1941 season at a training camp in Hershey, Pennsylvania, he declared, "This is the finest squad I've ever worked with in the National Football League." But Rooney disagreed. Stopping at Hershey for a day on his way to Saratoga to bet on the races, he sat in the bleachers and watched practice. A Pittsburgh sportswriter asked what he thought. "Those new uniforms they're wearing threw me off a bit, but once I saw them practice a couple of minutes, I could see they were the same, old Pirates," Rooney said.

The comment was a tacit acknowledgement that the Steelers simply were not good at football. Rooney would long regret what he said. The sportswriter quoted him in the next day's paper, and Pittsburgh's fans picked it up as a refrain with only a slight alteration. In the coming years, whenever their frustration boiled over as their team's losses mounted, they would simply utter three letters, SOS—"same old Steelers."

Though he had not played and coached as much as his partner, Rooney proved more adept than Bell at gauging the team's prospects. The Steelers went 1-9-1 in 1941 while the Eagles went 2-8-1 in their first year with Thompson as their owner. Bell's tenure as the Steelers' coach did not last long. They opened the 1941 season with a loss to the Rams in Cleveland, then lost their home opener to the Eagles, a particularly demoralizing result.

"We have to do something. At this rate, no one is going to come see us play," Bell lamented to Rooney after the loss to the Eagles.

"I know what we have to do, but you won't go for it," Rooney replied.

"Name it," Bell said.

"You have to quit!" Rooney roared.

Bell announced his resignation three days later; he would never coach in the NFL again. In a surprise, his replacement was Duquesne's head coach, Aldo "Buff" Donelli. It was not a surprise because Donelli was unknown; he was one of college football's more successful coaches. The surprise was Donelli would continue to coach Duquesne while also leading the Steelers. Yet again Rooney and Bell had come up with an unprecedented and highly unusual scheme. It seemed to be a coup for the Steelers, but Elmer Layden, the NFL's new commissioner, was appalled. Layden, who had been hired before the 1941 season, was a fabled former player; he had been the full-back in Notre Dame's Four Horseman backfield in the 1920s. More recently, he had coached the Fighting Irish. But he had coached at Duquesne before that—in fact, Donelli had played for him—and he believed it was unprofessional for Donelli to simultaneously coach pro and college teams. He forced Donelli to choose. Donelli agreed to coach the Steelers while serving as an "advisor" to his top assistant at Duquesne. That temporarily appeased Layden, even though it was clear Donelli was still effectively coaching both teams.

The Steelers briefly improved under Donelli; they did not win a game but nearly beat the Redskins. Meanwhile, Duquesne built an undefeated record. Donelli was able to make every game for both teams until a conflict arose. The Steelers were due to play the Eagles in Philadelphia a day after Duquesne played St. Mary's in California. Donelli could not make both games. Layden interceded again, telling him that he could no longer coach the Steelers if he was not in Philadelphia for their game. Donelli chose to go west with Duquesne, which served, in effect, as his resignation from the Steelers.

Rooney was not happy in the least that Donelli was no longer coaching his team. He blamed Layden, whom he had supported as a candidate for commissioner. "He could have helped us and helped the league, too," Rooney groused. Seeing little choice, Rooney tapped Walt Kiesling to coach the team for the rest of the 1941 season. Kiesling had been the head coach the year before and an assistant under Bell and Donelli; he was a favorite of Rooney's from the racetrack. As the 1941 season wound down, Kiesling performed what some in Pittsburgh regarded as a minor miracle. Somehow, he coached the Steelers to a victory over the Brooklyn Dodgers—their only triumph in yet another disappointing season.

16

POLITICAL WINDS

WHILE THEY JUGGLED FRANCHISES AND PLAYERS IN EARLY 1941, Bert Bell and Art Rooney joined their NFL colleagues in finishing off a crucial piece of league business—hiring a commissioner. Before the owners settled on Elmer Layden, the job was open for almost two years. Joe Carr had run the league office since 1921, but his title was president, not commissioner. Carr was a level-headed, effective executive who often wielded great influence on important matters, but when he died in May 1939 after suffering a heart attack, the owners sought to hire a bigger name, their version of Kennesaw Mountain Landis, major league baseball's imperious commissioner. A credible sports league needed a credible leader, they thought.

Carr's death gave them no choice but to settle for a fallback plan in 1939. Carl Storck had been Carr's lieutenant and the league's secretary-treasurer from the beginning, since 1921. He was the opposite of a high-profile hire. In fact, football was his second job; he worked full time for General Motors. But he knew the league's business and could keep things running well enough. The owners gave him a one-year contract.

After the 1939 season, they renewed their search. In Washington, George Preston Marshall had a conversation about the job with J. Edgar Hoover, the director of the Federal Bureau of Investigation. But Hoover was not interested. George Halas tried to hire Arch Ward, offering the *Chicago Tribune*'s innovative sports editor a ten-year contract worth $25,000 a year—a staggering amount. But Ward turned Halas down, saying he "could not overlook the splendid opportunities in my position with the *Chicago Tribune*." The owners pledged to make the hire when they met in New York in April 1940, but, lacking a candidate, ended up giving Storck another one-year contract. Marshall, though, was no fan of Storck, who had refused to overturn a controversial call that denied the Redskins a division title in 1939. In comments to reporters, Marshall made it clear Storck's tenure would not last much longer. "I think Storck is a fine executive, but I can name a better one," Marshall said. "However, I know of no available candidate now."

During the 1940 season, Halas again offered the job to Arch Ward, who again said no. This time, Ward himself suggested another candidate, Layden, who was also Notre Dame's athletic director as well as its football coach. Halas loved the idea. Although Layden had limited administrative experience, he was a famous sports figure who would generate good press. But other owners also had candidates in mind. Bell favored Jack Kelly, a wealthy Philadelphia contractor who had won three Olympic gold medals in rowing as a young man; Bell and Kelly had been friends since they served together in the Great War. Frank McCormick, athletic director at the University of Minnesota, was also under consideration.

At a meeting in Chicago on January 17, 1941, the owners amended the league constitution, inserting a clause enabling them to create the position of commissioner. They assigned Halas and Bell to interview Layden and Kelly by the end of the month. After conducting the interviews, Bell left for a vacation in Florida, believing a decision would not be made until the third candidate, McCormick, also had been interviewed. On the first day of his vacation, though, he received a shock. When he opened his morning newspaper, he read that Layden had been hired.

Knowing that Bell preferred Kelly, Halas had waited until Bell was in Florida and unavailable and spoke with the other owners who lived in Chicago, the Lions' Fred Mandel and the Cardinals' Charles Bidwill, selling them on Layden. Halas then asked Art Rooney to help him. Working the phones, Rooney obtained support for Layden from Marshall, Tim Mara, Curly Lambeau, and Cleveland's Edward Bruch. Emboldened, Halas offered Layden a five-year contract with a $20,000 annual salary. Layden accepted.

In interviews with the Associated Press, Bell, Alexis Thompson, and Brooklyn's Dan Topping accused their colleagues of skirting the league constitution in hiring Layden. (Thompson would swap franchises with Bell and Rooney weeks later.) The owners never voted as a body, Bell pointed out, adding that the announcement "came from Chicago, which is where Halas lives." Bell obviously believed Halas had manipulated the process. "Well, that's one thing Bell got right: I do live in Chicago," Halas snorted to the AP. He denied going behind Bell's back. "Bell knew all about the progress of negotiations. We interviewed Layden together last week in Pittsburgh. Then we talked to Thompson and Topping by phone. Layden's appointment was strictly legal," Halas said. "No announcement was made until Layden was handed an official binding agreement containing the signatures of a majority of our club owners."

Thompson explained to the AP that Bell and Halas were supposed to interview all three candidates before making a decision, but they "also were given authority to make an offer to one of the three and report back to the league." Halas had hijacked that authority while Bell was out of town, according to Thompson. "Bell wasn't even in on the signing of Layden," Thompson said. It was what some recognized, by that point, as a classic Halas maneuver. No one, including the other owners, doubted that he effectively ran the league. He always received unwavering support from Bidwill, who still cheered for the Bears despite owning the Cardinals. Halas also had arranged for Mandel, a young Chicago store owner, to buy the Lions when their prior owner, George "Dick" Richards, was forced to sell. That guaranteed Halas the support of three of the NFL's ten franchises on any issue—a powerful base.

The Lions' sale had been made possible by another Halas scheme. Richards, a flamboyant radio executive, had bought the Portsmouth Spartans in 1934, moved them to Detroit, and renamed them the Lions. They had developed a following and even won an NFL title in 1935 while Richards, a millionaire, bankrolled them through the Great Depression and became an influential owner, constantly pushing for bold measures, including firing Joe Carr, hiring a big-name commissioner, and putting games on the radio. But Richards irritated Halas, who was loyal to Carr, and Halas eventually orchestrated Richards's exit from the league.

When the Lions' owner fired his coach, "Gloomy Gus" Henderson, in 1940, Henderson took revenge, providing the other owners with letters proving Richards had bet large sums on the Lions. Fearing a gambling scandal, Halas leapt into action. He told the owners to keep the story quiet, then located a buyer, the thirty-one-year-old Mandel, who offered Richards $165,000, then a record price for an NFL team. Mandel did not have the cash, but Halas arranged for the ever-willing Bidwill to write a check making up the difference. Richards wanted to keep the team, but Halas was adamant, believing the Lions' owner was potentially toxic now. The sale of the Lions for a sizable profit bought Richards's silence.

Layden's hiring and Richards's exit exemplified one of the league's fundamental commandments: thou shalt not challenge George Halas. When Bell expressed concern about Layden's lack of executive experience—a fact that would soon enough prove problematic—his concern was drowned out by Halas's support. Marshall chimed in, calling Layden's hiring "the most constructive and finest move ever made" by the NFL. Rooney also offered praise. Storck was stunned. Other than Halas, no one had been associated with the NFL longer than him. He thought he had served the owners well since taking over for Carr. But the owners had other ideas, bigger plans. When they asked Storck to stay on as president under Layden, he resigned, criticizing his replacement as he departed. "I am convinced Layden is not qualified to handle the job, mostly due to his lack of administrative experience in professional sports," Storck said. "Layden was steamrolled into his job when George Halas and Arch Ward saw an opportunity."

Shortly thereafter, Storck suffered a stroke, which was followed by a series of health issues that he battled for almost a decade before dying in 1950 at age fifty-six. When his failing health drained his savings in his final years, Tim Mara alerted the owners, and they pitched in with several thousand dollars a year. But Storck's daughter said she believed her father's bitterness over his abrupt departure from the NFL led to his death. Halas may have been among the league's first owners and, among them, the most dedicated to the sport, but he was not the only person involved in the NFL's early history who saw pro football as a calling.

IN THE FALL OF 1941, CHARLES BIDWILL ADMITTED TO HALAS that owning the perennially mediocre Cardinals was not especially exciting. Bidwill asked Halas about the possibility of moving the team to Los Angeles. The NFL had been flirting with putting a team in Southern California, which was becoming an attractive sports market as its population exploded around midcentury. Five years earlier, the league had granted a "probationary franchise" to a Los Angeles group with the idea that it would develop a team that would, in turn, eventually join the league. The Los Angeles Bulldogs developed quickly, winning three of six games against NFL squads that traveled west for exhibitions in 1936. But the league broke its promise, establishing a new team in Cleveland rather than adding the Bulldogs in 1937. Most owners were against the idea of regular travel to the West Coast. Joe Carr, still in charge at the time, supported the idea of a team in Ohio, his home state.

After being turned down by the NFL, the Bulldogs joined the American Football League, Harry March's brainchild, then in its second and final season, and won the title with an 8-0 record in 1937. After that, they returned to independent status and continued to play exhibitions against NFL teams, then changed their name to the Hollywood Bears and joined a lesser league.

As sports teams on the West Coast played to larger and larger crowds, it was evident the NFL had to consider a franchise in Los Angeles. If Bidwill wanted to move the Cardinals there, Halas would not attempt to stop him. Halas certainly owed Bidwill, who had helped the league in many ways over the years; he had arranged for Halas to obtain a loan when Halas was on the verge of losing the Bears in 1932, and, more recently, he had provided money to help the sale of the Lions go through.

Bidwill's lukewarm interest in his own team was a source of amusement in league circles. In 1938, a reporter had asked whether he would be in New York to watch his Cardinals take on the Giants. No, Bidwill said, he would be in Chicago to watch the Bears. By the early 1940s, the gap between Chicago's two teams was widening. Halas had built a powerful squad that played to large, enthusiastic crowds. The Cardinals continued to lose and shrink further into the Bears' shadow. Moving them to the West Coast was one solution. But Halas asked Bidwill to keep the idea between them for the time being. The Los Angeles situation was delicate, as several West Coast groups also were interested in obtaining an NFL franchise. Hopefully, Halas told Bidwill, we can make it happen sooner rather than later. That pledge would cause more trouble than either man could have imagined.

IN 1939, FOR THE THIRD YEAR IN A ROW, THE REDSKINS AND Giants concluded the season by playing at the Polo Grounds for the East division title. Each team sported an 8-1-1 record. They had played a scoreless tie in October at Griffith Stadium. The rematch drew 62,404 fans on a gray December afternoon, another indication that the Giants had become a marquee sports attraction in their city, especially when the Redskins visited.

The defenses dominated. Neither offense produced a touchdown in the first three quarters as the Giants inched ahead with three field goals from two different kickers. But just when it appeared the 9-point lead would hold up, the Redskins rallied. They blocked a punt, quickly scored a touchdown, forced another punt, and drove the ball into scoring range. As the crowd fell quiet, the Redskins' Bo Russell lined up a 15-yard field goal attempt to win the game in the final seconds. The snap and hold were perfect. Russell put his right foot into the ball. Half of the Redskins Band, seated behind the end zone, erupted in celebration, thinking the kick was good. The other half groaned, believing the ball had flown wide of the uprights.

On the field, standing behind the offense, Bill Halloran, a veteran referee, signaled that the field goal was no good. His was the only opinion that counted. It produced bedlam. Washington coach Ray Flaherty rushed toward Halloran, furious. A half-dozen Washington players surrounded the 135-pound referee, shouting at him. As Halloran and the other officials tried to leave the field, one Redskin chased after them and threw a punch. A team of policemen had to form a wedge to protect the officials.

A few hours later, Tim Mara and George Preston Marshall shared a lavish dinner at a Manhattan restaurant. Marshall was livid; he was sure Halloran had robbed his team of a division title. But, still, he could joke about it. Noting Mara's luck that afternoon, he asked, "Tim, just tell me one thing, what church do you go to?" Marshall often infuriated Mara, but the two understood that the rivalry between their teams was good for each of their businesses, and for the league in general.

Both men quickly forgot about their conciliatory dinner, however. Marshall went on a rampage. First, he tried to convince Carl Storck, at that time still the league president, to overturn the call; Storck refused, which probably cost him his job a year later. In the meantime,

Marshall saw to it that Storck was relieved of an important duty, the assigning of referees to games. Starting in 1940, a committee of owners, led by Marshall, handled the assignments. Halloran's load was reduced. Mara believed Marshall was acting childishly, and their feud escalated. They began arguing over everything, including the hiring of the commissioner, the schedule, rules changes, and more. "The two moguls were squaring off," according to Rooney's biographers. Rooney had to calm them down with the reminder that the league's future required cooperation off the field.

Mara and Marshall were not the only owners whose relationship veered from friendly to acrimonious and back again. Halas and Mara "were so often on opposite sides that I grew up looking upon Halas as an enemy," Wellington Mara said. But they also could shake hands and work together. Halas and Lambeau had battled on and off the field for two decades, but the rivalry between the Bears and Packers helped keep both teams afloat. Bell was infuriated by Halas's hiring of Layden as commissioner, but Halas had great respect for Bell and for Rooney, especially after he tried to short the upstart Rooney on a game check in 1936 and was challenged to a fight. "Their relationship was one of great warmth," Virginia McCaskey said of Halas and Rooney. "Art's personal warmth may have gotten in the way of his having a good team at times, but it also benefitted the league. Helping people get along. He just wanted to be a good friend to everyone."

Months after Layden's hiring seemingly drove a wedge between them, Halas asked Bell for a favor. Virginia was attending college, having left Chicago for Drexel University in Philadelphia, and now she was dating a University of Pennsylvania student named Ed McCaskey. "Would you please check up on him and let me know what you find out?" Halas asked Bell, the Penn grad and lifelong Philadelphia resident. The request was a sign of the immense trust between the two owners. Halas's older brother, Walter, had been a coach and athletic administrator at Drexel since the late 1920s, but Halas asked Bell to "scout" his potential son-in-law.

McCaskey was on a partial scholarship that covered his tuition but left him constantly scrambling to pay for his meals, books, and rent. A resourceful young man, he took extra jobs waiting tables and working in Penn's athletic ticket office. The ticket manager, Bill Lenox, liked him and offered to help. Penn was a national power in football, drawing big crowds to its home games at Franklin Field. The demand for tickets was always high. Lenox let McCaskey sell cheap, obstructed-view seats and keep the proceeds. Bell knew Lenox and asked what he thought of McCaskey, explaining that the young man was dating Virginia Halas. Lenox said he thought highly of the diligent McCaskey.

Bell's scouting mission was not over. One day McCaskey reported for work at a restaurant near Penn's campus. His boss told him two men were waiting to speak to him. He was directed to a table occupied by Bell and Rooney. "Ed sat down with them. They asked how he was doing," Virginia McCaskey recalled. "The conversation went on for a while and finally ended when Bert said, 'Well, if you're OK with Bill Lenox, you're OK with me.'"

Bell contacted Halas to tell him the same. Halas remained unconvinced, but that changed after McCaskey married Virginia a year later and eventually became part of the NFL's fraternity of owners. McCaskey, it turned out, fit right in. "He and Art Rooney both loved horse racing," Virginia said. "They got to be real close."

17

DOG MEAT

THE STADIUM ANNOUNCER'S VOICE ECHOED THROUGH THE Polo Grounds shortly after 2 p.m., during the first quarter of a game between the Giants and Dodgers on December 7, 1941.

"Attention, please. Attention, please. Here is an urgent message," the announcer stated. "Will Colonel William J. Donovan call operator 19 in Washington immediately?"

Few in the crowd of 55,051 thought much of it. The Polo Grounds routinely reverberated with announcements during games. Season tickets were for sale. A car outside the stadium was parked with the motor running and the doors locked. A man's wife had gone into labor; please call home. Some fans surely recognized that this announcement was unusual, however: "Wild Bill" Donovan was widely known as a Great War hero and now headed the Office of the Coordination of Information, a forerunner of the Central Intelligence Agency. In attendance at the Polo Grounds because he rooted for the Giants, he surely was dealing with an important matter if he had to make an urgent call to Washington.

The NFL was concluding its season with a slate of Sunday games, including this one in New York, where the Dodgers were surprisingly ahead of the Giants early. In the Polo Grounds press box, a Western Union operator studied his news ticker and told the sportswriter next to him that the Cardinals also had gone ahead of the Bears in Chicago, another surprise.

A few minutes later, still looking at his ticker, the Western Union man said, "Oh, my God."

"What, Cardinals score again?" the sportswriter asked.

"No," the wire man said, "the Japs have attacked Pearl Harbor."

While the game went on, everyone in the press box gathered around the ticker as more details came through. *U.S. fleet in ruins. Thousands dead. President Roosevelt to meet with cabinet. Declaration of war imminent.* The news spread rapidly through the crowd, even without a stadium announcement. A team chaplain informed twenty-five-year-old Wellington Mara on the sidelines. "I didn't even know where Pearl Harbor was," the young Mara would recall.

The Giants' head coach, Steve Owen, told his players at halftime. "He gave us such a bad account of all the bad things that happened there, it was like we didn't want to go back out on the field," said Jim Poole, an end. Jock Sutherland, the Dodgers' coach, elected not to inform his players, fearing they would lose interest in the game. But they already knew. "What do we do now?" asked halfback Ace Parker as he paced the locker room. The teams played a listless second half. Near the end of Brooklyn's 21–7 victory, the public address announcer's voice rumbled through the stadium's loudspeakers again. "Attention, all officers and men of the Army and Navy are to report to their stations immediately. Repeat, all armed forces personnel will report to their stations immediately."

Tim Mara left the stadium deeply conflicted. Although the Giants had lost, they had already secured the East division title, earning them a place in the upcoming league championship game. That normally would have been cause for celebration, but it felt meaningless now. Thousands of Americans were dead and the country surely was going to war. At fifty-four, Mara was the elder statesman among the NFL's brotherhood of owners. As the son of Irish immigrants who had fled dire conditions in their homeland for a better life in America, Mara had strong feelings about his country. Though he was too old to serve, he would aid the impending war effort however he could. The fate of the Giants and the NFL seemed trivial in comparison.

Yet Mara could not help but worry about his team and the league. Two years earlier, New York had legalized pari-mutuel wagering, effectively putting the state's racetracks in charge of the gambling on their premises. Wagers were now placed with the house, not on a man-to-man basis in a betting enclosure. Legal bookmakers had been put out of business. In 1939, Mara's career as a bookie came to an end, cutting off what had been his steadiest source of income for many years. He still owned a fuel company (technically, his wife owned it, in the same way his sons owned the Giants) and had other interests, but the Giants were now the backbone of his business empire.

The Giants had become popular and profitable, owing to their consistent success on the field. But the continued existence of the league overall was far from assured. Even after two decades in business, the league was constantly held back by teams that were neither successful on the field nor profitable at the gate.

Recently, after barely surviving the economic depression of the 1930s, the NFL had finally started to gain a measure of security. Interest was growing, attendance surging. Now, though, the league faced another challenge. At the very moment its business appeared to be stabilizing, a war was beginning. Mara was old enough to remember life during the Great War. It had been a time of great uncertainty, when Americans were asked to conserve resources to support the war effort. If rationing was mandated again, Mara wondered, would the NFL be able to endure?

IN CHICAGO, THE STADIUM ANNOUNCER AT COMISKEY PARK broke the news from Pearl Harbor to the crowd of 18,879 that had gathered to watch the Bears play the Cardinals. "They announced it over the loudspeakers. It was a tremendous shock to everyone," re-called Sid Luckman, the Bears' quarterback.

The game was vitally important to the Bears, who needed to win to set up a one-game playoff with the Packers for the West division title. The Cardinals, concluding another losing season, had less to play for, but they always wanted to beat their heralded crosstown rivals and had taken an early lead. After the announcement, "the teams just didn't have the same emotions knowing our country had been attacked," Luckman said. There was talk of stopping the game. "I didn't know what to do. We decided the game should go on. Very few people left," Halas wrote later. His team continued to trail for most of the game, but finally took the lead in the fourth quarter when George McAfee caught a 39-yard touchdown pass from Luckman. McAfee then sealed the win with a 70-yard touchdown run.

Halas was briefly elated, but his thoughts quickly turned to the impending war. As a young man, he had volunteered for naval service during the Great War and requested that he be assigned duty at sea. He was disappointed when the navy instead installed him in the sports program at the Great Lakes Naval Training Base. After his discharge, he pledged to see more purposeful action if America ever went to war again. It was time to uphold that commitment. In the midst of his preparations for the playoff game with the Packers, he drove to the Great Lakes base, north of Chicago, and asked the commander, an old friend, if he could be "sent to sea." The commander told him he was too old. Halas was forty-six. "I'll send your name to Washington. Maybe someone will pick you up," the commander said.

Halas returned to Chicago and coached the Bears. Their game with the Packers drew 43,425 fans, a sizable figure, to Wrigley Field; it seemed people needed a respite from the grim war news in their newspapers. The Bears routed the Packers, then also routed the Giants, 37–9, in the 1941 championship game a week later. Few would dispute that Halas had put together the finest pro football team ever. The Bears had now won back-to-back NFL titles. But only 13,341 fans attended the title game at Wrigley Field. The public's interest in sports already was waning.

In the coming months, dozens of NFL players volunteered for military duty, leaving rosters depleted. When training camps opened in 1942, almost half of the NFL's players, more than 150, were in the service. The Giants had lost more than half of their 1941 division-winning squad. Twenty rookies made New York's roster in 1942. "I took one look at the squad and I felt like crying," fullback Tuffy Lee-mans said. The Steelers had lost so many players that they dressed just sixteen for their first preseason game. There was some talk that the league should suspend operations. But in early 1942 President Roosevelt penned a "green light letter" to Kennesaw Mountain Landis, suggesting he "keep baseball going" because the war effort would be taxing and people "ought to have a chance for recreation and for taking their minds off work." The NFL owners took that as a rationale to continue operating normally. When Bell and Rooney lobbied the other owners to at least shorten the 1942 season to nine games, their proposal was dismissed.

A powerful squad to begin with, the Bears lost fewer key players than other teams did and dominated their opponents once the 1942 season began. Led by Luckman and McAfee, they beat the Packers by 16 points, the Rams by 14, the Cardinals by 27, the Giants by 19, and the Eagles by 31. Their home attendance remained strong, with 38,000 fans attending the Cardinals game, and 32,000 paying to see the championship-game rematch with the Giants. At times, it was hard for Halas to tell the country was at war. But midway through the season, Halas finally received his military call-up; the navy reactivated him as a lieutenant commander and assigned him to a base in Norman, Oklahoma, where aircraft mechanics were trained. He wore his uniform on the sidelines of a home game against the Lions on November 1, 1942, his final contest before leaving. At halftime, players from both teams gathered around him at midfield, and an induction officer presented him with a sword. Halas also inducted his son into the navy as part of the ceremony. After the Bears won, 16–0,

Halas departed for Oklahoma, leaving his top assistants in charge of his undefeated team. There was no immediate falloff in the Bears' performance. They scored 162 points and gave up just seven while winning their next four games.

Halas arrived in Norman to find he was third in command at the base, with "many duties," he later wrote. Still, the assignment discouraged him. "I would not have chosen it," he wrote. "The duty I wanted was in the Pacific, fighting the Japs. I hoped an early transfer could be arranged."

In December, he wrangled a temporary leave and took a military flight to Washington to watch the Bears play the Redskins in the 1942 league championship game at Griffith Stadium. The Redskins had gone 10-1 during the regular season, finishing with nine straight wins after an early loss to the Giants. They still had Sammy Baugh at quarterback and a strong squad around him, but the undefeated Bears were favored to win. Chicago had scored 376 points and allowed just 84 during the season. The Redskins, however, were eager to avenge the 73–0 humiliation Chicago had dealt them two years earlier. Their fans felt the same. Meanwhile, the Bears had grown overconfident after winning eighteen straight games over two seasons. "We were beginning to think of ourselves as unbeatable. Coach Halas never would have allowed that," Luckman recalled.

A packed house of 36,006 crammed excitedly into Griffith Stadium but fell quiet when a burly Chicago tackle, Lee Artoe, picked up a fumble and rumbled 50 yards for the game's first touchdown. But the rout many expected did not happen. Eighteen Redskins were playing their final game before beginning their military deployments. Washington's coach, Ray Flaherty, was joining the navy in forty-eight hours. Displaying the passion one might expect in such circumstances, the Redskins stymied Luckman and the Chicago offense, which was accustomed to scoring easily.

The Redskins took a 7–6 lead on a stunning touchdown pass before halftime. Baugh dropped back and heaved the ball 50 yards, seemingly beyond the reach of his receivers. But Wilbur Moore caught up

George Halas, in his navy uniform, on the Bears' bench during the 1942 championship game. (Associated Press)

to it and grabbed it on a dead sprint for a score. The Redskins then scored another touchdown in the third quarter. Halas, seated on the Bears' bench, was shocked. Sensing victory, many Washington fans stood through the fourth quarter, encouraging the home team. In the final minutes, Luckman led a drive to the Washington 2 yard line, but several runs fell short of the goal line, and a fourth-down pass fell incomplete. Washington's fans flooded the field after the final gun. "The once mighty football empire of the Chicago Bears was forever crushed and ground," the *Washington Post* wrote the next day.

Disconsolate at first, Halas soon recovered, at least outwardly, wearing his naval uniform to the owners' post-championship meeting the next day. Marshall, in the mood to gloat, punctured his calm. "George, you're too old to fight a war. Why don't you take off the uniform and let a younger guy do the job?" Marshall said. Halas had to be pulled off his "best friend" who owned the Redskins. "I thought Halas would kill Marshall," Art Rooney recalled.

When Pearl Harbor was attacked, Rooney was forty, with five sons and several businesses to run. He was hardly an ideal candidate for combat. But after arguing with Kass, he went to a recruitment center and signed up. As he turned in the paperwork, though, an official sneered, "You're no big shot now!" Rooney tore up the duty application papers and walked away. His friends had suggested his energies would be better spent at home, helping people in need, boosting morale with his football games and boxing cards. He realized his friends were right. That winter, he staged patriotic-themed boxing cards at Duquesne Gardens, Pittsburgh's largest indoor venue. Servicemen received free admission, and Rooney sold war bonds between bouts. Months later, 19,000 fans came out for what sportswriters called the best boxing card ever staged in Pittsburgh, headlined by a bout between Ezzard Charles and Joey Maxim.

Rooney remained troubled that he was not fighting for his country. Several of his brothers and friends had volunteered, as had a booking agent in his boxing business who was two years older. Rooney sought to assuage his guilt by tending to the needs of those left behind. "He found people waiting for him every morning in the Fort Pitt Hotel lobby. Many counted on Art to intercede on their behalf or reach into his pocket," his biographers wrote.

He had hoped the NFL would cancel its 1942 season; too many players were in the service, he believed, and too many fans did not have enough money for tickets. After reading Roosevelt's "green light letter," he knew the league would remain open for business, but he still disagreed with that implicit decision and initially staged a quiet protest by failing to field a full roster of players. After watching the outmanned Steelers lose miserably to the Cleveland Rams in a preseason game, however, he changed his mind and went on a recruiting binge. The Steelers wound up fielding the most competitive team in their history.

Rooney also benefited from some good fortune. Months earlier he had drafted Bill Dudley, a supremely talented halfback from Virginia. Dudley promptly signed up to fight—typical Steeler luck, many observers lamented. But, over the summer, he received a furlough enabling him to play in 1942. He scored all four of the Steelers' touchdowns in their first two games, both defeats. Rooney sensed another losing season on the way, but Dudley was more confident. "This team is going to win some games," the young man told the owner.

Dudley was prescient. The Steelers won their next three games, helping lure a sellout crowd to their next home contest, against the Redskins. One sportswriter enthusiastically declared pro football finally had arrived in Pittsburgh. The Steelers lost, but it was clear they were vastly improved. The next week, they went to New York and beat the Giants as Dudley broke a 65-yard touchdown run to seal the victory. It was the start of a four-game winning streak, their longest run of success since they joined the NFL. For the first time, Pittsburgh ended a season with a winning record. But the war effort remained Rooney's priority. In the middle of the winning streak, the Steelers played a military team in a benefit exhibition game and raised $35,000, which went toward building a USO canteen in downtown Pittsburgh.

After the season, Rooney again suggested to his fellow owners that the NFL suspend operations, even though he had enjoyed his team's winning campaign. When the owners voted to keep playing, Rooney groused that his franchise would "go through the motions" in 1943. He did not think it was a tenable situation. By April, a third of the players on his roster had enlisted, and more were leaving every week. Bert Bell had sent recruiting letters to 250 prospects, but none signed up. Rooney feared offering a cheap product to the public. Fans might lose faith in what was still a fledgling league, at least compared to major league baseball.

His concerns gained support. By April 1943, the Cleveland Rams had only a handful of players under contract and petitioned the league to be allowed to suspend their own operations for the rest of the year. The owners approved the request. By June, Rooney and Bell were in a similar position, with just five players under contract. The rosters of the Eagles, Bears, and Cardinals also were thinning. At a league meeting in June, Rooney proposed that the Steelers and Eagles merge their squads for the 1943 season. The Bears and Cardinals also asked to merge. Fearing the power of a single Chicago team, the other owners passed a rule forbidding such mergers. But they quickly relaxed several conditions of the rule before voting on whether the Steelers and Eagles could merge.

Rooney had proposed a permanent merger of the league's two Pennsylvania franchises two years earlier, when he, Bell, and Alexis Thompson were negotiating their complex franchise sale and eventual swap. The other owners did not like the idea then, but it made sense now. Thompson, like Halas, was in the military, leaving the Eagles without an owner. But they did have sixteen players under contract, far more than Bell and Rooney in Pittsburgh. There also were larger issues to consider. The league needed eight teams to put on a season, and Cleveland was already out. If neither Philadelphia nor Pittsburgh could field squads, the 1943 season might have to be abandoned.

Some owners remained against the merger. George Preston Marshall feared that a combined Philadelphia-Pittsburgh squad would deny his Redskins a division title. Tim Mara also expressed doubts. When the proposal finally was put to a vote, it passed, but barely, by a 5–4 margin, and it included the stipulation that the merger expired at the end of the regular season. The other owners did not want the Philadelphia-Pittsburgh squad eligible to play in the championship game.

Though it had been his idea, Rooney was unhappy from the outset with the merger arrangement. It was decided that the team would wear green and white uniforms, the Eagles' colors, and practice in Philadelphia, which had a naval yard and more defense department jobs than Pittsburgh had, giving it access to more players. The home schedule would be split between the cities, but Philadelphia would host four of the six games. It almost seemed Pittsburgh had been cut out of the league. But Rooney kept his dissatisfaction to himself. He had agreed to the merger because the league needed it, not because it was in his or his city's best interests.

During training camp, it was hard to be optimistic about the "Steagles," as sportswriters quickly dubbed them. Pittsburgh's head coach, Walt Kiesling, and Philadelphia's head coach, Greasy Neale, were supposed to run the team together, but they did not get along, so Kiesling ran the defense, Neale ran the offense, and they spoke as little as possible. The team dressed just twenty-five players, eight below the limit. Most of the players were available because they were ineligible for military service. A tackle had bleeding ulcers. Another lineman was deaf in one ear. A receiver was blind in one eye. The situation appeared so bleak that Bell called Steve Owen, coach of the Giants, near the end of camp.

"Please help me, Steve," Bell said. "I hardly have enough men here to field a team. I'll take anyone you cut from your squad."

"Sorry, Bert," Owen replied. "I don't have anyone I can spare. All I have here is dog meat."

Surprisingly, though, the Steagles opened their season by winning a pair of home games over the Dodgers and Owen's "dog meat" Giants before decently sized crowds at Philadelphia's Shibe Park. That was followed a pair of lopsided road losses to the Bears and Giants, in which they allowed a combined 90 points. But their first game in Pittsburgh brought a win, and the Steagles held their own down the stretch, even defeating the Redskins in Washington. They finished with a 5-4-1 record and, more impressively, drew 34,294 fans to their last home game at Shibe Park.

Attendance was similarly strong in several other NFL cities. When the Giants and Redskins met in a playoff at the Polo Grounds to determine the East division title, the game drew 42,800. A week later, 34,320 came to Wrigley Field on the day after Christmas to watch the Bears win the league title over the Giants. Overall, some 1.1 million fans attended NFL games during the 1943 season, just short of the all-time record. It seemed that Americans wanted to watch football in wartime. There had always been, in the eyes of many, an undeniable connection between the two—the brutal sport and real battle—that underscored its appeal. Teddy Roosevelt had praised the game as an ideal training ground for military leaders. Author Stephen Crane had said he used his experiences as a football player and coach to help him write his acclaimed Civil War novel, *The Red Badge of Courage*. "I believe I got my sense of the rage of conflict on the football field," Crane said. Not long after Pearl Harbor, as the United States entered what became known as World War II, Commander Thomas J. Hamilton of the navy asserted that football was "the nearest thing to actual war."

Perhaps sports fans at home, being so far from the front, felt that supporting football was one way of connecting with the troops overseas. Attendance lagged at major league baseball games, which seemed peaceful by comparison. A game of football, however, reflected the general American experience of the early 1940s. When major college programs such as Alabama, Auburn, Stanford, Harvard, Michigan State, and many others elected not to field squads during the war, the NFL became one of the few places where fans could watch football. Even though many of its best players were overseas and its product was diluted, the NFL was thriving during the war. In fact, it was thriving *because of* the war.

Rooney, Bell, and Thompson all turned a profit with their merged squad in 1943, with Rooney making out the best because he had invested the least in the Philadelphia-based operation. At a league meeting in January 1944, though, Rooney said he would not merge the Steelers with the Eagles again. With Bell's help, he planned to field a team in Pittsburgh that year. Three months later, though, he only had five players under contract. The other owners came to Rooney with a request: Would he merge the Steelers with Charles Bidwill's Chicago Cardinals, who had gone winless in 1943 and badly needed help?

Reluctantly, Rooney assented, mostly because, again, it was what the league needed. Cleveland was back in for the 1944 season. The Eagles also were back, hoping to build on the unexpected success of pro football in Philadelphia the year before. A new team in Boston, known as the Yanks and owned by Ted Collins, a millionaire radio entrepreneur, was kicking off in 1944. That meant the league had eleven teams, but it wanted ten, a number that made scheduling easier. If the Steelers and Cardinals merged, the problem was solved. Thus was born the team known as Card-Pitt. "If we don't watch it, we could get arrested for polygamy," Steelers coach Walt Kiesling joked after the merger announcement.

After his success with a merged team the year before, and despite his reservations, Rooney was hopeful about the combined team's prospects. "We could put a weak team on the field and so could Chicago, but together, we are sure to be strong," he said. From the outset, though, this second merger was an abject disaster. Card-Pitt opened the season with a competitive loss, but the quarterback was drafted into the army before the next game, and the team never recovered. A handful of players were fined for not playing hard during a loss to the Bears, and the fined players almost quit the team entirely before meeting with Rooney and agreeing to pay what they owed. A loss to the Redskins featured a brawl so violent that police had to break it up. Rooney, the former boxer, ended up in the scrum and came close to throwing punches.

As the season unfolded, Card-Pitt lost so miserably that one sportswriter joked they should be called the "Car-pets" because everyone walked all over them. A star running back, Johnny Grigas, simply abandoned the team late in the season, explaining to Rooney that he was mentally exhausted after playing for the winless Cardinals the year before and now this winless team. In the end, Card-Pitt played ten games and lost them all, in the process tossing forty-one interceptions, a single-season league record. "We just didn't have it," Rooney lamented. Sportswriters lambasted him for merging with other teams in back-to-back seasons, depriving Pittsburgh of its own squad and of a quality product. Rooney did not even try to defend himself.

18

TWO WARS

A FTER TRAINING AIRPLANE MECHANICS AT THE BASE IN Norman, Oklahoma, for six months, George Halas received what he saw as a more desirable assignment in the spring of 1942. Finally, at age forty-seven, he went to war, joining the Seventh Fleet, the immense naval force supporting General Douglas MacArthur in the South Pacific.

Upon connecting with the fleet in Brisbane, Australia, he found he was a welfare and recreation officer, in charge of shipboard movie viewings and overseeing the construction of baseball diamonds, beer halls, and rec centers on bases. "I would have preferred a place on a warship, but looking back, I can see my years with the Bears did make me more useful in the duty the navy allocated to me," he later wrote. MacArthur personally asked him to accompany comedian Bob Hope and other celebrities on USO tours. Near the end of the war, the fleet's commander would award him a ribbon for "contributing to high morale."

While in uniform on the other side of the world, Halas managed to stay informed about the Bears, later recalling that Luke Johnsos, his coaching stand-in, would send a cable when they won and write a letter when they lost. "I think sometimes he put the letter in a bottle and dropped it in Lake Michigan," Halas wrote. When the world war ended, Halas came home to find himself immersed in a different conflict—a war in professional football that threatened the league he had worked so hard to build.

The conflict could be traced to Halas's actions before he rejoined the navy in 1942. He had all but promised a Los Angeles franchise to his friend, Charles Bidwill, who had grown tired of running the No. 2 team in a two-team town. When Bidwill suggested moving the Cardinals to the West Coast, Halas pledged to make it happen but asked Bidwill to keep the idea private while Halas cleared the way with the other owners. Then Arch Ward proposed a different plan for pro football in Los Angeles. Ward, the influential *Chicago Tribune* sports editor, was so respected by the owners that they had twice sought to hire him as their commissioner. Ward turned them down but remained in the league's inner circle. He convinced a powerhouse West Coast group to invest in pro football, and, at a league meeting in Washington on December 9, 1942, that group, led by Don Ameche, the popular movie actor, applied for a franchise for Buffalo, planning to move it to Los Angeles and begin playing when the war ended.

The day before the meeting, the Bears had played the Redskins in the championship game and lost, 14–6, at Griffith Stadium. Halas, already in the navy, had taken a brief leave to attend the game, but the real purpose of his trip was to wield his influence at the league meeting the next day. "I had promised Charley [Bidwill] I would back him when Los Angeles opened," Halas would remember. "I told Arch I could not go back on my promise to Charley. The league did not approve his [Ameche] application. Arch was furious. His anger was to prove costly."

Much like Harry March a few years earlier, Ward took revenge by forming a rival league. The timing was right, in Ward's view. No longer was the NFL widely dismissed as a poor imitation of the college game. The Bears, Redskins, and Giants were popular and profitable. Wealthy men in other cities wanted in. If he waited for the end of the war to start his league, Ward figured, Americans would be ready to spend on entertainment when the peace began, and a new league could prosper.

Helping his cause, the NFL moved cautiously without Halas present, fearful of taking a misstep. The owners were well aware that other cities wanted franchises and also knew that, structurally, their sport should eventually be able to support a second league; baseball had two leagues, after all. But the owners were skeptical of letting anyone into their exclusive club. With the country at war and several existing franchises still barely surviving, they tabled almost all expansion plans. The new franchise they approved for Ted Collins in Boston was an unusual case. When they licensed the franchise in 1943, to begin play in 1944, they did so to achieve an even number of teams and prevent scheduling headaches.

The owners' caution was apparent at a league meeting in Chicago in 1944. Prospective ownership groups from five cities made pitches. Four were so confident of receiving approval that they paid a $50,000 nonrefundable deposit, which the league had demanded. Bing Crosby headed Buffalo's group; the practice of attaching a celebrity face to an ownership group—still relatively common—has a long history. Anthony Morabito, a wealthy lumber magnate, led San Francisco's bid.

The owners turned them all down. They regarded the Buffalo market as too small because it did not have a major league baseball franchise. "Buffalo is not ready for the league," Tim Mara declared. George Preston Marshall advised Morabito to forget about pro football entirely. "We've got 10 clubs operating now. Only four have ever shown a profit. More than 40 other franchises have gone broke. Stay in the lumber business. You'll be better off," Marshall said. As the meeting ended, commissioner Elmer Layden told reporters, "We feel there is no hurry in deciding which way we want to go." But that did not satisfy Morabito. Before leaving Chicago, he met with Ward. He had heard the sports editor was recruiting prospective owners for a new league. Morabito's interest helped convince Ward it was time to launch the endeavor.

At the initial meeting in St. Louis on June 4, 1944, a name for the new league was decided on: it would be the All-America Football Conference. The form of the AAFC began to crystallize at a meeting in New York in September. The Ameche group, spurned by the NFL, would back a team in Los Angeles. Gene Tunney, the retired boxing champion, would start one in Baltimore. Morabito would have his San Francisco franchise. Arthur McBride, a taxicab entrepreneur in Cleveland, would field a team in that city. (His attempt to buy the NFL's Rams had failed.) Chicago, Buffalo, and New York also would have teams.

A few months later, the AAFC followed the NFL's lead and hired a member of Notre Dame's famed Four Horsemen backfield as its commissioner. Its choice, Jim Crowley, had gone on to coach winning teams at Michigan State and Fordham. A young lineman named Vince Lombardi had played for him at the latter school. Initially, the AAFC hoped Crowley and his former college teammate, Elmer Layden, could work together in what it called "a spirit of cooperation and friendliness," replicating baseball's arrangement with its American and National Leagues. But the NFL owners did not want to cede the monopoly they had worked so hard to build over a quarter century. Layden refused to meet with his former teammate or anyone from the AAFC and offered a tart public reply to the new league's handshake offer. "All I know of a new league is what I read in the newspapers. There is nothing to talk about as far as new leagues are concerned until someone gets a football and plays a game," Layden said in 1945. Meanwhile, Halas returned from naval duty to discover he was positioned opposite Ward in a conflict of escalating tensions and expanding size. "The rival league spoiled their friendship," Virginia McCaskey recalled. "That was such a sad development."

OTHER NFL OWNERS BESIDES HALAS ALSO FOUGHT IN THE war—the real war. Brooklyn's Dan Topping, just twenty-eight when Pearl Harbor was attacked, served in the Marines for forty-two months, twenty-six of which he spent out of the country, mostly in the Pacific. Wellington Mara enlisted in the navy as a lieutenant in early 1942 and served until the war ended, earning medals as a radar officer on aircraft carriers in both the Atlantic and Pacific theaters. Both of the Cleveland Rams' co-owners, Dan Reeves and Fred Levy, joined the Army Air Corps.

Their absences meant fewer people around the table at league meetings. Marshall, by now among the longest-tenured owners, became an even more dominant figure without Halas around, voicing his opinions so loudly he almost shook the walls. The wartime restrictions that shaped the lives of so many Americans had little impact on Marshall. He continued to spend and spend to keep the Redskins popular and successful, and he still lived extravagantly with Corinne Griffith.

Some insiders had thought the absence of hundreds of players due to the war would finally level the playing field, bringing losing teams such as the Eagles and Steelers more even with the Giants and Redskins. But the Redskins remained a power and still drew larger crowds than any team except the Giants. In 1943, when they won the East in a playoff before losing to the Bears in the championship game, they sold 206,540 tickets to six home contests, setting a franchise record.

Their head coach that year was Arthur "Dutch" Bergman, formerly the coach at Catholic University, which had discontinued football. Bergman replaced Ray Flaherty, who had gone into the navy after leading the Redskins to the league title in 1942. Marshall had never been afraid to interfere with his coaches, tell them who should be on the field, even call plays, but he had refrained with Flaherty, an authoritative former player who did not tolerate such meddling. Once Flaherty was gone, though, Marshall quickly resumed his invasive ways. Bergman lasted just one year. His replacement, one Dudley DeGroot, was a brainy Stanford graduate who held a doctorate in education and was a recognized expert in ornithology, the study of birds. He was the Redskins' sixth head coach in their thirteen-year ex-

Playing defense, the Redskins'
Sammy Baugh (33) closes in on
a tackle during a game in 1943.
(Bettmann)

istence and the easiest for Marshall to push around. "He would drive his limousine right out on the practice field and say, 'Change this guy over here,' like that,'" former Redskin Jack Doolan told sportswriter Dan Daly years later. "And DeGroot would say, 'Yeah, OK.' That's the kind of coach George wanted."

DeGroot put up with it in part because he had never coached such talent before. In 1944, the Redskins' backfield featured two star quarterbacks, Sammy Baugh and Frank Filchock. Baugh, now thirty, had received a military deferment with orders to produce beef at his Texas farm, deemed vital to the war effort. He spent his weeks in Texas and his weekends with the Redskins, a schedule that proved problematic when DeGroot, at Marshall's request, switched offenses, installing the T formation. Filchock, rejoining the team after two years in the navy, was around for practice and more able to learn the offense, but DeGroot was not about to bench Baugh. The quarterbacks split snaps on Sundays, shuttling back and forth between the sideline and field.

With Baugh flying between his Texas ranch and Washington so frequently, Marshall took out a $100,000 insurance policy on the quarterback, fearing he might die in a plane crash. Ever mindful of promotional angles, Marshall also sought to use the situation to generate headlines. The owner parked a plane by the Redskins' practice field and identified it for the press as the one Baugh used on weekends. That was just a ruse, though; the plane was a rudimentary "trainer" plane, incapable of traveling far. "I wouldn't go near that thing on a bet, let alone fly in it. It's just another of George's promotions," Baugh said with a laugh when reporters asked about the plane.

The Redskins started fast in 1944, winning five straight games after opening with a tie. Another division title seemed likely. On Sunday nights, after the latest win, Marshall and Griffith would make a grand entrance at the Blue Room of the Shoreham Hotel, where bandleader Barnee Breeskin performed. Breeskin and Griffith had cowritten "Hail to the Redskins" in the late 1930s, and now, when Breeskin saw Marshall and Griffith enter the Blue Room, he would stop his orchestra mid-song, tap his baton, and lead a rousing rendition of the city's beloved football fight song. Beaming, with his hair slicked back and a beautiful woman on his arm, Marshall appeared like a king, his mood as buoyant as ever even with America at war.

It did not last. Though they took an early lead over the Eagles before 35,540 fans at Griffith Stadium on November 19, the Redskins were crushed for the rest of the day and lost, 37–7. Suddenly, it felt like a burden to have two quarterbacks operating a new offense. Baugh's arrangement came under scrutiny and criticism from the parents of soldiers wondering why the quarterback was allowed to flout the travel restrictions in place during the war. The Redskins ended the season with a pair of losses to the Giants, who took the East title. The biggest surprise, perhaps, was that Dudley DeGroot survived Marshall's ire and kept his job.

ARCH WARD WAS NOT THE ONLY SPORTS ENTREPRENEUR WHO believed America would be ready for another pro football league after the war. Two other leagues, the Trans-America Football League and the United States Football League, also appeared, with plans to begin play when the war ended.

The TAFL boldly proposed a merger with the NFL that would result in a sixteen-team league—eleven from the NFL and five from the TAFL. The NFL owners immediately dismissed the idea. Though their league was still not on firm footing, they did not see the benefit in merging with a league composed of teams that had never played a down. In the end, the TAFL folded before a game was played.

The USFL lasted somewhat longer, having received a flurry of attention after announcing Red Grange as its commissioner. Now an author and broadcaster, Grange was still football royalty. But his league's demise was effectively sealed on the day it announced it had eight teams and planned to kick off in 1945. "Our club owners are all good businessmen, not millionaires," Grange told reporters. He did not realize that a new league needed millionaires. Lacking the necessary backing, the USFL never got off the ground.

Ward's AAFC was in much better shape with an ownership group that included millionaires such as McBride and Morabito, as well as James Brueil, an oilman from Buffalo; Ben Lindheimer, a developer and race track owner from Chicago, who was Ameche's coinvestor in the Los Angeles franchise; and John Keeshin, a Chicago trucking magnate. The AAFC had the resources to present a serious challenge to the NFL.

On February 13, 1945, the new league announced the signing of Paul Brown, a highly regarded thirty-seven-year-old coach who had won at Ohio State and, before that, at a high school in Massillon, Ohio. During the war, he had coached at the Great Lakes Naval Training Base, where Halas served during World War I. Most fans had expected Brown to return to Ohio State, but McBride lured him to Cleveland's AAFC franchise with an unprecedented offer, a five-year deal worth $25,000 per season, which was more than the league's commissioner made. Now no one in the NFL could doubt that the AAFC was a true threat.

Two months later, in early May, the real war in Europe ended with Germany's surrender. Japan surrendered in August, days after American planes dropped atomic bombs on Hiroshima and Nagasaki. As the rhythm and rituals of normal American life slowly resumed, NFL players returned from military service to find the landscape of professional football changed. Though the AAFC would not begin playing until 1946, Crowley told reporters that the league already had 150 players under contract, including some from the Redskins and Bears.

For its part, the NFL experienced a strange season in the fall of 1945. Dozens of players returned from the war and put their football uniforms back on, and the status quo exploded. The Giants, Bears, and Packers—three of the four teams that had long dominated on the field—fell out of playoff contention. Alexis Thompson's Eagles rose up and challenged the Redskins for the East division title. The Rams shot to the top of the West division behind Bob Waterfield, a rookie quarterback from UCLA whose pro debut had been delayed by an injury and the war.

Some things remained the same. After two years of shotgun mergers with other teams, Art Rooney brought the Steelers back to Pittsburgh, determined to go it alone. But with an assistant coach in charge of a no-name roster, the team won just two games. The Redskins shut them out twice. Marshall's team still controlled the East. After beating Pittsburgh a second time, the Redskins just needed to defeat the Giants in their season finale at Griffith Stadium on December 9 to wrap up their fifth division title in nine years in Washington.

But, several days before the game, Marshall and the other owners received a shock. On December 6, 1945, Dan Topping, who had owned the league's Brooklyn franchise since 1931, called a press conference in New York to announce he was abandoning the NFL and jumping to the AAFC starting in 1946. Now the new league *really* had the NFL's attention. Though just thirty-three, Topping was wealthier than Halas, Bell, Rooney, and the NFL's other decision-makers—perhaps wealthier than all of them combined. Topping's grandfather, Daniel Reid, had amassed a fortune in the tin-plate business; started the American Can Company; invested in railroads, tobacco, and banks; and left most of his estate, valued at between $40 million and $50 million, to Topping's mother. Topping could do as he pleased. Earlier in 1945, he and two partners had spent $2.8 million to buy baseball's New York Yankees, the most storied and probably the most valuable franchise in the sport.

The sale had included Yankee Stadium, the majestic ballpark in the Bronx where the Yankees had played since 1923. That meant Topping now owned a stadium, a claim no other NFL owner could make; they all rented their home fields. That only increased Topping's desire to change his football team's status quo. He was tired of owning a Brooklyn team that played in the long shadow of Tim Mara's Giants. A handsome playboy who would marry six times, Topping thought he deserved better. He had more money than Mara. He owned the Yankees. He thought *he* belonged in the spotlight, not Mara.

But there was a problem with his grand vision. Mara had held the NFL's territorial rights to New York since the 1920s. Any league matter involving the city had to go through him. The other NFL owners were sympathetic to Topping's plight. His Brooklyn franchise had lost what little following it had during the war. Brooklyn and Ted Collins's Boston Yanks had been forced to merge for the 1945 season. Chafing at the situation, Topping had told the owners he was set on moving his team from Ebbets Field to Yankee Stadium in 1946. Reluctantly, Mara had agreed to work with him to find a peaceful way forward. They met at Mara's office in late November 1945 to divide up home dates for the next season, so Mara's Giants and Topping's Yanks—the name he wanted to use—would never play at home on the same day. Each wanted as many home dates as possible later in the year, after the baseball season ended, when football attendance always picked up.

Mara took some dates and offered Topping others. The Giants' owner thought the meeting went well and expected to hear soon that Topping had submitted prospective home dates to Elmer Layden for league approval. But the next time Mara and Topping spoke was a few minutes before the December press conference at which Topping announced he was leaving the NFL for the AAFC. Topping wanted to give Mara the news personally before making it public.

At the press conference, held in the Yankees' offices at Yankee Stadium, Topping issued what amounted to a declaration of war. He announced he was hiring Ray Flaherty, the former Giant who had won two NFL titles as the Redskins' coach, to coach his New York Yanks in the AAFC. The team would be filled with players from his defunct NFL team, he said. He reminded all present that Yankee Stadium could hold as many as 90,000 fans for football games, and he planned to fill it.

The NFL had previously faced competition from rival leagues such as the "Grange League" in 1926 and the American Football League in the 1930s. Every time, the new league had attempted to establish itself initially in New York, turning Mara and the Giants into the NFL's first line of defense. In the previous instances, Mara and the Giants had held their ground, prompting the rival league to fold. This latest challenge appeared far more formidable, however. According to the *New York Times*, "It had been the contention of observers ever since the AAFC was first conceived that it could not quite attain the status of a major football circuit until it operated a franchise in New York. Now that this has been achieved, and with the vast Yankee Stadium and its proposed 90,000 capacity providing the setting, the path of the new league to a major ranking seems assured." The *Times* added, "Everything is set for a war to the hilt for local patronage."

Mara was among the NFL's most respected owners, but his colleagues were perturbed with him now. Topping would not have bolted, they thought, if Mara had granted him more late-season dates at Yankee Stadium. Asked to comment on Topping's defection, Mara launched into an emotional defense of his franchise, as if he and it were under attack. "We've spent years of time and heaps of money building up the Giants to where they are today," he declared. "I wouldn't take a million dollars for the franchise. It may not be worth that much but it is to the Mara family." He sought to downplay the significance of Topping's defection. "All it has done has been to balance our league better," he told the *Times,* explaining that it would have proved awkward to have two teams in Manhattan and eleven overall. Marshall made a similar claim, telling the paper the move "will help our league by clearing things up all around." Marshall added dryly, "I hope that Topping does better in the new league than he did in the old one."

Halas did not comment. He had just reentered civilian life in November, having received a Bronze Star from the navy. With his return, all seats at the NFL's ownership table finally were filled for the first time since 1942, and important league business could once again be decided.

The war years had scarred certain teams in the NFL. To survive, five had been forced to merge with another for at least one season, and another had skipped a season altogether. None could pledge to their fans a rosy future. Once again, the trajectory of the league was not one of constant ascent but, rather, of advances followed by challenges and setbacks. Overall, though, the decision to continue playing during the war years could not have worked out better. If the NFL had halted operations, it might have lost many fans who simply forgot about pro football and never returned; the country was hardly obsessed with the sport at the time, after all. Resuming play after such a prolonged hiatus, the league could well have been fatefully diminished. At a minimum, it would have begun its conflict with the AAFC on almost equal footing, a dangerous proposition.

The AAFC, with its millionaire owners and big plans, had loosed a counterproductive line of thinking among the NFL's owners. They had always grasped that they needed to work together, that the good of the league should supersede their own interests. But, with the AAFC looming, that focus on the collective had given way to the idea that it might be time for them to look out for themselves. Topping certainly had done that. In the coming weeks, Bert Bell, a true insider, would meet with Jim Crowley, commissioner of the AAFC, and discuss the possibility of putting a team in Philadelphia, Bell's hometown. Dan Reeves, the Rams' owner, would demand that he be allowed to move his struggling franchise from Cleveland to Los Angeles. If the other owners did not allow it, he said, he was through with them.

Suddenly, it seemed everything was up for grabs. Although the NFL had survived the real war with palpable momentum in many cities, it was under siege like never before, both from outside and from within. With Halas back, though, it was fully armed for the looming conflict with the AAFC—a conflict that, indeed, would test the strength of the collaborative instincts the NFL had developed over the years.

19

THE RIGHT GUY IN CHARGE

Days before the Rams played the Redskins for the league championship on December 16, 1945, eighteen inches of snow fell on Cleveland. Another front moved in on the day of the game. The temperature was eight below zero in the morning and around zero at kickoff. Dan Reeves, owner of the Rams, had hoped for a crowd that demonstrated Cleveland had arrived as a legitimate pro football town. The Rams had mostly struggled since joining the NFL eight years earlier and had even suspended operations for a season during the war. Now, though, they had a winning team and a marketable young quarterback, Bob Waterfield, who was married to Jane Russell, the sultry Hollywood actress.

Cleveland's fans had gone wild for Waterfield and the Rams, prompting Reeves to move the site of the championship game. His team normally played at League Field, a deteriorating brick bandbox with 30,000 seats. Anticipating a much larger crowd with a title on the line and the powerful Redskins visiting Cleveland for the first time, Reeves rented Municipal Stadium, the cavernous home of the Indians, the city's major league baseball team. It could hold more than 80,000 fans.

Some 40,000 tickets had been sold, a record for the Rams, but Reeves was disappointed not to sell more, and now, given the weather, some of those 40,000 fans would surely stay home and listen to the game on the radio rather than venture outside. Many streets across Cleveland still had not been plowed. When George Preston Marshall and his wife, Corinne Griffith, arrived at the stadium and took their seats before kickoff, they were surprised to see fans departing. The stadium was adjacent to Lake Erie. Brutal winds howled around the bowl. "I didn't think I could take it," Griffith would later write. "Icy gusts of wind, leftovers from the recent blizzard, swept frozen bits of snow high in the air and held them there to diffuse an already pale winter sun. Other stray blasts, roaring through the stadium, blew in relentless spasms against the early arrivals."

Marshall and Griffith did stay, and, in the end, 32,178 fans witnessed a dramatic contest. Reeves had thought of an ingenious way to protect the field before the blizzard arrived. He ordered bales of hay and paid a crew of city workers to spread the straw on the turf before the storm hit. The workers returned hours before kickoff and shoveled the snow and hay off the field. The process left slush piled high behind the benches and end zones, but the playing field was relatively clear. Even with the whipping winds, Waterfield and the Redskins' Sammy Baugh could operate as normal.

The Rams scored first on a fluke play. With the ball on the Redskins' 5 yard line, Baugh took a snap and retreated into the end zone to throw a pass. He saw an open receiver and fired the ball in his direction, but it hit one of the goalpost uprights and fell to the turf in the end zone. According to the rules, when a pass fell incomplete without crossing the goal line, the defensive team was awarded a safety. Cleveland led, 2–0. In his seat, Marshall cursed the little-known rule. He and the other owners had moved the posts to the goal line to enhance scoring by making field goals easier to convert. That change had worked, but this "safety" rule, an addendum, was in Marshall's sights now. It would be gone from the rulebook by the start of the next season. From then on, a pass that fell to the turf in the end zone was just another incompletion.

Baugh soon left the game with bruised ribs, but his replacement, Frank Filchock, threw a 37-yard touchdown pass to give the Redskins the lead in the second quarter. The Rams regained it before halftime on a Waterfield touchdown pass. Waterfield's extra point attempt—he also kicked and played safety—was partially blocked, but it fluttered to the goal posts and landed on the crossbar for a tantalizing second before rolling across, giving the Rams a point that eventually proved decisive.

Waterfield hurled another touchdown pass in the third quarter, but he missed the extra point, leaving the Rams ahead, 15–7. The Redskins rallied before the quarter ended, with Filchock leading a long drive that ended with a short touchdown pass. Trailing by a point, the Redskins threatened to score throughout the fourth quarter, but Waterfield saved a touchdown by tripping up a Washington back in an otherwise open field, and the Redskins' kicker, Joe Aguirre, missed field goal attempts of 46 and 31 yards. When the final gun sounded, a few fans stormed the field to celebrate the Rams' victory—but most headed for home or the nearest bar to warm up.

Reeves had mixed emotions. It was exhilarating to win, particularly against a league standard-bearer such as the Redskins, but between the stadium rental and hay purchase, he had invested so much in the game that he ended up losing money; not even the largest pro football crowd in Cleveland history could save him. He also had lost money on the season—a *championship* season. And now the AAFC was bringing a team to Cleveland, and, with Paul Brown as its coach, the competition for the city's fans would be formidable. Meanwhile, Reeves had coveted the possibility of moving to Los Angeles for several years, expressing his desire to his fellow owners. They had denied him. Now, emboldened by his championship and his celebrity quarterback, and unenthused by the prospect of a turf war in Cleveland, he was determined to go.

Marshall himself also was weighing a change, though of a different kind. Despite the defeat in Cleveland, the Redskins were winners, and consistently profitable, too. Marshall was having so much fun and making so much money that he no longer wanted to run a team *and* a chain of laundries. Within months, he would sell his controlling interest in the Palace Laundry and Dry Cleaning Corporation to his partner, an old friend named John Chevalier.

When the Redskins opened training camp the next summer, they were favored to win the East again. Marshall could focus solely on his team. At fifty, he was known now as a sportsman, not a laundryman. Baseball's Washington Senators had descended into mediocrity, drawing puny crowds. In less than a decade, the Redskins had come to rule Washington. But World War II was over, and society was changing in ways he did not—could not—comprehend. Marshall and his team would be left behind. Indeed, the game he had just witnessed in Cleveland was the last championship contest he would see his beloved Redskins play.

THE NATION'S NEWSPAPERS REPORTED THAT THE NFL OWNERS had decided to meet in a special session at the Commodore Hotel in New York in early January 1946. But, in reality, only one owner thought the meeting was necessary. With the AAFC threat looming, Halas believed the league could not hesitate to move on what he saw as a series of critical issues.

Most sportswriters covering the session did not expect fireworks. The owners needed to strike a new deal with Elmer Layden, whose five-year contract as commissioner was expiring. But it was widely assumed Layden would keep the job. Halas had other ideas. He got along well with the mild-mannered Layden, but he thought the league needed a more combative leader if it was going to beat back the AAFC. Layden was friendly with Arch Ward and hesitant to confront him. Layden also had bungled the Dan Topping situation, Halas believed, by neglecting to treat Topping's festering dissatisfaction. A more able commissioner never would have allowed Topping to defect, Halas believed. Working the phones before the special session began, Halas garnered support for a change. It turned out the other owners also were not happy with Layden. His hiring had brought attention to the league five years earlier, but Marshall and Art Rooney wanted a more imposing personality to lead the league. When the owners gathered informally the night before the New York meeting began, Marshall remarked that Layden would continue as commissioner "over my dead body."

Shortly after Layden opened the meeting the next morning, a vote was taken on whether to approve extending his contract. Only three owners voted for him. Layden, surprised and saddened, was told to leave the meeting and wait in his hotel room. Once the former Notre Dame fullback was gone, a discussion commenced on who should replace him. Halas asked Bert Bell to leave the room, too. Halas wanted to make Bell the commissioner.

Some of the other owners expressed doubt, wondering whether Bell, with his ready smile and gregariousness, had the necessary gravitas. His record in the sport certainly did not shine. He had lost money and games as an owner and coach in both Philadelphia and Pittsburgh. How did that make him a viable candidate to run the league?

But Halas saw him differently, believing Bell was one of the few men with the right vision for professional football and for the NFL in particular. It had been Bell who proposed a draft to make the league more competitive—a goal that was finally being realized. Bell also had sat on the league's management council, so he had a hand in numerous major decisions. From his role in the various franchise swaps and mergers that had enabled the Eagles and Steelers to survive during the war, it was clear he was a skilled dealmaker. "Bell's mission in life was football. He had a sure instinct for conducting the business of the game," Halas said later. Halas held Bell in such high regard that he had even asked for a scouting report on a prospective son-in-law.

But most important, in Halas's view, was that Bell was a member of the small fraternity of men who had run the league for several decades. "There were other guys in the room, but Halas, Marshall, Bell, Rooney, Mara, and Bidwill were in charge. It was a crucial moment for the league and they thought it was time for one of their own to become the commissioner," Rooney's son, Dan, recalled. "And Bert could do it. Halas couldn't do it. Marshall couldn't do it. But Bert could."

Halas called for a vote. Seven owners supported Bell—a majority. Still, Halas asked for another vote, thinking it was important that the league show its unanimous support for Bell. A second vote produced just that.

Returning to the room, Bell was overjoyed at the decision. He had long ago wasted his fortune, and, though he and his family were comfortable, he had typical financial concerns. The commissioner's job, with its $20,000 salary, would provide security for his wife and three children. He also would make money selling his half-interest in the Steelers to Rooney—a stipulation of his taking the new job.

In a session with reporters after the owners' meeting, he mused about changes he wanted to make. He wanted to start the season earlier, so it could end in early December. Never again, he said, should a title be decided in wintry conditions such as those the Rams and Redskins had just endured in Cleveland. He also thought that more night games would boost attendance and that NFL radio announcers should be taught to emphasize to their audiences what was different and special about the pro game, drawing a starker contrast to college football. The pro game held up well in such comparisons, Bell told reporters, as it boasted more passing, scoring, and excitement.

Most of the other owners were excited about Bell. "Now we have a pro running our league and they have an amateur," Marshall said, referring to the AAFC's Jim Crowley, whose main qualification was that he had been one of the Four Horsemen. (Layden, of course, had been another.) The football press also gave the hiring its approval. Bell "speaks the pro football language," the *New York Times* wrote, and "is aware of the problems of each and every owner, as well as the league itself. He seems admirably equipped for the job, even though he takes over in a time of crisis. It's almost as if the NFL said to the AAFC,

Left to right, seated, at a league meeting after World War II: Art Rooney; Wellington Mara; commissioner Bert Bell; Curly Lambeau, Packers; Fred Mandel Jr., Lions. Standing: Dan Reeves, Rams; Walter Halas, Bears; Jack Mara, Giants; Roy Benningsen, Cardinals; George Preston Marshall; Al Ennis, Eagles; Ralph Brizzolara, Bears. (Associated Press)

'OK, you asked for a fight and we'll give it to you because Bert Bell is the best scrapper we have.'"

Privately, Bell marveled at the twisting path he had taken to reach this moment. His father had helped found the NCAA, which oversaw college football. Bell had championed the college game as a young man, disdaining the pros. But now he was a pro league's most prominent and capable defender. At age fifty, the former quarterback and Philadelphia socialite had a sizable paunch, but he had not lost any of his passion for the sport.

When he banged the gavel to open his first meeting as commissioner on January 12, 1946, he was immediately greeted with an epic crisis. Dan Reeves had not relented on his demand to move the

Rams from Cleveland to Los Angeles. Reeves's general manager, Chile Walsh, stood by the head table and argued passionately for moving the team while Reeves sat quietly, listening. He needed eight votes for approval. Six owners supported him. Leading the opposition was Halas, who argued that travel to the West Coast would be unaffordable for the rest of the teams, an argument he had made many times to keep Los Angeles vacant. A vote was scheduled. Reeves stood up to leave. Before he departed, he turned and spoke solemnly to the group. "Gentlemen," he said, "you who know me know that I never bluff. I am not trying to force you into any action you might consider detrimental to the league. But when I return to this room after you have voted on my proposal, I am announcing that unless you go along with me, all of my stock in the Cleveland club will be for sale. I am getting out. No bolting, understand, for I do not expect to go with the All America Conference. But I am leaving the National Football League."

Los Angeles's pro football vacancy had caused the fissure between Arch Ward and Halas, so upsetting Ward that he started another league. Now it appeared the Los Angeles issue might produce more unsettling headlines. Bell called a recess and told Halas, Marshall, and Bidwill to go speak to Reeves. Bell wanted to figure out a way to satisfy Reeves, even if meant allowing him to move. Bell was not opposed. The AAFC was starting a franchise in Los Angeles, and whatever costs the move would impose on the NFL's other teams, the necessity of competing with the upstart league in one of the country's largest markets seemed to outweigh them.

Halas had known that his fellow owners would eventually turn against him on this issue. He had prepared himself for this moment in two ways, by accepting its inevitability and by persuading Bidwill to back away from the idea of moving to Los Angeles. Halas had told his longtime friend that the Bears and Cardinals needed to work together to defeat the well-funded AAFC team that was coming to Chicago with the intent to win over the city. Halas exhorted Bidwill to redouble his effort to make the Cardinals flourish in Chicago. Ever amenable, Bidwill agreed to try. That meant Halas could bless the move of another owner into Los Angeles, and he did not have any particular objections to that owner being Reeves.

Sitting in Reeves's hotel room, Halas, Reeves, Marshall, and Bidwill negotiated the terms for the Los Angeles team. League rules stipulated that home teams guaranteed visitors $5,000 for regular-season games. Reeves agreed to guarantee $10,000 for his home games, which would help defray the visitors' travel costs. That allowed the deal to go through. On Bell's first day as commissioner, he had helped orchestrate the most momentous franchise move in league history.

THE OWNERS' SPECIAL SESSION TURNED INTO A MARATHON LASTing almost a week. Bell's agenda grew and grew. He brought in travel agents to explain the air and rail options for trips to California. One day was devoted to the draft. Bell advised teams not to reveal their selections to anyone outside the room so they could negotiate with their players without interference from the AAFC.

The owners and their new commissioner girded themselves for war. They announced a five-year ban of players who signed with the AAFC. They ratified an amendment to the league constitution limiting the NFL to ten franchises—the current number—in the belief that that would discourage any AAFC owners who secretly hoped to end up in the NFL if the leagues merged. Instinctively, Bell decided on an approach for dealing with the AAFC in public. He would ignore it. In the coming years, he would seldom comment on any aspect of the rival league, even when reporters prompted him.

When the marathon meeting finally adjourned, Bell took a train home to Philadelphia. By the time he walked in his front door, another crisis had erupted, this time with him in the middle of it. Jim Crowley, commissioner of the AAFC, had told the Associated Press that the NFL's new commissioner had recently considered jumping to the new league. Crowley and Bell had met in Philadelphia to discuss the possibility, Crowley claimed. Two other men were part of a potential ownership group for an AAFC team in

Philadelphia, according to Crowley, and Bell was involved because—this was a bombshell—he had taken out a lease on the football rights to Shibe Park, one of the city's main sports venues. The lease deal seemed to support the allegation that Bell truly had considered joining the AAFC. Why else would the Pittsburgh Steelers' co-owner take out a stadium lease in another city?

Following up, the New York *Daily News* intimated that Bell was interested in the AAFC until George Halas heard about it and came up with a solution. One AAFC owner told the paper "it is pretty plain" that Halas guaranteed Bell the commissioner's job to ensure he did not jump leagues. That claim was debatable. In fact, the NFL owners had hired Bell for a multitude of reasons, one of which was that he could think on his feet. He now put that skill to use trying to stamp out the story. It was true he had spoken to Crowley, he said, but he denied any interest in owning an AAFC team, claiming the other prospective owners had brought him into their conversation with Crowley only because he held the Shibe Park lease.

One of those other prospective owners corroborated Bell's story. "Bert at no time represented us," said Walter Donovan, owner of Garden State Park, a racetrack. But why had Bell leased Shibe Park? He had an answer: he wanted to keep an AAFC team from playing there. "There was no secret about it. The whole [NFL] knew," Bell said. He also denied that Halas had promised him the commissioner's job to keep him in the NFL.

The story lingered for several days, with one Philadelphia paper suggesting that Bell had considered trying to run the Eagles out of business by refusing to allow them to continue to play in Shibe Park, where they had averaged 30,804 fans for six home games in 1945. Then Bell's Steelers could move to Philadelphia, the paper suggested. But this accusation made little sense. The Eagles, after struggling for years, finally were winning games and drawing crowds. Why would Bell want to kill off the team he had founded? In any case, the Eagles themselves supported Bell's version of the story. "We knew Bert was talking to Crowley," the team's general manager said. "We thought it was smart to have him find out as much as possible about the new league. Everyone in the NFL has the highest respect for Bert."

The story died. Bell went to work. He moved the commissioner's office from Chicago, where Layden lived, to New York but quickly tired of commuting. The owners let him operate out of Philadelphia. He opened an office in a second-floor space over a men's clothing shop near the Penn campus. A sportswriter visiting him there said customers in the men's shop could easily hear the NFL's most powerful man conducting the league's business in his booming voice. Bell later moved the office to Center City.

Both at home and wherever he worked, Bell had a telephone in his ear as he conversed with owners, coaches, and other league officials. "There was a phone in the bedroom. A phone on the landing. A phone on the first floor. A phone in what he called his office. You could just about kill yourself on those long extension cords he had running all over the place," his son, Upton, would later write, describing the scene at home. "He'd be walking back and forth, a cigarette in his left hand and a phone in his right, talking to owners like George Preston Marshall."

His immediate priority was finalizing the schedule for the 1946 season. The owners had failed to agree on one at the meeting in Philadelphia; as always, various stadium conflicts and individual requests, as well as personal jealousies, had prevented a solution. "All of the clubs were very jealous of the schedules and no one trusted anyone. After a while people started walking out of the meetings and saying 'Let Bert do it,'" Wellington Mara would recall. Bell sat down with the list of conflicts and requests. He decided to build the schedule around the idea that the weaker teams should play each other early in the season, enabling some of them to win games, stay in contention longer, and hopefully sell more tickets. He drew up a schedule, tested it with different owners, and made corrections. After settling on a version that seemed to satisfy everyone, he sold it to the owners at a league meeting in April. Bell called it the most harmonious meeting he had ever attended. "Only once did anyone raise his voice. That was

George Marshall," Bell commented. "I told him, 'Keep your shirt on, George.' He apologized."

By the end of the year, the owners would raise Bell's annual salary to $30,000 and add two more years to his original three-year deal. He would receive another extension soon enough. From a most surprising place—the lower echelon of its franchises—the NFL had found its ideal commissioner. Indeed, Bell would keep the job for the rest of his life, becoming one of the most important and influential figures in league history.

PART FOUR

20

BACK ACROSS THE COLOR LINE

A MERICANS WERE READY TO ENJOY THE PEACE THAT FOL-lowed their country's military victory. The war effort had provided jobs for millions, and, with restrictions lifted and triumph in the air, people crowded into bars, restaurants, movie theaters, and ballparks, ready to spend their money.

Sports experienced a soaring renewal. On May 4, 1946, the Kentucky Derby, America's foremost horse race, drew more than 100,000 spectators for the first time, according to the race's organizers. A colt named Assault won, and then he also won the Preakness Stakes and Belmont Stakes to capture the sport's Triple Crown as millions listened on the radio. In June, boxers Joe Louis and Billy Conn fought for a title at the Polo Grounds in another event that captured headlines, with Bert Bell among the celebrities sitting ringside.

No sport was seen as more distinctly American than baseball—during the war, Japanese soldiers had taunted US soldiers with cries of "Fuck Babe Ruth!"—and no sport came back stronger. Dan Topping's Yankees drew 2.265 million fans to seventy-seven home games in 1946, smashing their season attendance record. The Brooklyn Dodgers, Detroit Tigers, and Boston Red Sox also set records for season attendance. Overall, major league crowds nearly tripled compared to three years earlier. The radio rights to the World Series sold for $150,000, a record fee, and the Red Sox and St. Louis Cardinals played a taut series that mesmerized the nation.

College football rosters had been so gutted by the war that some schools could not field teams. But the sport returned in 1946, and so did its fans. Notre Dame twice drew more than 70,000 to games and never played before fewer than 50,000. Michigan and Illinois drew 85,938 to an October game in Ann Arbor, Michigan. Southern Cal and UCLA played before 93,714 at the Los Angeles Memorial Coliseum in November. For the second year in a row, the college football season peaked with what the media dubbed "the Game of the Century." A year earlier, Army and Navy had been ranked No. 1 and No. 2 when they played in a sold-out Municipal Stadium in Philadelphia; it was such an event that President Harry Truman had attended. Now, a year later, Army and Notre Dame were No. 1 and No. 2 when they met at the Polo Grounds, with war heroes General Dwight Eisenhower and Admiral Chester Nimitz in the crowd.

The NFL owners believed they could take a similar leap forward. Although they now had to contend for gate receipts with the AAFC, the NFL had the advantage of a quarter century of tradition, and, though the league had experienced various troubles during the war, there had been positive signs as well. The strongest teams—the Giants, Bears, and Redskins—had drawn large crowds, and formerly lesser teams such as the Eagles and Rams had finally become competitive. The Bears' Sid Luckman had commented at one point during the war that so many players were missing that the NFL had become a semi-professional league, but with dozens of popular players back now, that was no longer the case. The owners expected their product to become more exciting and interesting.

But pro football still lagged behind baseball, horse racing, boxing, and college football. The NFL's 1945 championship game had drawn a crowd of 32,178, a pittance compared to the teeming throngs that gathered for major horse races and boxing matches and important games in other sports. The radio rights to the NFL championship game had sold for a fraction of what the rights to the World Series sold for. Outside of Chicago, New York, and Washington, sports fans still—after twenty-five years—paid comparatively little attention to the NFL. Part of the problem was the league was still very much a regional enterprise, confined to the East Coast and Midwest. Much of the country simply never saw pro games. That would change with Dan Reeves's move to Los Angeles, as would another longstanding feature of the NFL: its all-white racial composition.

THE RAMS WANTED TO PLAY AT THE LOS ANGELES MEMORIAL Coliseum, a massive public venue. The team's general manager, Chile Walsh, appeared at a meeting of the nine-man commission that ran the stadium on January 15, 1946, asking for a lease deal. Haley Harding, a sports reporter for the *Los Angeles Tribune*, a black weekly newspaper, took the floor at the meeting and pointed out that no NFL team had employed a black player since 1933. Harding suggested it was wholly inappropriate to use a taxpayer-funded stadium to effectively sanction segregation. The commission agreed. Pledging that no player would be barred from the Coliseum because of his skin color, it approved a lease deal with the Rams on the condition that they attempt to integrate.

Walsh promised they would grant tryouts to black players. Two months later, on March 21, they signed Kenny Washington, a black receiver who had earned All-American honors while playing for UCLA before the war. Now twenty-seven, he had played for semipro teams and worked as a policeman to make ends meet. "I have heard many fine things about Washington, both as a player and as a man, and I feel certain he will be a credit to our ball club and to his race," Chile Walsh said. "I look for other teams in the league to accept him in good grace, just as he has always been given fair treatment and won the respect of all who have played with him and against him in intercollegiate football and in his professional play on the West Coast during the past five seasons."

Walsh's comment amounted to a warning to the other NFL owners and teams to accept the signing of Washington. It was a delicate subject, to put it mildly. The league had fielded entirely white rosters for more than a decade. But the Rams had no choice but to integrate. Within weeks, they reached a deal with Woody Strode, another black receiver who had played at UCLA.

Bob Snyder, the Rams' backfield coach, later conceded that financial concerns, rather than tolerance or even special concern for the situation of black Americans, guided the Rams' decision making. They needed Washington and Strode to obtain a lease on the Coliseum. "I doubt we would have been interested in Washington if we had stayed in Cleveland," Snyder said. If the Rams hoped the rest of the league would understand, they were quickly disappointed. "All hell broke loose," Snyder said. Although the owners would always deny they had agreed to exclude black players for more than a decade, it seems clear in hindsight that they had an understanding. Several dozen black players had suited up for NFL teams from the league's first year in 1920 through 1933, but rosters had gone entirely white starting in 1934.

This was not unusual at the time. Many major American institutions were still segregated or otherwise governed by Jim Crow–era attitudes in 1946. Major league baseball would not integrate until Jackie Robinson debuted with the Brooklyn Dodgers a year later. America's military forces had been segregated for decades and would remain so until 1948, when President Harry Truman signed an executive order forcing their integration.

If, in fact, all hell did break loose in the NFL after the Rams leapt across the league's color line, it is likely George Preston Marshall voiced his displeasure most vehemently. He had impacted the NFL in many positive ways during his fifteen years as an owner, pushing for rules to promote scoring, for the owners to make their games more of a show, and for the league to be divided into two divisions with the season culminating in a championship contest. But his position on integration was a negative influence. The Redskins' owner was, simply, a racist. Blacks belonged in their place, he believed, and that place was not the NFL. Although Marshall seldom discussed his attitude publicly, when he did, his distaste for the idea of integration was manifest. "In ordinary conversation, Marshall refers to Negroes in a manner which leaves little doubt that his objection to them is based purely along racial lines," *Sport* magazine would write about him.

Years earlier, Marshall had told another interviewer it was a bad idea to mix black and white players on a team because the whites might harm the blacks. Indeed, in the 1930s and 1940s, college football in the South remained strictly segregated and some southern players now in the NFL were opposed to playing with and against African Americans. But the majority of professional-caliber white players had no problem with it. After Kenny Washington played for the College All-Stars against the Green Bay Packers in 1940, a New York columnist urged Tim Mara to sign him. "He played on the same field with boys who are going to be scattered throughout the league. And he played against the champion Packers. There wasn't a bit of trouble anywhere," Jimmy Powers wrote in the *Daily News*.

Marshall was resolute. He also maintained a business rationale for keeping NFL rosters white. His team in Washington was the league's southernmost franchise, and, from the start of his time there, he had sought to profit from the situation, selling the Redskins as the South's pro team. They had a regional network of radio stations that broadcast their games deep into the South. Marshall encouraged his coaches to sign players from southern colleges, reinforcing the bond between the Redskins and the region. Marshall had long assumed that fans of his team, both in Washington and beyond, preferred not to see African Americans playing for *either* team in an NFL game.

By 1946, however, racial strictures and attitudes were beginning to change, at least in some parts of the country. President Franklin Roosevelt had integrated the defense industry during the war, a prelude to the integration of the military that would soon occur. Baseball's Dodgers had signed Robinson in October 1945, anticipating that he would need a year of grooming in the minor leagues before braving the majors, where, indeed, he was greeted with fury and contempt by many fans.

George Halas had considered integrating the Bears before the war, after watching Kenny Washington play in the College All-Star Game in 1940. Washington had led the nation in total offense as a senior at UCLA, and, after he made several sparkling runs against the Packers, Halas asked that he stay in Chicago after the game, perhaps while Halas tried to talk the other NFL owners into letting him sign Washington. But Washington eventually went home unsigned.

Art Rooney also had contemplated signing black players after watching several perform for a military team against the Steelers in a wartime charity exhibition game. Rooney's attitude on race was far different than Marshall's. Rooney "practiced civil rights before it became fashionable," said a relative of Cum Posey, a black sports entrepreneur who owned the Homestead Grays, Pittsburgh's powerhouse team in baseball's Negro leagues. Rooney and Posey had developed a close friendship after meeting in the early 1920s. Both were former athletes who had turned to the business side of sports. Rooney's semipro baseball teams barnstormed with the Grays for many years. Posey, a decade older, advised Rooney on organizing and operating teams. Later, Rooney lent Posey money that kept the Grays afloat.

Around Pittsburgh, Rooney was viewed as a progressive on race. He had never hesitated to put black players on his semipro rosters in the 1920s and early 1930s. The Steelers were one of the last NFL teams to field a black player before the league went all-white starting in 1934. In the end, though, Rooney cooperated with the NFL's unwritten all-white dictum—probably out of "deference to the league and his coaches," according to his biographers. Even after the Rams reintegrated in 1946, he hesitated to follow their lead; the Steelers did not sign a black player until 1952. The *Pittsburgh Courier,* the city's black newspaper, praised Rooney's many shows of tolerance in an editorial in 1947 but also chided him about the Steelers' all-white roster. "What about the Steelers, Mr. Rooney?" the *Courier* asked.

Rooney's slow response to the Rams' reintegration was typical of the entire league's reaction. After the Rams signed Washington and Strode in 1946, two years passed before another black player joined the NFL. In 1951, the Bears, Steelers, and Redskins still fielded all-white teams.

The AAFC's Cleveland Browns were the only other pro football team to integrate in 1946. As they opened training camp that summer, Paul Brown signed Bill Willis, a black defensive lineman who had played for him at Ohio State. After Willis quickly proved in practice that he deserved a starting spot, Brown signed another black player, fullback Marion Motley, who had starred for Brown's Great Lakes Naval Training Base team during the war.

Willis and Motley performed so well for the Browns in 1946 that they were named to the all-league team. Their teammates accepted them, and the Browns certainly did not suffer at the gate because of them. Cleveland went wild for Paul Brown's team in a way it never did for the Rams. On their way to capturing the AAFC title, the Browns drew an average of 57,000 fans per game—far more than any NFL team had ever averaged in a season. The Browns' success was a rebuke to any NFL owner who feared turning off fans by using black players.

That is not to say the integration of the Browns passed without incident. Motley and Willis had to stay apart from their teammates on the road whenever the Browns stayed at segregated hotels. Both players endured racist taunts from opponents. They could not play in a game in Miami, where municipal law prohibited integrated sports events.

Washington and Strode had similar experiences with the Rams in 1946. Their teammates accepted them, and their presence did not offend fans; the Rams drew an average crowd of more than 41,000 at the Coliseum. But some opposing players and fans in other cities taunted them, and they could not stay at segregated hotels on trips to Chicago, New York, Green Bay, Detroit, and Boston. According to author Thomas Smith, "Strode did not relish being a racial pioneer. As

The Los Angeles Rams reintegrated the league with Kenny Washington (standing, left) and Woody Strode (on his knees, far right). (Associated Press)

Washington's roommate on the road, he had to share the humiliation of eating and staying overnight at separate establishments from their teammates. 'If I have to integrate heaven,' Strode told a reporter, 'I don't want to go.'"

Unlike Willis and Motley, Washington and Strode were veterans with ebbing skills. Washington had undergone multiple knee surgeries and lost his quickness. Unable to use him at halfback or receiver, the Rams gave him a shot at quarterback during the 1946 preseason. He threw an interception and was tackled for a safety. They tried him at fullback once the regular season began, and he caught some passes out of the backfield, but he suffered another knee injury. Eventually, Washington did not play much at all. Neither did Strode, who was thirty-two and had been signed mostly so Washington would not have to live alone on the road.

In many respects, Washington and Strode faced the same obstacles as Jackie Robinson did after he debuted with the Dodgers on April 15, 1947. And they stared down the challenge with the same stony calm as Robinson, who had played football and baseball with Washington and Strode at UCLA. Why did Robinson attain far greater renown as a symbol of racial progress? It helped that he was a fantastic talent who came to the majors in his prime. Just as importantly, though, he played America's favorite sport, its national obsession. The story of Washington, Strode, and the reintegration of the NFL would gain more attention after the fact, but the collective shrug that greeted it at the time was, if anything, an indication of pro football's secondary place in American sports.

ART ROONEY COULD HARDLY WAIT FOR THE 1946 SEASON TO begin. The Steelers had seldom won since they joined the league, but Rooney had finally achieved one of his longstanding goals and hired Jock Sutherland as the team's head coach. Rooney was confident that would make all the difference.

Sutherland was a football god in Pittsburgh, owing to his magnificent run as coach of the Pitt Panthers between 1924 and 1938. Sutherland's teams had won seven eastern championships, made four Rose Bowl appearances, and played before sellout crowds at home. When the school's administrators instituted tighter controls on his program, he resigned and eventually took a job with Dan Topping's Brooklyn Dodgers. He had left the Dodgers after two years, though, to serve in the navy during the war. Now, Sutherland finally was ready to come back to Pittsburgh.

Knowing how badly Rooney wanted him, Sutherland did not sign a deal until Rooney gave him a lucrative package that included a $12,500 salary, 25 percent of the team's profits *plus* stock options. But Rooney got his man and was so elated he effectively handed the franchise over to his new coach. Sutherland was given control of scouting, drafting, negotiating contracts, promoting the team, and selling tickets. A notorious micromanager, Sutherland wanted no less.

The hiring accelerated a shift in the makeup of the city's football fans that was already underway. Pitt was no longer a power. Duquesne, which had fielded ranked teams in the 1930s, was deemphasizing the sport. The Steelers had a chance to take over, and, with Sutherland as their public face, they began doing just that. During the spring and summer of 1946, Sutherland traveled around Western Pennsylvania giving speeches about how he expected to turn the Steelers into winners. He always returned to Rooney's office at the Fort Pitt Hotel with a stack of season-ticket pledges.

Rooney's only job was to sign the checks that paid for whatever Sutherland wanted, which Rooney gladly did in most cases. At times, though, he hesitated over the checks for player salaries. The price for football talent was rising sharply now that AAFC teams also were bidding for players. The new league's cadre of wealthy owners knew how to compete for college stars. They signed forty of the sixty-six players on the College All-Star squad that took on the Rams, the reigning NFL champions, in the exhibition game in August 1946. Dozens of former NFL players also signed with the new league, despite the NFL's pledge to permanently ban players who jumped. (A pledge the league did not keep when it proved impractical.) Although NFL owners insisted to one another and to the football public that AAFC teams would play inferior football, it was becoming clear the new league would put a decent product on the field.

Rooney had always needed to limit his payroll because the Steelers did not win enough games or draw enough fans to cover his large costs. But he was not going to cut corners after finally hiring a coach who could turn the team around. Sutherland, a shrewd judge of talent, put together a solid team heading into training camp. The offense was built around Bill Dudley, the elusive tailback who had led the NFL in rushing as a rookie in 1942 before heading off to war. Back in shape after returning to the team, he appeared ready for a strong season. Sutherland drove the players hard during training camp in

Hershey, Pennsylvania. The Steelers practiced in pads for two hours in the mornings and three hours in the afternoons, sometimes scrimmaging during both sessions. Sutherland spiked the drinking water on the sidelines with oatmeal to make it unpalatable; at the time, drinking water while playing was thought to make a player "soft." After working out with the team one day, a Pittsburgh sportswriter who had played at Alabama wrote, "There will only be two kinds of men on the Pittsburgh Steeler roster this year—those that are in shape and those that are dead."

To help the team get off to a good start, Sutherland asked Rooney to lobby Bert Bell to move the date of a game between the Steelers and Cardinals, scheduled for December at Forbes Field. Make it the season opener, Sutherland suggested. Rooney agreed to ask Bell, who approved of the idea and convinced Charles Bidwill to go along. Fans snapped up tickets to Sutherland's debut. The Friday night contest sold out several days beforehand. "First time anything like that has happened out there," Bell told reporters. By the day of the game, Rooney had sold $185,000 worth of tickets to the opener and to other games later in the season. That was far more than he had ever sold before any season. "I've never seen anything like it," he said. "We've had them waiting in line for days, and I remember, not so long ago, when we used to be happy to deliver two tickets to any customer, just so he would buy them."

A steady rain that fell on the day of the season opener did not dampen the city's enthusiasm. Baseball's Pirates were finishing up a losing season. Pittsburgh was focused on pro football. Almost thirty-three thousand fans crammed into Forbes Field that night. Rooney, scarcely believing his eyes, watched scalpers outside the stadium selling tickets for more than their face value.

As evident from his training camp, Sutherland preached toughness as the key to winning. His offense employed the single wing, a bruising alignment from football's yesteryear. His defense beat up opponents. The Cardinals featured a daunting lineup of offensive stars such as Marshall Goldberg, a fleet halfback who had played for

Sutherland at Pitt, but the Steelers shut them down. Dudley tossed an early touchdown pass, then set up another score with a long run before halftime. Goldberg caught a touchdown in the third quarter, but the Steelers held on to win, 14–7. When the final gun sounded, the fans loosed a roar and filed out into the streets, not caring in the least that they were soaking wet. They would fill Forbes Field all season, turning a Steeler ticket into such a valued commodity that the city agreed to add seats on the field, expanding the stadium's capacity to nearly 40,000.

Rooney had been right about Sutherland's ability to turn the franchise around. The change was instantaneous and profound. After barely surviving the war years, the Steelers battled the Eagles, Giants, and Redskins for the East division title in 1946.

On November 3, the Redskins visited Pittsburgh. A record crowd of 36,995 fans came to see the Steelers take on an opponent that had dealt them much misery over the years. The Steelers brought a 3-2-1 record into the game. They badly needed to win. Their scoring had dropped off since their opponents realized Dudley constituted most of their offense and focused on him. The fans roared when Dudley intercepted a Sammy Baugh pass and returned it 80 yards for a touchdown in the first quarter. That was the game's only score until the Steelers again reached the end zone early in the fourth quarter. Baugh directed a touchdown drive a few minutes later, but the Steelers won, 14–7.

Unlike some owners, Rooney had rarely squabbled with George Preston Marshall. Nonetheless, he relished the victory over the Redskins and their loudmouth owner. The Steelers followed it up with another home win over the Eagles, putting them in control of the division race. If they won their final two games, they would capture the division title. But those final games were on the road, and the players were exhausted after four months of Sutherland's challenging practices. The Giants beat them, 7–0, and then they lost to the Eagles, 10–7. The Steelers finished tied for third behind the division-winning Giants.

Sutherland was undaunted, telling reporters it took five years to develop a consistent winner. The Steelers were well on their way, he claimed, and Pittsburgh's fans believed him. They would buy more than 21,000 season tickets in 1947, doubling the total from the year before. It seemed that pro football finally had arrived in Pittsburgh.

Rooney was not as sure about that, though. The Steelers had lost money in 1946 despite their improved attendance. The problem was player salaries, which had risen sharply because of competition from the AAFC. The rising payroll had offset Rooney's higher revenues. Rooney was constantly in touch with his fellow owners during the season, and they offered the same lament. They were not coming out ahead. League-wide, the player payroll had risen 250 percent from 1945. No business could survive for long in such a situation.

Some teams had fared worse than others. The Lions and Boston Yanks had lost a lot of money. Failing to draw as well as they hoped in their first year in Los Angeles, the Rams also ran a sizable deficit. The Eagles lost less, but they sold out almost every game now that they had a competitive team, and their owner, Alexis Thompson, was disturbed by the absence of a profit. The only NFL teams that made money in 1946 were the Giants and Bears, who won the division titles, and the Redskins. And Tim Mara was not comforted by his slim profit. His player payroll had been under $100,000 in 1945 and now it was close to $300,000. He feared what might happen if he had to continue to compete with the AAFC and Dan Topping in New York.

The owners had hoped the new league would collapse quickly. That was what happened to the "Red Grange league" in 1926 and the American Football League a decade later. But if the AAFC's inaugural season was any indication, the latest upstart league was not going to fold. Its championship team, the Browns, had drawn massive home crowds and probably could have competed against the NFL's best squads. Tony Morabito's San Francisco 49ers had fared reasonably well at the gate, as had Topping's Yankees despite their ill-advised idea of playing home games on Saturday nights.

But every AAFC team other than the Browns had lost money, quite a bit in some cases. Their player payrolls were just as high as the NFL's, and they had given away tickets to cultivate interest in their product. Most teams had lost at least $100,000. The Miami franchise went under. The Chicago franchise was a disaster. Still, there was enough strength in the AAFC's coalition to assure its continued existence. It was a thorny reality the NFL owners would have to confront. When they met in New York in April 1947, Bert Bell spoke rapturously to them and to reporters about the record attendance the league had achieved in 1946 and his belief that interest in the NFL was on the rise. It sounded great. But, when speaking privately, the owners grumbled that this was no way to run a business. Art Rooney was the primary example in their minds. He finally had a competitive team and a devoted fan base but still faced the same financial problems that had threatened individual franchises, and the league, from the beginning. That was not encouraging.

21

SCANDAL

EVEN WITH HIS PLAYER PAYROLL SOARING, TIM MARA surely saw a lot to like when he contemplated the Giants' circumstances on the eve of the 1946 championship game. His son Wellington, now thirty, was back from the war and again in charge of scouting college talent, drafting players, and negotiating contracts. The Giants had started the 1946 season with four wins in their first five games and, after slumping at midseason, finished strong to earn a division title. By sundown on December 14, 1946, the day before the title game, they had finished preparations and were ready to play the Chicago Bears before what was likely going to be a record crowd at the Polo Grounds. The NFL championship game had never drawn more than 49,000 fans, but New Yorkers had stood in long ticket lines all week, and Mara was going to be disappointed if Sunday's crowd did not surpass 60,000.

The Giants had never been more popular. Bert Bell had permitted them to host an extra home game in 1946—only one of their last eight contests was on the road—so they could compete with the AAFC's Yankees for local headlines and fans. The Giants had taken full advantage, generating increasing excitement in the city with their winning season. They had averaged 51,705 fans per game, easily their highest attendance figure ever. The AAFC's Yankees had also fielded a division-winning team that fall, but they averaged just 27,800 fans per game at the cavernous stadium where baseball legends Babe Ruth and Lou Gehrig once played—an impressive figure for a new team, but still far behind the Giants. For Tim Mara, building the Giants into a viable concern, in a city that was the capital of major league baseball, had been a daunting challenge. But, in 1946, it was clear his Giants had carved out a sizable niche.

Best of all from his point of view, it seemed they were poised for a long run of success. Before the season, the Giants' longtime coach, Steve Owen, had asked Mara to trade for Frank Filchock, a dual-threat tailback on the Redskins whose opportunities were limited because of Sammy Baugh. Owen thought Filchock had the right skills to run his unusual "A formation" offense; the agile twenty-eight-year-old from Pennsylvania's coal country could throw a deep pass and was also a gifted runner. Mara made the trade, and Filchock had delivered for the Giants just as Owen envisioned, passing and rushing for a total of 1,633 yards during the season. No player had contributed more to the team's success, and it seemed Filchock was in New York to stay, having signed a three-year contract before the season. "He's going to be a Giants star for a long, long time," Owen told reporters.

But, after sunset on the eve of the championship game, Mara received a phone call that soured his optimistic view. His son, Jack, who ran the Giants, was on the line with ominous news: William O'Dwyer, the mayor of New York, wanted to see them both at City Hall—immediately. Tim and Jack arrived to discover O'Dwyer also had summoned Bert Bell and several of the city's top law enforcement officials. O'Dwyer explained the urgency. Undercover detectives working in the Giants' security detail had discovered that Filchock and a teammate, Merle Hapes, had a relationship with a gambler, Alvin Paris, who was well known to New York police. The men had spent several evenings together with their wives, and according to the police, Paris had offered the players bribes to intentionally lose the championship game.

Filchock and Hapes, a fullback from Ole Miss, were contacted and also told to come to City Hall. O'Dwyer questioned them separately as Bell listened. Soon, "both were in tears," according to Bell's biographer. Hapes admitted Paris had offered him a bribe. Filchock denied it.

After midnight, the mayor was notified that Paris had been arrested and taken to a precinct on West Fifty-Fourth Street. The entire party, included Filchock, rushed to meet him there. Hapes was permitted to leave. Near dawn, Paris signed a statement admitting he had offered the players $2,500 apiece to throw the game. In an unusual dark-of-night press session, Bell announced Hapes was suspended for the championship game later that day, but Filchock could play. Reporters, who had arrived after listening in on police radio chatter, asked why one could play but not the other. Bell responded that Filchock was "absolutely in the clear" but Hapes had delayed telling Owen about the bribe offer, raising doubts about his intentions.

Tim Mara did not sleep that night. He went home, showered, changed, attended morning mass, and headed to the Polo Grounds. He was worried. Although he had been involved in legal gambling for decades, he was familiar with the underbelly of that world. It was no secret that gamblers and bookies targeted athletes and tried to influence games. Major league baseball had nearly fallen apart as a result of the "Black Sox" gambling scandal in 1919. More recently, New York police had uncovered a betting ring involving Brooklyn College's basketball varsity.

Mara was not naïve. He knew a betting scandal would generate headlines and could linger, threatening a team's business and even its survival. He hoped the story would die quietly. His players had rebuffed Paris, after all. By the start of the game that afternoon, though, the story's impact was evident. The crowd did not surpass 60,000, as Mara had expected. And the fans at the Polo Grounds voiced their opinion, giving Filchock—a popular player who had led the team all season—a nasty welcome. A chorus of boos echoed through the stadium when he jogged onto the field before kickoff.

The Bears took an early 14–0 lead as Filchock's troubles continued with a hit that broke his nose. Doggedly playing on, he tossed a pair of touchdown passes that tied the score by the middle of the third quarter. But the Bears' Sid Luckman led two late-scoring drives, and, when the final gun sounded, the visitors celebrated a 24–14 victory.

The gambling story did not die there. In fact, it took a darker turn. At Paris's trial several weeks later, Filchock testified that he had lied to the mayor the night before the title game. Yes, Paris had offered him a bribe. Paris was a front man for three New Jersey bookies, it turned out. Mara was dismayed, as were the other owners. Bert Bell was outraged. He had been commissioner for only a year, but he had been in the league since 1933 and seen it through the challenges of the Great Depression and World War II. This, though, was the gravest threat the NFL had faced, he believed. Even though they had not taken a bribe, Filchock and Hapes had undermined the league's credibility by consorting with a gambler.

At a league meeting in late January 1947, Bell warned the owners that he was embarking on a crusade. The NFL needed to take a strong position against gambling. Bell, like Mara, was no innocent on the subject; he had lost a fortune betting on horse racing years earlier and had even bet on himself as a player at Penn, losing a new car in the process. But his youthful foolishness bore little resemblance to a mobster trying to change the outcome of a championship game. The league needed to make clear to its fans, Bell told the owners, that NFL games were legitimate.

At the meeting, the owners approved a measure allowing Bell to ban for life "without appeal" any player or team official who withheld knowledge of a plot to fix a game. He could also ban anyone he deemed "undesirable" from a locker room or stadium. The commissioner feared "city slicker" gamblers taking advantage of "country boy" players, believing Paris had done that to Filchock and Hapes. Before the meeting adjourned, the owners added a warning about gambling

Bert Bell (right) hands suspension papers to Frank Filchock. (Associated Press)

to the league's standard player contract and agreed to put the warning on posters that hung in locker rooms.

Continuing his crusade a few months later, Bell enacted a league rule forcing teams to publicize all news about player injuries. Coaches had previously sought to keep such information out of the papers, thinking, rightly, that they benefitted from keeping their opponents in the dark. But injury news was what prompted gamblers to try to infiltrate locker rooms in the first place; armed with insider knowledge, a gambler could beat a point spread if, for instance, he alone knew that an important player on a given team was unlikely to play. Making injury news public would eliminate the desire for the information, Bell believed, and deny gamblers the potential edge.

In early April, Bell announced Filchock and Hapes were suspended indefinitely from the NFL. He had wanted to trigger his new lifetime ban option but, in the end, decided that would not be fair because the ban was not in effect when Filchock and Hapes received bribe offers. Some fans and sportswriters were surprised by the penalty's severity; the players had not actually accepted bribes, after all. But Bell shrugged off the distinction. "Professional football cannot continue to exist unless it is based on absolute honesty," he explained. "The players must be not only absolutely honest, but above suspicion."

Filchock never played again for the Giants. He spent the rest of his career in the Canadian Football League except for a few games in 1950 after Bell lifted his suspension. Hapes also played in Canada and never returned to the NFL, although Bell lifted his suspension in 1954.

As it turned out, Mara was right to suspect that the scandal would have a grave impact on his team. Stripped of their starting backfield, the Giants went into a nightmarish decline. Early in the 1947 season, they lost seven games in a row for the first time in the franchise's history. They had never finished a season in last place, but they achieved that dubious franchise first in 1947 with a record of two wins, eight defeats, and two ties. Many fans simply abandoned them. Their total ticket sales dropped almost by half, from 361,937 the year before to 190,173. Their December showdown with the Redskins drew just 25,594 fans after attracting more than 60,000 the year before.

As Mara's revenues declined, his player payroll continued to increase. Suddenly, his team was operating at a deficit. Meanwhile, Dan Topping's Yankees fielded another division winner that fall, and thousands of fans appeared to have adopted the new team.

Topping and the football Yankees were formidable rivals. New York fans approved of the Yankees' coach, Ray Flaherty, a former Giant. The Yankees also had a dynamic running back, one Orban Eugene "Spec" Sanders, a former University of Texas star who, with Filchock gone, became New York's premier pro football figure in 1947, rushing for 1,432 yards and eighteen touchdowns. As the Yankees drove toward a division title, more and more fans came to their games. On November 23, while the Giants hosted Green Bay before 27,939 fans at the Polo Grounds, the Yankees hosted the Cleveland

Browns, the AAFC's top team, before more than 70,000 at Yankee Stadium. Those fans witnessed a classic contest. The Yankees scored the game's first 28 points. The Browns responded with 28 straight of their own. After the game, which ended in a tie, supporters were spent from hours of shouting. Although the Yankees gave away tickets to boost attendance, they were gaining on the Giants.

Mara was anxious, and he was not alone among the NFL owners in this respect. Other members of the league's ruling class also experienced challenging seasons in 1947. The Redskins won just four games. The Packers went a month without a win and slipped from contention. The Bears won eight straight games at one point, but they lost the first two and final two games on their schedule, and those defeats denied them a division title. The NFL's world had been turned upside down. Now, the teams on top were the ones that had spent years being humiliated by the Giants, Bears, Redskins, and Packers. Those four teams had combined to win sixteen of the past eighteen NFL championships, but in 1947 the Cardinals, long entrenched as Chicago's No. 2 team, won the West division, and the Eagles and Steelers tied for first in the East. None of the three had ever come close to winning a division title.

The tie in the East meant the Eagles and Steelers met for a one-game playoff on December 21 to determine who would play the Cardinals for the league championship. The Eagles won, 21–0, disappointing a sellout crowd at Forbes Field. A week later, the Eagles and Cardinals played for the title before just 30,759 fans at Comiskey Park on Chicago's South Side. It was the smallest crowd for a league title game in six years, well short of the stadium's capacity. More than twice as many people attended the AAFC title game at the Polo Grounds and watched the Browns defeat the Yankees. Although the AAFC, like the NFL, was operating in the red because of high player salaries, it was clearly appropriating a significant slice of the pro football pie. The new league actually seemed more popular at times than the NFL. No NFL team had ever encountered anything like the Browns' success on and off the field.

In the end, though, the Browns' impressiveness damaged the league. Quite simply, they were *too* good. In the AAFC's first two seasons, they won twenty-four of twenty-eight regular-season games and a pair of championships. In 1947, they defeated the Baltimore Colts, 42–0; the San Francisco 49ers, 37–14; the Brooklyn Dodgers, 55–0; and the Buffalo Bills, 28–7. The league lacked suspense, and if the Browns were removed from the calculations, it clearly was struggling. The other seven teams in the AAFC were hemorrhaging money, losing an estimated $1.5 million between them in 1947 alone. Jim Crowley, the AAFC's original commissioner, had resigned after one year to take over the Chicago franchise, called the Rockets; he had been a winning college coach. But the Rockets went 1-13 while playing in mostly empty Soldier Field. The AAFC's Baltimore and Brooklyn teams also were foundering.

Strangely, the sudden decline of the NFL's ruling class worked in the older league's favor. Although fans of the Bears, Giants, Redskins, and Packers bombarded their teams' offices with unhappy letters and phone calls in 1947, those franchises could count on their histories and traditions to sustain them through dismal seasons. Their owners might lose money in the short run, but the teams could return to profitability. It was more important to the NFL's health that its lesser franchises become more competitive. Leveling the playing field had long been a goal of the men who ran the league, and that goal was being realized. The Cardinals, Eagles, and Steelers were winning and drawing crowds. Although the NFL still had several troubled franchises, most of its teams were now capable of winning a championship. The AAFC could not credibly make the same claim.

The Cardinals' success was exactly what the owners had envisioned when they instituted a draft in 1936. In 1947 the Cardinals relied on what sportswriters dubbed the "Million Dollar Backfield," a group of big-name former college stars. Players of that caliber never would have signed with the lowly Cardinals before a draft existed, when any player could sign with any team. But the Cardinals had secured their rights by drafting them, and then offered them enough money to sign.

Marshall Goldberg, the halfback from Pitt, had been the No. 12 over-all selection in 1939. Paul Christman, a quarterback from Missouri, was the No. 13 overall pick in 1941. Pat Harder, a fullback from Wisconsin, went No. 2 overall in 1944. Charlie Trippi, a halfback from Georgia, was the very first pick in the 1945 draft. Elmer Angsman, a Notre Dame halfback, was the No. 16 overall pick in 1946.

When World War II ended, and the players returned from military duty, each became the subject of a bidding war with an AAFC team. The Cardinals seemed unlikely to sign them all, or even just one. Dozens of players were decamping for the AAFC. The Cardinals, perennial losers, were not a glamorous option. But when the AAFC put a team in Chicago, Charles Bidwill uncharacteristically became motivated to win. He knew John Keeshin, the trucking magnate who was backing Chicago's AAFC team. Both men operated horse racing tracks. Keeshin irritated Bidwill when he told him that three pro football teams were too many for Chicago and the Cardinals should just leave for another city. Bidwill had seemingly never minded seeing his team lose, but now he wanted nothing more than to win games and put Keeshin out of business. Bidding aggressively, he landed all five players, including Trippi, who had seemed likely to sign with Dan Topping's Yankees until Bidwill offered him a $100,000 contract, by far the largest any pro player had received. Trippi joined the Cardinals, and, in the 1947 championship game against the Eagles, he scored touchdowns on a 44-yard run and a 75-yard punt return, all while wearing tennis shoes for better traction on an icy field.

Sadly, Bidwill did not get to see his new signings lead the Cardinals to the title. In the spring of 1947, after he had signed the players but before the NFL season began, he contracted pneumonia and died on April 19. He was just fifty-one. His fellow owners raised a toast to him at the first league meeting after the Cardinals won the title. They also toasted the lamentable state of the AAFC's Chicago franchise. Keeshin had sold it after one disastrous season. Bidwill had won that contest, too.

As they looked ahead to 1948, the Giants needed to reverse course—and quickly. They had won just two games the year before. The Yankees had stolen their headlines. Now, yet another New York–area AAFC team was offering a challenge. Branch Rickey, the forward-thinking baseball executive who had integrated the major leagues by signing Jackie Robinson, had followed the AAFC's rise. He believed the franchise-building fundamentals that worked in baseball could also work in pro football, and he convinced the board that ran baseball's Brooklyn Dodgers to buy the AAFC franchise with the same name. It had floundered in 1946 and 1947, but Rickey believed he would have the football Dodgers winning games and drawing fans to Ebbets Field in 1948.

A showdown occurred early in 1948, long before the football season. The Dodgers had the AAFC rights to Charlie Conerly, a quarterback who had set passing records at Ole Miss during the previous two seasons after returning from the war. The Giants also wanted Conerly. Wellington Mara believed he could make Owen's offense hum and, hopefully, lure New York fans back to the Polo Grounds. Wellington asked his father to approve a trade with the Redskins, who had drafted Conerly while he was in the service. Tim Mara told his son to go ahead, and the Giants sent Washington two players in exchange for Conerly's rights. Now they had to sign him.

A master showman, Rickey made headlines when he offered Conerly a $110,000 deal. The baseball man was sure he had landed a quarterback who could turn the Dodgers around. Tim Mara contemplated his response. The Giants would not get into a bidding war, he decided. He believed Conerly was skeptical about the AAFC. Mara also understood that it would offend the Giants' veterans to pay a rookie as much as Rickey was offering. He instructed his son to offer a $62,500 deal. Conerly signed with the Giants.

Furious, Rickey predicted the Giants would have "a morale problem" because Conerly had taken the lesser offer. "It seems un-American to me," said Rickey, who was known for making lowball offers to his best baseball players, including Ralph Branca, a twenty-one-game winner in 1947. "Maybe the kid figures he'll have greater security with the Giants than with an organization that puts such a [low] price on a 21-game winner," Mara replied dryly. "Or maybe he looked over the All-America conference and realized we've been here 24 years, whereas Brooklyn has had three, four owners. I don't know where this guy [Rickey] gets off talking about morale problems and stuff, considering the business he's in."

The Dodgers opened the 1948 season with six straight defeats. Baseball savvy did not translate to football, it turned out. Rickey's team was a laughingstock. His recruits included Pepper Martin, a forty-four-year-old retired baseball star. The Dodgers ended the season with two wins and a dozen defeats, playing in a nearly empty stadium. O'Malley gave up the franchise after the season, having lost $300,000. The AAFC's Yankees also struggled badly in 1948. After beating the Dodgers to open the season, they lost four games in a row. A trip to Cleveland resulted in a 35–7 loss to the Browns, who would go undefeated and win a third straight league title. The Yankees now played before smaller crowds. Their final game drew less than 19,000 fans.

The Giants did not fare that much better, comparatively. Early in the 1948 season, they lost successive road games in Washington and Philadelphia by a combined 86–10 score. Owen's signature unit, his bruising defense, had fallen apart. Another losing season was soon assured. Fans wrote letters demanding Owen's firing. But the signing of Conerly would eventually make the fans' suffering well worth it. Resembling a young Sammy Baugh, he tossed twenty-two touchdown passes and piled up 2,175 passing yards in 1948. The Giants' defense was weak, but they now had one of the league's most exciting offenses. Conerly would wear their uniform for thirteen years, winning three East division titles and a league championship before he retired.

The Giants also added Emlen Tunnell in 1948. An African American who had played halfback at Iowa, he had not signed with a team by that summer; although the Rams and Browns had broken pro football's color line two years earlier, no other black players had been signed since then. Tunnell, from near Philadelphia, simply showed up at the Giants' offices in New York one day.

"I'm looking for a job," he told Wellington Mara.

"What kind of a job?" Mara asked.

"Playing football. I'm a football player and I think I can make your club," Tunnell replied.

The team's scouts had heard of him, and the Giants signed him. The southern players on their roster embraced him when training camp began, easing a fear that may have discouraged other owners from integrating. Tunnell became the Giants' first black player, and, as a rookie in 1948, he ran back punts and emerged as a star defensive back, intercepting seven passes.

Toward the end of the season, Tunnell returned an interception 43 yards for a touchdown against the Packers in a game the Giants won, 49–3. Two weeks later, Conerly dropped back on almost every down against the Steelers in Pittsburgh, attempting fifty-three passes and completing thirty-six, three for touchdowns. The Giants rolled up thirty-one first downs and 463 offensive yards, mostly through the air. Although they lost, 38–28, Conerly was the talk of the town in New York the following week.

His performance in Pittsburgh was indicative of important changes occurring in the NFL. Passing offenses were evolving; it was no longer just Sid Luckman in Chicago who could march a team downfield through the air. Conerly could. The Rams' Bob Waterfield could. And, because an effective passing offense was hard to stop, a talented quarterback could make all the difference. Where once a team needed reliable players at many positions, more and more the focus would be on the quarterback. With players like Conerly and Waterfield, the modern game was coming into view.

For decades, football's appeal had rested on its ability to build character, its inherent violence, its approximation of war. Those elements were not ebbing in the eyes of fans, but as the sport evolved, becoming as much about skill and speed as toughness, other elements became equally paramount, none more than the sheer brilliance of the talent—in the NFL, especially. In the coming decade, as it became a league of quarterbacks, the pro game's capacity to entrance sports fans, to *dazzle,* would catapult it to heights not even the most optimistic insider ever envisioned.

22

EVERYONE LOSES

AFTER WATCHING JOCK SUTHERLAND COACH HIS TEAM FOR two years, Art Rooney believed the Steelers were on the cusp of glory. They had tied for the East division title in 1947 with an 8-4 record. Other owners in the league now saw them as a power. In March 1948, Sutherland left Pittsburgh for an annual driving trip through the South to scout talent and reconnect with his college contacts. In early April, the Steelers received a call from a Kentucky sheriff whose deputies had found Sutherland wandering through a field, disoriented. He had a headache, he said, and could not account for his recent whereabouts. Several Steeler assistants flew to Kentucky, collected him, and brought him back to Pittsburgh, where he underwent surgery to determine what was wrong. The surgeon found an inoperable brain tumor. Sutherland died on April 11 at age fifty-nine.

It was a fateful development for the Steelers. Sutherland had planned to coach until 1950 and then hand over the team to a young assistant he was grooming. That handoff now took place sooner, before the assistant was ready. The Steelers' rise abruptly halted, and they descended into mediocrity again. More than two decades would pass before their fortunes significantly changed.

But although Rooney simply could not manage to push his team into the NFL's upper ranks, he continued to wield influence in the league's inner circle. He had been an owner for fifteen years when Sutherland died, making him one of the longest-tenured men at the owners' table. The commissioner was his former business partner and one of his closest friends. Halas and Marshall, who together practically ran the league, trusted his instincts and relied on him to mediate their disputes. Tim Mara, his friend from the horse racing world, felt similarly about him. With his kind nature and calm demeanor, Rooney could be counted on to sort through the clutter and render sound judgments that benefitted the league.

In 1948, a furious internal dispute arose over how to deal with the AAFC. Weary of losing money, the Eagles' Alexis Thompson suggested the NFL should at least cooperate with the new league on a draft, which would eliminate the outrageous bidding wars that were driving salaries so high. Halas and Marshall vehemently disagreed. The war with the AAFC was personal to them, especially Halas, whose feud with Arch Ward had started it. Halas and Marshall wanted to put the AAFC out of business, not cooperate with it, and Mara agreed. As usual, their opinion was all that mattered. When Thompson's general manager raised the possibility of a common draft at an owners' meeting, the idea was rejected with little discussion and no vote.

But, other than Halas and Marshall, everyone in the NFL, including Mara and Rooney, was operating in the red. They wanted to end the war, even if it meant working with the AAFC. Although they dismissed Thompson's idea this time as a show of solidarity, they actually were open to it.

The AAFC's owners also wanted to negotiate. Except for Cleveland's Mickey McBride, they were all losing money, too, and no longer able to deny that their league faced significant problems. Trying to make games more competitive in 1948, they engineered a dubious personnel swap in which winning teams simply gave players to losing teams. It was a ridiculous exercise that, predictably, failed. The

Browns won fourteen games without a loss during the 1948 season and easily defeated the Buffalo Bills in the championship game, 49–7. The Browns and San Francisco 49ers were the only teams that posted winning records. The Yankees faltered. Branch Rickey's Brooklyn experiment had come to nothing. Chicago's franchise stayed afloat only because the Los Angeles Dons' owner, Ben Lindheimer, underwrote it.

But the NFL's owners did not exult in the AAFC's woes. They had problems of their own in 1948. Dan Reeves sold a minority share of the Rams to keep from going under. After losing several hundred thousand dollars in six years, Fred Mandel sold the Lions for $40,000 less than he had paid for them. The Eagles defeated the Cardinals in a Philadelphia snowstorm to win the championship game, but Thompson continued to lose money and preach cooperation with the AAFC. "We'll either get smart and make peace, or we'll all go bust," he said.

The Steelers won just four games in 1948. The enthusiastic crowds that flocked to Forbes Field the year before vanished. Rooney still sold enough tickets to gross $900,000 in revenues, but he ended the season $40,000 in the red and did not expect that to change in 1949 as long as the AAFC still existed.

Rooney occupied a unique seat in the league's hierarchy. Although he was close with Halas, Marshall, and Mara, he understood the plight of teams that lost games and money season after season. For years, he had demanded that the owners guarantee the road team a sizable cut of the attendance receipts at every game—a safeguard that kept some losing teams from folding. Bell, who was commissioner now but had endured terrible seasons in Philadelphia and Pittsburgh, had a similar firsthand grasp of what it was like to run a losing team. In their daily phone conversations, Rooney and Bell agreed on the need for a solution that ended the war. Halas and Marshall had to be talked out of trying to obliterate the AAFC. It was time to shake hands and make peace. Too many people were losing too much money. If Halas and Marshall could not relate to the less successful owners, they needed to be convinced that a truce was in the NFL's best interests.

From his office in Pittsburgh, Rooney orchestrated a campaign. As always, he also had other businesses to tend to; he still promoted fight cards and had bought a horse farm in Maryland, where he bred his own thoroughbreds for racing. But in phone conversations with Halas and Marshall during the 1948 season, he pointed out that virtually every other team was suffering and a truce with the AAFC was imperative. He had little trouble convincing Halas, who had originated the principle of putting the league's best interests ahead of your own when the situation demanded it. Marshall was more reluctant, but, once Halas was swayed, he began to relent, too. "The time is ripe for peace. Certainly we can sit down and work out a sensible solution," Halas told the Chicago media.

The AAFC took Halas's remark as a signal that the NFL was open to talks. Within days, a group from the rival league met with Bell. The commissioner made a stark proposal: the NFL would take on the Browns and 49ers, but the other AAFC teams would disband without a settlement of any amount from the NFL. The owners of the AAFC's Buffalo and Los Angeles franchises would have the option of investing in an NFL team as minority owners.

Most of the AAFC owners were ready to accept Bell's terms. But the AAFC's Baltimore franchise, the Colts, scuttled the deal. The Colts wanted to join the NFL, and almost every NFL owner was ready to allow it. The lone holdout was Marshall, who believed a team in nearby Baltimore would infringe on his market. Marshall eventually softened his position, saying he would accept $200,000 from the Colts' owner, Abraham Watner, in exchange for letting the Colts join the NFL. But Watner said that was too high a price, leaving the situation unsettled. Meanwhile, the AAFC owners had said they would sign off on the deal only if every team approved it. With the Colts in limbo, the AAFC chose to continue operating in 1949.

Mike McGee, a horse trainer whose father conditioned Rooney's thoroughbreds starting in the late 1940s, recalled a conversation with Rooney about Marshall. "We would talk about things. He told me

Marshall was the most cantankerous man he'd ever met," McGee said. "Rooney told me that 'everyone would agree on something, except George. You couldn't do a lot of things until he came around, and he was very bullheaded, hard to deal with.'"

But, though initial negotiations between the NFL and AAFC failed, largely because of Marshall, they provided a starting point for dialogue. Talks continued through the spring and summer of 1949 and intensified during the football season. The need for a deal became obvious. Attendance in both leagues declined. Teams continued to lose money. Rooney took a public stand, saying the Steelers would not field a team in 1950 unless the NFL and AAFC struck a compromise to end the war.

By December 1949, the AAFC was ready to capitulate. It only had seven teams, most of which were losing money. Lindheimer, whose money supported two franchises, had suffered a heart attack and lost interest. The Browns were about to win their fourth straight title, but even they were losing money now because their home attendance had dropped; their fans were bored with watching them roll over overmatched opponents. But, even though both sides were ready to deal, relationships among the principals held the negotiations back. Cleveland's Paul Brown criticized Marshall for blocking a merger. Marshall fired back, insisting he would be open to one. Bell and the AAFC's third commissioner in four years, O. O. "Scrappy" Kessing, a retired navy admiral, found little common ground.

Finally, a baseball man interceded. Horace Stoneham owned baseball's New York Giants and the Polo Grounds, which made him a football landlord. The football Giants had played at the Polo Grounds since 1925, and, in the 1949 season, another NFL team also played there after Ted Collins moved his downtrodden Boston franchise and rechristened them the New York Bulldogs. Stoneham watched both of his tenants lose money in 1949, and he knew Dan Topping's football Yankees were doing no better. Fearing that pro football in New York was about to fail and end one of his sources of revenue, Stoneham arranged for Bert Bell to meet with George Weiss, the baseball

Yankees' general manager. Bell agreed to try to negotiate a settlement with a lone representative of the AAFC, J. Arthur Friedlund, general counsel for the baseball and football Yankees.

Bell and Friedlund met at the commissioner's office in Philadelphia. Bell presented an offer similar to the one he had made a year earlier. The NFL would take the Browns and 49ers, and it would also take the Colts if Watner could agree with Marshall on a price. The rest of the AAFC would go out of business. Not wanting to block a deal, Marshall lowered his asking price to $150,000. Watner, who had already lost a great deal of money on the Colts, continue to negotiate and eventually paid Marshall just $50,000. But that finalized the deal. A series of other details were worked out. The NFL's Bulldogs would buy out Topping's Yankees, change their nickname to the Yanks, and play their home game at Yankee Stadium rather than the Polo Grounds. The players on disbanding AAFC teams would be dispersed in a draft, separate from the annual college draft. Bell, seeking to ensure the Browns' support, quietly agreed to give Cleveland three of Buffalo's best players—a side deal that enraged Halas and Marshall when they learned of it.

On December 9, 1949, Bell and Friedlund called a press conference in Philadelphia and announced the two leagues were merging into an entity known as the National-American Football League. It would have thirteen teams, with the divisional alignments to be determined. Bell would be the commissioner.

The war was over. It had cost millions, pushing the owners and the two leagues to the brink. Finally, though, there was peace again in pro football—of a sort.

Two days after the merger announcement, the NFL completed its 1949 regular season with a slate of games on December 11, a Sunday. The Eagles, who had already clinched a third straight East division title, defeated the Giants to finish with an 11-1 record, best in the league. The Rams routed the Redskins to win the West and secure a spot in the league title game for the first time since they moved to Los Angeles.

Bert Bell made plans to travel to California to attend the championship game on December 18 but canceled his trip several days beforehand. He had barely slept while hammering out the merger deal, and his doctor told him he needed to rest. Bell reluctantly stayed home. At fifty-four, he was not in the best physical shape, and his job was increasingly stressful.

He still became embroiled in a controversy over the championship game, even though he was at the other end of the continent. The Rams had hoped to sell 70,000 tickets, but a hard rain fell in Los Angeles in the days before the game, and, according to forecasters, it was not going to stop in time for kickoff. With a much smaller crowd anticipated and the Los Angeles Memorial Coliseum field a muddy mess, the owners of the Rams and Eagles wanted to postpone the game for a week in hopes of better weather and better attendance. But Bell said the game had to be played on the scheduled date. He had negotiated deals for national radio and regional television broadcasts, and the networks did not want to change their schedules at the last moment. The Los Angeles press crucified Bell after 27,980 fans sat through a driving rainstorm as the Eagles defeat the Rams, 14–0, on a field that was barely playable. "Bertie sat back there in his Philadelphia apartment and . . . pulled one of the biggest bloomers of his career," the *Los Angeles Times* wrote.

Whether or not he was right to force the game to be played, Bell was right to skip the long trip. He was going to need all his energy and savvy for the owners' meeting, the first since the merger, scheduled to begin on January 19, 1950, in Philadelphia. Many aspects of the reconfigured league remained undecided. With strong-willed men from two leagues coming together for the first time, there were certain to be acrimonious disputes.

A mix of snow and rain was falling outside when Bell banged a gavel to begin the meeting at the Bellevue-Stratford Hotel in Philadelphia's City Center. It was a Thursday, shortly after noon, and the familiar cadre of NFL owners had gathered, led by George Halas, Tim Mara, George Preston Marshall, and Art Rooney, who, along with Bell, Curly Lambeau, and Charles Bidwill, had guided the league's affairs through most of the 1930s and 1940s. "We owners were a tight little group," Halas would write. "We had gone through a lot together. We had helped one another. We had to the best of our abilities become professionals dedicated to the game of football."

By 1950, though, Bidwill had died, and Lambeau was being forced out in Green Bay. His purchase of a year-round training facility had strained the Packers' finances just as salaries escalated. Unable to keep pace with wealthier teams in larger markets, the Packers had sunk to the bottom of the West division. The team's board of directors also was quietly unhappy that Lambeau was on his third marriage and spent his offseasons in California. Without Bidwill and Lambeau, the "tight little group" was even tighter. Bell was in charge, with four men constantly whispering in his ear: Halas, whose tenure dated to the league's birth; Mara, who had doggedly fought for and defended his New York franchise since 1925; Marshall, whose innovations and prejudices had shaped the league in fundamental ways; and Rooney, the affable peacekeeper.

That they still controlled the league soon became evident. Within weeks of the Philadelphia meeting, the owners would toss out the awkward name they had come up with, the National-American Football League, and return to the more familiar National Football League.

But during the meeting, the newcomers made their presence felt. Paul Brown, the Cleveland Browns' head coach, was not only one of the sport's best strategists, but also a shrewd boardroom tactician, unafraid to voice strong opinions, and he never let anyone take advantage of him. Brown could not stand Marshall. It irritated him that Marshall was so determined to keep African Americans from playing for the Redskins. Marshall also had not hidden his scorn for the AAFC throughout the league's four years. In 1947, the AAFC's commissioner at the time, Jonas Ingram, a retired navy admiral, had proposed that the champions of the two leagues play, with the proceeds going to charity. Marshall haughtily responded that Ingram should have the AAFC winner play Navy's varsity. Now, in Philadelphia, Brown observed Marshall at a league meeting for the first time and found him "obnoxious." What really bothered Brown, he said later, was Marshall's "habit of sleeping most of the day" after carrying on in nightclubs all evening "and showing up at the meetings late in the afternoon. By that time all of us were pretty tired and ready to adjourn, but he was rested and mentally sharp. That was when he tried to work some of his little deals." Brown's personal and professional opposition to Marshall represented the start of a decline in Marshall's power—an ebbing that would continue through the 1950s.

On the first day of the meeting, prospective ownership groups from Buffalo, Houston, and Oakland lobbied to join the league. Although the initial merger agreement had provided for a total of thirteen teams, some owners wanted to let in one more. Making out the schedule would be easier, and several cities were viable candidates, it seemed. Buffalo had more than 14,000 season ticket pledges. Houston was proposing to build an 110,000-seat indoor stadium. But most of the "tight little group," led by Halas, was dubious about letting anyone else in. "As with most organizations, we were perhaps too unresponsive to newcomers wanting to join our league." Halas would write. "We liked things the way they were. We did our best to keep things that way." Bell announced that a vote for adding another team had to be unanimous. That was not going to happen. "Plans here are the proverbial dime-a-dozen. There is a Marshall Plan, a Mara Plan, and three or four other plans," the *New York Times* reported. When a procedural voice vote fell short of unanimity, Bell called off the whole process. There would be thirteen teams in the NFL.

The next item on the agenda was organizing those thirteen teams into two divisions. Everyone agreed there would be two six-team units and a "swing" team that would alternate between competing in one division one year and the other division the next year. But whenever one owner proposed a particular alignment, an argument erupted. When Marshall suggested the Browns should be the swing team, Brown glared at him and threatened to pull out of the league. Rooney, as was his custom, took the floor and preached for calm. Bell offered a threat: if the owners did not settle on a plan soon, they could find a new commissioner. "I banged down the gavel and started for the doors," Bell would recall. "Someone stopped me. I cooled off for the minute and they put the action through."

The owners voted on a two-division setup with Baltimore as the swing team. The motion passed, 12–1, with Bell casting the dissenting vote on behalf of Marshall, who, according to Bell's biographer, had "left the meeting in a huff when he realized he couldn't put through a motion to have any team other than Baltimore named the swing team." The Associated Press would credit Bell for negotiating "the most important decision in the new league . . . a decision that seemed impossible until Bell waved his gavel and threatened direct action. From all indications, the owners would have been in conference, arguing, until next week, if Bell hadn't called a halt."

Another complex matter was how to distribute the players from the disbanding AAFC teams. The situation was hopelessly complex. Everyone agreed that there was going to be a draft, but should the NFL allow its weaker teams to select more players, seeing as they needed more help? And should the AAFC teams entering the league get to keep all their players, include those on their developmental "reserve" list? That did not seem fair, as the NFL teams were only going to be able to "protect" so many from being eligible for the dispersal draft.

After arguing for almost five hours on January 21, the owners threw the problem to Bell, who retreated to his hotel room for an entire afternoon before returning with a proposal. The three teams entering the NFL from the AAFC could protect thirty-two active players and three on reserve. The Packers and Colts, as the weakest teams in the merged league, would receive five extra selections. New York's two franchises, the Giants and Yanks, could split up most of the talent from the AAFC's Yankees. It was not an entirely equitable solution, but there did not seem to be an alternative. The men in the inner circle had always instinctively known when to prioritize the league's best interests ahead of their own, and this surely was such a moment. Marshall, who was back at the table, seconded Bell's plan, and Halas "never kicked," Bell said, despite getting "the worst of it." The proposal passed easily.

The owners also conducted a college draft, approved several rules changes, and gave Bell a ten-year contract. When the commissioner wrapped up the meeting on January 24, he was described by the *Times* as "shirt-sleeved and dead tired." The "portly" Bell had somehow navigated a minefield of conflicting agendas and opinions without blowing up the fragile coalition he now oversaw.

WHILE NEWS FROM PHILADELPHIA CONCERNING FRANCHISE BIDS, divisional alignments, and drafts generated headlines across the country, a seemingly minor rule change barely made the papers: after experimenting with allowing teams to make unlimited substitutions during games in 1949, the NFL was making the rule permanent. The AAFC had permitted unlimited substitutions throughout its four-year history, and the owners and coaches from that league believed the freedom to move players in and out of huddles markedly improved the game. The NFL was adopting its former rival's inventive stance on the issue.

Restrictions on substitutions had been in place from the very start of the sport. In 1922, the NCAA mandated that a player who came out of a game in the first half could not return until the second half, and a player who came out in the second half was finished for the day. Deferring to the college game, far more popular at the time, the NFL simply utilized the same rule. At both levels, it became routine for players to have roles on both offense and defense, and seldom leave the field. Don Hutson became famous as the Packers' brilliant receiver, but he also accumulated thirty interceptions during his eleven-year career as a defensive back. The Giants' Mel Hein was a center on offense and a linebacker on defense.

The endurance required to play "both ways" was seen as an essential burden the game placed on players, part of the physical challenge that made football so compelling for spectators. When players suddenly were in scarce supply during World War II, however, both college and pro football were forced to adapt. The NFL went with unlimited substitutions. In the college game, a player who left the field had to sit out at least one play before returning. When the war ended, the NFL reinstituted limits on substitutions, allowing only three players to enter a game at a time. The college game continued with a freer approach, allowing teams to switch out as many players as they wanted on possession changes. But the purists in the college game believed this violated the game's nature, changing it beyond recognition. Robert Neyland, a former army brigadier general who coached at Tennessee, famously referred to football with unlimited substitutions as "chickenshit football."

In 1953, the NCAA would reinstitute limits on substitutions. A player could enter a game only once per quarter. The doughty two-way player, a staple of the game's past, was valued again. But the college game was making a mistake, looking backward instead of ahead. The unlimited-substitution rule was a cornerstone of football's future. It led to teams developing two separate units, an offense and defense. Now, a strong-armed quarterback just played offense; he did not have to risk injury playing defense, too. Coaches could separate their teams into units, enabling players to remain fresher and to become true specialists, thereby raising the quality of play across a single team and the entire sport. The Giants' Charlie Conerly was a case in point. He was born to play quarterback, and, under the new rules, he could focus on developing the skills necessary for succeeding at that position.

Not surprisingly, Paul Brown had already figured out how to take advantage of the unlimited substitution rule—indeed, it had been central to his team's success in the AAFC. Throughout the sport's history, players on the field had always called the offensive signals, but Brown was able to exert more control; he called his offense's plays from the sideline, sending in his instructions via a pair of guards who shuttled between the sideline and huddle on every play. College football was more storied, but the pro game had become more innovative and dynamic. With one rule change that received almost no attention at the time, the NFL had set in motion a fateful inversion. By the time the college game recognized its mistake and moved to unlimited substitutions in 1965, the NFL had surpassed it and pro football was well on the way to becoming America's most popular sport.

23

THE LITTLE BLACK BOX

ONE DAY IN EARLY 1947, GEORGE HALAS DROPPED BY THE *Chicago Tribune* newsroom to visit Don Maxwell, the newspaper's city editor. The two had been friends since the 1920s, when Maxwell edited the sports section and Halas wanted coverage for his new pro football team. Halas found Maxwell staring at "a little black box, about two feet square, with a glass front on which fuzzy pictures were moving about," Halas would write.

"There it is, George—television," Maxwell said.

Halas was not impressed. "The picture is so small, Don, and so fuzzy," he said. "Will it ever be anything more than a toy for adults?"

Maxwell smiled and said, "George, that little box with the fuzzy picture is going to change the American way of life." He explained that the picture quality would soon improve, and the ability to transmit a picture "miles away" to sets in living rooms would transform the news, sports, and entertainment industries.

"Television is coming, George," Maxwell said. "What are you going to do about it?"

Halas had no answer. But after listening to Maxwell, he began "asking questions." Within weeks, the NFL owners addressed the issue "for the first time" during a meeting in Chicago. Though focused on the Filchock gambling scandal, the owners voted to permit teams to sell the television rights to their home games in 1947. It was not deemed a significant matter. The rights to local radio broadcasts of NFL games had grown to the point that teams now received between $15,000 and $35,000 per year. But that amount, although not a pittance, did not significantly impact a team's business, and there was no reason to believe television income would, either; just 44,000 sets were in use in America in 1947, compared to 40 million radios.

Halas approached Chicago's single television station about broadcasting the Bears' home games in 1947. The station agreed to do it, paying the team $900 per game for the rights. "I could not believe it. The money was an unexpected bonus," Halas wrote. He viewed the arrangement less as a driver of profits than as an experiment. The Bears were coming off a championship season in which they averaged 42,291 fans per game. Halas wondered whether his customers would stop buying tickets once they could watch the Bears for free, on television, either at home or in a bar. Sure enough, even with a fuzzy picture and few sets in use, his attendance dropped 9 percent in 1947. Nonetheless, he signed another deal to televise his games the following year, in the belief that the broadcasts helped publicize the team. The Bears fared better at the gate that season, with an average crowd of 43,672. Their attendance was actually up after two years of televised home games.

During the 1948 season, though, Halas soured on the experiment. He realized Maxwell had been right about television's impact. Radio industry powerhouses such as the Columbia Broadcasting System and National Broadcasting Company had launched TV divisions that were off to promising starts. The American Broadcasting Company and DuMont Television Network were also airing programming. Meanwhile, the country was buying TV sets in greater numbers. There were 350,000 sets in use in America early in 1948, and the total would rise to 2 million within a year and 7.7 million by 1950.

As Maxwell had predicted, television was changing Americans' habits. Instead of going to movies or listening to the radio, more and more people just turned on their sets for entertainment. Television was becoming so prevalent so quickly that Halas believed his fear would be realized—fans would stop coming to see the Bears if given the option of staying home and watching for free. "So many sets were coming into Chicago homes that I lacked enthusiasm for having our games televised," he wrote.

The success of a comedy show, the *Texaco Star Theater*, revealed TV's potential to influence a sizable portion of the public. The program, which starred Milton Berle, a rubber-faced former vaudevillian, debuted on ABC in 1948, and a year later, when Berle jumped to NBC, the *Texaco Star Theater* became a phenomenon, drawing 80 percent of the television audience during its Tuesday night slot. It was rumored that restaurants and movie houses began closing that night because so many of their customers stayed home to watch Berle. On May 16, 1949, the comedian made the cover of *Time* magazine.

Several sports also thrived in these early years of television. Broadcasts of boxing matches proved popular, sparking renewed interest in a sport that had declined. Broadcasts of major horse races turned thoroughbreds into household names. If Berle was television's first superstar, a gray colt named Native Dancer was the second.

Of all the sports, however, baseball was the biggest draw on television. Major league teams quickly struck deals with local stations and networks, and, suddenly, the national pastime was available for free. The viewing experience was far from optimal, with the small ball difficult to see on a small screen, and, thus, the action difficult to follow. But it was still a revelation. Many fans began to stay home and watch games rather than buy tickets. Major league attendance, which had spiked after World War II, declined sharply. The average crowd for a game was 16,447 in 1949. Within four years, it was 11,831. Halas and the football owners saw that as a reason to avoid embracing television, but, surprisingly, most major league club owners did not mind seeing their attendance plummet. In 1946, the New York Yankees became the first club to sell their local television rights, receiving $75,000 for that season. The market for rights fees quickly escalated. Within a decade, the Brooklyn Dodgers received $800,000 for the rights to televise one hundred games per year.

But baseball's owners were the only ones profiting. The televising of major league games crippled minor league baseball, long a popular diversion in smaller American cities. Millions of minor league fans simply gave up on their teams, choosing instead to follow major league clubs on television. The number of minor leagues would shrink from fifty-nine to twenty-one within a decade as attendance dropped 65 percent. College football also suffered once games were televised. The sport's overall attendance dropped 5 percent in 1950 and another 5 percent in 1951. Though that was not as precipitous as baseball's decline, it was enough for the NCAA to act. In 1951, it passed a regulation limiting the number of games that could be shown on television—seven per season in each region of the country.

Most NFL owners experienced similarly ominous results with their initial television broadcasts. Attendance dropped throughout the league in 1948 and 1949, significantly in several cases. Teams in the AAFC also televised games and saw their attendance drop. The war between the leagues did not help, but NFL owners believed the televising of games was the root of the decline.

Halas permitted just one game at Wrigley Field to be broadcast in Chicago in 1949. The $5,300 he received in return constituted his entire television income for the year. "I, a most cautious man with no outside income to speak of, was most careful to preserve ticket sales," Halas later wrote.

Most of his fellow owners followed his example. Although they recognized television's increasing prominence, they still feared its impact on ticket sales. They also could not envision their rights fees soaring as high as baseball's; their sport simply was not as popular. In 1950 the owners of the newly merged league continued to adhere to an informal agreement the NFL owners had reached the year before: teams would not televise home games.

The Rams were granted an exemption. Their owner, Dan Reeves, was so bullish on television's potential that he had arranged for all his team's games, home and away, to be televised in 1949. The Rams fielded a talented team led by Bob Waterfield, won a division title, and their attendance rose. Reeves negotiated the same deal for the 1950 season, with one important, new provision: if his attendance did drop, the Rams' television sponsors would reimburse him for the lost revenues. The new provision soon went into effect. Although the Rams won another division title in 1950, their attendance declined precipitously, and Reeves's sponsors had to pay him $200,000.

Halas and the other owners were not surprised by such an outcome. It seemed there was no doubt about the correlation between television broadcasts and lower attendance. Yet so many Americans were buying TV sets now that more than half of the homes in the country would have one by 1953. The NFL owners knew that could not be ignored. "I determined to increase our effort to make it work for the Bears," Halas wrote later. But how?

THE HARDEST TASK THE COMMISSIONER FACED EVERY YEAR WAS setting the regular-season schedule. For weeks, sometimes months, Bell sat at his kitchen table, smoked cigarettes, and scribbled versions, then called owners for their reactions. Marshall always took issue with Bell's proposals. Halas was seldom lacking objections. It was impossible to satisfy everyone's idea of what was fair. In the end, Bell went with the schedule that made the most owners the least angry.

Whether it was a skill he developed or an innate talent, Bell was a superb scheduler. That was never more apparent than in 1950. To open pro football's first post-merger season, he chose the game that fans across the country had yearned for: the Philadelphia Eagles, two-time defending NFL champions, would host the Cleveland Browns, winners of the AAFC every year the league existed.

Fans had debated the merits of the rival leagues since the AAFC kicked off. Several columnists had suggested the champions should meet on the field at the end of the season and put an end to the arguments. The leagues never got along well enough for that to occur, but now that Bell controlled the situation, he addressed it immediately. No one could accuse him of lacking a showman's touch.

The demand for tickets was high enough in Philadelphia that the Eagles switched the site from Shibe Park, the 33,000-seat baseball park where they usually played, to Municipal Stadium, the 100,000-seat behemoth that hosted the Army-Navy game. That famous college rivalry always sold out, and the Eagles-Browns game did not—an indication, perhaps, that college football still commanded more interest. But the crowd of more than 71,000 was easily the largest in Eagles history, and *that* was an indication of what lay ahead for pro football.

The Eagles expected to win, perhaps easily. Led by Steve Van Buren, a relentless running back, they had rolled through the NFL for two years. The NFL's owners, players, and fans had no doubt their football was superior to the AAFC's. "The worst team in our league could beat the best team in theirs," Marshall had said. That remark—representative of a general smugness in NFL circles—served to motivate Paul Brown and his Cleveland squad, which contained five future Hall of Fame inductees, including Marion Motley and quarterback Otto Graham. Anticipating the showdown, Brown had scouted the rainy 1949 NFL championship game between the Eagles and Rams. The Eagles' coach, Greasy Neale, never deigned to scout the Browns. "I would say that there was never another team in the history of sports, anywhere in the world, that was as prepared, physically and emotionally, to play a ballgame. We would have played the Eagles for a keg of beer or a milkshake," Graham said.

Bell was in the large crowd that stood and cheered when the opening kickoff flew through the air on a warm September evening in Philadelphia. Midway through the first quarter, the Eagles' veteran quarterback, Tommy Thompson, led a long drive. Van Buren, holder of six NFL rushing records, was out with a broken toe, but his backup

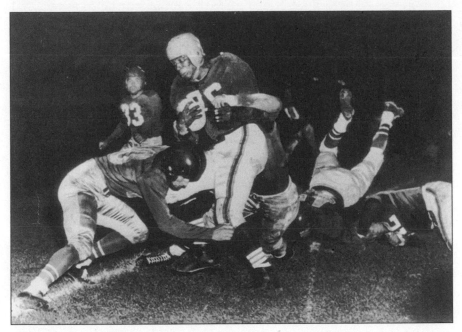

Fullback Marion Motley carries the ball during the Browns' season-opening victory in Philadelphia. (Associated Press)

gouged Cleveland's defense for gains and the Eagles kicked a field goal for a 3–0 lead. Late in the first quarter, Graham retreated to pass, scanned the field, and saw a receiver running behind the defense. His long pass hit Dub Jones in stride, and the receiver raced to the end zone to complete a 59-yard scoring play.

A tight, back-and-forth game developed. Trailing 7–3, the Eagles drove to a first down at the Cleveland 2 yard line in the second quarter. It appeared the home team would regain the lead. But Motley—so useful he still played both ways, despite Brown's emphasis on specialization—led a defensive stand that kept the Eagles out of the end zone on four plays. That galvanized the visitors. Graham threw a touchdown pass before halftime and another in the third quarter. The Eagles finally reached the end zone in the fourth quarter, but the Browns kept adding to their lead. The final score was 35–10, an unimaginable result for the NFL. "We whetted our appetite for that game for about three years," said Brown, unable to hide his immense satisfaction.

Bell was noticeably subdued after the game, but he soon received some encouraging information. A coaxial cable had been laid that could carry a television signal from the East Coast as far west as Omaha, Nebraska. (The cable would reach the West Coast in 1951, making "national" broadcasts possible.) Bell had tried to coax NBC and CBS into televising the Eagles-Browns game as far as the cable could carry the signal. Those networks passed, but DuMont, the struggling fourth network, was desperate for programming and signed a deal to televise the season-opening game, several other regular-season contests, and the NFL championship game. The viewing audience for the opening game was large, it turned out.

The contract with DuMont was Bell's second national television deal of the year. ABC had already agreed to televise fifteen regular-season games across the coaxial cable. The money was minimal: teams earned just $8,000 apiece from the ABC and DuMont deals. But the quasi-national broadcasts introduced pro football to areas of the country where college football had long ruled and, in some cases, pro results barely made the newspapers.

The timing was exquisite. With unlimited substitutions and daring offenses led by strong-armed quarterbacks and speedy receivers, pro football was becoming a spectacle. Meanwhile, many college coaches still relied on slow-moving ground games.

Although the Browns-Eagles contest was one-sided, Bell and the rest of the NFL learned that it was surely the most-watched league game ever. The next year, DuMont released data showing that national broadcasts of NFL games attracted 17.1 percent of the television audience in their time slot. By 1954, that figure had had risen to 36.1 percent on Sunday afternoons. That meant millions were watching. For Halas and the other owners who had feared television might ruin them, the Browns-Eagles game was a watershed. Here was the way to make the new medium work for them. Yes, if given a chance, thousands of fans in their home cities would stay home and watch games for free. But by televising games in other cities and states, particularly those that did not have teams of their own, franchises could expand their reach and attract new fans.

Halas contacted stations in eight cities in Chicago's orbit. He rented coaxial cable space on Sunday afternoons and struck a deal with WGN, a Chicago station, to televise his home games as well as those of the Cardinals. WGN's broadcasts of Chicago pro football were shown in Omaha, Minneapolis, Cincinnati, Louisville, Nashville, and several other cities. The Bears paid for the broadcasts, but the out-of-town stations sold advertising to help defray the team's costs. "It was quite an operation. We took a big gamble," Halas wrote. When 1951 season ended, the Bears had lost $1,750 on the venture. "But more people have seen the Bears play this year than the first 30 years of our existence put together," Halas said. The next year, stations in fifteen cities wanted the signal, and Halas picked up a major advertiser when Standard Oil paid $30,000 for 50 percent of the commercial time.

Several other owners adopted the same strategy. The Giants sold game broadcasts to stations throughout the Northeast. The Redskins developed a network of affiliates in the football-mad South, which did more than anything to realize George Preston Marshall's long-held ambition to make his team the South's team. By the end of the decade, the Bears' network would consist of seventy-seven stations in nineteen states, the Redskins' network of thirty-seven stations in nine states, and the Giants' network of fourteen stations in seven states.

Inevitably, problems arose. Some teams either were not as adept at selling themselves or could not match the interest that the Bears, Redskins, and Giants generated. By the end of the decade, the Eagles' network would consist of just three stations beyond Philadelphia. The Steelers and Lions had six stations apiece. There were "have" and "have not" television franchises, and the differences often translated to the field as certain franchises became much wealthier and thus had more to spend on players.

The league also had to go to court to protect its television policy. After the Rams' disastrous experiment in 1950, the league enacted a rule that games could not be televised within a seventy-five-mile radius of the home city—an obvious attempt to preserve ticket sales. But a station in Erie, Pennsylvania, sued the league for restraint of trade when a game between the Eagles and Browns in Cleveland was "blacked out" in Erie, seventy miles from the game. After more than two years of legal wrangling culminating in a federal trial in Philadelphia, the league was found guilty of three antitrust violations. But the judge upheld the legality of the seventy-five-mile blackout policy, giving the league an important victory. The owners had protected their ticket sales and gained control of their television broadcasts. They unanimously voted not to appeal the decision.

Between regional broadcasts and Bell's network deals, television income soared. In 1951, NBC paid $100,000 to broadcast the league championship game from "coast to coast," a first. In 1957, CBS offered $1 million for the broadcast rights to the entire NFL season. The league declined the offer, mostly because Halas, Mara, and Marshall were reluctant to break up their lucrative regional networks. Even with their television money growing from a pittance to a pile, the inner circle still operated with the instincts honed in the 1920s. They were protective of any gains, distrustful of outsiders, and watchful of one another's best interests.

BY THE MID-1950S, THE GREEN BAY PACKERS HAD BECOME A nuisance to the rest of the league. They were a historic franchise, but they still played in a high school stadium with just 26,000 seats, and with their winning days just a memory, they rarely sold out even that small venue. As a run of losing seasons mounted in the 1950s, they could not build a viable regional network of television and radio affiliates. Other owners, especially those relatively new to the league, no longer saw the romance in having a team in "little Green Bay." Art Rooney had rammed through a 60-40 gate-split rule, ensuring that visiting teams received 40 percent of the gate receipts for every game, but after playing profitable games before large crowds on the road, the

Packers could not reciprocate when opponents came to Green Bay. The visitors' take was virtually nothing.

The Packers' future seemingly rested on the fact that they now played several games a year in Milwaukee. The city, much larger than Green Bay, was having a sports boom. It had built a new multisport stadium with 54,000 seats, and that had attracted a major league baseball franchise, the Braves, who set attendance records and became a pennant contender soon after moving from Boston in 1953. Although the Packers did not draw nearly as well in Milwaukee, the other NFL owners broached the idea of the team moving there permanently. The last of the NFL's small-town franchises, a holdover from the days of sandlot and semipro teams, looked as though it might fail and bring an era to an end.

But Halas and his "tight little group" did not want the Packers to move. When Bell was struggling in Philadelphia in the 1930s, the board of directors who oversaw the Packers had loaned him money. He never forgot it, later telling a Green Bay sportswriter that there would always be an NFL team in the city. Halas was loyal to Green Bay, too. The Packers had been the Bears' primary rivals for more than three decades, and the enmity between the franchises ran deep. But Halas knew a rivalry was good for business; fans love to hate. Halas also knew that Green Bay had steadfastly supported its team through many years when other cities showed little interest in professional football.

Bell suggested to the Packers' board that the team needed a new stadium. The funding for one was floated as a bond referendum in Green Bay in April 1956. Halas drove up from Chicago and stumped for the project, and the referendum passed. Seventeen months later, the Packers upset the Bears at City Stadium, their new home venue, before a sellout crowd that included Bell and Richard Nixon, the US vice president, a noted pro football fan.

With the completion of the new stadium, the Packers' future in Green Bay was ensured. Although they would hit a low point with an 0-11-1 season in 1958, that miserable performance was followed by a fateful coaching change. Out went Raymond "Scooter" McLean, who played cards with his players on road trips. In came a strict, little-known Giants assistant coach named Vince Lombardi.

At that critical moment in the mid-1950s, when the members of the league's inner circle were deciding whether to continue to support a team in Green Bay, they were also considering what would happen next with television. They were far more encouraged by its possibilities now. Although they were still cutting their own deals with regional networks, Bell was negotiating network contracts from which all teams profited. As viewership and rights fees spiraled upward, the owners could envision the wealth that would result—and how that wealth, properly shared, would benefit the entire league. It was a remarkable prospect for them to consider, but a team in Green Bay could make just as much as a team in New York.

24

ALL-WHITE REDSKINS

THREE YEARS AFTER THEY REINTRODUCED AFRICAN AMERican players to the NFL in 1946, the Rams crossed another threshold, becoming the first team in the league to sign a player from an all-black college. Paul "Tank" Younger, a halfback and linebacker from Grambling College in Louisiana, was not among the 251 players selected in the 1949 draft, but the Rams had scouted him—in itself a progressive act—and liked him. They signed him shortly after the draft.

The press ignored the move, as did the rest of the NFL. Many pro scouts and coaches still believed *all* black players, even those on integrated major college teams, were not equipped to play in the pros. Players on historically black college teams such as Grambling, Bethune-Cookman in Florida, and Morgan State in Baltimore were widely dismissed as inferior.

When the Giants and Lions finally followed the Rams' example in 1948, they signed black players from integrated major college teams. The Giants, with Tim Mara's blessing, added Emlen Tunnell, a defensive back from Iowa. The Lions signed Melvin Groomes, a halfback from Indiana, and Bob Mann, a receiver from Michigan.

Tunnell and Mann earned starting jobs as rookies and demonstrated they belonged on the field with the league's best white players.

Questions about race were at the forefront of America's sports culture in the late 1940s and early 1950s. After Jackie Robinson broke in with baseball's Brooklyn Dodgers at the start of the 1947 season, four other black players were called up to the major leagues that year. By the end of the 1940s, almost a dozen were in the majors. In 1950, Althea Gibson became the first African American to play in the United States Lawn Tennis Association's national tournament. That same year, a court order forced the American Bowling Congress to remove a clause in its constitution restricting membership to whites. The National Basketball Association integrated in 1951 when the Boston Celtics drafted Chuck Cooper, a black forward from Duquesne.

Once the NFL allowed a few black players in, most of the owners examined their biases. Playing both ways as a six-foot-three, 225-pound rookie in 1949, Younger totaled more than 300 rushing and receiving yards, forced four fumbles, leveled opposing halfbacks with fierce tackling, and helped the Rams win a division title. Scouts began to look differently at black players, especially those from historically black colleges. The 1950 season brought more irrefutable evidence that black players belonged in the league. Marion Motley and Bill Willis had helped the Browns dominate the AAFC, but the NFL was dubious of the brand of football played in its rival league. Once the Browns joined the NFL, though, they won the championship in their first year with Motley and Willis performing well enough to earn All-Pro honors.

On November 25, 1951, George Halas brought his Bears to Cleveland to face the Browns for the first time. The Bears still had an all-white team, as did Art Rooney's Steelers and George Preston Marshall's Redskins. Marshall, descended from Confederate soldiers, was unambiguous on the subject of integration. "I have nothing against Negroes but I want an all-white team," he told the *Pittsburgh Courier,* that city's black newspaper, in 1950. At the very least, the end of the color line in other sports had led him to make his stance on the issue public. By contrast, it is not clear why Halas and Rooney failed to integrate their teams.

Halas certainly was not opposed to having African Americans play for the Bears. In 1940, he had tried to talk the other owners into letting him sign Kenny Washington. In 1949, the Bears had become the first NFL team to draft a black player when they took George Taliaferro, a halfback from Indiana. But Taliaferro turned Halas down to play for the AAFC's Los Angeles Dons, and the Bears were still an all-white squad when they traveled to Cleveland to play the Browns two years later.

Perhaps Halas and Rooney did not integrate their teams because they were not under pressure to do so. Even as America's racial laws and attitudes began to change in the early 1950s, segregated institutions and public venues remained commonplace. Few in the mainstream press—the white press—expressed anything close to outrage. Halas would always deny that the absence of blacks from his roster in these years was purposeful. Much later on, he would point out that scouting was in its infancy and teams had little information on players from all-black colleges—an incomplete explanation at best. At least one of Halas's biographers said he was influenced by his friendship with Marshall.

Whatever caused Halas to hesitate, his trip to Cleveland in 1951 resulted in a humbling the likes of which he had not often experienced, and it changed his mind. The game between the Bears and Browns was not only a battle of first-place teams but also Halas's first opportunity to make a statement with his team about the caliber of the AAFC relative to the NFL. "He really tried to get us up that week. I don't think I ever saw him want to win a game more," said Don Kindt, one of the Bears' defensive leaders. But in front of a howling crowd of 40,969 at Municipal Stadium, the Browns—faster, quicker—dismantled Halas's squad. Cleveland led by two touchdowns at halftime and built a 42–7 lead before settling for a 42–21 victory. Browns halfback Dub Jones, who scored six touchdowns, took the next day's headlines, as did the officials, who flagged the teams for thirty-seven penalties combined, but the Browns' three black players all played central roles in the victory. Willis disrupted Chicago's offense from his middle guard spot. Motley rushed for gains. Horace Gillom, a punter, continually pinned the Bears deep in their territory.

It was clear now to Halas that he was hurting his team by not employing black players. Two months later, he made Eddie Macon, a black halfback from College of the Pacific, his second-round pick and the twentieth overall selection in the 1952 draft. A year after that, the Bears used their first-round pick on Billy Anderson, another black halfback, from Compton Community College in Los Angeles.

Neither Macon nor Anderson fared well. Macon fumbled eight times as a rookie in 1952 and was released after two seasons. Anderson, the son of a famous actor, Rochester Anderson, was a bust. But it seemed that Halas had left behind whatever biases or even prejudice that had characterized his earlier thinking. With a second-round pick in 1955, he selected Bobby Watkins, a black halfback from Ohio State, who became a starter. The next year, he drafted Willie Galimore, a halfback from Florida A&M, and J. C. Caroline, a defensive back from Illinois, both of whom also became valuable starters.

By the time the Browns humbled Halas and the Bears in 1951, Rooney and the Steelers had already grown accustomed to Cleveland embarrassing them. The teams had been assigned to the same division after the merger, which meant they played twice a year. In 1950, the Browns won in Pittsburgh, 30–17, and in Cleveland, 45–7. In 1951, the Steelers, still fielding an all-white team, lost both games of the home-and-home series by a combined 45–0 score.

Why did Rooney, otherwise a man of principle and substance, wait so long to integrate his team? It could be that, like Halas, he was loyal to Marshall. He may not have wanted to overrule his coaches, who either doubted that black players were skilled enough for the pros or did not want to deal with the locker room tension that might arise between a black player and white southerners from segregated colleges. Whatever the explanation, the Steelers, like the Bears, finally integrated in 1952. Joe Bach, just hired as the team's head coach, told reporters that jobs would go to the best players, period, regardless of skin color—a clear indication that a new era was coming into view. It was long overdue, embarrassingly so. Pitt, the city's foremost college team, had integrated seven years earlier.

In the 1952 draft, hours after Halas took Eddie Macon in the second round, the Steelers drafted a black player for the first time, Jack Spinks, a 235-pound fullback from Alcorn State, a historically black college in Mississippi. He went in the eleventh round, and fourteen rounds later, the Steelers took Bill Robinson, a halfback from Lincoln, a historically black college in Missouri.

With a rare blend of speed and strength, Spinks was a promising prospect. But the Steelers' assistant coaches eyed him suspiciously during training camp. One lamented that Spinks did not even own a sports coat to wear on the road, as if that were a reason to cut him. After hearing that, one of Rooney's brothers loaned Spinks a coat.

Robinson, a Pittsburgh native, was a long-shot prospect. The Steelers' coaches thought so little of him that they did not even want to bring him to training camp. "We're wasting our time with him," Walt Kiesling said. But Rooney intervened; his son Dan had played on youth teams with Robinson. In the end, Robinson was invited to camp, but he played little. Rooney requested that he at least be given a shot. "All I'm asking is that you put him on the kickoff and we'll see what he can do," he said before a preseason game against the Giants. The owner then called Steve Owen, the Giants' head coach, and asked, "Would you see that your guy kicks the ball to him?"

Owen said he would happily kick to Robinson. "Do you want him to go all the way?" the coach joked.

During the game, the Giants' kicker drove the ball to Robinson, standing deep in the end zone. One of Robinson's teammates urged him to down the ball, but Robinson brought it out, thinking this might be his only chance to make an impression. A few yards past the goal line, he realized he had made a mistake and tried to return to the end zone to down the ball, but the Giants tackled him for a safety. "I told you he couldn't play!" Kiesling told Rooney.

Robinson did not make the team, but Spinks did, becoming the Steelers' first black player since Ray Kemp in 1933. And indeed, as some people affiliated with the team no doubt expected, several of his white teammates resented him. In *Ruanaidh,* his book on his father, Art Rooney Jr. wrote that, after Spinks ran over a white defensive back in practice one day, the white player cursed him with racial slurs and threw a football in his face from point-blank range. Mimicking Jackie Robinson, who had responded to racial abuse with a steely, dignified silence, Spinks returned to the huddle without speaking. According to *Ruanaidh,* Art Rooney either saw the incident or heard about it, and counseled Spinks, "Jack, the guy who threw that football at you is a good kid, but the next time that happens, I want you to punch him out."

Another rookie, Ed Modzelewski, beat out Spinks for the starting fullback job. Spinks carried the ball just twenty-two times during the 1952 season and was cut from the team the next year. The Cardinals picked him up, and he continued to draw a paycheck in the NFL through 1957, also playing for the Packers and Giants and switching positions to offensive guard before his career came to an end.

After their "experiment" with Spinks in 1952, the Steelers were cautious about black players. The next year they drafted Jack "Cy" Mc-Clairen, an end from Bethune-Cookman, in the twenty-sixth round. But an army stint kept McClairen out of pro football until 1955, and, in the intervening years, the Steelers remained entirely white.

IN 1949, THE LAST YEAR BEFORE THE MERGER WITH THE AAFC, five black players had jobs in the NFL. In 1950, after the merger, there were nineteen. The total would steadily increase over the decade. But, despite those gains, black players were pro football's second-class citizens. They faced taunts from opponents and fans. They stayed apart from their teammates on the road, in lesser accommodations, when their teams stayed at segregated hotels.

In 1951, the Giants and Redskins played a preseason game in Birmingham, Alabama, that was sponsored by the local Chamber of Commerce and benefitted an all-white hospital. Birmingham's city leaders made it known that they did not want black players in the game. Rather than stand up for their players, the Giants acquiesced, telling Tunnell and Bob Jackson not to suit up. Teams received sizable payments from cities to stage these preseason games, and neither wanted to lose the paycheck.

Teams also routinely signed blacks that played the same few positions, usually offensive end, defensive back, and offensive tackle or guard, then made them compete for jobs, ensuring that there would only be so many on the final roster. The originator of this practice, known as "stacking," has never been identified, but teams seldom had more than three or four black players at a time, and many players were sure an off-the-books quota existed. "I doubt it was written, you couldn't prove it in court, every owner would deny it, but it was there," said Jim Brown, who joined the Browns in 1957.

By the time Brown was drafted, though, fans had at least become accustomed to seeing black NFL players take the field for their teams, which represented progress over the previous decade. The Cardinals had drafted Ollie Matson, a running back from the University of San Francisco, with the third overall pick in the 1952 draft; a future Hall of Famer, he scored eight touchdowns as a rookie. Dick "Night Train" Lane, an agile defensive back, also with the Cardinals, led the league as a rookie with fourteen interceptions in 1952, then led the league again in 1954. Lenny Moore, a halfback-receiver from Penn State, earned the league's Rookie of the Year award in 1956 after the Baltimore Colts made him their first-round pick. When the Giants reemerged as a power that year, a pair of dominating black linemen anchored their interior play. Moore's former college teammate, Rosey Grier, a defensive end, had been a third-round draft pick in 1955. Rosey Brown, a gigantic offensive tackle from Morgan State, had been picked in the twenty-eighth round of a thirty-round draft in 1953. He was the league's best tackle. Ever so slowly, teams were moving in the right direction on a sensitive issue—with one glaring exception.

THE FIRST BONA FIDE EPIDEMIC OF PRO FOOTBALL FEVER HAD broken out in Washington, DC, after the Redskins came to town in 1937. Within a few years, Griffith Stadium hosted enthusiastic sellout crowds as Sammy Baugh led them to five division titles and two championships in their first nine years in the nation's capital. The Redskins' success had helped stabilize the NFL. But, by the mid-1950s, they had regressed. They had not won a division title since 1945. They no longer drew sellout crowds at home. George Preston Marshall still rolled out a marching band and staged elaborate half-time shows, but what the fans really wanted was winning football, and they were not getting it. Starting in 1946, the Redskins finished under .500 six times in an eight-year span.

"I went to a game in Washington in the late 1940s. It wasn't very crowded, nothing like it is today," recalled Mike McGee, a thorough-bred horse trainer whose father worked for Art Rooney starting in the late 1940s. "Rooney had given me a pass to get into any NFL game. I walked in there. They had a cyclone fence around back on one side. There was a crowd, but I thought, 'Jeez, this isn't a big deal.'"

Marshall took solace in the fact that his profits were up even though his gate receipts were down; his regional television network produced more and more income in the form of rights fees and advertising profits. Only Halas and the Bears had a larger network than Marshall and the Redskins.

As for the team itself, Marshall, with typical bombast, insisted it was only a matter of time until the Redskins reigned again. When pressed to explain their years of defeat, he fell back on a set of convenient excuses. Baugh had retired. Several coaches had failed to do the job expected of them. The draft had not brought relief. His rationale omitted the fact that, first, he made many important personnel decisions himself, and, second, he often selected players based on promotional value, not their value to the team. Ever focused on winning newspaper headlines and selling tickets, he used high draft picks on prospective offensive stars, largely ignoring the blockers and tacklers that served as a team's foundation. Almost every year, the Redskins drafted a quarterback or running back with their top pick.

Marshall also thought he could sway the public with "name" coaching hires, such as Curly Lambeau, the fading Green Bay legend, whom he brought to Washington in 1952, and who won ten games with the Redskins over two years before he was fired, never to coach again. It did not help that Marshall continually harangued and second-guessed whoever coached his team. He continued to pick up the private phone line connecting the owner's box and the sideline during games and suggest substitutions or play calls. The coaches and players tried to ignore him. "We had those big capes for cold weather, and sometimes we'd hang one over the phone at the bench, to muffle the sound," running back Jim Podoley told the *Washington Post*. "When Marshall saw what was happening, he'd send his chauffeur down to take the cape off the phone."

An equally if not more daunting problem was Marshall's steadfast refusal to employ black players. Even as they emerged as role players and stars on other teams, Marshall stuck to an all-white policy. His fondness for an older world, one in which the hierarchies of his youth were still in place, was readily apparent. His beloved halftime shows occasionally featured entertainers in blackface. In the late 1950s he briefly changed a lyric in his team's fight song from "fight for old D.C." to "fight for old Dixie." Surely, he abhorred the idea of paying blacks to play football and truly detested the thought of granting them leverage in salary negotiations.

At first, he attempted to avoid making news on the subject by obfuscating. Although he had told the *Pittsburgh Courier* in 1950 that he wanted an all-white team, he told a Washington columnist in 1953 that he "would like very much to sign a colored player. But it seems the other guys always beat me to them." It helped him that the Senators, Washington's baseball team, also had not integrated by the end of the 1953 season. Soon, though, his intentions became too obvious to ignore. In the 1954 draft, other teams combined to select thirteen black players, but the Redskins spent all thirty of their picks on white players. Then, on September 6, 1954, five months after the Supreme Court declared segregation in public schools unconstitutional, the Senators broke their color line with Carlos Paula, a black outfielder from Cuba. Now Marshall had the only all-white team in Washington.

That fall, the Redskins won just four games. On November 21, Ollie Matson scored four touchdowns against them in a 38–16 win for the Cardinals in Chicago. It was evident the Redskins were falling behind by ignoring black players. The pressure on Marshall began to build. Sam Lacy, an influential black sportswriter for the *Baltimore Afro-American,* called for black fans to boycott the team. Lacy had traveled with Jackie Robinson in 1947, the year Robinson integrated the major leagues. A DC native, he had stopped covering the Redskins in 1950 because of Marshall.

But Marshall paid little attention to criticism from Lacy or from other reporters, including the *Washington Post*'s Shirley Povich. In 1955, the Redskins had the NFL's only all-white team and surprisingly went 8-4 to finish second in the East. Dick McCann, their general manager, proclaimed it "the greatest reconstruction job since the Civil War," a comparison his boss surely enjoyed. The next year, Washington finished 6-6.

Whenever the subject of race and football came up, Marshall insisted fans in Washington wanted an all-white team. But his rationale was dated. It was true that Washington had been imbued with a southern sensibility when Marshall brought the team to town in 1937. (Ironically, though, Griffith Stadium was one of the few public facilities open to blacks at that time.) But the city was undergoing a dramatic transformation. Its population had soared to 1.5 million, and, after discrimination in federal hiring was outlawed in 1950,

African Americans flooded the capital in search of work. Between 1938 and 1956, the percentage of blacks in the federal workforce grew from 3 percent to 24.4 percent. By the mid-1950s, Washington's public schools, Catholic schools, restaurants, and theaters were no longer segregated, and it was much harder to claim that its sports fans desired an all-white team.

Marshall was apt to point out that the Redskins' fans in the Deep South still had a strong bias against black players. In 1956, the team's games were broadcast on sixty radio and twenty-nine television stations, covering Virginia, the Carolinas, and even Florida, where the top college teams remained all white. The Redskins barnstormed through the region every summer, playing preseason games in stadiums with separate seating for blacks and whites. Marshall did not want to tamper with a profitable arrangement.

Opposition to his position was growing, though. In January 1957, when the NFL owners met at the Bellevue-Stratford Hotel in Philadelphia to conduct the final rounds of that year's draft, they were surprised to find anti-Marshall protestors picketing the building. The Washington branch of the National Association for the Advancement of Colored People had organized the protest.

The owners rallied around their colleague, unanimously passing a resolution in his honor: "George Marshall, having completed 25 years in professional football, is the greatest asset sports has ever known with his honesty, integrity, and his perfect frankness in expressing what he believes." The resolution remains a blemish on the records of Halas, Bell, Rooney, Mara, and the entire NFL. Povich, a long-time critic of Marshall's, was appalled by it. "There are those who will contend," he wrote, "that a more debatable statement has never been uttered in the entire history of the spoken word."

IN THE FIRST ROUND OF THE 1957 DRAFT, THE BROWNS SE-lected Jim Brown, who had played at Syracuse. The Colts selected

Jim Parker, a tackle from Ohio State. Both were African Americans, destined for the Hall of Fame. The Redskins selected Don Bosseler, a fullback from Miami, who was white and destined for a solid if work-manlike eight-year pro career. After Bosseler, they drafted twenty-nine more white players. That fall, they went 5-6-1 to begin a run of nine straight losing campaigns.

The 1958 season brought more indignity for Marshall and his team. After Brown rushed for 152 yards and several scores in a vic-tory for the Browns in Washington, Povich wrote that the powerful running back, "born ineligible to play for the Redskins, integrated their end zone three times yesterday." Povich would later note that the Redskins' colors were "burgundy, gold and Caucasian." The Redskins finished that season 4-7-1 and then fell off badly, going 3-9 in 1959 and just 1-9-2 in 1960. "There were only so many good players, and when you eliminated half of them, it was tough. Very tough," recalled running back Jim Podoley, who played for the Redskins from 1957 to 1960. But Marshall was defiant. "We'll start signing Negroes when the Harlem Globetrotters start signing whites," he said.

On December 27, 1960, the owners gathered in Philadelphia for the annual college draft. Owing to their recent failures, the Redskins were in a prime position, holding the second and third picks in the first round. After the Minnesota Vikings, an expansion team, selected Tommy Mason, a white halfback from Tulane, with the first over-all pick, it was the Redskins' turn. The pool of draftees included fu-ture stars such as Bernie Casey, a speedy back from Bowling Green; Herb Adderly, a cornerback from Michigan State; Houston Antwine, a guard from Southern Illinois, and Ernie Ladd, a massive lineman from Grambling—all African Americans.

The Redskins took two white players: Norm Snead, a quarter-back from Wake Forest, and Joe Rutgens, a tackle from Illinois. Both would play well in the pros, but they could not change the fortunes of the all-white Redskins, who went 1-12-1 in 1961, reaching an embar-rassing nadir. "In modern pro football, Marshall is an anachronism, as out of date as the drop-kick," Povich wrote. "The other club owners have passed him by. Marshall, with his dedication to white supremacy on the football field, is still hearing a cry that doesn't exist."

Marshall dismissed Povich's criticism as a publicity stunt—for whom, it was not clear. His colleagues at the owners' table knew better, but they could not dissuade him. Marshall was going to run the Washington Redskins as he damn well pleased.

25

FORTY MILLION VIEWERS

A T SOME POINT IN THE 1930S, TIM MARA HAD PLEDGED TO treat the Giants' office staff to lunch every workday. He was still doing it more than two decades later even though it had become an expensive proposition as pro football became a bigger business, and the Giants' staff swelled with coaches, scouts, and administrators. Mara also had promised to take care of the Giants' head coach, Steve Owen, who, remarkably, had never signed a contract for longer than one year since first taking the job in 1930. Though the succession of one-year contracts may have suggested otherwise, Mara trusted Owen, who had won two league titles as the Giants' coach.

By the end of the 1953 season, though, Mara was weary of being the patient, rational owner who preached trust and continuity. The Giants, one of the oldest and most successful franchises in the league, had stopped winning, and he needed to make changes. It had been seven years since their last division title, a severe drought for a team that had played in eight league championship games between 1933 and 1946. After a low point in the late 1940s after the Filchock gambling scandal, the team briefly recovered; they tied for a division title in 1950 and posted winning records in 1951 and 1952. But in

1953, the Giants won just three games. And it was not just that they lost but *how* they lost that bothered Mara. Everywhere he looked, he saw teams playing more sophisticated and effective football. The league championship games of 1950 and 1951 had featured spectacular aerial duels between the Browns' Otto Graham and the Rams' Bob Waterfield. The Detroit Lions had won the league title in 1952 with another daring quarterback, Bobby Layne, leading the way. Those teams mixed old-fashioned power running with innovation and deception. The Giants, meanwhile, still ran Owen's A formation attack, in which the primary deception was the center snapping the ball to one of three players lined up in the backfield. They looked predictable and slow in comparison to the other teams. The Browns had embarrassed them, 62–14, near the end of the 1953 season.

Mara feared that fans were losing interest. The Giants had developed a loyal following after nearly three decades in business, but baseball had always been a more popular sport in New York, and that was truer than ever in the 1950s. The three major league teams in the city had launched something of a golden age of New York baseball. By the fall of 1953, the Yankees had won five straight World Series titles. In four of those five years, another New York–area team, either the Giants or Brooklyn Dodgers, had won the National League pennant before losing in the Series. With luminous stars such as Mickey Mantle, Willie Mays, and Jackie Robinson hitting home runs and stealing bases, baseball was dominant. In 1953, the Yankees, Dodgers, and Giants combined to sell 3.51 million tickets, even with many games televised. That fall, Mara's Giants sold just 147,056, an average of 24,509 per game—their lowest figure in several decades. Although the availability of games on the team's regional television network likely was a factor, it was just as likely that the product on the field was the primary problem.

When the Giants had fallen apart in the late 1940s, Mara went to his sons, who still ran the team, and asked whether Owen was the problem. As fond as Mara was of the coach, he was willing to replace him. His sons assured him the problem was not Owen but the talent, or lack of it, on the squad. Their opinion seemingly was validated when the Giants began winning again with Owen still in charge.

By late in the 1953 season, though, Mara's sons thought otherwise. Their roster featured promising young players, all recent draft picks, such as Kyle Rote, a receiver from SMU; Frank Gifford, a triple-threat halfback from Southern Cal; and Rosey Brown, a tackle from Morgan State. Their veteran quarterback, Charlie Conerly, could still play at a high level. The Giants had talent. But their whole approach seemed dated. Cleveland's Paul Brown and Detroit's Buddy Parker were mastermind coaches, always inventing new schemes. Owen had devised a new defensive alignment, a 6-1-4 setup known as the "umbrella" defense, to blunt opposing passing attacks, but the league had already figured out how to beat it. Sports columnists in New York called for Owen's ouster, and "as much as the Maras hated to admit it, they had to agree that the gridiron parade had passed by their old warhorse," wrote Don Smith, the team's director of publicity, years later.

A day after the 62–14 loss in Cleveland, Tim Mara and his sons summoned Owen for a meeting. "What's up?" Owen asked as he sat down in Tim's office. He listened silently, shocked, as his bosses informed him that his long run was over; he was being fired. Jack Mara later described it as "the toughest thing I ever had to do; Steve was like family." Owen coached the Giants' 1953 finale, which was his last game with the team. He did not speak to the Maras for years afterward.

But, though the firing of Owen was personally difficult for the Mara family, it was the correct move. The Maras replaced Owen with Jim Lee Howell, an easygoing native of Lonoke, Arkansas, who had played receiver and defensive back for the Giants before and after World War II. Howell put one of his assistants in charge of the offense and another in charge of the defense—a relatively new practice, one that followed the unlimited substitutions rule. To run the offense, Howell hired Army's backfield coach, Vince Lombardi, a tenacious former Fordham classmate of Wellington Mara's. The defense was handed to an active defensive back, Tom Landry, a tall Texan with a sharp strategic mind.

Of course, Lombardi and Landry would become head coaches, win championships, and make the Hall of Fame. As young assistants in the mid-1950s, they worked together to orchestrate a drastic turnaround for the Giants. Landry designed a defensive alignment featuring four linemen and three linebackers in front of a four-man umbrella of defensive backs, an update on Owen's approach. Lombardi designed a methodical offense built around Gifford, a nimble natural athlete who could run for gains, catch passes, and throw. The Giants posted a 7-5 record in 1954, in their first year under Howell, with Conerly throwing seventeen touchdown passes. The quarterback had considered retiring, not wanting to play another losing season, but now that the Giants were headed in the right direction, Conerly would play for them into the early 1960s.

In 1955, Conerly alternated with a young quarterback, Don Heinrich, while Gifford made All-Pro and fullback Alex Webster regularly plowed up the middle for chunks of yardage. The Giants started slowly, losing four of their first five games, but, by late in the season, no one wanted to play them. They went unbeaten in their final five games. On the Sunday after Thanksgiving, the Browns visited the Polo Grounds, and an epic game unfolded. The Giants went ahead, 14–0. The Browns, destined to win the league title, rallied to lead, 21–14. The Giants then staged a rally of their own, going up 28–21 as Conerly fired completions and Gifford twisted away from defenders to move the ball downfield. Back and forth the offenses went, with Conerly and Otto Graham matching big plays, until Graham moved his unit into position for a short field goal that would win the game in the final seconds. But the Giants blocked the kick. The final score was 35–35. The teams had combined for 770 yards of offense. Two years after Owen's firing, the Giants were playing thrilling football. They had drawn just 7,000 fans for a home game against the Cardinals earlier that season, but 45,699 watched them play the Browns.

That fall, Bert Bell phoned Tim Mara with some surprising news. A pair of Texas oilmen had offered to buy the Giants.

"But . . . the Giants aren't for sale," Mara sputtered.

"I know that," Bell responded.

Curious, Mara asked what the oilmen were offering.

"They'd pay $1 million," Bell said, "but they want to move the home games to Yankee Stadium."

Mara was amazed, both by the amount of the offer and the proposed venue change. "You know," he told his sons, "if we're worth $1 million in Yankee Stadium and they don't want any part of us in the Polo Grounds, maybe we ought to think about moving to Yankee Stadium."

Until that point, Mara had little interest in moving to Yankee Stadium because of his poor relationship with Dan Topping, who still owned the Yankees and the stadium. Mara remembered with some bitterness how Topping had cut off negotiations over home dates for their respective teams and jumped to the AAFC a decade earlier. But, as he had with Owen, Mara saw that necessity dictated that he put aside his personal feelings. The Polo Grounds had served the Giants well, but it was originally built in 1890 and, perhaps not surprisingly, starting to fall apart. The baseball Giants had stopped drawing big crowds to the stadium even though they had winning teams. Yankee Stadium was larger, which meant the Giants could sell more tickets, and it featured wider concourses and better sight lines. Fans also equated it with success, owing to the Yankees. Mara turned down the Texas oilmen, but, with Bert Bell's encouragement, he moved out of the Polo Grounds. The Giants signed a lease to begin playing in Yankee Stadium in 1956.

That year, they added another player who would prove vital, when Sam Huff, a ferocious rookie from West Virginia, joined the defense. They already had a stout unit with Rosey Grier and Andy Robustelli anchoring the line, and Emlen Tunnell leading the secondary. Tom Landry devised another new scheme around a third linebacker stationed in the middle of the defense, behind the line and in front of the secondary, responsible for stopping both runs and passes. Previously, most defenses had used two linebackers, one on each edge of the line, but with Huff roaming the field as a newfangled "middle" linebacker, Landry's defense yielded the fewest yards in the NFL in 1956.

The Giants began the season with three road games, winning two, as baseball preoccupied the city's sports fans. Contesting the sixth all–New York World Series in eight years, the Yankees and Dodgers played seven games before a winner was determined. (Yankees, again.) By the time the football Giants hosted their first game at Yankee Stadium on October 21, though, baseball was over, and the city was ready to turn its attention to them. The Giants promptly routed the Steelers, 38–10, before 48,108 fans. Three weeks later, they defeated the Cardinals, 23–10, in front of 62,410. It was their fifth straight victory.

The Browns had won six straight East division titles since the merger, but the Giants were now the superior team. Although they showed some weakness down the stretch, at one point winning just once in a month, they claimed the division title, their first in a decade, before the final Sunday of the season.

A throwback championship-game matchup was finalized when the Bears routed the Lions on the final Sunday to win the West. The Giants and Bears had met in the NFL's first two championship games, in 1933 and 1934, after George Preston Marshall had proposed the idea of a title game; and they had played again in 1941 and 1946. Now, after a decade in the wilderness for both teams, they were meeting again for the title.

George Halas had coached the Bears in their previous championship games against the Giants, but in 1956 he had handed the head coaching duties over to his friend and longtime assistant, Paddy Driscoll. Halas still effectively ran the team (and the league, though to a lesser extent than before), conducting meetings and putting sixty-four-year-old Clark Shaughnessy, his favorite football strategist, in charge of the defense.

Early in the week leading up to the title game, Tim Mara announced that he wanted to speak to the players, a rare request. After practice, he came to the locker room, still a commanding figure at age sixty-eight, over six feet tall, always dressed as if he were headed to the opera. The weather in the city had been frigid for weeks, and the forecast for Sunday was for more of the same. "Boys, we played the

Bears for the title back in '34 in weather this bad, and we nearly lost," Mara told the players. He explained how the Giants fell behind on a frozen field, then rallied to win after they changed into sneakers after halftime. "We're going to do the same thing this year, only we don't have to steal the sneakers," Mara said.

He pointed to Robustelli, who owned a sporting goods store. "Andy, can you fill an order for a good pair of sneakers for every man on the team by the end of week?" he asked. "You betcha, Mr. Mara," Robustelli said.

As predicted, the weather on game day was below freezing and blustery. An hour before kickoff, Howell put one player in cleats and another in sneakers and asked them to test the field. It was an easy choice. "We all go with sneakers!" Howell exclaimed.

The weather limited the Yankee Stadium crowd to 58,836, but the fans were rewarded for braving the conditions. The Giants scored an early touchdown and led by 13 points at the end of the first quarter. Near the end of the second quarter, they blocked a Chicago punt in the end zone and fell on the ball for a touchdown that gave them a 34–7 lead. Shaughnessy's defense could not stop Lombardi's varied attack. Conerly tossed a pair of touchdown passes. Gifford totaled 161 rushing and receiving yards. Webster also went over 100 yards from scrimmage. The final score was 47–7. A national television audience, watching on CBS, saw a caliber of football no college team could possibly reach. The Giants were almost frighteningly fierce on defense. Their offense dazzled the Bears. Like rubber-faced Milton Berle a decade earlier, New York's football Giants had become must-see TV.

ALTHOUGH THEY HAD BECOME FAMOUS LARGELY FOR LOSING time and time again to the Yankees in the World Series, baseball's Brooklyn Dodgers were popular and profitable. Ebbets Field was sold out for many of their games. They shared a lucrative local television contract with the Yankees and Giants. Baseball fans around the country knew their lineup and rooted for them to topple the widely reviled Bronx Bombers. Nonetheless, Walter O'Malley, who owned the club, was restless by 1956. Ebbets Field was small, with just a 32,000-seat capacity. A few years earlier, the worst team in the National League, Boston's Braves, had left behind a cramped, empty ballpark and moved into a large new stadium in Milwaukee. Now they were winning, drawing big crowds, and generating profits. O'Malley was jealous. Brooklyn supported his team, but he wanted a new place to play.

Various New York City politicians had different ideas about the best site for a new ballpark. There was a lot of discussion but no decision making, and O'Malley began to look elsewhere. Los Angeles beckoned. The West Coast metropolis was now larger than all but three cities with major league teams. It already had a successful NFL team, and the city's elected officials wanted a baseball franchise. O'Malley quietly began negotiating with politicians in Los Angeles, who offered to build him a new stadium if he moved the Dodgers. When the media learned of the talks, O'Malley at first denied that he would leave Brooklyn. But when New York officials still did not react as he wanted, he offered a warning early in 1957: "Unless something is done within six months, I will have to make other arrangements."

O'Malley called Horace Stoneham, owner of baseball's Giants, who was in a similar position. His attendance was plummeting. After drawing 1.16 million fans with a pennant-winning team in 1954, the Giants had drawn just 824,000 in 1955 and a paltry 629,000 in 1956. The Polo Grounds, like Ebbets Field, was dated. Tim Mara had moved out, taking the football Giants to Yankee Stadium. O'Malley asked Stoneham whether he, too, was pondering a move, and Stoneham said yes.

In May 1957, the other National League owners gave O'Malley and Stoneham permission to leave New York as long as they confirmed their intentions by October, which they did. New York sports fans were heartbroken. They had lived at the epicenter of the baseball world for decades, their clashing loyalties energizing the city. Now, though, they would only have one major league team.

The 1957 baseball season was solemn in New York. On September 24, the Dodgers played their final game at Ebbets Field. Between innings, the stadium organist played such songs as "Don't Ask Me Why I'm Leaving" and "Thanks for the Memories." Within a week, the Giants played their last game at the Polo Grounds.

Less than three weeks later, Tim Mara's Giants, the reigning NFL champions, were welcomed with a roar when they routed Pittsburgh in their first home game of the 1957 season. A palpable transformation was underway. No longer the capital of professional baseball, New York was turning to pro football. The Giants of the mid- to late 1950s were ideal objects of such affection. Gifford, glib and handsome, was destined for magazine covers and a career as a broadcaster. He began receiving the endorsement offers that had previously gone to baseball stars, as did Conerly, the drawling quarterback, and Huff, the fierce defender with an incongruously sunny personality. Football players had long been lesser figures in the city than baseball players, but that was shifting. Now, when a Giant drank at Toots Shor's, the iconic New York City watering hole, or dined at 21, it made the tabloid gossip columns.

The football Giants' season ticket sales grew quickly, as did their overall attendance. The 290,667 tickets they sold for six home games in 1957 was nearly double the amount they had sold just four years earlier. And the number of fans watching in person was small compared to the television viewership. Although the Giants' games were blacked out in the city, their regional network reached throughout the Northeast. Fans in the city drove to Connecticut, Long Island, and New Jersey on Sundays to watch games on stations outside the seventy-five-mile radius.

For much of the 1957 season, it appeared the Giants would win a second consecutive league title and launch a dynasty. When they defeated the Cardinals on November 24, they had a 7-2 record and trailed first-place Cleveland by just a half game in the East. But they faltered in December, losing their final three games. The division title went to the Browns.

Despite that disappointment, the Giants remained New York's darlings. In 1958, they played to even larger crowds and again battled Cleveland for the division title. After a midseason slump, they trailed by one game heading into their final regular-season contest, against the Browns at Yankee Stadium. Before 63,192 fans, they won, 13–10, on a field goal in the final minute. That meant the teams had to play again a week later, also at Yankee Stadium, to decide the division, and the Giants won again to advance to the league championship game for the second time in three years. They would play the Baltimore Colts, a new team in the league's championship mix.

The Colts were a Bert Bell creation, palpable evidence of the commissioner's vision and influence. The Baltimore franchise that joined the NFL from the AAFC in 1950 had lasted just one year before folding. Two years later, when a team in Dallas failed, Bell moved it to Baltimore and put a new owner in charge, Carroll Rosenbloom, a wealthy clothing manufacturer whom Bell had coached on the football squad at Penn in the 1920s. Rosenbloom quickly put the franchise on solid footing.

But the central figure in the Colts' rise was their quarterback, Johnny Unitas, a crew-cut Pittsburgh native whom Art Rooney already saw as one of his biggest mistakes. The Steelers, forever struggling, had given Unitas a tryout at their training camp in 1955, but they cut him without letting him throw a pass in the preseason. After playing semipro ball in Pittsburgh for a year, Unitas received a tryout offer from the Colts in 1956. He won the starting job and now, in his third pro season, operated the league's most dangerous passing attack.

Much like the revived Giants in New York, the Colts played before sellout crowds—fans so enthusiastic a Chicago sportswriter would label the scene in Baltimore "the world's largest outdoor insane asylum." Seven thousand Baltimore fans bought tickets to the 1958 championship game against the Giants and traveled to New York to cheer on their team. For the third straight Sunday, Yankee Stadium was brimming with pro football diehards.

When the game began at 3 p.m., fans across the country settled in to watch NBC's live broadcast from New York. Other sports that had initially benefitted from television's power were now struggling. Interest in boxing had plummeted because of overexposure. Horse racing had simply balked, refusing to televise many major races out of fear that attendance at tracks would drop. Baseball had made inroads, but the game was not always easy to follow on a small, black-and-white screen. The union of pro football and television, however, amplified the power of both the sport and the medium.

By using blackout rules and regional networks to control their television audience, the NFL's inner circle—Halas, Bell, Marshall, Rooney, and Mara—had boosted interest outside of their home cities while protecting their attendance figures and thus their gate receipts. The ratings for NFL broadcasts were up, and so was attendance. In 1950, the average crowd for an NFL game was 25,356. By 1958, it was 43,167. The inner circle had always believed in their game and their league and hoped that one day it would reach the same heights of popularity and influence as baseball and college football. Now, through television, pro football appeared poised to do just that.

The game itself was chiefly responsible for the surge in interest. For years, the prominent owners had tinkered with the rules, always with an eye toward making the game more accessible and exciting. In 1933, they had eliminated restrictions on the forward pass. Three times, they had voted to move the hash marks nearer the middle of the field. In 1950, they permitted unlimited substitutions. By the late 1950s, their game was a wide-open blend of brute force, athleticism, and daring. It was ideal for television. The 100-yard stage offered a tighter focus than baseball's. It was easy to see the hits and follow the significantly larger ball on the screen. The 1958 championship game introduced a final, and necessary, ingredient: high drama.

The Colts led at halftime, 14–3, with costly Giant fumbles having wasted one scoring chance and set up one for Baltimore. Unitas seemed in total control of the flow of the game, his pinpoint passes allowing him to move the Colts against Tom Landry's vaunted umbrella defense. Yet the Giants rallied. Rote fumbled near midfield after catching a pass, but Alex Webster scooped up the loose ball and raced to the Baltimore 1 yard line before being tackled. That set up a New York touchdown. Early in the fourth quarter, the Giants drove deep into Baltimore territory on a long pass from Conerly to receiver Bob Schnelker, and another pass, from Conerly to Gifford, produced a touchdown. The Giants now led, 17–14.

The game was decided by a late Baltimore drive. Starting at his 14 with two minutes to play, Unitas moved the ball forward with completions to Raymond Berry, a spidery wide receiver and future Hall of Fame inductee whose precise footwork enabled him to shake free from defenders. The drive penetrated deep into New York territory as the clock ticked down. The fans screeched, barely able to watch the tense scene.

With seven seconds to play, the Colts lined up for a 20-yard field goal that would tie the score. Bell, watching from the Yankee Stadium stands with Rooney and other league officials, knew what was at stake, but few fans and players did. The league had a "sudden death overtime" rule for its championship game. In the event of a tie after four quarters, play would continue until one team scored to win the game. The league had passed the rule more than a decade earlier, but it had never been used.

After the Colts' kicker, Steve Myhra, booted the ball through the uprights to tie the score at 17–17, players on both teams initially thought they would simply share the title. A few even shook hands and headed for their locker room until an official intervened, explaining that the game would continue.

A coin flip at midfield determined who would get the ball first. The Giants won the flip, but their offense could not pick up a first down, leading to a punt. Now Unitas had the ball again. The big crowd quieted when he threw passes to Berry and Alan Ameche, his fullback, for first downs. Ameche picked up 22 yards on a run. A completion to

Berry moved the ball to New York's 8 yard line. Any score would win the game, but, rather than settle for another field goal, Unitas wanted a touchdown. He completed a pass to an end, Jim Mutscheller, moving the ball to the 1. Now Unitas called a running play, and Ameche took the handoff and bulled into the end zone for a touchdown. The Colts had won.

"Up in the grandstand, a man was crying tears of joy. It was Bert Bell," columnist Frank Graham wrote in the *New York Journal-American.* The commissioner immediately and fully comprehended the significance of the moment. The NFL had staged a championship contest that was more than just another game. It had been a dramatic, unpredictable spectacle, just as compelling on television as it was in person. Ratings experts would estimate that 40 million people had watched the Colts and Giants on NBC. Forty million! That was roughly one-fifth of the country's population.

George Halas watched the game on a black-and-white television set in his den in Chicago. George Preston Marshall also watched from his home. Tim Mara was in his seat on the Giants' side of the field, distraught over how the game ended but aware that the show had been a success. Art Rooney sat in the stands next to Bell, his great friend. The five of them had worked together and encouraged one another for several decades even as their teams competed ferociously on the field. They had made many poor choices but many more good ones. With their determination to cooperate, their relentless, often unfounded optimism, and their skill as both football men and businessmen, they had built out of nothing something that was substantial and profitable, something millions now cared about. In that sense, their job was done.

EPILOGUE

B Y THE FALL OF 1957, THE NFL'S PLAYERS WERE WELL aware of the league's television bonanza and knew the owners could no longer cry poverty in salary negotiations. The players wanted to form a union and collectively bargain for a minimum salary, preseason pay, and support for injured players. The owners were split on how to respond.

George Preston Marshall led the opposition to a union, which was no surprise. A staunch political conservative, he had fought against the New Deal and opposed unionization in any context. And his stinginess was legendary. He was furious when he heard the Lions had started paying players fifty dollars to participate in preseason games. George Halas also opposed the union, unwilling to give up the leverage he had always wielded in salary talks.

Marshall and Halas had fought with each other through the years, but when they aligned on a league issue, they usually got their way. This time, though, they did not. Art Rooney lived in a union town and had a softer heart. He believed the players needed the help and could unionize without putting the owners out of business. Bert Bell's first instinct may have been to side with Halas and Marshall, but the commissioner understood that unionization probably was inevitable and that it would be better for business than the alternative, given the political climate. A congressional antitrust subcommittee was investigating restraint of trade in pro sports because the leagues had been so slow to expand. Bell had told the subcommittee that he was not opposed to the players forming a union, then filed a statement with the subcommittee in August 1957 saying he planned to formally recognize the players' nascent union as legitimate.

The night before Bell released the statement, Marshall lectured him over a meal in Washington. "You're going to get fired, Bert. What are you going to do? You can't get a job anywhere," Marshall said. Bell shrugged and replied, "If I get fired, I get fired." He was accustomed to threats. A year earlier, Tony Morabito, the volatile lumberman who owned the 49ers, was so upset by an officiating call that went against his team that he said he would "try to get Bert Bell's job." Morabito called Bell "a dictator." But that potential revolt never materialized after Halas defended the commissioner, and now, though Marshall envisioned another revolt, Bell actually had broad support on the issue. Other than Marshall and Halas, no owner was vehemently opposed to the players forming a union. After Bell said he would recognize it, the other owners stood by him. "There's no doubt Bell has the right to negotiate any differences between the players and owners," Jack Mara said.

The NFL officially dealt with the matter at an owners' meeting in Philadelphia on December 2, 1957. According to Art Rooney's son Dan, who attended the meeting, Halas and Marshall still did not want to recognize the union. "My father was the guy who got up and said, 'You have to vote so the players can have a union,'" Dan Rooney said. "Marshall and Halas were yelling at him and he said, 'Listen, Bert went before Congress and said he would get this done. If you don't do this, his effectiveness as commissioner is finished.'" Rooney forced a vote and the issue carried by a 10–2 margin, the minimum required for passage.

Halas, who had long acted as a shadow commissioner, was accustomed to getting his way, but he had been overruled. He grudgingly said he would support the union as long as players from every team belonged, but in a demonstration of his stubbornness and lingering power, the Bears' players did not join until 1962.

The conflict over the union was the last great debate between Halas, Bell, Marshall, Rooney, and Mara.

On February 16, 1959, six weeks after the Giants' loss to Baltimore in the overtime championship game that had been televised across the nation, Tim Mara suffered a heart attack and died at his Park Avenue apartment. Though his health had declined and his death was not unexpected—his family, the Giants' team doctor, and a priest were by his side—it was still a shock. Until recently, Mara had still been arriving at the Giants' offices every day at 7 a.m., as he had for years. In fact, at age seventy-one, he had never been more optimistic about the team. Season tickets were selling briskly after two championship-game appearances in three years. "We're going to sell out next year!" Mara exclaimed.

His death made national news. "Pro Football Pioneer Dies," read a banner headline in the *Chicago Tribune*. Although Mara's sons had effectively run the team for years, Mara had founded the franchise that gave the NFL a credible presence in New York, the country's largest media market. He had kept the Giants afloat through the stock market crash, the Great Depression, World War II, and a gambling scandal involving the team's quarterback. Only George Halas had been associated with the NFL longer than Tim Mara. Art Rooney had regarded Mara as a wise older brother, both in football and at the racetrack, going so far as to name a son after him. Rooney and the other owners traveled to New York for Mara's funeral. According to Rooney's biographers, Rooney was stoic at the funeral, "finding solace in his faith." But Bert Bell, who was anything but stoic, became agitated and suffered a minor heart attack during the event.

After that scare, a doctor advised Bell, who was sixty-six, to stop attending NFL games; it was possible his heart could not take the stress, the doctor said. Bell dismissed the warning. "I'd rather die watching football than in my bed with my boots off," he said. He

would get his wish. Seven months later, while taking in a game between the Eagles and Steelers at Franklin Field in Philadelphia on
October 12, 1959, Bell suffered a fatal heart attack.

It happened after the Eagles, headed for victory, scored an insurance touchdown with less than two minutes to play on a pass to
Tommy McDonald, a young wide receiver destined for the Hall of
Fame. McDonald would recall looking up and seeing the fans cheering except for those in one section, who were calling for help. Bell had
slumped after seeing his beloved team score.

His son, Upton, was also at the game, seated across the stadium.
"There was a commissioner's box, which he never sat in. He always
moved around, talking to people," Upton said. "I remember looking
across the field and seeing a guy wearing a tan suit down. He always
wore a tan suit in the summer and a blue suit in the winter.

"I said to my friend, 'Give me the binoculars.' He was gone by the
time I got to him."

Though devastated, Upton Bell understood that it was a fitting
end for his father, the lifelong football man whose devotion to the city
of Philadelphia, and to the NFL, was unrivaled. "What better way
was there for him to go out? He was watching an NFL game between
the two teams in the league he had owned. The Eagles had just scored
the winning touchdown," Upton Bell said. A sportswriter would later
characterize it as "like Caruso dying in the third act of Pagliacci."

The news of his death startled the rest of the league. Rooney, who
also attended the game, said later he was so dazed he wandered in
front of a streetcar as he left Franklin Field and was nearly killed. The
Packers' first-year head coach, whom Bell had helped steer to Green
Bay, had to take a seat and compose himself when reporters told him
about Bell after the Packers' game. "I don't know how we'll replace
him," Vince Lombardi said.

It would not be easy. Bell's record as an owner and coach in Philadelphia and Pittsburgh had been lamentable, but almost from the
day he joined the NFL in 1933, he had been a central figure in league
circles. It had been his idea to stimulate competitive balance with an

annual draft of college talent. "That move alone probably saved the league," Upton Bell said. As commissioner since the end of World War II, Bell had fended off and co-opted the AAFC and deftly steered the league through the reintegration of rosters, television's rise, and the start of a players' union. Over the course of his tenure, he had taken the league from uncertainty to security, from a tenuous financial state to clear profitability, and from the lowly status of a secondary sport to the game of the television age.

After his death, the tributes rolled in. "There is no such thing as an indispensable man. But Bert Bell came closer to it than most in his role as commissioner," Arthur Daley wrote in the *New York Times*. Edwin Anderson, the Lions' team president, remarked that Bell "has done more for professional football than any other man," quite a statement given that he worked alongside Halas.

"He's certainly the only commissioner in sports history who played the game, coached the game, owned a team, and became commissioner. No one else in sports history has ever had that background," Upton Bell recalled. "If there was a problem with a player, he knew what it felt like to have his nose broken and his face kicked in. If there was a problem with an owner, and there were many, he'd done that so he could tell them off."

More than a half century later, Upton Bell said his father was preparing to give up the commissioner's job when he died. "He was going to buy the Eagles back. He had a deal for $900,000," Upton said. That went unreported at the time, probably because it was not widely known. Bell had been the commissioner for so long that the owners could not imagine anyone else in the job. They battled through twenty-three ballots at the next league meeting before they finally agreed on a replacement: Pete Rozelle, the Rams' general manager.

A thirty-three-year-old, perpetually tanned former public relations man, Rozelle would attain legendary status as he guided the NFL through an era of exponential growth. As the league became a slick, wildly profitable corporate entity, the pre-Rozelle years would become something of a curiosity. It seemed impossible that the commissioner of America's preeminent sports institution had once doodled the schedule while sitting at his kitchen table and talking on the phone with the owners. But that had been the NFL when Bert Bell was in charge.

BEFORE THEIR TEAMS PLAYED IN WASHINGTON ON AN OCTOBER afternoon in 1964, George Halas and George Preston Marshall found themselves having an impromptu conversation. Marshall's limousine happened to pull up to the stadium just as the Bears' team bus arrived. Halas leapt from the bus and rushed over to greet Marshall. "George!" Halas exclaimed with his hand extended. "So good to see you, Chief. So really good to see you." According to a *Washington Star* reporter who witnessed the scene, Marshall began to cry. "It's like old times," Halas said cheerfully. After a brief silence, Halas added, "If there's anything you need, George just let me know. I'll be glad to help."

Marshall nodded. Two years earlier, he had undergone a hernia operation. It was successful, but complications kept him in the hospital. Then he suffered a stroke. For decades, the Redskins' owner had been the loudest voice in the NFL. But now he was seldom able to speak at all. Marshall no longer attended the league meetings he had once dominated, and he had been too ill to attend the dedication of the Hall of Fame in Canton, Ohio, on September 7, 1963, when seventeen men became the Hall's charter class of inductees. Marshall was one of the seventeen, enshrined with playing legends including Sammy Baugh, Don Hutson, Red Grange, and Bronko Nagurski, and also Halas, Tim Mara, and Bert Bell. (Art Rooney was enshrined a year later.)

Few men had done more than Marshall to popularize pro football. He had pushed for rules that opened up the passing game. He had invented the postseason with his idea of separating the teams into two divisions and having the winners meet in a championship game. He had enlivened a dour sport with halftime pageants and marching bands.

More recently, though, Marshall had drawn only criticism for his refusal to sign African Americans players, earning himself a reputation as the NFL's fiercest racist. He was forced to relent when no less an authority than the US government began pressuring him. A new sports venue, D.C. Stadium, was opening in Washington in 1961. It seated more fans than Griffith Stadium, where the Redskins had always played, and thus offered the possibility of higher gate receipts. But the new stadium was located on federal land and overseen by the National Park Service. Stewart Udall, secretary of the interior under President John F. Kennedy, informed Marshall that the Redskins could play in the stadium only if they followed federal hiring laws. That meant no discrimination.

Marshall was furious. But support for him had eroded within the league. Mara and Bell were dead. Halas and Rooney recognized that their longtime colleague's position was untenable. They encouraged Pete Rozelle to talk to Marshall. To that point, the new commissioner had avoided confronting a league elder over an embarrassing situation, but the NFL had signed a large network television contract and could no longer afford to broadcast the games of a segregated franchise. In the calculus of what finally turned the league against Marshall, it seemed, sadly, that profits and public perception were a larger factor than principle—a prioritization some believe is still in effect today as the league grapples with player protests over civil issues and a questionable record of minority hiring among coaches.

After Rozelle spoke to him, Marshall claimed he was interested in drafting a black player with his top pick later that year. Udall grudgingly allowed the Redskins to play in D.C. Stadium as an all-white team in 1961, provided they agreed to desegregate after the season. They won just one of fourteen games that fall while protestors picketed outside D.C. Stadium on Sundays. Critics in the press and civil rights activists wondered whether Marshall would break his promise, but the Redskins selected Ernie Davis, a black All-American halfback from Syracuse, with the first pick in the 1962 draft. When Davis said he did not want to play for Marshall, the Redskins traded his rights to the

Cleveland Browns for Bobby Mitchell, another black halfback. Mitchell and two other black players suited up for the Redskins in 1962.

Long before he lost that battle, Marshall's life had begun to disintegrate. His marriage to Corinne Griffith fell apart. He saw little of his children. He sold a minority interest in the Redskins to Edward Bennett Williams, a powerful Washington lawyer. His friends wondered whether the years of turmoil caused by his stance against integration contributed to his declining health.

Decades later, his name is still invoked for a different, though broadly related, reason. The team name he had selected in 1933—Redskins—has been deemed by many to be racist and offensive to Native Americans. Among the critics are Native American groups. There are calls for the franchise to change its name, as well as many fans who want to keep it in place. The team's current owner, Dan Snyder, sides with the latter group. But as a result of the current controversy, Marshall has received new scrutiny, and his record on race is as embarrassing as ever to the NFL.

In the late 1960s, as Marshall relinquished control of the Redskins, it became clear he would not live much longer. Halas and Rooney traveled to Washington for a final visit. Marshall was now partially paralyzed. "He couldn't take part in the conversation, so we had to talk in front of him. It was very hard," Rooney recalled. "Finally, Halas asked the nurse for a drink and she brought a quart of whiskey."

Rooney, who had given up alcohol several decades earlier, demurred. But Halas, who seldom drank, poured a large glass and guzzled it. "Now he got loose, real loose, talking to Marshall about things that happened in the past," Rooney recalled. "Pretty soon Marshall was laughing and crying. I told Marshall I'd need his wheelchair to get Halas home. Marshall laughed some more. I was real proud of Halas that day."

Despite all the trouble he had caused the league in prior years, and despite his repellent racial views, the NFL gave Marshall a hero's treatment after he died on August 9, 1969. Rozelle, speaking at his funeral, said, "Mr. Marshall was an outspoken foe of the status quo when most were content with it. We are all beneficiaries of what his dynamic personality helped shape over three decades."

It would have been hard for the league to criticize him in death, but not impossible. Yet it chose not to bring up race, the issue that now dominates, and tarnishes, Marshall's legacy. For his part, Marshall had put in his will a proviso for the creation of a charitable foundation in his name, but it came with a caveat: the foundation's funds would not support "the principle of racial integration in any form."

GEORGE HALAS WORE A DARK SUIT WHEN HE ENTERED A CON-gressional subcommittee room on Capitol Hill in Washington, DC, on December 10, 1981. After taking a seat in front of a panel of politicians, he cleared his throat and began to speak, occasionally looking up through thick glasses. "I am George Halas of the Chicago Bears Football Club," he said. "I was born February 2, 1895, in Chicago. Chicago has been my home for 86 years."

The panel was studying potential antitrust violations in professional sports, specifically whether franchise relocations, which always agitated fans, might rise to that level. Pete Rozelle was scheduled to address the committee and had brought along Halas for support. Halas was more than just a central figure in pro football history. Halas *was* pro football.

"On September 17, 1920, 12 independent teams met in Canton, Ohio, in Ralph Hay's automobile showroom. Chairs were few. I sat on the running board of a Hupmobile," Halas told the committee. "All agreed we needed a league. In two hours, our league, the American Professional Football Association, was born." In a strong voice belying his age, he proceeded to detail how the league survived. "Our league was then, and still is, best exemplified as a wheel. In 1920, we were 12 independent spokes. But spokes, if they are to serve a useful purpose and make a contribution, must have a rim. A spoke may weaken, even break, but the rim prevents collapse. Our league was and is our rim. The credo of sharing became the foundation of our league. On this foundation, professional football was built. This sharing concept was unprecedented in sport."

He detailed examples of how the NFL's owners had worked together, citing the draft, scheduling, and national television deals. It was a history lesson. Halas had owned and operated the Bears for more than six decades, since the start of the 1920s. He had coached them for forty of those years, winning six championships, most recently in 1963, and had not retired from coaching until he was seventy-two.

"When I started going to Bears games at age five, my brothers and I sat on an army blanket by the bench while our grandfather coached," recalled Patrick McCaskey, one of Halas's grandsons. "We heard a lot of things. One time, he told an official, 'No man is completely worthless. You can always serve as a horrible example.' It's hard to forget that. After the games, we would wait for him outside the locker room, and regardless of how the Bears did, he always reached out to each of us and said, 'Hi, pal, how about a kiss for Grandpa?'"

By the 1970s, Halas had relinquished the job of coaching the Bears and had given up most of his front office responsibilities. Younger men, including his son, directed the affairs of his team and the league. But he continued to have a role. "The business of the league still very much occupied him," Patrick McCaskey explained. "He was on the board of NFL Charities. He was chairman of the Bears. He went to league meetings." McCaskey added, "He didn't talk much about the past. When a Bears fan asked for an autograph, he always complied. He lived the Bears and appreciated any sign that a fan did, too."

Halas had groomed his son, George Jr., to run the Bears. Known to all as Mugs, the younger Halas had many of his father's qualities, according to another of Halas's grandsons. "Mugs was so sharp, so quick, fast on his feet. Both guys were quick thinkers, not just about sports, but about politics, current events, anything," George McCaskey said. Mugs joined the Bears' front office at age twenty-five in 1950 and became the team president in 1963, the same year his father coached the Bears to a title for the last time. Mugs was a fixture in league circles when he suffered a fatal heart attack at age fifty-four on the last day of the 1979 regular season, a traumatic blow for Halas, whose wife, Min, had died thirteen years earlier.

When Halas spoke on Capitol Hill in 1981, he was still shaken about Mugs but, as always, determined to carry on. More than two decades earlier, when Lamar Hunt, the scion of a Texas oil fortune, had sought to buy the Chicago Cardinals, the team's owner, Walter Wolfner, who despised Halas, predicted the demise of his crosstown rival. "Halas is way up there in years. He's liable to pass away anytime soon," Wolfner told Hunt. Wolfner died in 1963. Halas was eighty-six and still in good health when he spoke on Capitol Hill in 1981. He told the committee,

"I have devoted all my energies to professional football. No other business enterprises command my attention. No other professions demand my time. When I returned to civilian life after World War II, I was asked to run for Congress with the guaranteed backing of the *Chicago Tribune*. I declined. I would not and could not walk out on my responsibilities to my profession, my Bears, and our NFL.

"In 60 years, I have watched our ugly duckling of a league grow into a majestic eagle. . . . The National Football League was not and is not an accident. Our league did and does demand hard work, planning, experimentation, and solid management. It will continue to grow and bring professional football to new communities only if the foundation and principles on which it was built are permitted to survive."

Within a year, Halas would learn he had pancreatic cancer. He died on October 31, 1983. "When he was dying, he had every intention of beating his cancer and getting back to work," Patrick Mc-Caskey recalled. "He was an optimist. America needed optimists during the last century because of the depression and two world wars. His era shaped him. He maintained a great enthusiasm for work. There weren't any problems, only opportunities."

WHEN ART ROONEY WAS HONORED WITH INDUCTION INTO THE Hall of Fame in 1964, it was strictly for his influential role in the

NFL's decision-making apparatus for more than three decades. His credentials as a team owner did not merit consideration. The Steelers had played twenty-nine seasons by then, not counting the two years during the war when they merged with other teams. In those twenty-nine years, they had posted just seven winning records. They had never won a division title outright, never played in the league championship game, and stood at fifty-three games under .500 since kicking off in 1933. The lament Rooney had inadvertently invented years earlier—"same old Steelers"—was as apt in the 1960s as it had been in the 1930s.

Still, most people in the game understood that Rooney was fully deserving of his Hall induction. He had provided wise counsel at the owners' table and served as a peacemaker in many disputes, helping the league grow and mature. He was arguably the best example of an owner more concerned about the league than his own team's success. Asked what Rooney contributed to the inner circle that ran the league, Virginia McCaskey, Halas's daughter, replied, "Integrity, certainly. But mostly, he was a wonderful man. My father's relationship with him was very warm. And his warmth benefited the league. Helping people get along. He just wanted to be a good friend to everyone." Upton Bell could also attest to Rooney's generosity, recalling that, "at one point, he was sending cash in an envelope to my father to keep the Eagles afloat."

That was typical, said one of Rooney's five sons, Art Jr. "My dad was the guy who would pay his toll on the highway and also pay the toll of the guy waiting behind him in line. He really liked people," Art Jr. said. "During the season, he would go down to the trainers' room and play cards with the injured players. One time we had a guy who had been out for two years, and when he came back, we cut him. Well, my dad came around to talk to him as he was leaving, asked how he was doing, how his wife and kids were. My dad left and the guy told the trainer, 'I've never seen anything like that. I'm bumming a free ride off him and he remembers my name and my wife's name and my kids' names?'"

When he went into the Hall in 1964, Rooney was portrayed in newspaper coverage of the event as a man who possessed more character than football acumen. The *Pittsburgh Post-Gazette* said he was "simply a great guy" but also labeled him "a philosopher," defining the term, in a football context, as "an owner who has never won a league pennant." The contrast bothered Rooney, despite how he presented himself to the world. "There is the image of me as the benevolent loser, that even though my teams have never won anything, it doesn't bother me. Well, that's foolishness," he would say later. "I keep a lot to myself, but you'd better believe that I hurt inside every time we lose."

He only spoke from the podium briefly on the day he was inducted, but he sounded an optimistic note, predicting the Steelers' time still might come. Most observers scoffed. The team went 5-9 in 1964 and embarked on a new run of abject failure—eight straight losing seasons, including back-to-back records of 1-13 in 1969 and 2-11-1 in 1970. Rooney's squad had never looked worse. "All those years, he never had a good team. He was always hiring his friends as coaches, and I think his personal liking for players influenced his decisions," Virginia McCaskey said.

But quietly—so quietly no one noticed at first—things began to change in Pittsburgh. Rooney's son Dan was running the team by 1969. Art told him to hire a new coach without taking congeniality into consideration. Dan tapped Chuck Noll, a clever Paul Brown disciple who had been the Baltimore Colts' defensive coordinator. Meanwhile, Art Jr. led a scouting department that produced talented draft picks, including defensive tackle Joe Greene, quarterback Terry Bradshaw, cornerback Mel Blount, linebacker Jack Ham, and running back Franco Harris.

The pieces started coming together in 1972 when the Steelers won a division title, their first ever. Two years later, they won a Super Bowl. Then they won another. Before the 1970s ended, they had won four under Noll.

"After we'd won one or two Super Bowls, George Halas came to me at a league meeting and said he wanted to take me to dinner," Art

Jr. recalled. "I said, 'Oh, I'll tell Dad,' and he said, 'No, I don't want your dad, I want to go just with you and [your wife] Kathleen.' We had dinner with him and his family, and when it was over, he said, 'OK, get your chair over here next to me, and Kathleen, get your chair over here, too.' He says, 'You know, you did the greatest personnel job in the history of the National Football League.' Coming from old man Halas, that was big."

When Halas died in 1983, Rooney became the last surviving member of the NFL's old guard, a kindly presence known for his ever-present cigar.

"We'd go to training camp and he'd say, 'I'd like to talk to these kids and I want to use their names,'" Art Jr. recalled. "He was very, very elderly. I would stand with him. A player would be coming off the field. He'd say, 'Who's that?' I'd say, 'John Miller.' He was a redhead and my dad would say, 'Hey Red, come over here. I'm Art Rooney. I own this team. How ya doing? Where ya from?' They'd give an answer and he'd say, 'Oh, yeah, I know that place. You know so and so?' Sometimes they did. He would do that with all of the players."

When Rooney died on August 25, 1988, it was widely reported as "the end of an era." Pro football had become a billion-dollar enterprise whose owners looked to maximize revenue streams, not play cards with the players. It was the fate of any industry that had grown so large and profitable.

Today, the NFL is one of the nation's premier sources of entertainment, having overtaken the other sports, even baseball. The game itself has changed, with players much larger, faster, and stronger than ever before, and with offenses and defenses more inventive every year. The dangers the game entails are newly apparent, too, leading some to question how long football can survive. Mara, Bell, Marshall, Rooney, and Halas would have felt at home debating the ominous subject. For them, survival was always the preeminent question, and they always seemed to find their way, together, to an answer.

Acknowledgments

THIS BOOK GREW OUT OF A CONVERSATION BETWEEN SCOTT Waxman, my literary agent, and Dan Gerstle, a senior editor at Basic Books. Dan wanted to publish a book about the men who built the NFL. When he asked Scott to recommend an author, my name came up. Having written several books about pro football, I had long regarded the sport's first decades as promising storytelling terrain. A deal was struck. Dan and Scott, many thanks for making it possible for me to dive headlong into such a fascinating subject.

I still work full time as a "daily" sportswriter, as has been the case for nearly four decades. These days, I'm writing columns on the digital channels operated by the Baltimore Ravens of the National Football League. I really appreciate that Michelle Andres, the team's senior vice president for digital media and broadcasting, allows me to juggle my job responsibilities with writing books.

Kevin Byrne, the Ravens' senior vice president for public and community relations, introduced me to his colleagues from several other NFL teams, helping me include important voices in the narrative. The New York Giants' Pat Hanlon set up my interview with John Mara in East Rutherford, New Jersey. The Chicago Bears' Scott Hagel set up my interviews with Virginia McCaskey, George McCaskey, and Patrick McCaskey in Lake Forest, Illinois. The Pittsburgh Steelers' Burt Lauten set up my interview with Dan Rooney in Hershey, Pennsylvania, and told me how to contact Art Rooney Jr. in Pittsburgh. Upton Bell was enthusiastic about the project from the outset and helpful throughout. Dan Gray put me in touch with his father, Mike McGee. I thank them all for their time and effort.

I traveled twice to the Pro Football Hall of Fame in Canton, Ohio, to spend time at the Ralph Wilson Jr. Pro Football Research and Preservation Center. Jon Kendle, the center's archivist, oversaw my visits and directed me to the right research materials, which included newspaper coverage of many of the events depicted in the book. The online archives of the *New York Times, Chicago Tribune,* and *Washington Post* were also helpful. My go-to resource for checking any score or statistic was pro-football-reference.com.

As always, I'm most grateful to Mary Wynne Eisenberg, my wife of thirty-four years who, by now, is an expert in her own right at what it takes to write a book. Once again, I love you, MW, and I can't thank you enough for everything.

—*John Eisenberg*

Note on Sources

THIS BOOK RELIES ON ORIGINAL INTERVIEWS, NEWSPAPER AND magazine articles, web research, primary sources, and previous books on the central figures and the early days of pro football and the NFL. An important primary source, located at the Pro Football Hall of Fame, is a volume containing the official minutes of every league meeting dating back to 1920.

I have not invented conversations; everything that appears within quotation marks is cited, as are numbers that are not commonly in the public record, such as financial profit and loss figures. Football scores, statistics, and attendance figures are not cited, as they are widely available. The central characters in the book are well-known, even legendary, figures, and I have sought to stick to a factual accounting of their lives and actions, as opposed to interpreting their thoughts.

Interviews with Upton Bell, John Mara, George McCaskey, Patrick McCaskey, Virginia McCaskey, Mike McGee, Art Rooney Jr., and Dan Rooney provided invaluable insight. Robert Lyons's Bert Bell biography, *On Any Given Sunday*, was extremely helpful, as was George Halas's autobiography, *Halas by Halas*, and *Rooney: A Sporting Life*, by Rob Ruck, Maggie Jones Patterson, and Michael P. Weber. It would have been impossible for me to accurately depict the NFL's early years without *Joe Carr: The Man Who Built the National Football League*, by Chris Willis, and the splendid work of Dan Daly, author of *The National Forgotten League* and coauthor of *The Pro Football Chronicle*.

BIBLIOGRAPHY

Ashby, Steven K., and C. J. Hawkins. *Staley: The Fight for a New American Labor Movement*. Urbana: University of Illinois Press, 2009.

Bell, Upton, with Ron Borges. *Present at the Creation: My Life in the NFL and the Rise of America's Game*. Lincoln: University of Nebraska Press, 2017.

Boswell, Thomas, Richard Justice, Tony Kornheiser, et al. *Redskins: A History of Washington's Team*. Washington, DC: Washington Post Books, 1997.

Coenen, Craig R. *From Sandlots to the Super Bowl: The National Football League*. Knoxville: University of Tennessee Press, 2005.

Cowen, Tyler. *What Price Fame?* Boston: Harvard University Press, 2000.

Daly, Dan. *The National Forgotten League: Entertaining Stories and Observations from Pro Football's First Fifty Years*. Lincoln: University of Nebraska Press, 2012.

Daly, Dan, and Bob O'Donnell. *The Pro Football Chronicle: The Complete (Well, Almost) Record of the Best Players, the Greatest Photos, the Hardest Hits, the Biggest Scandals and the Funniest Stories in Pro Football*. New York: Collier Books, 1990.

Davis, Jeff. *Papa Bear: The Life and Legacy of George Halas*. New York: McGraw Hill, 2005.

DeVito, Carlo. *Wellington: The Maras, the Giants and the City of New York*. Chicago: Triumph Books, 2006.

Didinger, Ray, and Robert S. Lyons. *The New Eagles Encyclopedia*. Philadelphia: Temple University Press, 2014.

Doxsie, Don. *Iron Man McGinnity: A Baseball Biography*. Jefferson, NC: McFarland, 2009.

Elfin, David. *Washington Redskins: The Complete Illustrated History*. Minneapolis, MN: MVP Books, 2011.

Erghott, Robert. *Mr. Wrigley's Ball Club: Chicago and the Cubs During the Jazz Age*. Lincoln: University of Nebraska Press, 2013.

Freedman, Lew. *The Chicago Bears: The Complete Illustrated History*. Minneapolis, MN: MVP Books, 2008.

Gotterher, Barry. *The Giants of New York: The History of Professional Football's Most Fabulous Dynasty*. New York: G. P. Putnam's Sons, 1963.

Griffith, Corinne. *My Life with the Redskins*. New York: A. S. Barnes, 1947.

Halas, George, with Gwen Morgan and Arthur Veysey. *Halas by Halas: The Autobiography of George Halas*. New York: McGraw-Hill, 1979.

Helyar, John. *Lords of the Realm: The Real History of Baseball*. New York: Villard Books, 1994.

Holley, Joe. *Slingin' Sam: The Life and Times of the Greatest Quarterback Ever to Play the Game.* Austin: University of Texas Press, 2012.

Hudson, Sam. *Philadelphia and Its Public Men.* Philadelphia: Hudson and Joseph, 1909.

Loverro, Thom. *Hail Victory: An Oral History of the Washington Redskins.* Hoboken, NJ: Wiley, 2007.

Lowenfish, Leo. *Branch Rickey: Baseball's Ferocious Gentleman.* Lincoln: University of Nebraska Press, 2007.

Lyons, Robert S. *On Any Given Sunday: A Life of Bert Bell.* Philadelphia: Temple University, 2010.

MacCambridge, Michael. *America's Game: The Epic Story of How Pro Football Captured a Nation.* New York: Random House, 2004.

———. *Lamar Hunt: A Life in Sports.* Kansas City, MO: Andrews McMeel, 2012.

Nelson, David M. *The Anatomy of a Game: Football, the Rules, and the Men Who Made the Game.* Newark: University of Delaware Press, 1994.

Oberholtzer, Ellis Paxson. *Philadelphia: A History of the City and Its People; A Record of 225 Years.* Vol. 4. Philadelphia: S. H. Clark, 1912.

O'Toole, Andrew. *Fight for Old DC: George Preston Marshall, the Integration of the Redskins and the Rise of a New NFL.* Lincoln: University of Nebraska Press, 2016.

Page, Joseph S. *Pro Football Championships Before the Super Bowl: A Year-by-Year History.* Jefferson, NC: McFarland, 2010.

Peterson, Robert W. *Pigskin: The Early Years of Pro Football.* New York: Oxford University Press, 1994.

Poole, Gary Andrew. *The Galloping Ghost: Red Grange, an American Football Legend.* Boston: Houghton Mifflin Harcourt, 2008.

Roberts, Randy. *A Team for America: The Army-Navy Game That Rallied a Nation at War.* Boston: Houghton Mifflin Harcourt, 2011.

Rooney, Art, Jr., with Roy McHugh. *Ruanaidh: The Story of Art Rooney and His Clan.* Pittsburgh: Self-published, 2008.

Ross, Charles K. *Outside the Lines: African Americans and the Integration of the National Football League.* New York: New York University Press, 1999.

Ruck, Robert, Maggie Jones Patterson, and Michael P. Weber. *Rooney: A Sporting Life.* Lincoln: University of Nebraska Press, 2010.

Skaler, Robert Morris, and Thomas H. Keels. *Philadelphia's Rittenhouse Square.* Charleston, SC: Arcadia, 2008.

Smith, Thomas G. *Showdown: JFK and the Integration of the National Football League.* Boston: Beacon Press, 2011.

Snider, Rick. *100 Things Redskins Fans Should Know and Do Before They Die.* Chicago: Triumph Books, 2014.

Tindall, George Brown, and David E. Shi. *America: A Narrative History.* Vol. 2. New York: W. W. Norton, 2012.

Whittingham, Richard. *What a Game They Played: An Inside Look at the Golden Era of Pro Football.* Lincoln, NE: Bison Books, 2002.

Will, George. *A Nice Little Place on the North Side: Wrigley Field at 100.* New York: Crown, 2014.

Willis, Chris. *Joe F. Carr: The Man Who Built the National Football League.* Lanham, MD: Scarecrow Press, 2010.

NOTES

PROLOGUE

3 **"words of congratulation":** Chris Willis, *Joe F. Carr: The Man Who Built the National Football League* (Lanham, MD: Scarecrow Press, 2010), 335.

5 **it marked the first time Marshall, Halas, Bell, Rooney, and Tim Mara were together in the same room:** Official minutes, Pro Football Hall of Fame, Canton, Ohio.

5 **"They fought with each other":** Author interview with Upton Bell.

5 **"The credo of sharing":** George Halas speech to Congress on December 10, 1981, transcript at NFL.com (*Commissioner Paul Tagliabue NFL Report,* Winter 1999), www.nfl.info/nflmedia/news/PT_NFLReport Articles/Winter%201999.htm.

6 **"They were on their own":** Author interview with Upton Bell.

CHAPTER 1: HALAS: THE FOUNDER

11 **"stresses and strains":** George Halas, with Gwen Morgan and Arthur Veysey, *Halas by Halas: The Autobiography of George Halas* (New York: McGraw-Hill, 1979), 50.

12 **"a very determined man":** Halas, *Halas by Halas,* 53.

12 **competed in an industrial league:** Don Doxsie, *Iron Man McGinnity: A Baseball Biography* (Jefferson, NC: McFarland, 2009), 153–155.

13 **"You're the expert":** Halas, *Halas by Halas,* 54–55.

14 **"tired of constant wars":** Josefa Humpal Zeman, *The Bohemian People of Chicago,* http://media.pfeiffer.edu/lridener/DSS/Addams/hh6.html.

14 **"One would find men of education":** Zeman, *Bohemian People of Chicago.*

15 **"quite suddenly":** Halas, *Halas by Halas,* 24.

16 **"Just when I teach you fellows how to play football":** Ibid., 35.

16 **"govern the rest of my life"**: Ibid.

17 **"I ached for the excitement of a good game"**: Ibid., 50.

18 **"The season deepened my love for football"**: Ibid., 52.

18 **scale-house clerk**: Steven K. Ashby and C. J. Hawkins, *Staley: The Fight for a New American Labor Movement* (Urbana: University of Illinois Press, 2009), 8.

18 **"I assured the men"**: Ashby and Hawkins, *Staley,* 8

19 **"I believe in rough games"**: Christopher Klein, "How Teddy Roosevelt Saved Football," September 6, 2012, www.history.com/news/how-teddy -roosevelt-saved-football.

20 **"indifferent and vague"**: Halas, *Halas by Halas,* 60.

20 **"Chairs were few"**: Ibid.

20 **"I sat on a runningboard"**: Ibid.

21 **"meanest, toughest player alive"**: George Trafton biography, www .profootballhof.com/players/george-trafton/biography/.

22 **Halas wanted to win so badly that he signed Paddy Driscoll:** Jeff Davis, *Papa Bear: The Life and Legacy of George Halas* (New York: McGraw Hill, 2005), 61.

23 **"confirmed my belief"**: Halas, *Halas by Halas,* 66.

23 **"There were a lot of pioneers, but Joe Carr was the one"**: Author interview with Dan Rooney.

24 **"seethed about that 'lost title'"**: Davis, *Papa Bear,* 62.

26 **suspended by the league when Carr discovered they were also playing for a nonleague team in Philadelphia:** Dan Daly and Bob O'Donnell, *The Pro Football Chronicle: The Complete (Well, Almost) Record of the Best Players, the Greatest Photos, the Hardest Hits, the Biggest Scandals and the Funniest Stories in Pro Football* (New York: Collier Books, 1990), 10–11.

27 **"robs the great American game"**: Yost speech transcript, *Michigan Alumnus* 28 (1922): 471.

28 **"College athletes have something to fight for"**: "The Inquiring Reporter," *Chicago Tribune,* October 29, 1922.

28 **Stagg . . . advocated taking away the varsity letters of college players who eventually turned pro:** Daly and O'Donnell, *Pro Football Chronicle,* 15.

28 **"Under the guise of fair play"**: Ibid.

28 **"Professional football will never replace college football"**: Ibid., 40.

29 **he sold enough tickets to turn a $21,600 profit:** Ibid., 14.

29 **"I lacked enthusiasm"**: Halas, *Halas by Halas,* 91.

29 **"Football players are bigger than baseball players"**: Ibid., 76.

30 **"In truth, . . . the Bears lived hand-to-mouth"**: Ibid., 89.

CHAPTER 2: MARA: THE PROMOTER

31 **"He was one of those people"**: Author interview with John Mara.

32 **"live best and work the least"**: Carlo DeVito, *Wellington: The Maras, the Giants and the City of New York* (Chicago: Triumph Books, 2006), 6.

32 **"He didn't have a lot of education"**: Author interview with John Mara.

33 **"Little can be said"**: "The New York Giants Before They Were Giants," January 10, 2012, http://www.boweryboyshistory.com/?s=The+Giants +Before+They+Were+Giants.

34 **"Doc March was looking for an angel"**: Dan Daly, *National Forgotten League: Entertaining Stories and Observations from Pro Football's First Fifty Years* (Lincoln: University of Nebraska Press, 2012), 56.

35 **"I never passed up the chance to promote anything"**: Willis, *Joe F. Carr*, 185.

35 **"I'm not sure you can still live the kind of life he did"**: Author interview with John Mara.

35 **"He knew about boxing and horse racing"**: Ibid.

35 **"Say, maybe you'd be interested in this, Tim"**: Barry Gotterher, *The Giants of New York: The History of Professional Football's Most Fabulous Dynasty* (New York: G. P. Putnam's Sons, 1963), 25–26.

35 **"Now what do I do?"**: Gotterher, *Giants of New York*, 26.

36 **"He just thought, 'I'm a promoter'"**: Author interview with John Mara.

36 **"The Giants were born out of a combination of brute strength and ignorance"**: Willis, *Joe F. Carr*, 186.

38 **"Well, I'm going to see if I can put pro football over in New York"**: DeVito, *Wellington*, 19–20.

38 **"Isn't that the greatest run you've ever seen?"**: Gotterher, *Giants of New York*, 29.

38 **"He made that switch"**: Author interview with John Mara.

39 **"Pro Elevens Clash Before 27,000 Here"**: Alison Danzig, *New York Times*, October 19, 1925.

39 **"a far cry"**: Danzig, "Pro Elevens Clash Before 27,000 Here."

39 **"New York evidently is ready"**: Ibid.

40 **"Pro football will never amount to anything"**: Willis, *Joe F. Carr*, 200.

40 **"run me right out of the house"**: Ibid.

41 **Partially successful STOP**: DeVito, *Wellington*, 22.

41 **"Grange will play in the Giants-Bears game"**: Gotterher, *Giants of New York*, 34.

42 **"there was almost a riot"**: Gotterher, *Giants of New York*, 34.

43 **added up to $143,000**: Ibid., 37.

43 **"I was about ready to toss in my hand until Grange turned pro":** Ibid., 38.

44 **played seventeen games before slightly fewer than 300,000 spectators:** Daly and O'Donnell, *Pro Football Chronicle,* 24.

44 **He and Grange netted some $250,000:** Willis, *Joe F. Carr,* 209.

45 **"I have the biggest star in football":** Ibid., 215.

45 **"No blasted Irishman":** Ibid., 213.

46 **"I didn't make enough money last year to stuff a hat brim":** Ibid., 215.

46 **"Oh, it's a great game":** Ibid.

47 **"There's no one over there, either!":** Ibid., 225.

47 **Pyle and the Yankees lost $100,000. . . . Mara lost $40,000:** DeVito, *Wellington,* 34.

48 **"It was a challenge just to stay afloat":** Author interview with John Mara.

CHAPTER 3: MARSHALL: THE SHOWMAN

50 **blue and gold:** Thomas G. Smith, *Showdown: JFK and the Integration of the National Football League* (Boston: Beacon Press, 2011), 3.

50 **the first man able to palm a basketball:** Betty Hoover DiRisio, "Horse Gillum: Giant of a Man," by Lawrence County (Pennsylvania) Historical Society website, May 16, 2014, www.lawrencechs.com/horse-gillium -giant-of-a-man/.

51 **Meyer Davis Palace Five Orchestra:** "Champion Celtic Basketball Teams Are Strengthened," *Washington Post,* November 29, 1925.

51 **"a big business requiring more of my personal attention":** "Capital Team Quits Basketball," *Washington Post,* January 3, 1928.

51 **"I went to a few games":** Author interview with Virginia McCaskey.

52 **"fine Jacksonville hare":** George Preston Marshall, "Pro Football Is Better Football," *Saturday Evening Post,* November 19, 1938.

52 **"I've been guilty of promotional ideas":** Marshall, "Pro Football Is Better Football."

52 **descended from Confederate officers:** Joe Holley, *Slingin' Sam: The Life and Times of the Greatest Quarterback Ever to Play the Game* (Austin: University of Texas Press, 2012), 60.

52 **"making as much as twenty-five dollars per contest:** Marshall, "Pro Football Is Better Football."

52 **He liked to call himself the Magnificent Marshall:** Holley, *Slingin' Sam,* 61.

52 **"I persisted in the conviction that I was a budding Barrymore":** Marshall, "Pro Football Is Better Football."

53 **"My playing days were over":** Ibid.

53 **"considered it a lost opportunity were he not the center of attention":** Smith, *Showdown*, 3.

53 **"is not always offensive":** Ibid., 3.

54 **"more time for baseball, football, and basketball":** Marshall, "Pro Football Is Better Football."

55 **"thrilling" contest:** Ibid.

55 **"Why can't we have a football team":** Ibid.

55 **"My worst nature got the best of me":** Ibid.

CHAPTER 4: BELL: THE PROFLIGATE SON

56 **richest 10 percent . . . owned 75 percent:** George Brown Tindall and David E. Shi, *America: A Narrative History*, vol. 2 (New York: W. W. Norton, 2012), 589.

56 **"home to more millionaires per square foot":** Robert Morris Skaler and Thomas H. Keels, *Philadelphia's Rittenhouse Square* (Charleston, SC: Arcadia, 2008), 7.

57 **he married Fleurette at her family's mansion:** Robert S. Lyons, *On Any Given Sunday: A Life of Bert Bell* (Philadelphia: Temple University, 2010), 2.

57 **a lawyer and Civil War veteran who had been a Republican Congressman and close confidant of two presidents:** Lyons, *On Any Given Sunday*, 2.

58 **De Benneville eventually renounced the privileged life of an aristocrat:** Nelson Simonson and John Morgan, *George De Benneville, Universalist mystic*, http://archive.uuworld.org/2003/03/lookingback.html.

58 **"one of the interesting weddings of the week":** *Times of Philadelphia*, December 14, 1890.

59 **"yielded to the persistent demand":** Ellis Paxson Oberholzer, *Philadelphia: A History of the City and Its People; A Record of 225 Years*, vol. 4 (Philadelphia: S. H. Clark, 1912), 376.

59 **"brilliant" and "leading chemists of the world":** Oberholzer, *Philadelphia*, 376.

59 **"by a very nattering majority":** Ibid.

59 **"followed faithfully the traditions of the office":** Ibid.

59 **"position is evident to all":** Ibid.

59 **"amid such turn of the century wealth":** Lyons, *On Any Given Sunday*, 1.

60 **"had a nanny when he was 2":** Ibid.

60 **"For a fellow like me":** Ibid., 4.

60 **"wanted to follow in his father's footsteps":** John Cromwell Bell Jr. biography, Pennsylvania Historical and Museum Commission, www.phmc.state.pa.us/portal/communities/governors/1876-1951/john-bell.html.

61 "**If you don't think I had to fight many times**": Lyons, *On Any Given Sunday*, 1.

61 "**hero of countless football, baseball, and basketball battles**": Ibid., 4.

61 "**one of the best athletes in the history of the school**": Ibid., 4.

61 "**most sarcastic" and "best kidder**": Ibid., 52.

61 "**Although he came from a proper conservative Republican family**": Ibid., 1.

61 "**He'll go to Penn or he'll go to hell!**": Ibid., 3.

61 "**never came to class if the weather was bad outside**": Ibid., 20–21.

62 "**peppery little guy**": Ibid., 8.

62 "**great field general**": Ibid., 10.

62 "**piloted the team in masterful fashion**": Ibid., 6.

62 "**faultless**": Ibid., 9.

63 "**used such a varied selection of plays**": Ibid., 11.

63 **The unit received commendations**: Ibid., 12–14.

64 "**almost never talked about his war experience**": Author interview with Upton Bell.

64 "**Penn seems destined to take the leading position**": Lyons, *On Any Given Sunday*, 16.

64 "**squarely**": Ibid., 18–19.

64 "**My father and mother gave me everything I ever asked for**": W. C. Heinz, "Boss of the Behemoths," *Saturday Evening Post*, December 3, 1955.

65 **wagered his Marmon roadster**: Lyons, *On Any Given Sunday*, 19.

65 "**all the money I had and could borrow**": Ibid.

65 "**despite their philosophical differences, Bert was my grandfather's favorite child**": Ibid., 31.

66 "**reportedly dropped $50,000**": Ibid., 30.

66 "**Dammit, you're thirty-something**": Ibid.

67 "**reluctantly**": Ibid.

67 "**And I ain't marrying that broad**": Ibid.

67 "**Well, Bert**": Ibid., 30–31.

68 **even suited up for one AFL game**: Ibid., 45.

69 **turned Marshall down after consulting with Bell**: Willis, *Joe F. Carr*, 284.

69 **The group paid a $2,500 guarantee to the NFL and assumed $11,000 in debts**: Lyons, *On Any Given Sunday*, 47.

CHAPTER 5: ROONEY: THE GAMBLER

70 "**clanging, smoke-belching metropolis**": Robert Ruck, Maggie Jones Patterson, and Michael Weber, *Rooney: A Sporting Life* (Lincoln: University of Nebraska Press, 2010), 6.

71 **snow on their blankets:** Art Rooney Jr., with Roy McHugh, *Ruanaidh: The Story of Art Rooney and His Clan* (Pittsburgh: Self-published, 2008), 5.

72 **had no idea he was breaking the law:** Rooney Jr., *Ruanaidh*, 9.

72 **spent an entire day at church praying for her:** Ibid., 6.

72 **"Boy, could they punch":** Ibid., 5.

72 **he defeated a lightweight who later won the gold medal:** Ibid., 7.

72 **"wiggling, squirming, and serpentine runs":** Ibid., 12.

73 **"head and shoulders above his companions":** Ibid.

73 **Penn State offered him a cut of the proceeds:** Ibid., 13.

73 **played simultaneously for Indiana Normal . . . and Duquesne:** Ibid., 13–14.

74 **"the Red Grange of the independents":** Ibid., 32.

75 **"How much money do you make?":** Ibid., 12–13.

75 **"born to play the horses":** Ibid., 37.

76 **"I can make more money at the racetrack":** Ibid., 25.

76 **His co-owner was a notorious card shark:** Ibid., 22.

76 **bootleggers and ward heelers:** Ruck, Patterson, and Weber, *Rooney*, xiii.

76 **"was no angel," "uncorroborated hearsay," and "scant evidence indicating that he was more than peripherally engaged":** Ibid.

77 **"every racetrack from here to Tijuana":** Ibid., 83.

77 **"He answers the phone":** Author interview with Art Rooney Jr.

CHAPTER 6: ALMOST BROKE

82 **"We couldn't pay our guarantee":** Halas, *Halas by Halas*, 132.

82 **"The split hurt the team":** Ibid.

82 **"I think Pete Rozelle was the first commissioner he didn't control":** Author interview with George McCaskey.

82 **his modest proceeds from program sales were all that had kept the team in the black:** Halas, *Halas by Halas*, 132.

82 **"He would try anything, whatever came along":** Author interview with Virginia McCaskey.

82 **"who never let him forget it":** Ibid.

83 **"I was probably ten or eleven":** Ibid.

83 **"The time had come for Dutch and me to stop coaching":** Halas, *Halas by Halas*, 136.

83 **"astonished":** Ibid.

83 **"I believed him":** Ibid.

84 **"We had a drawer full of bills and we were overdrawn at the bank":** Ibid., 147.

85 **"a colorful crowd of nearly 60,000":** "Twenty Grand and the Kentucky

Derby, 1931," April 20, 2010, http://colinsghost.org/2010/04/twenty -grand-and-the-kentucky-derby-1931.html.

87 **"raised $5,000 from a bank that was already closed":** Halas, *Halas by Halas,* 147.

87 **"I called everyone I knew":** Ibid., 148.

88 **"He had a good partner":** Author interview with Virginia McCaskey.

90 **"If I get my price":** Halas, *Halas by Halas,* 150.

90 **"one of the old-fashioned brawls":** Wilfrid Smith, "Packers Whip Bears, 2–0," *Chicago Tribune,* October 17, 1932.

91 **"the elephants had been there":** Author interview with Virginia McCaskey.

91 **"It was all a bit puzzling at times":** Ibid.

93 **"some of the greatest players in history":** Author interview with George McCaskey.

CHAPTER 7: NEW IDEAS

95 **Buffalo, Milwaukee, Pittsburgh, St. Louis, San Francisco, and Baltimore all were larger:** From https://www.biggestuscities.com/1930.

95 **Tim Mara presented a motion. Halas seconded it:** Official minutes, Hall of Fame.

97 **"lost by a roll call vote":** Ibid.

97 **"I realize you men know your football inside and out":** Ibid.

97 **"Gentlemen, it's about time we realized we're not only in the football business":** Willis, *Joe F. Carr,* 302.

98 **"Nagurski will pass from anywhere so why not make it legal?":** Joseph S. Page, *Pro Football Championships Before the Super Bowl: A Year-by-Year History* (Jefferson, NC: McFarland, 2010), 21.

98 **"In every sport but football":** Daly and O'Donnell, *Pro Football Chronicle,* 9.

98 **"We think we have overcome the balance previously held by the defense":** Ibid., 8–9.

99 **"Marshall was way ahead of everybody":** David Elfin, *Washington Redskins: The Complete Illustrated History* (Minneapolis, MN: MVP Books, 2011), 14.

99 **the operation was $46,000 in the red:** Willis, *Joe F. Carr,* 299.

100 **"The fact that we have in our head coach, Lone Star Dietz, an Indian":** Travis Waldron, "The 81-Year-Old Newspaper Article That Destroys the Redskins' Justification for Their Name," May 30, 2014, https://think progress.org/the-81-year-old-newspaper-article-that-destroys-the -redskins-justification-for-their-name-e76bf65b3985/.

100 **He just wanted to avoid any confusion with baseball's Braves:** Waldron, "The 81-Year-Old Newspaper Article That Destroys the Redskins' Justification for Their Name."

101 **Lillard joined the Cardinals in 1932:** Charles K. Ross, *Outside the Lines: African Americans and the Integration of the National Football League* (New York: New York University Press, 1999), 39–45.

102 **"Negro Star of the Chicago Eleven Thrills 18,000 by Dazzling Runs as Cardinals Down Boston"** Ross, *Outside the Lines,* 40.

102 **"Great player, elusive as all outdoors":** Daly, *National Forgotten League,* 100.

102 **"We've got to get that damn nigger the hell out of there:"** Ibid.

102 **"I was mad, naturally":** Ibid., 100–101.

103 **"He said, 'There's no reason this should be happening'":** Ibid., 101.

103 **"It was my understanding that there was a gentleman's agreement":** Smith, *Showdown,* 28.

103 **"For myself and most of the owners":** Ross, *Outside the Lines,* 40.

103 **"in no way, shape, or form":** Ibid.

103 **many historians trace to the influence of Marshall:** Ibid., 50.

CHAPTER 8: BENNY AND THE GIANTS

104 **$40,000 debt:** Gotterher, *Giants of New York,* 64.

105 **"We need Friedman":** DeVito, *Wellington,* 49.

106 **"the time to pass is on first or second down":** Gotterher, *Giants of New York,* 65.

106 **"Polo Grounds Crowd Watches Brilliant Aerial Display":** *New York Times,* October 21, 1929.

107 **"most enthusiastic professional crowd of the year":** Arthur Daley, "Green Bay Blasts Giants Title Hopes," *New York Times,* November 25, 1929.

109 **more than $20,000 ahead:** Gotterher, *Giants of New York,* 78.

110 **"See the Four Horseman Ride Together Again":** Ibid., 79.

110 **"Take it easy on us":** Ibid., 81.

111 **Friedman left his apartment in Brooklyn early in the morning:** Ibid., 72.

111 **"I've got to build for the future":** Harold F. Parrott, "Benny Friedman Plans to Quit Pro Football for Chance to Coach," *Brooklyn Daily Eagle,* February 13, 1931.

112 **$35,000 profit:** Gotterher, *Giants of New York,* 91.

112 **"I'm sorry, Benny, but this is a family business":** Ibid., 92.

112 **"My timing was off":** Daly and O'Donnell, *Pro Football Chronicle,* 40.

113 **"probably the most spectacular game of the year" and "brilliant display of offensive firepower":** "Bears Cop Pro Gridiron Title by 23–21 score," Associated Press, December 18, 1933.

114 **"It was a game worthy of its surroundings":** Arthur Daley, "55,000 See Chicago Bears Down Giants on Last-Minute Field Goal," *New York Times,* November 19, 1934.

115 **"I know it doesn't look good":** Gotterher, *Giants of New York,* 115.

116 **"It was a freakish way to lose":** Halas, *Halas by Halas,* 180.

116 **"Enthusiasm turned to delirium":** Wilfrid Smith, "Giants Whip Bears for Pro Title, 30–13," *Chicago Tribune,* December 10, 1934.

CHAPTER 9: INSTITUTING A DRAFT

117 **"They had maids and butlers":** Upton Bell, with Ron Borges, *Present at the Creation: My Life in the NFL and the Rise of America's Game* (Lincoln: University of Nebraska Press, 2017), 23.

117 **"he was a man about town":** Bell, *Present at the Creation,* 21.

117 **"She was the only person who could ever say no":** Ibid.

118 **demanded that Bell give up drinking:** Lyons, *On Any Given Sunday,* 37.

118 **his future wife loaned him the necessary money:** Ibid., 47.

118 **a free car wash:** Ray Didinger and Robert S. Lyons, *The New Eagles Encyclopedia* (Philadelphia: Temple University Press, 2014), 200.

119 **"I asked him point blank if he would sign with the Eagles":** "Back's Refusal to Sign Led to Grid Draft," Associated Press, January 30, 1957.

119 **"I knew what was in his mind":** "Back's Refusal to Sign Led to Grid Draft."

120 **"Finally, Curly sent me a contract and I just went ahead and signed it":** Richard Whittingham, *What a Game They Played: An Inside Look at the Golden Era of Pro Football* (Lincoln, NE: Bison Books, 2002), 121–122.

120 **"I told Kelly I couldn't do that because I had already signed with Curly":** Whittingham, *What a Game They Played,* 122.

121 **Lambeau's had been posted seventeen minutes earlier:** Willis, *Joe F. Carr,* 339.

121 **"Something has to be done":** Ibid., 338.

122 **"I thought the proposal sound":** Ibid., 343.

122 **"was a hazard we had to accept for the benefit of the league":** DeVito, *Wellington,* 84.

122 **"Gentlemen, I've always had the theory that pro football is like a chain":** Lyons, *On Any Given Sunday,* 57.

122 **"Bert was a very persuasive man"**: Art Rooney, "I Remember Bert Bell," game program, Kansas City Chiefs vs. New York Jets, September 29, 1975, Pro Football Hall of Fame.

123 **clergymen of varying faiths:** Lyons, *On Any Given Sunday*, 55.

123 **Edwin "Alabama" Pitts:** Ibid., 53–54.

123 **"Bert, the only thing you haven't done is hire a good football team":** Ibid., 55.

123 **On February 8, 1936, the owners gathered:** Official minutes, Hall of Fame.

125 **"There were plenty of cigars, and the liquor flowed":** Frank Fitzpatrick, "First NFL Draft, Held at Philly's Ritz-Carlton, Went Unnoticed," *Philadelphia Inquirer*, April 8, 2017.

125 **"new ruling":** "Chicago Bears Get First Call on Berwanger," *Chicago Tribune*, February 10, 1936.

125 **Only twenty-four of the eighty-one players selected in 1936 suited up for a game that season:** Willis, *Joe F. Carr*, 351.

125 **"I haven't decided what I will do":** Ken Crippen, "The First NFL Draft," *National Football Post*, April 20, 2014.

126 **"He asked me what I wanted":** Frank Litsky, "Jay Berwanger, 88, Winner of the First Heisman Trophy," *New York Times*, June 28, 2002.

126 **he founded a company that made plastic and sponge-rubber strips:** "Jay Berwanger, 88, Winner of the First Heisman Trophy."

126 **John McCauley, the second pick, took a job with a tool company:** Rice Athletic Hall of Fame program, presentation of awards, November 21, 1970, http://grfx.cstv.com/photos/schools/rice/genrel/auto_pdf/2011-12 /misc_non_event/FirstHOF.pdf.

126 **Bill Wallace . . . also went into business:** Ibid.

126 **Harry Shuford . . . went to law school:** Obituary, *Dallas Morning News*, May 17, 2007.

126 **Al Barabas . . . chose minor league baseball:** Hall of Fame series, go columbialions.com, July 22, 2014, www.gocolumbialions.com/ViewArticle .dbml?ATCLID=209600296.

126 **John "Jac" Weller . . . opened a real estate and insurance business:** Biography, National Football Foundation website, www.footballfoundation .org/Programs/CollegeFootballHallofFame/SearchDetail.aspx?id=30066.

126 **Pepper Constable . . . went to Harvard Medical School:** "Dr. W. Pepper Constable, 72, Ex-official of Jersey Hospital," *New York Times*, August 17, 1986.

126 **Shakespeare, the third overall pick, opted to work for the Thor Power Tool Company in Aurora, Illinois:** "Bill Shakespeare, Star Halfback at Notre Dame in 1930s, Dies," *New York Times*, January 19, 1974.

CHAPTER 10: BETTING BONANZA

130 **Harp Vaughan and Warren Heller were two of Rooney's old friends from the Northside. Cap Oehler had worked in the coal mines. Dave Ribble carried a Teamsters card:** Ruck, Patterson, and Weber, *Rooney*, 104.

130 **The quintessential early Pirate was Mose Kelsch:** Ibid., 111.

131 **The argument escalated until Rooney suggested they settle it with their fists:** Ibid., 106.

131 **drew an average of 12,489 fans per game:** Ibid., 113.

131 **"In those days, nobody got wealthy in sports":** Ibid.

133 **Bach was so incensed that he and Rooney came to blows:** Ibid., 116.

133 **"Halas, mistrustful by nature, may have been testing this younger man":** Ibid., 114.

134 **"George, you were no sure thing to win that fight":** Ibid.

134 **"Aside from Halas, Marshall, Curly Lambeau and Mara, I guess I, like most of the other owners, didn't pay enough attention to football":** Pat Livingston, "Long Wait Sweetens Rooney Victory," *Sporting News*, January 6, 1973.

135 **"three or four":** Red Smith, "Rooney Recalls Day at the Races," *New York Times*, April 13, 1972.

135 **between $19,000 and $25,000:** Ruck, Patterson, and Weber, *Rooney*, 119.

135 **"Stick that dough in your kick":** Ibid.

136 **"What's your next move, Artie?":** Ibid.

136 **close to $100,000:** Ibid., 123.

136 **"It's Art but They Don't Like It":** Ibid.

137 **Mara estimated it was between $250,000 and $380,000:** DeVito, *Wellington*, 88.

137 **"When George gives up the broads, I'll give up gambling":** Ruck, Patterson, and Weber, *Rooney*, 124.

CHAPTER 11: MOVE TO DC

139 **singing about slaves in the Old South and serving mint juleps:** Smith, *Showdown*, 19.

139 **a Confederate flag that had been in his family since the Civil War:** Dan Daly, "The Man Who Gave the Redskins Their Name," *Washington Times*, September 6, 2001.

140 **"There were times on game day when the papers played the Radcliffe girls' field hockey team above our game":** Thomas Boswell, Richard Justice, Tony Kornheiser, et al., *Redskins: A History of Washington's Team* (Washington: Washington Post Books, 1997), 20.

141 **"The nice thing about owning a pro football team is that all you have to do to move is pack your trunks":** Daly and O'Donnell, *Pro Football Chronicle*, 70.

142 **"Bothered? I hope George Preston Marshall is in good voice":** Gotterher, *Giants of New York*, 145.

143 **"george, stop / guess what, stop":** Holley, *Slingin' Sam*, 77.

143 **"We'll get a much bigger gate in New York":** Thom Loverro, *Hail Victory: An Oral History of the Washington Redskins* (Hoboken, NJ: Wiley, 2007) 14.

144 **"Marshall Moves Boston Redskins to District":** *Washington Post*, December 17, 1936.

144 **Washington would grow from 486,000 residents in 1930 to 663,000 by the end of the decade:** Smith, *Showdown*, 43.

145 **"What size do you wear?":** Holley, *Slingin' Sam*, 98.

145 **"They're not for me, son":** Ibid.

145 **"My feet hurt":** Ibid., 99.

146 **"Which eye?":** Ibid., 111.

146 **Barnee Breeskin, leader of the hotel's orchestra, was on the line:** Corinne Griffith, *My Life with the Redskins* (New York: A. S. Barnes, 1947), 37.

146 **Marshall was initially unenthusiastic:** Griffith, *My Life with the Redskins*, 37.

146 **Griffith had the opposite reaction and quickly penned lyrics:** Ibid., 39.

146 **"Braves on the warpath":** Ibid.

146 **a brass ensemble composed of milk deliverymen from the Chestnut Farms Dairy:** 1948 Redskins media guide.

147 **"Mark me, there will be a new record for football crowds in Washington":** Shirley Povich, "Marshall Sees Team as Civic Unifier," *Washington Post*, November 19 1937.

147 **"envisions the Green Bay crowd as the last convincing argument to fling into the teeth of the doubters":** Povich, "Marshall Sees Team as Civic Unifier."

148 **"sweep the Giants aside like rubbish":** Smith, *Showdown*, 51.

148 **"The invading Washington rooters were much in evidence on the Eighth Avenue subway":** John Kieran, "The Massacre at Coogan's Bluff," *New York Times*, December 6, 1937.

149 **"new costumes of burgundy and gold, with white feather head-dresses, imported straight from Hollywood":** Griffith, *My Life with the Redskins*, 60.

149 **"They were simply full of loyalty and red feathers and other things":** Ibid., 61.

149 **"George Preston Marshall slipped unobtrusively into town today at the head of a 150-piece band and 10,000 fans":** Ibid.

149 **"paraded in a wild demonstration":** Shirley Povich, "DC Redskins Smear Giants, 49–14, to Win Eastern Title," *Washington Post,* December 6, 1937.

149 **"in a frenzy":** Arthur Daley, "58,285 See Redskins Keep Eastern Title by Routing Giants at Polo Grounds," *New York Times,* December 6, 1937.

150 **"hauled out their tomahawks":** Daley, "58,285 See Redskins Keep Eastern Title by Routing Giants at Polo Grounds."

150 **"gargantuan form" and "in a flash":** Ibid.

150 **"There is not a superlative":** Ibid.

150 **"joyously stampeded onto the field":** Povich, "DC Redskins Smear Giants, 49–14, to Win Eastern Title."

151 **The Redskins' season ticket total would soar from 958 in 1937 to 10,951 in 1940 and 31,444 by 1947:** Jack Walsh, "Marshall Made Redskins a Way of Life," *Washington Post,* August 10, 1969.

CHAPTER 12: BROTHERHOOD OF RIVALS

155 **"That man Halas is positively revolting!":** Griffith, *My Life with the Redskins,* 74.

155 **"Don't you dare say anything against Halas!":** Ibid.

156 **"They were the most unique set of men in American sports history":** Author interview with Upton Bell.

156 **"drawn together" and "love at first sight":** Griffith, *My Life with the Redskins,* 71.

158 **"The owners with the staying power were the ones who came away with the decent schedules":** Michael MacCambridge, *America's Game: The Epic Story of How Pro Football Captured a Nation* (New York: Random House, 2004), 39.

158 **two in the morning:** Official minutes, Hall of Fame.

159 **"It is absolutely vital to us":** Ibid.

159 **"I don't think there is a member here who would think it unreasonable":** Ibid.

159 **"I don't think that is a legal form of procedure":** Ibid.

159 **"get redder and redder":** DeVito, *Wellington,* 93.

159 **"There is no use putting to a vote something that is not right":** Official minutes, Hall of Fame.

159 **"I didn't say I think there should be a vote on it":** Ibid.

159 **"I don't see any reason why he should have six games at home and the Chicago Bears only have four":** Ibid.

160 **"The motion is lost":** Ibid.

160 **a guaranteed $40,000 payout every year:** Ibid.

161 **"I move that the president be directed to thank Mr. Runyon for his kind offer":** Ibid.

161 **an average of 35,717 fans:** Willis, *Joe F. Carr*, 363.

163 **"You gentlemen will destroy me":** Halas, *Halas by Halas*, 156.

163 **"was bitterly opposed":** DeVito, *Wellington*, 83–84.

163 **"An official went to retrieve a punt that had gone out of bounds":** Ibid., 172.

163 **Like Halas, Ray had played football for the Illini:** Seymour Smith, "Pro Football to Honor Ray," *Baltimore Sun*, September 14, 1966.

164 **The other owners agreed to the proposal:** Jimmy Jordan, "Hugh Ray and His Stopwatch Have Done Much for Football," Associated Press, September 9, 1945.

164 **"He pounded the rules into his officials":** Seymour Smith, "Pro Football to Honor Ray," *Baltimore Sun*, September 14, 1966.

165 **"my great contribution to the National Football League":** "Officials, Not Rams, Beat Us Sunday," *Chicago Tribune*, November 3, 1949.

CHAPTER 13: A STEP FORWARD

167 **"When I got there, he thought I was a kid who wanted his autograph":** DeVito, *Wellington*, 85.

167 **"but I was able to convince him that I was in fact a legitimate emissary":** Ibid.

168 **"The thinking was":** Author interview with Upton Bell.

168 **"It was a pretty remarkable thing":** Author interview with Virginia McCaskey.

169 **"I didn't think I had to put every name on that list":** DeVito, *Wellington*, 95–96.

169 **"They would gather for league meetings":** Author interview with Virginia McCaskey.

172 **"The band had seen enough":** John Kieran, "The Rout of the Redskins," *New York Times*, December 5, 1938.

172 **"A great game":** Gotterher, *Giants of New York*, 163.

172 **"Eddie, we don't need a band":** Ibid.

174 **"absolutely ferocious" and "No such blocking and tackling":** Arthur Daley, "Record Play-Off Throng Sees Giants Halt Packers at Polo Grounds," *New York Times*, December 12, 1938.

174 **"a contusion of the brain":** Daley, "Record Play-Off Throng Sees Giants Halt Packers at Polo Grounds."

174 **"This was the gridiron sport at its primitive best"**: Arthur Daley, "The Good Old Days" *New York Times,* December 12, 1937.

175 **$200,000 profit**: Gotterher, *Giants of New York,* 166.

CHAPTER 14: THE GREATEST ROUT

176 **"I was about the same age as their daughter"**: Author interview with Virginia McCaskey.

176 **"No one asked for his autograph"**: Ibid.

177 **The number of radios in use in America rose from 60,000 in 1922 to 3 million in 1924 to 16.6 million by 1932**: George Will, *A Nice Little Place on the North Side: Wrigley Field at 100* (New York: Crown, 2014), 47.

177 **The number of radio stations also rapidly grew, from 382 in 1922 to 681 in 1927**: Will, *Nice Little Place on the North Side,* 47.

177 **Eleven of the sixteen major league owners were skeptical enough to consider banning all radio game broadcasts**: Paul Dickson, "How Radio Gave Baseball Its Voice," February 26, 2016, thenationalpastimemuseum .com.

177 **he allowed WMAQ, a major Chicago station, to broadcast the Cubs' home games**: Dickson, "How Radio Gave Baseball Its Voice."

178 **The Cubs' gate rose 140 percent between 1925 and 1929**: Will, *Nice Little Place on the North Side,* 49.

178 **"Don't stop it"**: Ibid., 48.

178 **"He loved them"**: Author interview with Virginia McCaskey.

178 **"It wasn't a big deal to them"**: Ibid.

178 **WGN agreed to broadcast the home games of the Bears**: Phil Rosenthal, "Are the Bears Poised to Change Radio Stations?," *Chicago Tribune,* August 25, 2017.

178 **Halas made sure the broadcasts were promoted**: "Green Bay–Bears Game on WGN at 1:58 Today," *Chicago Tribune,* December 10, 1933.

179 **"I remember him having dinners with us"**: Author interview with Virginia McCaskey.

181 **"roamed the ball field, pulling down impossible passes"**: Halas, *Halas by Halas,* 183.

182 **"When the 1940 season began, I felt we were fit for anything or anybody"**: Ibid., 186.

182 **"I was ready to tear the referee limb from limb"**: Ibid., 187.

183 **"The Bears are a bunch of crybabies"**: Ibid., 188.

183 **"I did not let the players forget"**: Ibid.

183 **"Congratulations"**: Ibid.

183 **The Mutual Broadcasting System paid $2,500 for the right to broadcast the game nationally on the radio:** Ibid.

183 **"When we were ready to go out, he pointed to the clippings":** Ibid., 190.

184 **"They will show you whether the Redskins are staying with the defense they used":** Ibid.

184 **"I could see this was going to be a great day":** Ibid., 191.

184 **"Our adjusted plays had them confused":** Ibid., 192.

186 **"We wanted revenge and we got it":** Halas, *Halas by Halas,* 197.

186 **"If Charley had caught it, the score would have turned out 73–7":** Ibid., 196.

186 **"The weather was perfect. So were the Bears":** Arthur Daley, "Bears Overwhelm Redskins by Record Score," *New York Times,* December 9, 1940.

186 **The head linesman that day had been Irv Kupcinet:** Davis, *Papa Bear,* 159, 161.

187 **"the greatest team professional football has ever produced":** Ibid., 161.

187 **"The Bears were wonderful, weren't they?":** Holley, *Slingin' Sam,* 170.

CHAPTER 15: SAME OLD PIRATES

188 **cost just $5,000:** Ruck, Patterson, and Weber, *Rooney,* 164.

188 **finished $35,000 in the red, pushing Rooney's deficit since he joined the NFL to more than $100,000:** Ibid., 154.

189 **"We're not playing this week":** Ibid., 150.

190 **"On most teams, the coach worries about where the players are on the night before a game":** Ira Berkow, "When Johnny Blood Rode," *New York Times,* July 11, 1982.

190 **"felt for a long time that Sutherland was the best coach in the profession":** Ruck, Patterson, and Weber, *Rooney,* 164.

191 **"In that sense, they were opposites":** Author interview with Upton Bell.

191 **made the only, and thus winning, bid:** MacCambridge, *America's Game,* 43.

192 **Bell brought the fifty or so diehards who attended the game into the press box:** Didinger and Lyons, *New Eagles Encyclopedia,* 7.

192 **"It's days like that when it takes a very good sense of humor":** Ibid.

192 **Bell accepted the loan, which he repaid the following year:** Lyons, *On Any Given Sunday,* 72–73.

192 **"Everyone out, time for practice!":** Ibid., 76.

193 **The Pirates had lost $8,000 during the season:** Ruck, Patterson, and Weber, *Rooney,* 170.

193 **George Preston Marshall found a wealthy Washingtonian:** Ibid.

193 **"They tell me around here that I'm fighting a losing battle"**: Ibid., 170–171.

193 **"I'm definitely going to keep the team in Pittsburgh for another season"**: Ibid., 174.

193 **"No matter what you call a grapefruit, it still squirts in your eye"**: Ibid., 175.

194 **he offered Sutherland only a $7,500 annual salary, which Dan Topping easily doubled**: Ibid., 173.

194 **"I wish Art Rooney all the luck in the world"**: Ibid.

194 **"Say, George"**: Ibid., 179.

194 **"broke the Halas spell"**: Ibid.

195 **"woeful gang"** that **"made a mockery of themselves and the league"**: Ibid., 182.

195 **Povich estimated that Rooney had saved $2,000 but damaged the NFL's credibility**: Ibid.

195 **losing an exhibition game to a minor-league team**: Daly, *National Forgotten League,* 166.

195 **"After I turned him down three times in a row"**: Ruck, Patterson, and Weber, *Rooney,* 182.

195 **"more effective resolving NFL matters than he was in addressing the Steelers' woes"**: Ibid., 176.

196 **"You can't blame the guy"**: Ibid., 183.

197 **Thompson announced in February 1941 that his team would stay in Pittsburgh with a new name**: Ibid., 186.

197 **Rooney took him out for an evening at a popular Pittsburgh saloon**: Ibid.

197 **Neale, Thompson, Bell, and Rooney met at the Racquet Club in Philadelphia to divide up the players**: Lyons, *On Any Given Sunday,* 89.

197 **"This is the finest squad I've ever worked with in the National Football League"**: Ibid., 90.

198 **"Those new uniforms they're wearing threw me off a bit"**: Ibid.

198 **"We have to do something"**: Ibid.

198 **"You have to quit!"**: Ibid.

199 **"He could have helped us and helped the league, too"**: Daly and O'Donnell, *Pro Football Chronicle,* 95.

CHAPTER 16: POLITICAL WINDS

201 **had a conversation about the job with J. Edgar Hoover**: Willis, *Joe F. Carr,* 395.

201 **"could not overlook the splendid opportunities"**: Ibid., 394.

201 **"I think Storck is a fine executive":** Ibid., 394–395.

201 **Ward himself suggested another candidate, Layden:** Ibid., 395.

202 **When he opened his morning newspaper, he read that Layden had been hired:** Lyons, *On Any Given Sunday,* 86.

202 **"came from Chicago":** Ibid.

202 **"Well, that's one thing Bell got right":** Ibid.

202 **"Bell knew all about the progress of negotiations":** Ibid.

202 **"also were given authority to make an offer to one of the three":** Ibid.

203 **"the most constructive and finest move ever made":** Ibid.

204 **"I am convinced Layden is not qualified":** Willis, *Joe F. Carr,* 396.

205 **But Halas asked Bidwill to keep the idea between them:** Davis, *Papa Bear,* 196.

206 **"Tim, just tell me one thing, what church do you go to?":** Gotterher, *Giants of New York,* 173.

207 **Marshall saw to it that Storck was relieved of an important duty:** Daly and O'Donnell, *Pro Football Chronicle,* 84.

207 **"The two moguls were squaring off":** Ruck, Patterson, and Weber, *Rooney,* 176.

207 **"were so often on opposite sides that I grew up looking upon Halas as an enemy":** Halas, *Halas by Halas,* 156.

207 **"Their relationship was one of great warmth":** Author interview with Virginia McCaskey.

207 **"Would you please check up on him":** Ibid.

208 **"Ed sat down with them":** Ibid.

208 **"He and Art Rooney both loved horse racing":** Ibid.

CHAPTER 17: DOG MEAT

209 **"Attention, please":** Gotterher, *Giants of New York,* 178.

210 **"Oh, my God":** Ibid.

210 **"I didn't even know where Pearl Harbor was":** Mike Lupica, "Mara Facing Another Tough Sunday," New York *Daily News,* September 14, 2001.

210 **"He gave us such a bad account":** Dave Anderson, "The Day Colonel Donovan Was Paged," *New York Times,* December 1, 1991.

210 **"What do we do now?":** Gotterher, *Giants of New York,* 179.

210 **"Attention, all officers and men of the Army and Navy are to report to their stations immediately":** DeVito, *Wellington,* 100.

211 **"They announced it over the loudspeakers":** Davis, *Papa Bear,* 169.

212 **"the teams just didn't have the same emotions":** Ibid.

212 **"I didn't know what to do":** Halas, *Halas by Halas,* 202.

212 **"I'll send your name to Washington":** Ibid., 203.

213 **When training camps opened in 1942:** Ruck, Patterson, and Weber, *Rooney,* 203.

213 **Twenty rookies made New York's roster in 1942:** Gotterher, *Giants of New York,* 184.

213 **"I took one look at the squad and I felt like crying":** Ibid.

213 **they dressed just sixteen for their first preseason game:** Ruck, Patterson, and Weber, *Rooney,* 203.

213 **"keep baseball going":** From text of Roosevelt letter, www.baseball -almanac.com/prz_lfr.shtml.

214 **"many duties" and "I would not have chosen it":** Halas, *Halas by Halas,* 204.

214 **"We were beginning to think of ourselves as unbeatable":** Ibid., 205.

215 **"The once mighty football empire of the Chicago Bears":** Lew Freedman, *The Chicago Bears: The Complete Illustrated History* (Minneapolis, MN: MVP Books, 2008), 50–51.

215 **"George, you're too old to fight a war":** Halas, *Halas by Halas,* 206.

215 **"I thought Halas would kill Marshall":** Ibid.

216 **"You're no big shot now!":** Ruck, Patterson, and Weber, *Rooney,* 198.

216 **Rooney tore up the duty application papers and walked away:** Ibid.

216 **"He found people waiting for him every morning":** Ibid.

217 **"This team is going to win some games":** Ibid., 205.

217 **After the season, Rooney again suggested to his fellow owners that the NFL suspend operations:** Ibid., 208.

217 **"go through the motions":** Ibid., 212.

217 **Bert Bell had sent recruiting letters to 250 prospects:** Ibid.

219 **A tackle had bleeding ulcers. Another lineman was deaf in one ear:** Chris Strauss, "70 years ago, the Steelers and Eagles were One Team," *USA Today,* December 5, 2013.

219 **"Please help me, Steve":** Arthur Daley, "A Mighty Stout Fella," *New York Times,* May 18, 1964.

219 **"Sorry, Bert":** Daley, "A Mighty Stout Fella."

220 **"I believe I got my sense of the rage of conflict on the football field":** Rick Burton, "The Author of Red Badge Loved the Game More Than His Studies," *New York Times,* March 13, 2010.

220 **"the nearest thing to actual war":** Randy Roberts, *A Team for America: The Army-Navy Game That Rallied a Nation at War* (Boston: Houghton Mifflin Harcourt, 2011), 60.

221 **"If we don't watch it, we could get arrested for polygamy":** Ruck, Patterson, and Weber, *Rooney,* 215.

221 **"together, we are sure to be strong":** Ibid.

221 **"We just didn't have it":** Ibid.

CHAPTER 18: TWO WARS

222 **"I would have preferred a place on a warship":** Halas, *Halas by Halas*, 206–207.

222 **"contributing to high morale"** Ibid., 207.

223 **"I think sometimes he put the letter in a bottle and dropped it in Lake Michigan":** Ibid., 211.

223 **"I had promised Charley [Bidwill] I would back him":** Ibid., 206.

224 **"Buffalo is not ready for the league":** Craig R. Coenen, *From Sandlots to the Super Bowl: The National Football League* (Knoxville: University of Tennessee Press, 2005), 112.

224 **"We've got 10 clubs operating now. Only four have ever shown a profit":** Coenen, *From Sandlots to the Super Bowl*, 114.

225 **"a spirit of cooperation and friendliness":** Ibid., 119.

225 **"All I know of a new league is what I read in the newspapers":** Ibid.

225 **"The rival league spoiled their friendship"** Author interview with Virginia McCaskey.

225 **Dan Topping . . . served in the Marines for forty-two months:** Topping bio, Society for American Baseball Research, https://sabr.org/bioproj /person/f12c897a.

226 **Wellington Mara enlisted in the navy as a lieutenant in early 1942:** De-Vito, *Wellington*, 101.

227 **"He would drive his limousine right out on the practice field":** Daly, "Man Who Gave the Redskins Their Name."

228 **"I wouldn't go near that thing on a bet, let alone fly in it":** Ibid.

229 **"Our club owners are all good businessmen, not millionaires":** *New York Times*, November 28, 1944.

230 **Crowley told reporters that the league already had 150 players under contract:** AAFC chronology, AAFC-NFL folder, Pro Football Hall of Fame, Canton, Ohio.

232 **"It had been the contention of observers ever since the AAFC was first conceived":** John Drebinger, "Topping's Eleven Joins New Circuit," *New York Times*, December 6, 1945.

233 **"We've spent years of time and heaps of money building up the Giants":** "Football Owners Head Is Surprised by Topping's Withdrawal," *New York Times*, December 6, 1945.

233 **"All it has done has been to balance our league better":** "Football Owners Head Is Surprised by Topping's Withdrawal."

233 **"will help our league by clearing things up all around":** Ibid.

233 **"I hope that Topping does better in the new league than he did in the old one":** Ibid.

CHAPTER 19: THE RIGHT GUY IN CHARGE

236 **"I didn't think I could take it":** Griffith, *My Life with the Redskins*, 170.

238 **Within months, he would sell his controlling interest in the Palace Laundry:** Jack Chevalier obituary, *Washington Post*, June 16, 1976.

239 **"over my dead body":** Lyons, *Any Given Sunday*, 113.

239 **"Bell's mission in life was football":** MacCambridge, *America's Game*, 38.

240 **"There were other guys in the room":** Author interview with Dan Rooney.

240 **"Now we have a pro running our league":** Lyons, *On Any Given Sunday*, 116.

240 **"speaks the pro football language":** Ibid.

242 **"Gentlemen," he said, "you who know me know that I never bluff":** Ibid., 118.

243 **Crowley and Bell had met in Philadelphia:** Ibid., 121.

244 **"it is pretty plain":** Ibid., 122.

244 **"Bert at no time represented us":** Ibid., 123.

244 **"We knew Bert was talking to Crowley":** Ibid., 123–124.

245 **"There was a phone in the bedroom":** Bell, *Present at the Creation*, 11.

245 **"All of the clubs were very jealous of the schedules":** MacCambridge, *America's Game*, 40.

245 **"Only once did anyone raise his voice":** Lyons, *On Any Given Sunday*, 128.

CHAPTER 20: BACK ACROSS THE COLOR LINE

249 **drew more than 100,000 spectators for the first time:** Alex Bower, "Derby Wins of Triple Crown Victors: Assault," *Blood-Horse*, April 25, 2017.

249 **"Fuck Babe Ruth!":** Tyler Cowen, *What Price Fame?* (Boston: Harvard University Press, 2000), 69.

249 **Dan Topping's Yankees drew 2.265 million fans:** From www.baseball-reference.com/teams/NYY/.

250 **The radio rights to the World Series sold for $150,000, a record fee:** "Through the Years: World Series Broadcast Rights Fees," *Sports Business Daily*, October 13, 2003.

251 **Haley Harding, a sports reporter for the *Los Angeles Tribune*, a black weekly newspaper, took the floor at the meeting:** Gretchen Atwood, "Unsung Heroes of Rams Football Integration," *LA Weekly*, June 10, 2009.

251 **"I have heard many fine things about Washington, both as a player and as a man":** Ross, *Outside the Lines*, 82.

252   "I doubt we would have been interested in Washington if we had stayed in Cleveland": Thomas G. Smith, "Outside the Pale," *Coffin Corner* 9, no. 4 (1989): 13.

252   "All hell broke loose": Coenen, *From Sandlots to the Super Bowl*, 123.

253   "In ordinary conversation, Marshall refers to Negroes": Smith, *Showdown*, 32.

253   it was a bad idea to mix black and white players on a team: Ibid., 32–33.

253   "He played on the same field with boys who are going to be scattered throughout the league": Smith, "Outside the Pale," 9.

254   "practiced civil rights before it became fashionable": Ruck, Patterson, and Weber, *Rooney*, 236.

254   Rooney lent Posey money that kept the Grays afloat: Ibid., 235.

254   "deference to the league and his coaches": Ibid., 236.

255   "What about the Steelers, Mr. Rooney?": Ibid., 236.

255   Rooney's slow response to the Rams' reintegration was typical: "Permanent Reintegration of Pro Football," February 19, 2010, www.profootballhof.com/permanent-reintegration-of-pro-football/.

255   "Strode did not relish being a racial pioneer": Smith, *Showdown*, 74.

259   "There will only be two kinds of men on the Pittsburgh Steeler roster this year" Daly and O'Donnell, *Pro Football Chronicle*, 102.

259   "First time anything like that has happened out there": Lyons, *On Any Given Sunday*, 129.

259   "I've never seen anything like it": Ruck, Patterson, and Weber, *Rooney*, 237.

261   They would buy more than 21,000 season tickets in 1947, doubling the total from the year before: Ibid.

261   The only NFL teams that made money in 1946 were the Giants and Bears, who won the division titles, and the Redskins: Coenen, *From Sandlots to the Super Bowl*, 126.

261   payroll had been under $100,000 in 1945 and now it was close to $300,000: Gotterher, *Giants of New York*, 209.

262   Most teams had lost at least $100,000: Coenen, *From Sandlots to the Super Bowl*, 126.

CHAPTER 21: SCANDAL

264   "He's going to be a Giants star for a long, long time": Gotterher, *Giants of New York*, 207.

265   "both were in tears": Lyons, *On Any Given Sunday*, 131.

265   "absolutely in the clear": Ibid.

266 **"without appeal" and "undesirable":** Ibid., 132.

266 **"city slicker" and "country boy":** Ibid.

268 **"Professional football cannot continue to exist unless it is based on absolute honesty":** Ibid., 134.

270 **were hemorrhaging money, losing an estimated $1.5 million between them in 1947 alone:** Coenen, *From Sandlots to the Super Bowl*, 128–129.

272 **"It seems un-American to me":** DeVito, *Wellington*, 113.

273 **"Maybe the kid figures he'll have greater security with the Giants":** Ibid.

273 **O'Malley gave up the franchise after the season, having lost $300,000:** Leo Lowenfish, *Branch Rickey: Baseball's Ferocious Gentleman* (Lincoln: University of Nebraska Press, 2007), 458.

274 **"I'm looking for a job":** Gotterher, *Giants of New York*, 211.

CHAPTER 22: EVERYONE LOSES

278 **"We'll either get smart and make peace, or we'll all go bust":** Coenen, *From Sandlots to the Super Bowl*, 132.

278 **Rooney still sold enough tickets to gross $900,000 in revenues, but he ended the season $40,000 in the red:** Ruck, Patterson, and Weber, *Rooney*, 276.

279 **"The time is ripe for peace":** Coenen, *From Sandlots to the Super Bowl*, 132.

279 **"We would talk about things":** Author interview with Mike McGee.

281 **eventually paid Marshall just $50,000:** Daly and O'Donnell, *Pro Football Chronicle*, 106.

282 **"Bertie sat back there in his Philadelphia apartment":** Lyons, *On Any Given Sunday*, 156.

283 **"We owners were a tight little group":** Halas, *Halas by Halas*, 233.

284 **Marshall haughtily responded:** Daly and O'Donnell, *Pro Football Chronicle*, 105.

284 **"obnoxious":** Daly, "Man Who Gave the Redskins Their Name."

284 **"habit of sleeping most of the day":** Ibid.

284 **"As with most organizations, we were perhaps too unresponsive":** Halas, *Halas by Halas*, 233.

284 **"Plans here are the proverbial dime-a-dozen":** Louis Effrat, "Buffalo Franchise Bid Gains Favor at Football Meeting," *New York Times*, January 20, 1950.

285 **"I banged down the gavel and started for the doors":** Lyons, *On Any Given Sunday*, 161.

285 **"left the meeting in a huff":** Ibid.

285 **"the most important decision in the new league"**: Ibid., 161–162.

286 **"never kicked" and "the worst of it"**: Ibid., 162–163.

286 **"shirt-sleeved and dead tired" and "portly"**: Effrat, "Buffalo Franchise Bid Gains Favor at Football Meeting."

287 **"chickenshit football"**: David M. Nelson, *The Anatomy of a Game: Football, the Rules, and the Men Who Made the Game* (Newark: University of Delaware Press, 1994), 298.

287 **In 1953, the NCAA would reinstitute limits on substitutions**: Robert W. Peterson, *Pigskin: The Early Years of Pro Football* (New York: Oxford University Press, 1994), 193.

CHAPTER 23: THE LITTLE BLACK BOX

289 **"a little black box, about two feet square"**: Halas, *Halas by Halas*, 239.

289 **"There it is George, television"**: Ibid.

289 **"The picture is so small"**: Ibid.

289 **"George, that little box with the fuzzy picture is going to change the American way of life"**: Ibid., 240.

289 **"Television is coming, George"**: Ibid., 241.

289 **"asking questions"**: Ibid.

290 **"for the first time"**: Lyons, *On Any Given Sunday*, 132–133.

290 **teams now received between $15,000 and $35,000 per year**: Coenen, *From Sandlots to the Super Bowl*, 154.

290 **just 44,000 sets were in use in America in 1947, compared to 40 million radios**: From www.tvhistory.tv/1947%20QF.htm.

290 **"I could not believe it"**: Halas, *Halas by Halas*, 244.

291 **"So many sets were coming into Chicago homes that I lacked enthusiasm for having our games televised"**: Ibid., 245.

291 **Within four years, it was 11,831**: Coenen, *From Sandlots to the Super Bowl*, 161.

292 **In 1946, the New York Yankees became the first club to sell their local television rights, receiving $75,000**: Michael J. Haupert, "The Economic History of Major League Baseball," https://eh.net/encyclopedia/the-economic-history-of-major-league-baseball/.

292 **Within a decade, the Brooklyn Dodgers received $800,000 for the rights**: John Helyar, *Lords of the Realm: The Real History of Baseball* (New York: Villard Books, 1994), 52.

292 **Attendance dropped 65 percent**: Coenen, *From Sandlots to the Super Bowl*, 161.

292 **seven per season in each region of the country**: Ibid., 160–161.

292 **"I, a most cautious man"**: Halas, *Halas by Halas*, 246.

293 "I determined to increase our effort to make it work for the Bears": Ibid.

294 "The worst team in our league could beat the best team in theirs": MacCambridge, *America's Game*, 64.

294 "I would say that there was never another team in the history of sports": Lyons, *On Any Given Sunday*, 171.

295 "We whetted our appetite for that game for about three years": Ibid.

296 teams earned just $8,000 apiece from the ABC and DuMont deals: Coenen, *From Sandlots to the Super Bowl*, 156.

296 The next year, DuMont released data: Ibid., 161.

297 "It was quite an operation": Halas, *Halas by Halas*, 247.

297 "But more people have seen the Bears play this year than the first 30 years of our existence put together": Coenen, *From Sandlots to the Super Bowl*, 155.

297 Standard Oil paid $30,000 for 50 percent of the commercial time: Halas, *Halas by Halas*, 248.

297 By the end of the decade, the Bears' network would consist: Coenen, *From Sandlots to the Super Bowl*, 156.

297 The Steelers and Lions had six stations: Ibid.

298 NBC paid $100,000 to broadcast the league championship game from "coast to coast": Halas, *Halas by Halas*, 249.

299 there would always be an NFL team in the city: Lyons, *On Any Given Sunday*, 240.

CHAPTER 24: ALL-WHITE REDSKINS

301 were not equipped to play in the pros: Ross, *Outside the Lines*, 114.

302 "I have nothing against Negroes but I want an all-white team": Andrew O'Toole, *Fight for Old DC: George Preston Marshall, the Integration of the Redskins and the Rise of a New NFL* (Lincoln: University of Nebraska Press, 2016), 1.

303 "He really tried to get us up that week": Stan Grosshandler, "The Day Dub Jones Ran Wild," *Coffin Corner* 18, no. 4 (1996): 1.

305 "We're wasting our time with him": Ruck, Patterson, and Weber, *Rooney*, 280.

305 "All I'm asking is that you put him on the kickoff": Ibid.

305 "Would you see that your guy kicks the ball to him?": Ibid.

305 "Do you want him to go all the way?": Ibid.

305 "I told you he couldn't play!": Ibid., 281.

306 "Jack, the guy who threw that football at you is a good kid": Rooney Jr., *Ruanaidh*, 113.

307   **"I doubt it was written"**: Ross, *Outside the Lines*, 135.

308   **"I went to a game in Washington"**: Author interview with Mike McGee.

309   **"We had those big capes for cold weather"**: Boswell et al., *Redskins*, 45.

309   **"would like very much to sign a colored player"**: Ross, *Outside the Lines*, 132.

310   **"the greatest reconstruction job since the Civil War"**: Boswell et al., *Redskins*, 50.

311   **"George Marshall, having completed 25 years in professional football, is the greatest asset sports has ever known"**: Dave McKenna, "Fight for New Dixie," *Washington City Paper*, September 2, 2011.

311   **"There are those who will contend"**: McKenna, "Fight for New Dixie."

312   **"born ineligible to play for the Redskins"**: Leonard Shapiro, "Post Sports Columnist Shirley Povich Dies," *Washington Post*, June 5, 1998.

312   **"burgundy, gold and Caucasian"**: Shapiro, "Post Sports Columnist Shirley Povich Dies."

312   **"There were only so many good players"**: Boswell et al., *Redskins*, 53.

312   **"We'll start signing Negroes when the Harlem Globetrotters start signing whites"**: Rick Snider, *100 Things Redskins Fans Should Know and Do Before They Die* (Chicago: Triumph Books, 2014), 5.

312   **"In modern pro football, Marshall is an anachronism, as out of date as the drop-kick"**: Ryan Basen, "Fifty Years Ago, Last Bastion of N.F.L. Segregation Fell," *New York Times*, October 6, 2012.

CHAPTER 25: FORTY MILLION VIEWERS

316   **"as much as the Maras hated to admit it, they had to agree"**: DeVito, *Wellington*, 124.

316   **"What's up?"**: Ibid.

316   **"the toughest thing I ever had to do"**: Ibid.

317   **"But . . . the Giants aren't for sale"**: Arthur Daley, "Westward Course of Empire," *New York Times*, December 3, 1972.

318   **"They'd pay $1 million"**: Daley, "Westward Course of Empire."

318   **"maybe we ought to think about moving to Yankee Stadium"**: DeVito, *Wellington*, 133.

319   **"Boys, we played the Bears for the title back in '34 in weather this bad, and we nearly lost"**: Ibid., 137.

320   **"We're going to do the same thing this year"**: Ibid.

320   **"You betcha, Mr. Mara"**: Ibid., 138.

320   **"We all go with sneakers!"**: Ibid.

321   **"Unless something is done within six months, I will have to make other arrangements"**: Helyar, *Lords of the Realm*, 55.

323 **"the world's largest outdoor insane asylum":** Sportswriter Cooper Rollow's obituary, *Chicago Tribune*, April 1, 2013.

324 **By 1958, it was 43,167:** Coenen, *From Sandlots to the Super Bowl*, 163.

326 **"Up in the grandstand, a man was crying tears of joy":** Lyons, *On Any Given Sunday*, 291.

EPILOGUE

328 **"You're going to get fired":** Lyons, *On Any Given Sunday*, 264.

328 **"If I get fired, I get fired":** Ibid.

328 **"try to get Bert Bell's job" and "a dictator":** Ibid., 242.

328 **"There's no doubt Bell has the right to negotiate any differences":** Ibid., 265.

328 **"You have to vote so the players can have a union":** Ibid., 266.

329 **suffered a heart attack and died:** "Tim Mara, Pro Football Pioneer, Dies," *Chicago Tribune*, February 17, 1959.

329 **his family, the Giants' team doctor, and a priest were by his side:** "Tim Mara, Pro Football Pioneer, Dies."

329 **"We're going to sell out next year!":** DeVito, *Wellington*, 147.

329 **"finding solace in his faith":** Ruck, Patterson, and Weber, *Rooney*, 311.

329 **"I'd rather die watching football than in my bed with my boots off":** "Former FBI Agent Temporarily Acting as Commissioner of Pro Grid League," Associated Press, *York (Pennsylvania) Gazette and Daily*, October 13, 1959.

330 **"There was a commissioner's box, which he never sat in":** Author interview with Upton Bell.

330 **"What better way was there for him to go out?":** Ibid.

330 **"like Caruso dying in the third act of Pagliacci":** Lyons, *On Any Given Sunday*, 306.

330 **"I don't know how we'll replace him":** Ibid., 310.

331 **"That move alone probably saved the league":** Author interview with Upton Bell.

331 **"There is no such thing as an indispensable man":** Lyons, *On Any Given Sunday*, 310.

331 **"has done more for professional football than any other man":** Ibid.

331 **"He's certainly the only commissioner in sports history":** Author interview with Upton Bell.

331 **"He was going to buy the Eagles back":** Ibid.

332 **"So good to see you, Chief":** Morris Siegel, "Tears Flow as Marshall and Halas Hold Reunion," *Washington Star*, October 26, 1964.

334 **"He couldn't take part in the conversation":** Ruck, Patterson, and Weber, *Rooney*, 375.

334 **"Now he got loose, real loose":** Ibid.

334 **"Mr. Marshall was an outspoken foe of the status quo":** Marshall biography, www.profootballhof.com/players/george-preston-marshall/biography/.

335 **"the principle of racial integration in any form":** Michael Tomasky, "The Racist Redskins," *Daily Beast,* June 1, 2013.

335 **"I am George Halas of the Chicago Bears Football Club":** George Halas speech to Congress on December 10, 1981.

336 **"When I started going to Bears games at age five":** Author interview with Patrick McCaskey.

336 **"Mugs was so sharp":** Author interview with George McCaskey.

337 **"Halas is way up there in years":** Michael MacCambridge, *Lamar Hunt: A Life in Sports* (Kansas City: Andrews McMeel, 2012), 83.

337 **"When he was dying":** Author interview with Patrick McCaskey.

338 **"Integrity, certainly":** Author interview with Virginia McCaskey.

338 **"at one point, he was sending cash in an envelope to my father":** Author interview with Upton Bell.

338 **"My dad was the guy who would pay his toll":** Author interview with Art Rooney Jr.

339 **"simply a great guy" and "a philosopher" and "an owner who has never won a league pennant":** Vince Johnson, "Rooney Unique in Pro Football Hall of Fame," *Pittsburgh Post-Gazette,* September 7, 1964.

339 **"There is the image of me as the benevolent loser":** From unlabeled 1972 magazine profile, page 8c, Rooney folder, Pro Football Hall of Fame, Canton, Ohio.

339 **"All those years, he never had a good team":** Author interview with Virginia McCaskey.

339 **"After we'd won one or two Super Bowls":** Author interview with Art Rooney Jr.

340 **"We'd go to training camp and he'd say, 'I'd like to talk to these kids'":** Ibid.

Index

PHIL HOFFMANN

JOHN EISENBERG was an award-winning sports columnist for the *Baltimore Sun* for two decades and is the author of nine previous books. A native Texan and University of Pennsylvania graduate, he also has written for *Sports Illustrated* and *Smithsonian Magazine*. His columns now appear on the digital channels operated by the Baltimore Ravens of the National Football League.